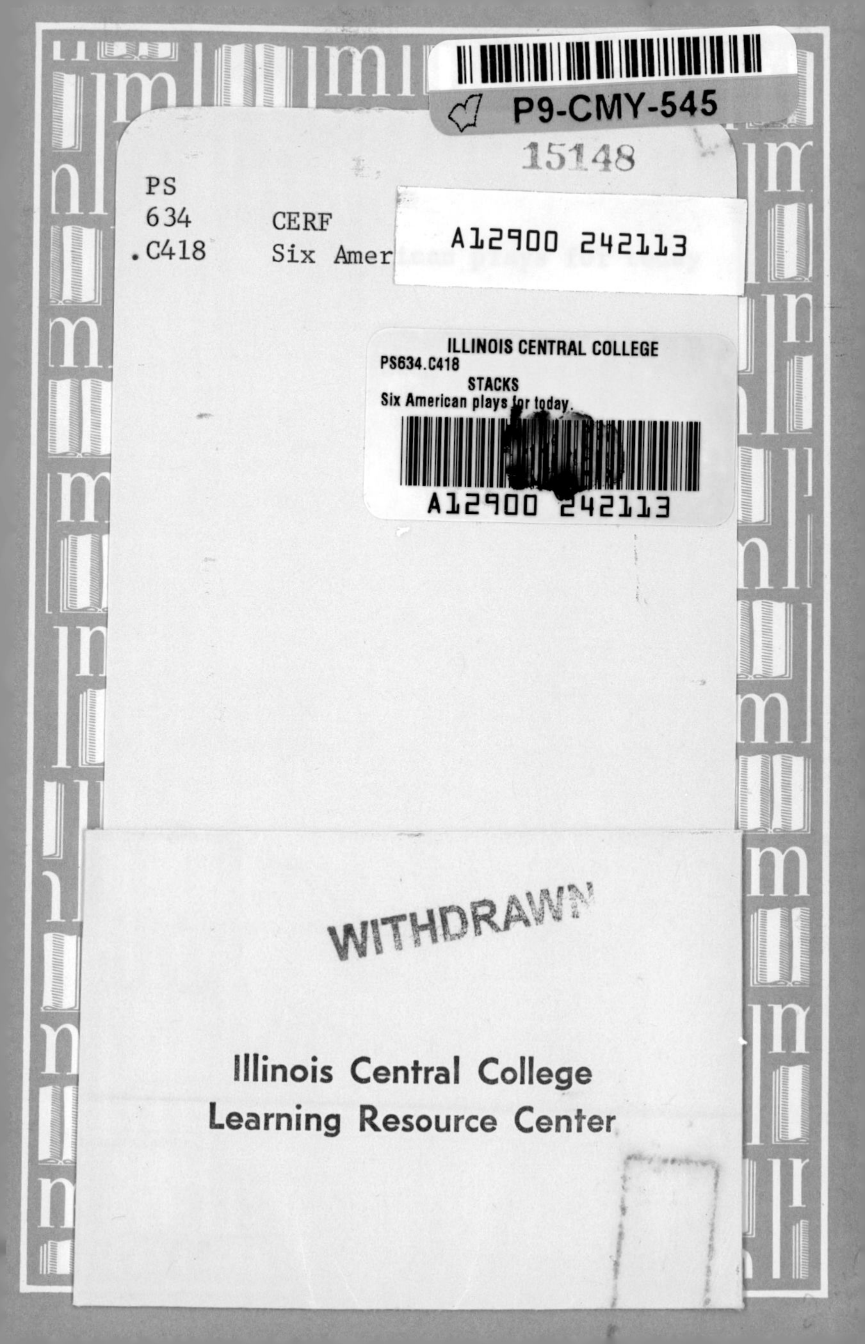

THE MODERN LIBRARY
OF THE WORLD'S BEST BOOKS

Six American Plays for Today

Six American Plays for Today

selected, and with biographical notes,

by Bennett Cerf

The Modern Library

NEW YORK

Library of Congress Catalog Card Number: 61–11189

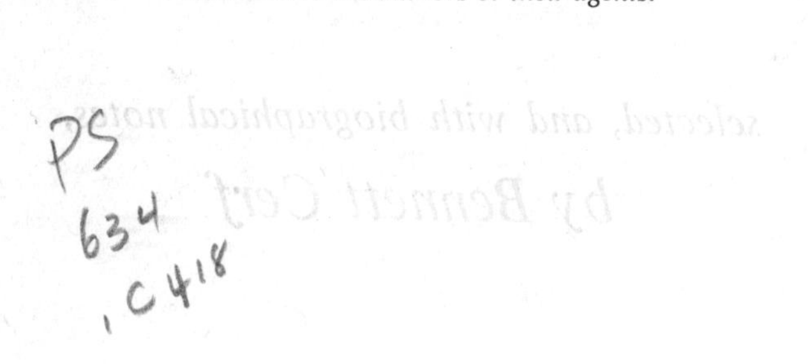

Random House IS THE PUBLISHER OF *The Modern Library*

Manufactured in the United States of America, by H. Wolff

CONTENTS

Six American Plays
for Today

Tennessee Williams

Camino Real

"In the middle of the journey of our life I came to myself in a dark wood where the straight way was lost."
***Canto I, Dante's* INFERNO**

FOR ELIA KAZAN

Manufactured in the United States of America by H. Wolff

FOREWORD*

It is amazing and frightening how completely one's whole being becomes absorbed in the making of a play. It is almost as if you were frantically constructing another world while the world that you live in dissolves beneath your feet, and that your survival depends on completing this construction at least one second before the old habitation collapses.

More than any other work that I have done, this play has seemed to me like the construction of another world, a separate existence. Of course, it is nothing more nor less than my conception of the time and world that I live in, and its people are mostly archetypes of certain basic attitudes and qualities with those mutations that would occur if they had continued along the road to this hypothetical terminal point in it.

A convention of the play is existence outside of time in a place of no specific locality. If you regard it that way, I suppose it becomes an elaborate allegory, but in New Haven we opened directly across the street from a movie theatre that was showing *Peter Pan* in Technicolor and it did not seem altogether inappropriate to me. Fairy tales nearly always have some simple moral lesson of good and evil, but that is not the secret of their fascination any more, I hope, than the philosophical import that might be distilled from the fantasies of *Camino Real* is the principal element of its appeal.

To me the appeal of this work is its unusual degree of

* Written prior to the Broadway premiere of *Camino Real* and published in the New York *Times* on Sunday, March 15, 1953.

freedom. When it began to get under way I felt a new sensation of release, as if I could "ride out" like a tenor sax taking the breaks in a Dixieland combo or a piano in a bop session. You may call it self-indulgence, but I was not doing it merely for myself. I could not have felt a purely private thrill of release unless I had hope of sharing this experience with lots and lots of audiences to come.

My desire was to give these audiences my own sense of something wild and unrestricted that ran like water in the mountains, or clouds changing shape in a gale, or the continually dissolving and transforming images of a dream. This sort of freedom is not chaos nor anarchy. On the contrary, it is the result of painstaking design, and in this work I have given more conscious attention to form and construction than I have in any work before. Freedom is not achieved simply by working freely.

Elia Kazan was attracted to this work mainly, I believe, for the same reason—its freedom and mobility of form. I know that we have kept saying the word "flight" to each other as if the play were merely an abstraction of the impulse to fly, and most of the work out of town, his in staging, mine in cutting and revising, has been with this impulse in mind: the achievement of a continual flow. Speech after speech and bit after bit that were nice in themselves have been remorselessly blasted out of the script and its staging wherever they seemed to obstruct or divert this flow.

There have been plenty of indications already that this play will exasperate and confuse a certain number of people which we hope is not so large as the number it is likely to please. At each performance a number of people have stamped out of the auditorium, with little regard for those whom they have had to crawl over, almost as if the building had caught on fire, and there have been sibilant noises on the way out and demands for money back if the cashier was foolish enough to remain in his box.

I am at a loss to explain this phenomenon, and if I am being facetious about one thing, I am being quite serious about another when I say that I had never for one minute supposed that the play would seem obscure and confusing to anyone who was willing to meet it even less than halfway. It was a costly production, and for this reason I had to read it aloud, together with a few of the actors on one occasion, before large groups of prospective backers, before the funds to produce it were in the till. It was only then that I came up against the disconcerting surprise that some people would think that the play needed clarification.

My attitude is intransigent. I still don't agree that it needs any explanation. Some poet has said that a poem should not mean but be. Of course, a play is not a poem, not even a poetic play has quite the same license as a poem. But to go to *Camino Real* with the inflexible demands of a logician is unfair to both parties.

In Philadelphia a young man from a literary periodical saw the play and then cross-examined me about all its dream-like images. He had made a list of them while he watched the play, and afterward at my hotel he brought out the list and asked me to explain the meaning of each one. I can't deny that I use a lot of those things called symbols, but being a self-defensive creature, I say that symbols are nothing but the natural speech of drama.

We all have in our conscious and unconscious minds a great vocabulary of images, and I think all human communication is based on these images as are our dreams; and a symbol in a play has only one legitimate purpose which is to say a thing more directly and simply and beautifully than it could be said in words.

I hate writing that is a parade of images for the sake of images; I hate it so much that I close a book in disgust when it keeps on saying one thing is like another; I even get disgusted with poems that make nothing but comparisons between one thing and another. But I repeat that symbols, when used respectfully, are the purest language of plays. Sometimes it would take page after tedious page of exposition to put across an idea that can be said with an object or a gesture on the lighted stage.

To take one case in point: the battered portmanteau of Jacques Casanova is hurled from the balcony of a luxury hotel when his remittance check fails to come through. While the portmanteau is still in the air, he shouts: "Careful, I have—" —and when it has crashed to the street he continues—"fragile—mementoes . . ." I suppose that is a symbol, at least it is an object used to express as directly and vividly as possible certain things which could be said in pages of dull talk.

As for those patrons who departed before the final scene, I offer myself this tentative bit of solace: that these theatregoers may be a little domesticated in their theatrical tastes. A cage represents security as well as confinement to a bird that has grown used to being in it; and when a theatrical work kicks over the traces with such apparent insouciance, security seems challenged and, instead of participating in its sense of freedom, one out of a certain number of playgoers will rush back out to the more accustomed implausibility of the street he lives on.

To modify this effect of complaisance I would like to admit to you quite frankly that I can't say with any personal conviction that I have written a good play, I only know that I have felt a release in this work which I wanted you to feel with me.

TENNESSEE WILLIAMS

AFTERWORD

Once in a while someone will say to me that he would rather wait for a play to come out as a book than see a live performance of it, where he would be distracted from its true values, if it has any, by so much that is mere spectacle and sensation and consequently must be meretricious and vulgar. There are plays meant for reading. I have read them. I have read the works of "thinking playwrights" as distinguished from us who are permitted only to feel, and probably read them earlier and appreciated them as much as those who invoke their names nowadays like the incantation of Aristophanes' frogs. But the incontinent blaze of a live theatre, a theatre meant for seeing and for feeling, has never been and never will be extinguished by a bucket brigade of critics, new or old, bearing vessels that range from cut-glass punch bowl to Haviland teacup. And in my dissident opinion, a play in a book is only the shadow of a play and not even a clear shadow of it. Those who did not like *Camino Real* on the stage will not be likely to form a higher opinion of it in print, for of all the works I have written, this one was meant most for the vulgarity of performance. The printed script of a play is hardly more than an architect's blueprint of a house not yet built or built and destroyed.

The color, the grace and levitation, the structural pattern in motion, the quick interplay of live beings, suspended like fitful lightning in a cloud, these things are the play, not words on paper, nor thoughts and ideas of an author, those shabby things snatched off basement counters at Gimbel's.

My own creed as a playwright is fairly close to that expressed by the painter in Shaw's play *The Doctor's Dilemma:* "I believe in Michelangelo, Velasquez and Rembrandt; in the might of design, the mystery of color, the redemption of all things by beauty everlasting and the message of art that has made these hands blessed. Amen."

How much art his hands were blessed with or how much mine are, I don't know, but that art is a blessing is certain and that it contains its message is also certain, and I feel, as the painter did, that the message lies in those abstract beauties of form and color and line, to which I would add light and motion.

In these following pages are only the formula by which a play could exist.

Dynamic is a word in disrepute at the moment, and so, I suppose, is the word *organic,* but those terms still define the dramatic values that I value most and which I value more as they are more deprecated by the ones self-appointed to save what they have never known.

TENNESSEE WILLIAMS

June 1, 1953

EDITOR'S NOTE

The version of *Camino Real* here published is considerably revised over the one presented on Broadway. Following the opening there, Mr. Williams went to his home at Key West and continued to work on this play. When he left six weeks later to direct Donald Windham's *Starless Night* in Houston, Texas, he took the playing version with him and reworked it whenever time allowed. It was with him when he drove in leisurely fashion back to New York. As delivered to the publisher, the manuscript of *Camino Real* was typed on three different typewriters and on stationery of hotels across the country.

Three characters, a prologue and several scenes that were not in the Broadway production have been added, or reinstated from earlier, pre-production versions, while other scenes have been deleted.

Camino Real is divided into a Prologue and Sixteen "Blocks," scenes with no perceptible time lapse between them for the most part. There are intermissions indicated after Block Six and Block Eleven.

The action takes place in an unspecified Latin-American country.

Camino Real was first produced by Cheryl Crawford and Ethel Reiner, in association with Walter P. Chrysler, Jr., and following tryouts in New Haven and Philadelphia, it had its Broadway premiere on March 19, 1953, at the Martin Beck Theatre. The production was directed by Elia Kazan, with the assistance of Anna Sokolow; the setting and costumes were designed by Lemuel Ayers; and incidental music was contributed by Bernardo Ségall. Production associate: Anderson Lawler. Tennessee Williams was represented by Liebling-Wood.

Cast of the Broadway Production

GUTMAN	Frank Silvera
SURVIVOR	Guy Thomajan
ROSITA	Aza Bard
FIRST OFFICER	Henry Silva
JACQUES CASANOVA	Joseph Anthony
LA MADRECITA DE LOS PERDIDOS	Vivian Nathan
HER SON	Rolando Valdez
KILROY	Eli Wallach
FIRST STREET CLEANER	Nehemiah Persoff
SECOND STREET CLEANER	Fred Sadoff
ABDULLAH	Ernesto Gonzalez
A BUM IN A WINDOW	Martin Balsam
A. RATT	Mike Gazzo
THE LOAN SHARK	Salem Ludwig
BARON DE CHARLUS	David J. Stewart
LOBO	Ronne Aul
SECOND OFFICER	William Lennard

A GROTESQUE MUMMER	Gluck Sandor
MARGUERITE GAUTIER	Jo Van Fleet
LADY MULLIGAN	Lucille Patton
WAITER	Page Johnson
LORD BYRON	Hurd Hatfield
NAVIGATOR OF THE FUGITIVO	Antony Vorno
PILOT OF THE FUGITIVO	Martin Balsam
MARKET WOMAN	Charlotte Jones
SECOND MARKET WOMAN	Joanna Vischer
STREET VENDOR	Ruth Volner
LORD MULLIGAN	Parker Wilson
THE GYPSY	Jennie Goldstein
HER DAUGHTER, ESMERALDA	Barbara Baxley
NURSIE	Salem Ludwig
EVA	Mary Grey
THE INSTRUCTOR	David J. Stewart
ASSISTANT INSTRUCTOR	Parker Wilson
MEDICAL STUDENT	Page Johnson
DON QUIXOTE	Hurd Hatfield
SANCHO PANZA	(*Not in production*)
PRUDENCE DUVERNOY	(*Not in production*)
OLYMPE	(*Not in production*)

STREET VENDORS: Aza Bard, Ernesto Gonzalez, Charlotte Jones, Gluck Sandor, Joanna Vischer, Ruth Volner, Antony Vorno.

GUESTS: Martin Balsam, Mary Grey, Lucille Patton, Joanna Vischer, Parker Wilson.

PASSENGERS: Mike Gazzo, Mary Grey, Page Johnson, Charlotte Jones, William Lennard, Salem Ludwig, Joanna Vischer, Ruth Volner.

AT THE FIESTA: Ronne Aul, Martin Balsam, Aza Bard, Mike Gazzo, Ernesto Gonzalez, Mary Grey, Charlotte Jones, William Lennard, Nehemiah Persoff, Fred Sadoff, Gluck Sandor, Joanna Vischer, Antony Vorno, Parker Wilson.

PROLOGUE

As the curtain rises, on an almost lightless stage, there is a loud singing of wind, accompanied by distant, measured reverberations like pounding surf or distant shellfire. Above the ancient wall that backs the set and the perimeter of mountains visible above the wall, are flickers of a white radiance as though daybreak were a white bird caught in a net and struggling to rise.

The plaza is seen fitfully by this light. It belongs to a tropical seaport that bears a confusing, but somehow harmonious, resemblance to such widely scattered ports as Tangiers, Havana, Vera Cruz, Casablanca, Shanghai, New Orleans.

On stage left is the luxury side of the street, containing the façade of the Siete Mares hotel and its low terrace on which are a number of glass-topped white iron tables and chairs. In the downstairs there is a great bay window in which are seen a pair of elegant "dummies," one seated, one standing behind, looking out into the plaza with painted smiles. Upstairs is a small balcony and behind it a large window exposing a wall on which is hung a phoenix painted on silk: this should be softly lighted now and then in the play, since resurrections are so much a part of its meaning.

Opposite the hotel is Skid Row which contains the GYPSY'S *gaudy stall, the* LOAN SHARK'S *establishment with a window containing a variety of pawned articles, and the "Ritz Men Only" which is a flea-bag hotel or flophouse and which has a practical window above its downstairs entrance, in which a bum will appear from time to time to deliver appropriate or contrapuntal song titles.*

Upstage is a great flight of stairs that mount the ancient wall to a sort of archway that leads out into "Terra Incognita," as it is called in the play, a wasteland between the walled town and the distant perimeter of snow-topped mountains.

Downstage right and left are a pair of arches which give entrance to dead-end streets.

Immediately after the curtain rises a shaft of blue light is thrown down a central aisle of the theatre, and in this light, advancing from the back of the house, appears DON QUIXOTE DE LA MANCHA, *dressed like an old "desert rat." As he enters the aisle he shouts, "Hola!", in a cracked old voice which is still full of energy and is answered by another voice which is impatient and tired, that of his squire,* SANCHO PANZA. *Stumbling with a fatigue which is only physical, the old knight comes down the aisle, and Sancho follows a couple of yards behind him, loaded down with equipment that ranges from a medieval shield to a military canteen or Thermos bottle. Shouts are exchanged between them.*

QUIXOTE (*Ranting above the wind in a voice which is nearly as old*) Blue is the color of distance!

SANCHO (*Wearily behind him*) Yes, distance is blue.

QUIXOTE Blue is also the color of nobility.

SANCHO Yes, nobility's blue.

QUIXOTE Blue is the color of distance and nobility, and that's why an old knight should always have somewhere about him a bit of blue ribbon . . .

(*He jostles the elbow of an aisle-sitter as he staggers with fatigue; he mumbles an apology*)

SANCHO Yes, a bit of blue ribbon.

QUIXOTE A bit of faded blue ribbon, tucked away in whatever remains of his armor, or borne on the tip of his lance, his—unconquerable lance! It serves to remind an old knight of distance that he has gone and distance he has yet to go . . .

(SANCHO *mutters the Spanish word for excrement as several pieces of rusty armor fall into the aisle.* QUIXOTE *has now arrived at the foot of the steps onto the forestage. He pauses there as if wandering out of or into a dream.* SANCHO *draws up clanking behind him.* MR. GUTMAN, *a lordly fat man wearing a linen suit and a pith helmet, appears dimly on the balcony of the Siete Mares, a white cockatoo on his wrist. The bird cries out harshly*)

GUTMAN Hush, Aurora.

QUIXOTE It also reminds an old knight of that green country he lived in which was the youth of his heart, before such singing words as *Truth!*

SANCHO (*Panting*) —Truth.

QUIXOTE *Valor!*

SANCHO —Valor.

QUIXOTE (*Elevating his lance*) *Devoir!*

SANCHO —Devoir . . .

QUIXOTE —turned into the meaningless mumble of some old monk hunched over cold mutton at supper!

(GUTMAN *alerts a pair of Guards in the plaza, who cross with red lanterns to either side of the proscenium where they lower black and white striped barrier gates as if the proscenium marked a frontier. One of them, with a hand on his holster, advances toward the pair on the steps*)

GUARD Vien aquí. (SANCHO *hangs back but* QUIXOTE *stalks up to the barrier gate. The* GUARD *turns a flashlight on his long and exceedingly grave red face, "frisks" him casually for concealed weapons, examines a rusty old knife and tosses it contemptuously away*) Sus papeles! Sus documentos!

(QUIXOTE *fumblingly produces some tattered old papers from the lining of his hat*)

GUTMAN (*Impatiently*) Who is it?

GUARD An old desert rat named Quixote.

GUTMAN Oh!—Expected!—Let him in.

(*The Guards raise the barrier gate and one sits down to smoke on the terrace.* SANCHO *hangs back still. A dispute takes place on the forestage and steps into the aisle*)

QUIXOTE Forward!

SANCHO Aw, naw. I know this place. (*He produces a crumpled parchment*) Here it is on the chart. Look, it says here: "Continue until you come to the square of a walled town which is the end of the Ca*mi*no Re*al* and the beginning of the *Ca*mino *Re*al. Halt there," it says, "and turn back, Traveler, for the spring of humanity has gone dry in this place and—"

QUIXOTE (*He snatches the chart from him and reads the rest of the inscription*) "—there are no birds in the country except wild birds that are tamed and kept in—" (*He holds the chart close to his nose*) *—Cages!*

SANCHO (*Urgently*) Let's go back to La Mancha!

QUIXOTE Forward!

SANCHO The time has come for retreat!

QUIXOTE The time for retreat never comes!

SANCHO *I'm* going back to *La Mancha!*

(*He dumps the knightly equipment into the orchestra pit*)

QUIXOTE *Without me?*

SANCHO (*Bustling up the aisle*) With you or without you, old tireless and tiresome master!

QUIXOTE (*Imploringly*) *Saaaaaan-chooooooooo!*

SANCHO (*Near the top of the aisle*) I'm going back to La *Maaaaaaaaan-chaaaaaaa . . .*

(*He disappears as the blue light in the aisle dims out. The* GUARD *puts out his cigarette and wanders out of the plaza. The wind moans and* GUTMAN *laughs softly as the* ANCIENT KNIGHT *enters the plaza with such a desolate air*)

QUIXOTE (*Looking about the plaza*) —Lonely . . . (*To*

his surprise the word is echoed softly by almost unseen figures huddled below the stairs and against the wall of the town. QUIXOTE *leans upon his lance and observes with a wry smile—)* —When so many are lonely as seem to be lonely, it would be inexcusably selfish to be lonely alone.

(He shakes out a dusty blanket. Shadowy arms extend toward him and voices murmur)

VOICE Sleep. Sleep. Sleep.

QUIXOTE *(Arranging his blanket)* Yes, I'll sleep for a while, I'll sleep and dream for a while against the wall of this town . . . *(A mandolin or guitar plays "The Nightingale of France")* —And my dream will be a pageant, a masque in which old meanings will be remembered and possibly new ones discovered, and when I wake from this sleep and this disturbing pageant of a dream, I'll choose one among its shadows to take along with me in the place of Sancho . . . *(He blows his nose between his fingers and wipes them on his shirttail)* —For new companions are not as familiar as old ones but all the same—they're old ones with only slight differences of face and figure, which may or may not be improvements, and it would be selfish of me to be lonely alone . . .

(He stumbles down the incline into the Pit below the stairs where most of the Street People huddle beneath awnings of open stalls. The white cockatoo squawks)

GUTMAN Hush, Aurora.

QUIXOTE And tomorrow at this same hour, which we call madrugada, the loveliest of all words, except the word alba, and that word also means daybreak—

—Yes, at daybreak tomorrow I will go on from here with a new companion and this old bit of blue ribbon to keep me in mind of distance that I have gone and distance I have yet to go, and also to keep me in mind of—

(The cockatoo cries wildly. QUIXOTE *nods as if in agree-*

ment with the outcry and folds himself into his blanket below the great stairs)

GUTMAN (*Stroking the cockatoo's crest*) Be still, Aurora. I know it's morning, Aurora. (*Daylight turns the plaza silver and slowly gold. Vendors rise beneath white awnings of stalls. The* GYPSY'S *stall opens. A tall, courtly figure, in his late middle years* (JACQUES CASANOVA) *crosses from the Siete Mares to the* LOAN SHARK'S, *removing a silver snuff box from his pocket as* GUTMAN *speaks. His costume, like that of all the legendary characters in the play (except perhaps* QUIXOTE) *is generally "modern" but with vestigial touches of the period to which he was actually related. The cane and the snuff box and perhaps a brocaded vest may be sufficient to give this historical suggestion in* CASANOVA'S *case. He bears his hawklike head with a sort of anxious pride on most occasions, a pride maintained under a steadily mounting pressure*) —It's morning and after morning. It's afternoon, ha ha! And now I must go downstairs to announce the beginning of that old wanderer's dream . . .

(*He withdraws from the balcony as old* PRUDENCE DUVERNOY *stumbles out of the hotel, as if not yet quite awake from an afternoon siesta. Chattering with beads and bracelets, she wanders vaguely down into the plaza, raising a faded green silk parasol, damp henna-streaked hair slipping under a monstrous hat of faded silk roses; she is searching for a lost poodle*)

PRUDENCE Trique? Trique?

(JACQUES *comes out of the* LOAN SHARK'S *replacing his case angrily in his pocket*)

JACQUES Why, I'd rather give it to a street beggar! This case is a Boucheron, I won it at faro at the summer palace, at Tsarskoe Selo in the winter of—

(*The* LOAN SHARK *slams the door.* JACQUES *glares, then shrugs and starts across the plaza.* OLD PRUDENCE *is crouched over the filthy gray bundle of a dying mongrel by the fountain*)

PRUDENCE Trique, oh, Trique!

(*The Gypsy's son,* ABDULLAH, *watches, giggling*)

JACQUES (*Reproving*) It is a terrible thing for an old woman to outlive her dogs. (*He crosses to* PRUDENCE *and gently disengages the animal from her grasp*) Madam, that is not Trique.

PRUDENCE —When I woke up she wasn't in her basket . . .

JACQUES Sometimes we sleep too long in the afternoon and when we wake we find things changed, Signora.

PRUDENCE Oh, you're Italian!

JACQUES I am from Venice, Signora.

PRUDENCE Ah, Venice, city of pearls! I saw you last night on the terrace dining with—Oh, I'm so worried about her! I'm an old friend of hers, perhaps she's mentioned me to you. Prudence Duvernoy? I was her best friend in the old days in Paris, but now she's forgotten so much . . . I hope you have influence with her! (*A waltz of Camille's time in Paris is heard*) I want you to give her a message from a certain wealthy old gentleman that she met at one of those watering places she used to go to for her health. She resembled his daughter who died of consumption and so he adored Camille, lavished everything on her! What did she do? Took a young lover who hadn't a couple of pennies to rub together, disinherited by his father because of *her!* Oh, you can't do that, not now, not any more, you've got to be realistic on the Camino Real!

(GUTMAN *has come out on the terrace: he announces quietly*—)

GUTMAN Block One on the Camino Real.

BLOCK ONE

PRUDENCE (*Continuing*) Yes, you've got to be practical on it! Well, give her this message, please, Sir. He wants her back on any terms whatsoever! (*Her speech gathers furious momentum*) Her evenings will be free. He wants only her mornings, mornings are hard on old men because their hearts beat slowly, and he wants only her mornings! Well, that's how it should be! A sensible arrangement! Elderly gentlemen have to content themselves with a lady's spare time before supper! Isn't that so? Of course so! And so I told him! I told him, Camille isn't well! She requires delicate care! Has many debts, creditors storm her door! "How much does she owe?" he asked me, and, oh, did I do some lightning mathematics! Jewels in pawn, I told him, pearls, rings, necklaces, bracelets, diamond ear-drops are in pawn! Horses put up for sale at a public auction!

JACQUES (*Appalled by this torrent*) Signora, Signora, all of these things are—

PRUDENCE —What?

JACQUES *Dreams!*

(GUTMAN *laughs. A woman sings at a distance*)

PRUDENCE (*Continuing with less assurance*) —You're not so young as I thought when I saw you last night on the terrace by candlelight on the—Oh, but—Ho ho! I bet there is *one* old fountain in this plaza that hasn't gone dry!

(*She pokes him obscenely. He recoils.* GUTMAN *laughs.* JACQUES *starts away but she seizes his arm again, and the torrent of speech continues*)

PRUDENCE Wait, wait, listen! Her candle is burning low. But how can you tell? She might have a lingering end, and charity hospitals? Why, you might as well take a flying leap into the Streetcleaners' barrel. Oh, I've told her and told her not to live in a dream! A dream is nothing to live in, why, it's gone like a—Don't let her elegance fool you! That girl has done the Camino in carriages but she has also done it on foot! She knows every stone the Camino is paved with! So tell her this. You tell her, she won't listen to me!—Times and conditions have undergone certain changes since we were friends in Paris, and now we dismiss young lovers with skins of silk and eyes like a child's first prayer, we put them away as lightly as we put away white gloves meant only for summer, and pick up a pair of black ones, suitable for winter . . .

(*The singing voice rises: then subsides*)

JACQUES Excuse me, Madam.

(*He tears himself from her grasp and rushes into the Siete Mares*)

PRUDENCE (*Dazed, to* GUTMAN) —What block is this?

GUTMAN Block One.

PRUDENCE I didn't hear the announcement . . .

GUTMAN (*Coldly*) Well, now you do.

(OLYMPE *comes out of the lobby with a pale orange silk parasol like a floating moon*)

OLYMPE Oh, there you are, I've looked for you high and low!—mostly low . . . .

(*They float vaguely out into the dazzling plaza as though a capricious wind took them, finally drifting through the Moorish arch downstage right. The song dies out*)

GUTMAN (*Lighting a thin cigar*) Block Two on the Camino Real.

BLOCK TWO

After GUTMAN'S *announcement, a hoarse cry is heard. A figure in rags, skin blackened by the sun, tumbles crazily down the steep alley to the plaza. He turns about blindly, murmuring: "A donde la fuente?" He stumbles against the hideous old prostitute* ROSITA *who grins horribly and whispers something to him, hitching up her ragged, filthy skirt. Then she gives him a jocular push toward the fountain. He falls upon his belly and thrusts his hands into the dried-up basin. Then he staggers to his feet with a despairing cry.*

THE SURVIVOR La fuente está seca!

(ROSITA *laughs madly but the other Street People moan. A dry gourd rattles*)

ROSITA The fountain is dry, but there's plenty to drink in the Siete Mares!

(*She shoves him toward the hotel. The proprietor,* GUTMAN, *steps out, smoking a thin cigar, fanning himself with a palm leaf. As* THE SURVIVOR *advances,* GUTMAN *whistles. A man in military dress comes out upon the low terrace*)

OFFICER Go back!

(THE SURVIVOR *stumbles forward. The Officer fires at him. He lowers his hands to his stomach, turns slowly about with a lost expression, looking up at the sky, and stumbles toward the fountain. During the scene that follows, until the entrance of* LA MADRECITA *and her* SON, THE SURVIVOR *drags himself slowly about the concrete rim of the fountain, almost entirely ignored, as a dying pariah dog in a starving country.* JACQUES CASANOVA *comes out upon the terrace of the Siete Mares. Now he passes the hotel proprietor's impassive figure, descending a step beneath and a little in advance of him, and without looking at him)*

JACQUES (*With infinite weariness and disgust*) What has happened?

GUTMAN (*Serenely*) We have entered the second in a progress of sixteen blocks on the Camino Real. It's five o'clock. That angry old lion, the Sun, looked back once and growled and then went switching his tail toward the cool shade of the Sierras. Our guests have taken their afternoon siestas . . .

(THE SURVIVOR *has come out upon the forestage, now, not like a dying man but like a shy speaker who has forgotten the opening line of his speech. He is only a little crouched over with a hand obscuring the red stain over his belly. Two or three Street People wander about calling their wares: "Tacos, tacos, fritos . . ."—"Lotería, lotería"—*ROSITA *shuffles around, calling "Love? Love?"—pulling down the filthy décolletage of her blouse to show more of her sagging bosom.* THE SURVIVOR *arrives at the top of the stairs descending into the orchestra of the theatre, and hangs onto it, looking out reflectively as a man over the rail of a boat coming into a somewhat disturbingly strange harbor)*

GUTMAN (*Continuing*) —They suffer from extreme fatigue, our guests at the Siete Mares, all of them have a degree or two of fever. Questions are passed amongst them like something illicit and shameful, like counterfeit money or drugs or indecent postcards— (*He leans forward and whispers*) —"What is this place? Where are we? What is the meaning of—*Shhhh!*"—Ha ha . . .

THE SURVIVOR (*Very softly to the audience*) I once had a pony named Peeto. He caught in his nostrils the scent of thunderstorms coming even before the clouds had crossed the Sierra . . .

VENDOR Tacos, tacos, fritos . . .

ROSITA Love? Love?

LADY MULLIGAN (*To waiter on terrace*) Are you sure no one called me? I was expecting a call . . .

GUTMAN (*Smiling*) My guests are confused and exhausted but at this hour they pull themselves together, and drift downstairs on the wings of gin and the lift, they drift into the public rooms and exchange notes again on fashionable couturiers and custom tailors, restaurants, vintages of wine, hair-dressers, plastic surgeons, girls and young men susceptible to offers . . . (*There is a hum of light conversation and laughter within*) —Hear them? They're exchanging notes . . .

JACQUES (*Striking the terrace with his cane*) I asked you what has happened in the plaza!

GUTMAN Oh, in the plaza, ha ha!—Happenings in the plaza don't concern us . . .

JACQUES I heard shots fired.

GUTMAN Shots were fired to remind you of your good fortune in staying here. The public fountains have gone dry, you know, but the Siete Mares was erected over the only perpetual never-dried-up spring in Tierra Caliente, and of course that advantage has to be—protected—sometimes by—martial law . . .

(*The guitar resumes*)

THE SURVIVOR When Peeto, my pony, was born—he stood on his four legs at once, and accepted the world!—He was wiser than I . . .

VENDOR Fritos, fritos, tacos!

ROSITA Love!

THE SURVIVOR —When Peeto was one year old he was wiser than God! (*A wind sings across the plaza; a dry gourd rattles*) "Peeto, Peeto!" the Indian boys call after him, trying to stop him—trying to stop the wind!

(THE SURVIVOR'S *head sags forward. He sits down as slowly as an old man on a park bench.* JACQUES *strikes the terrace again with his cane and starts toward* THE SURVIVOR. *The* GUARD *seizes his elbow*)

JACQUES Don't put your hand on *me!*

GUARD *Stay here.*

GUTMAN Remain on the terrace, please, Signor Casanova.

JACQUES (*Fiercely*) —*Cognac!*

(*The* WAITER *whispers to* GUTMAN. GUTMAN *chuckles*)

GUTMAN The Maître 'D' tells me that your credit has been discontinued in the restaurant and bar, he says that he has enough of your tabs to pave the terrace with!

JACQUES What a piece of impertinence! I told the man that the letter that I'm expecting has been delayed in the mail. The postal service in this country is fantastically disorganized, and you know it! You also know that Mlle. Gautier will guarantee my tabs!

GUTMAN Then let her pick them up at dinner tonight if you're hungry!

JACQUES I'm not accustomed to this kind of treatment on the Ca*mino* Re*al!*

GUTMAN Oh, you'll be, you'll be, after a single night at the "Ritz Men Only." That's where you'll have to transfer your patronage if the letter containing the remittance check doesn't arrive tonight.

JACQUES I assure you that I shall do nothing of the sort! —Tonight or ever!

GUTMAN Watch out, old hawk, the wind is ruffling your feathers! (JACQUES *sinks trembling into a chair*) —Give him a thimble of brandy before he collapses . . . Fury is a luxury of the young, their veins are resilient, but his are brittle . . .

JACQUES Here I sit, submitting to insult for a thimble of brandy—while directly in front of me— (*The singer,* LA MADRECITA, *enters the plaza. She is a blind woman led by a ragged Young Man. The* WAITER *brings* JACQUES *a brandy*) —a man in the plaza dies like a pariah dog!

—I take the brandy! I sip it!—My heart is too tir
break, my heart is too tired to—break . . .

(LA MADRECITA *chants softly. She slowly raises her*
to point at THE SURVIVOR *crouched on the steps from*
plaza)

GUTMAN (*Suddenly*) Give me the phone! Connect m
with the Palace. Get me the Generalissimo, quick, quick
quick! (THE SURVIVOR *rises feebly and shuffles very slowly toward the extended arms of "The Little Blind One"*) Generalissimo? Gutman speaking! Hello, sweetheart. There has been a little incident in the plaza. You know that party of young explorers that attempted to cross the desert on foot? Well, one of them's come back. He was very thirsty. He found the fountain dry. He started toward the hotel. He was politely advised to advance no further. But he disregarded this advice. Action had to be taken. And now, and now—that old blind woman they call "La Madrecita"?—She's come into the plaza with the man called "The Dreamer" . . .

THE SURVIVOR Donde?

THE DREAMER Aquí!

GUTMAN (*Continuing*) You remember those two! I once mentioned them to you. You said "They're harmless dreamers and they're loved by the people."—"What," I asked you, "is harmless about a dreamer, and what," I asked you, "is harmless about the love of the people?—Revolution only needs good dreamers who remember their dreams, and the love of the people belongs safely only to you—their Generalissimo!"—Yes, now the blind woman has recovered her sight and is extending her arms to the wounded Survivor, and the man with the guitar is leading him to her . . . (*The described action is being enacted*) *Wait one moment!* There's a possibility that the forbidden word may be spoken! Yes! The forbidden word is about to be spoken!

(THE DREAMER *places an arm about the blinded* SURVIVOR, *and cries out*)

THE DREAMER *Hermano!*

(*The cry is repeated like springing fire and a loud murmur sweeps the crowd. They push forward with cupped hands extended and the gasping cries of starving people at the sight of bread. Two Military Guards herd them back under the colonnades with clubs and drawn revolvers.* LA MADRECITA *chants softly with her blind eyes lifted. A Guard starts toward her. The People shout "NO!"*)

LA MADRECITA (*Chanting*) "Rojo está el sol! Roja está el sol de sangre! Blanca está la luna! Blanca está la luna de miedo!"

(*The crowd makes a turning motion*)

GUTMAN (*To the waiter*) *Put up the ropes!* (*Velvet ropes are strung very quickly about the terrace of the Siete Mares. They are like the ropes on decks of steamers in rough waters.* GUTMAN *shouts into the phone again*) The word was spoken. The crowd is agitated. Hang on! (*He lays down instrument*)

JACQUES (*Hoarsely, shaken*) He said "Hermano." That's the word for brother.

GUTMAN (*Calmly*) Yes, the most dangerous word in any human tongue is the word for brother. It's inflammatory. —I don't suppose it can be struck out of the language altogether but it must be reserved for strictly private usage in back of soundproof walls. Otherwise it disturbs the population . . .

JACQUES The people need the word. They're thirsty for it!

GUTMAN What are these creatures? Mendicants. Prostitutes. Thieves and petty vendors in a bazaar where the human heart is a part of the bargain.

JACQUES Because they need the word and the word is forbidden!

GUTMAN The word is said in pulpits and at tables of council where its volatile essence can be contained. But on the lips of these creatures, what is it? A wanton incitement to riot, without understanding. For what is a brother to them but someone to get ahead of, to cheat, to lie to, to undersell in the market. Brother, you say to a man whose wife you sleep with!—But now, you see, the word has disturbed the people and made it necessary to invoke martial law!

(*Meanwhile* THE DREAMER *has brought* THE SURVIVOR *to* LA MADRECITA, *who is seated on the cement rim of the fountain. She has cradled the dying man in her arms in the attitude of a* Pietà. THE DREAMER *is crouched beside them, softly playing a guitar. Now he springs up with a harsh cry*)

THE DREAMER *Muerto!*

(*The Streetcleaners' piping commences at a distance.* GUTMAN *seizes the phone again*)

GUTMAN (*Into phone*) Generalissimo, the Survivor is no longer surviving. I think we'd better have some public diversion right away. Put the Gypsy on! Have her announce the Fiesta!

LOUDSPEAKER (*Responding instantly*) Damas y Caballeros! The next voice you hear will be the voice of—the Gypsy!

GYPSY (*Over loudspeaker*) Hoy! Noche de Fiesta! Tonight the moon will restore the virginity of my daughter!

GUTMAN Bring on the Gypsy's daughter, Esmeralda. Show the virgin-to-be!

(ESMERALDA *is led from the* GYPSY'S *stall by a severe duenna,* "NURSIE," *out upon the forestage. She is manacled by the wrist to the duenna. Her costume is vaguely Levantine. Guards are herding the crowd back again*)

GUTMAN Ha ha! Ho ho ho! Music! (*There is gay music.* ROSITA *dances*) Abdullah! You're on!

(ABDULLAH *skips into the plaza, shouting histrionically*)

ABDULLAH Tonight the moon will restore the virginity of my sister, Esmeralda!

GUTMAN *Dance, boy!*

(ESMERALDA *is led back into the stall. Throwing off his burnoose,* ABDULLAH *dances with* ROSITA. *Behind their dance, armed Guards force* LA MADRECITA *and* THE DREAMER *to retreat from the fountain, leaving the lifeless* body of THE SURVIVER. All at once there is a discordant *blast of brass instruments.* KILROY *comes into the plaza. He is a young American vagrant, about twenty-seven. He wears dungarees and a skivvy shirt, the pants faded nearly white from long wear and much washing, fitting him as closely as the clothes of sculpture. He has a pair of golden boxing gloves slung about his neck and he carries a small duffle bag. His belt is ruby-and-emerald-studded with the word CHAMP in bold letters. He stops before a chalked inscription on a wall downstage which says: "Kilroy Is Coming!" He scratches out "Coming" and over it prints "Here!"*)

GUTMAN Ho ho!—a clown! The Eternal Punchinella! That's exactly what's needed in a time of crisis! Block Three on the Camino Real.

BLOCK THREE

KILROY (*Genially, to all present*) Ha ha! (*Then he walks up to the* OFFICER *by the terrace of the Siete Mares*) Buenas dias, señor. (*He gets no response—barely even a glance*) Habla Inglesia? Usted?

OFFICER What is it you want?

KILROY Where is Western Union or Wells-Fargo? I got to send a wire to some friends in the States.

OFFICER No hay Western Union, no hay Wells-Fargo.

KILROY That is very peculiar. I never struck a town yet that didn't have one or the other. I just got off a boat. Lousiest frigging tub I ever shipped on, one continual hell it was, all the way up from Rio. And me sick, too. I picked up one of those tropical fevers. No sick-bay on that tub, no doctor, no medicine or nothing, not even one quinine pill, and I was burning up with Christ knows how much fever. I couldn't make them understand I was sick. I got a bad heart, too. I had to retire from the prize ring because of my heart. I was the light heavyweight champion of the West Coast, won these gloves!—before my ticker went bad.—Feel my chest! Go on, feel it! Feel it. I've got a heart in my chest as big as the head of a baby. Ha ha! They stood me in front of a screen that makes you transparent and that's what they seen inside me, a heart in my chest as big as the head of a baby! With something like that you don't need the Gypsy to tell you, "Time is short, Baby—get ready to hitch on wings!" The medics wouldn't okay me for no more fights. They said to give up liquor and smoking and sex! —To give up sex!—I used to believe a man couldn't live without sex—but he can—if he wants to! My real true woman, my wife, she would of stuck with me, but it was all spoiled with her being scared and me, too, that a real hard kiss would kill me!—So one night while she was sleeping I wrote her good-bye . . . (*He notices a lack of attention in the* OFFICER: *he grins*) No comprendo the lingo?

OFFICER What is it you want?

KILROY Excuse my ignorance, but what place is this? What is this country and what is the name of this town? I know it seems funny of me to ask such a question. Loco! But I was so glad to get off that rotten tub that I didn't ask nothing of no one except my pay—and I got short-changed on that. I have trouble counting these pesos or Whatzit-you-call-'em. (*He jerks out his wallet*) All-a-this-here. In the States that pile of lettuce would make you a plutocrat!—But I bet you this stuff don't add up to fifty dollars American coin. Ha ha!

OFFICER Ha ha.

KILROY Ha ha!

OFFICER (*Making it sound like a death-rattle*) Ha-ha-ha-ha-ha.

(*He turns and starts into the cantina.* KILROY *grabs his arm*)

KILROY Hey!

OFFICER What is it you want?

KILROY What is the name of this country and this town? (*The* OFFICER *thrusts his elbow in* KILROY'S *stomach and twists his arm loose with a Spanish curse. He kicks the swinging doors open and enters the cantina*) Brass hats are the same everywhere.

(*As soon as the* OFFICER *goes, the Street People come forward and crowd about* KILROY *with their wheedling cries*)

STREET PEOPLE Dulces, dulces! Lotería! Lotería! Pasteles, café con leche!

KILROY No caree, no caree!

(*The Prostitute creeps up to him and grins*)

ROSITA Love? Love?

KILROY What did you say?

ROSITA *Love?*

KILROY Sorry—I don't feature that. (*To audience*) I have ideals.

(*The* GYPSY *appears on the roof of her establishment with* ESMERALDA *whom she secures by handcuffs to the iron railing*)

GYPSY Stay there while I give the pitch! (*She then advances with a portable microphone*) Testing! One, two, three, four!

NURSIE (*From offstage*) You're on the air!

GYPSY'S LOUDSPEAKER Are you perplexed by something? Are you tired out and confused? Do you have a fever? (KILROY *looks around for the source of the voice*) Do you feel yourself to be spiritually unprepared for the age of exploding atoms? Do you distrust the newspapers? Are you suspicious of governments? Have you arrived at a point on the Camino Real where the walls converge not in the distance but right in front of your nose? Does further progress appear impossible to you? Are you afraid of anything at all? Afraid of your heartbeat? Or the eyes of strangers! Afraid of breathing? Afraid of not breathing? Do you wish that things could be straight and simple again as they were in your childhood? Would you like to go back to Kindy Garten?

(ROSITA *has crept up to* KILROY *while he listens. She reaches out to him. At the same time a Pickpocket lifts his wallet*)

KILROY (*Catching the whore's wrist*) Keep y'r hands off me, y' dirty ole bag! No caree putas! No loteria, no dulces, nada—so get away! Vamoose! All of you! Quit picking at me! (*He reaches in his pocket and jerks out a handful of small copper and silver coins which he flings disgustedly down the street. The grotesque people scramble after it with their inhuman cries.* KILROY *goes on a few steps—then stops short—feeling the back pocket of his dungarees. Then he lets out a startled cry)* Robbed! My God, I've been robbed! (*The Street People scatter to the walls*) Which of you got my wallet? *Which* of you dirty—? Shh-Uh! (*They mumble with gestures of incomprehension. He marches back to the entrance to the hotel*) Hey! Officer! Official!—General! (*The* OFFICER *finally lounges out of the hotel entrance and glances at* KILROY.) Tiende? One of them's got my wallet! Picked it out of my pocket while that old whore there was groping me! Don't you comprendo?

OFFICER Nobody rob you. You don't have no pesos.

KILROY Huh?

OFFICER You just dreaming that you have money. You don't ever have money. Nunca! Nada! (*He spits between his teeth*) Loco . . .

(*The* OFFICER *crosses to the fountain.* KILROY *stares at him, then bawls out*)

KILROY (*To the Street People*) We'll see what the American Embassy has to say about this! I'll go to the American Consul. Whichever of you rotten spivs lifted my wallet is going to jail—calaboose! I hope I have made myself plain. If not, I will make myself plainer! (*There are scattered laughs among the crowd. He crosses to the fountain. He notices the body of the no longer* SURVIVOR, *kneels beside it, shakes it, turns it over, springs up and shouts*) *Hey! This guy is dead!* (*There is the sound of the Streetcleaners' piping. They trundle their white barrel into the plaza from one of the downstage arches. The appearance of these men undergoes a progressive alteration through the play. When they first appear they are almost like any such public servants in a tropical country; their white jackets are dirtier than the musicians' and some of the stains are red. They have on white caps with black visors. They are continually exchanging sly jokes and giggling unpleasantly together.* LORD MULLIGAN *has come out upon the terrace and as they pass him, they pause for a moment, point at him, snicker. He is extremely discomfited by this impertinence, touches his chest as if he felt a palpitation and turns back inside*) (KILROY *yells to the advancing Streetcleaners*) There's a dead man layin' here! (*They giggle again. Briskly they lift the body and stuff it into the barrel; then trundle it off, looking back at* KILROY, *giggling, whispering. They return under the downstage arch through which they entered.* KILROY, *in a low, shocked voice*) What *is* this place? What kind of a hassle have I got myself into?

LOUDSPEAKER If anyone on the Camino is bewildered, come to the Gypsy. A poco dinero will tickle the Gypsy's palm and give her visions!

ABDULLAH (*Giving* KILROY *a card*) If you got a question, ask my mama, the Gypsy!

KILROY Man, whenever you see those three brass balls on a street, you don't have to look a long ways for a Gypsy. Now le' me think. I am faced with three problems. One: I'm hungry. Two: I'm lonely. Three: I'm in a place where I don't know what it is or how I got there! First action that's indicated is to—cash in on something—Well . . . let's see . . .

(*Honky-tonk music fades in at this point and the Skid Row façade begins to light up for the evening. There is the* GYPSY'S *stall with its cabalistic devices, its sectional cranium and palm, three luminous brass balls overhanging the entrance to the* LOAN SHARK *and his window filled with a vast assortment of hocked articles for sale: trumpets, banjos, fur coats, tuxedos, a gown of scarlet sequins, loops of pearls and rhinestones. Dimly behind this display is a neon sign in three pastel colors, pink, green, and blue. It fades softly in and out and it says: "Magic Tricks Jokes." There is also the advertisement of a flea-bag hotel or flophouse called "Ritz Men Only." This sign is also pale neon or luminous paint, and only the entrance is on the street floor, the rooms are above the* LOAN SHARK *and* GYPSY'S *stall. One of the windows of this upper story is practical. Figures appear in it sometimes, leaning out as if suffocating or to hawk and spit into the street below. This side of the street should have all the color and animation that are permitted by the resources of the production. There may be moments of dancelike action (a fight, a seduction, sale of narcotics, arrest, etc.))*

KILROY (*To the audience from the apron*) What've I got to cash in on? My golden gloves? Never! I'll say that once more, never! The silver-framed photo of my One True Woman? Never! Repeat that! Never! What else have I got of a detachable and a negotiable nature? Oh! My ruby-and-emerald-studded belt with the word CHAMP on it. (*He whips it off his pants.*) This is not necessary to hold on my pants, but this is a precious reminder of the sweet used-to-be. Oh, well. Sometimes a man has got to hock his sweet used-to-be in order to finance his present situation . . .

(*He enters the* LOAN SHARK'S. *A Drunken* BUM *leans out the practical window of the "Ritz Men Only" and shouts*)

BUM O Jack o' Diamonds, you robbed my pockets, you robbed my pockets of silver and gold!

(*He jerks the window shade down*)

GUTMAN (*On the terrace*) Block Four on the Camino Real!

BLOCK FOUR

There is a phrase of light music as the BARON DE CHARLUS, *an elderly foppish sybarite in a light silk suit, a carnation in his lapel, crosses from the Siete Mares to the honky-tonk side of the street. On his trail is a wild-looking young man of startling beauty called* LOBO. CHARLUS *is aware of the follower and, during his conversation with* A. RATT, *he takes out a pocket mirror to inspect him while pretending to comb his hair and point his moustache. As* CHARLUS *approaches, the Manager of the flea-bag puts up a vacancy sign and calls out:*

A. RATT Vacancy here! A bed at the "Ritz Men Only"! A little white ship to sail the dangerous night in . . .

THE BARON Ah, bon soir, Mr. Ratt.

A. RATT Cruising?

THE BARON No, just—walking!

A. RATT That's all you need to do.

THE BARON I sometimes find it suffices. You have a vacancy, do you?

A. RATT For you?

THE BARON And a possible guest. You know the requirements. An iron bed with no mattress and a considerable length of stout knotted rope. No! Chains this evening, metal chains. I've been very bad, I have a lot to atone for . . .

A. RATT Why don't you take these joy-rides at the Siete Mares?

THE BARON (*With the mirror focused on* LOBO) They don't have Ingreso Libero at the Siete Mares. Oh, I don't like places in the haute saison, the alta staggione, and yet if you go between the fashionable seasons, it's too hot or too damp or appallingly overrun by all the wrong sort of people who rap on the wall if canaries sing in your bed-springs after midnight. I don't know why such people don't stay at home. Surely a Kodak, a Brownie, or even a Leica works just as well in Milwaukee or Sioux City as it does in these places they do on their whirlwind summer tours, and don't look now, but I think I am being followed!

A. RATT Yep, you've made a pickup!

THE BARON Attractive?

A. RATT That depends on who's driving the bicycle, Dad.

THE BARON Ciao, Caro! Expect me at ten.

(*He crosses elegantly to the fountain*)

A. RATT Vacancy here! A little white ship to sail the dangerous night in!

(*The music changes.* KILROY *backs out of the* LOAN SHARK'S, *belt unsold, engaged in a violent dispute. The* LOAN SHARK *is haggling for his golden gloves.* CHARLUS *lingers, intrigued by the scene*)

LOAN SHARK I don't want no belt! I want the gloves! Eight-fifty!

KILROY No dice.

LOAN SHARK Nine, nine-fifty!

KILROY Nah, nah, nah!

LOAN SHARK Yah, yah, yah.

KILROY I say nah.

LOAN SHARK I say yah.

KILROY The nahs have it.

LOAN SHARK Don't be a fool. What can you do with a pair of golden gloves?

KILROY I can remember the battles I fought to win them! I can remember that I used to be—CHAMP!

(*Fade in Band Music: "March of the Gladiators"—ghostly cheers, etc.*)

LOAN SHARK You can remember that you *used to be*—Champ?

KILROY Yes! I used to be—CHAMP!

THE BARON Used to be is the past tense, meaning useless.

KILROY Not to me, Mister. These are my gloves, these gloves are gold, and I fought a lot of hard fights to win 'em! I broke clean from the clinches. I never hit a low blow, the referee never told me to mix it up! And the fixers never got to me!

LOAN SHARK In other words, a sucker!

KILROY Yep, I'm a sucker that won the golden gloves!

LOAN SHARK Congratulations. My final offer is a piece of green paper with Alexander Hamilton's picture on it. Take it or leave it.

KILROY I leave it for you to *stuff* it! I'd hustle my heart on this street, I'd peddle my heart's true blood before I'd leave my golden gloves hung up in a loan shark's window between a rusted trombone and some poor lush's long ago mildewed tuxedo!

LOAN SHARK So you say but I will see you later.

THE BARON The name of the Camino is not unreal!

(*The* BUM *sticks his head out the window and shouts*)

BUM Pa dam, Pa dam, Pa dam!

THE BARON (*Continuing the* BUM'S *song*)

Echoes the beat of my heart!

Pa dam, Pa dam—*hello!*

(*He has crossed to* KILROY *as he sings and extends his hand to him*)

KILROY (*Uncertainly*) Hey, mate. It's wonderful to see you.

THE BARON Thanks, but why?

KILROY A normal American. In a clean white suit.

THE BARON My suit is pale yellow. My nationality is French, and my normality has been often subject to question.

KILROY I still say your suit is clean.

THE BARON Thanks. That's more than I can say for your apparel.

KILROY Don't judge a book by the covers. I'd take a shower if I could locate the "Y."

THE BARON What's the "Y"?

KILROY Sort of a Protestant church with a swimmin' pool in it. Sometimes it also has an employment bureau. It does good in the community.

THE BARON Nothing in this community does much good.

KILROY I'm getting the same impression. This place is confusing to me. I think it must be the aftereffects of fever. Nothing seems real. Could you give me the scoop?

THE BARON Serious questions are referred to the Gypsy. Once upon a time. Oh, once upon a time. I used to wonder. Now I simply wander. I stroll about the fountain and hope to be followed. Some people call it corruption. I call it—simplification . . .

BUM (*Very softly at the window*) I wonder what's become of Sally, that old gal of mine?

(*He lowers the blind*)

KILROY Well, anyhow . . .

THE BARON Well, anyhow?

KILROY How about the hot-spots in this town?

THE BARON Oh, the hot-spots, ho ho! There's the Pink Flamingo, the Yellow Pelican, the Blue Heron, and the Prothonotary Warbler! They call it the Bird Circuit. But I don't care for such places. They stand three-deep at the bar and look at themselves in the mirror and what they see is depressing. One sailor comes in—they faint! My own choice of resorts is the Bucket of Blood downstairs from the "Ritz Men Only."—How about a match?

KILROY Where's your cigarette?

THE BARON (*Gently and sweetly*) Oh, I don't smoke. I just wanted to see your eyes more clearly . . .

KILROY Why?

THE BARON The eyes are the windows of the soul, and

yours are too gentle for someone who has as much as I have to atone for. (*He starts off*) Au revoir . . .

KILROY —A very unusual type character . . . (CASANOVA *is on the steps leading to the arch, looking out at the desert beyond. Now he turns and descends a few steps, laughing with a note of tired incredulity.* KILROY *crosses to him*) Gee, it's wonderful to see you, a normal American in a— (*There is a strangulated outcry from the arch under which* THE BARON *has disappeared*) Excuse me a minute! (*He rushes toward the source of the outcry.* JACQUES *crosses to the bench before the fountain. Rhubarb is heard through the arch.* JACQUES *shrugs wearily as if it were just a noisy radio.* KILROY *comes plummeting out backwards, all the way to* JACQUES) I tried to interfere, but what's th' use?!

JACQUES No use at all!

(*The Streetcleaners come through the arch with* THE BARON *doubled up in their barrel. They pause and exchange sibilant whispers, pointing and snickering at* KILROY)

KILROY Who are they pointing at? At me, Kilroy? (*The* BUM *laughs from the window.* A. RATT *laughs from his shadowy doorway. The* LOAN SHARK *laughs from his*) *Kilroy is here and he's not about to be there!*—If he can help it . . . (*He snatches up a rock and throws it at the Streetcleaners. Everybody laughs louder and the laughter seems to reverberate from the mountains. The light changes, dims a little in the plaza*) Sons a whatever you're sons of! Don't look at me, I'm not about to take no ride in the barrel!

(THE BARON, *his elegant white shoes protruding from the barrel, is wheeled up the Alleyway Out. Figures in the square resume their dazed attitudes and one or two Guests return to the terrace of the Siete Mares as*—)

GUTMAN Block Five on the Camino Real!

(*He strolls off*)

BLOCK FIVE

KILROY (*To* JACQUES) Gee, the blocks go fast on this street!

JACQUES Yes. The blocks go fast.

KILROY My name's Kilroy. I'm here.

JACQUES Mine is Casanova. I'm here, too.

KILROY But you been here longer than me and maybe could brief me on it. For instance, what do they do with a stiff picked up in this town? (*The* GUARD *stares at them suspiciously from the terrace.* JACQUES *whistles "La Golondrina" and crosses downstage.* KILROY *follows*) Did I say something untactful?

JACQUES (*Smiling into a sunset glow*) The exchange of serious questions and ideas, especially between persons from opposite sides of the plaza, is regarded unfavorably here. You'll notice I'm talking as if I had acute laryngitis. I'm gazing into the sunset. If I should start to whistle "La Golondrina" it means we're being overheard by the Guards on the terrace. Now you want to know what is done to a body from which the soul has departed on the Camino Real!—Its disposition depends on what the Streetcleaners happen to find in its pockets. If its pockets are empty as the unfortunate Baron's turned out to be, and as mine are at this moment—the "stiff" is wheeled straight off to the Laboratory. And there the individual becomes an undistinguished member of a collectivist state. His chemical components are separated and poured into vats containing the corresponding elements of countless others. If any of his vital organs or parts are at all unique in size or structure, they're placed on exhibition in bottles containing a very foul-smelling solution called formaldehyde. There is a charge of admission to this museum. The proceeds go to the maintenance of the military police.

(*He whistles "La Golondrina" till the* GUARD *turns his back again. He moves toward the front of the stage*)

KILROY (*Following*) —I guess that's—sensible . . .

JACQUES Yes, but not romantic. And romance is important. Don't you think?

KILROY Nobody thinks romance is more important than me!

JACQUES Except possibly me!

KILROY Maybe that's why fate has brung us together! We're buddies under the skin!

JACQUES Travelers born?

KILROY Always looking for something!

JACQUES Satisfied by nothing!

KILROY Hopeful?

JACQUES Always!

OFFICER Keep moving!

(*They move apart till the* OFFICER *exits*)

KILROY And when a joker on the Camino gets fed up with one continual hassle—how does he get *off* it?

JACQUES You see the narrow and very steep stairway that passes under what is described in the travel brochures as a "Magnificent Arch of Triumph"?—Well, that's the Way Out!

KILROY That's the way out?

(KILROY *without hesitation plunges right up to almost the top step; then pauses with a sound of squealing brakes. There is a sudden loud wind*)

JACQUES (*Shouting with hand cupped to mouth*) Well, how does the prospect please you, Traveler born?

KILROY (*Shouting back in a tone of awe*) It's too unknown for my blood. Man, I seen nothing like it except through a telescope once on the pier on Coney Island.

"Ten cents to see the craters and plains of the moon!"— And here's the same view in three dimensions for nothing!

(*The desert wind sings loudly:* KILROY *mocks it*)

JACQUES Are you—ready to cross it?

KILROY Maybe sometime with someone but not right now and alone! How about you?

JACQUES I'm not alone.

KILROY You're with a party?

JACQUES No, but I'm sweetly encumbered with a—lady . . .

KILROY It wouldn't do with a lady. I don't see nothing but nothing—and then more nothing. And then I see some mountains. But the mountains are covered with snow.

JACQUES Snowshoes would be useful!

(*He observes* GUTMAN *approaching through the passage at upper left. He whistles "La Golondrina" for* KILROY'S *attention and points with his cane as he exits*)

KILROY (*Descending steps disconsolately*) Mush, mush.

(*The* BUM *comes to his window.* A. RATT *enters his doorway.* GUTMAN *enters below* KILROY)

BUM It's sleepy time down South!

GUTMAN (*Warningly as* KILROY *passes him*) Block Six in a progress of sixteen blocks on the Camino Real.

BLOCK SIX

KILROY (*From the stairs*) Man, I could use a bed now.—I'd like to make me a cool pad on this camino now and lie down and sleep and dream of being with someone—friendly . . .

(*He crosses to the "Ritz Men Only"*)

A. RATT (*Softly and sleepily*) Vacancy here! I got a single bed at the "Ritz Men Only," a little white ship to sail the dangerous night in.

(KILROY *crosses down to his doorway*)

KILROY —You got a vacancy here?

A. RATT I got a vacancy here if you got the one-fifty there.

KILROY Ha ha! I been in countries where money was not legal tender. I mean it was legal but it wasn't tender. (*There is a loud groan from offstage above*) —Somebody dying on you or just drunk?

A. RATT Who knows or cares in this pad, Dad?

KILROY I heard once that a man can't die while he's drunk. Is that a fact or a fiction?

A. RATT Strictly a fiction.

VOICE ABOVE *Stiff in number seven! Call the Streetcleaners!*

A. RATT (*With absolutely no change in face or voice*) Number seven is vacant.

(*Streetcleaners' piping is heard. The* BUM *leaves the window*)

KILROY Thanks, but tonight I'm going to sleep under the stars.

(A. RATT *gestures "Have it your way" and exits.* KILROY, *left alone, starts downstage. He notices that* LA

MADRECITA *is crouched near the fountain, holding something up, inconspicuously, in her hand. Coming to her he sees that it's a piece of food. He takes it, puts it in his mouth, tries to thank her but her head is down, muffled in her rebozo and there is no way for him to acknowledge the gift. He starts to cross. Street People raise up their heads in their Pit and motion him invitingly to come in with them. They call softly, "Sleep, sleep . . .")*

GUTMAN (*From his chair on the terrace*) Hey, Joe.

(*The Street People duck immediately*)

KILROY Who? Me?

GUTMAN Yes, you, Candy Man. Are you disocupado?

KILROY —That means—unemployed, don't it?

(*He sees* OFFICERS *converging from right*)

GUTMAN Jobless. On the bum. Carrying the banner!

KILROY —Aw, no, aw, no, don't try to hang no vagrancy rap on me! I was robbed on this square and I got plenty of witnesses to prove it.

GUTMAN (*With ironic courtesy*) Oh?

(*He makes a gesture asking "Where?"*)

KILROY (*Coming down to apron left and crossing to the right*) Witnesses! Witness! Witnesses! (*He comes to* LA MADRECITA) You were a witness! (*A gesture indicates that he realizes her blindness. Opposite the* GYPSY'S *balcony he pauses for a second*) Hey, Gypsy's daughter! (*The balcony is dark. He continues up to the Pit. The Street People duck as he calls down*) You were witnesses!

(*An* OFFICER *enters with a Patsy outfit. He hands it to* GUTMAN)

GUTMAN Here, Boy! Take these.

(GUTMAN *displays and then tosses on the ground at* KILROY'S *feet the Patsy outfit—the red fright wig, the big crimson nose that lights up and has horn rimmed glasses attached, a pair of clown pants that have a huge footprint on the seat*)

KILROY What is this outfit?

GUTMAN The uniform of a Patsy.

KILROY I know what a Patsy is—he's a clown in the circus who takes prat-falls but *I'm no Patsy!*

GUTMAN Pick it up.

KILROY Don't give me orders. Kilroy is a free agent—

GUTMAN (*Smoothly*) But a Patsy isn't. Pick it up and put it on, Candy Man. You are now the Patsy.

KILROY So you say but you are completely mistaken. (*Four* OFFICERS *press in on him*) And don't crowd me with your torpedoes! I'm a stranger here but I got a clean record in all the places I been, I'm not in the books for nothin' but vagrancy and once when I was hungry I walked by a truck-load of pineapples without picking one, because I was brought up good— (*Then, with a pathetic attempt at making friends with the* OFFICER *to his right*) and there was a cop on the corner!

OFFICER Ponga selo!

KILROY What'd you say? (*Desperately to audience he asks*) What did he say?

OFFICER Ponga selo!

KILROY What'd you say? (*The* OFFICER *shoves him down roughly to the Patsy outfit.* KILROY *picks up the pants, shakes them out carefully as if about to step into them and says very politely*) Why, surely. I'd be delighted. My fondest dreams have come true.

(*Suddenly he tosses the Patsy dress into* GUTMAN'S *face and leaps into the aisle of the theatre.*)

GUTMAN Stop him! Arrest that vagrant! Don't let him get away!

LOUDSPEAKER Be on the lookout for a fugitive Patsy. The Patsy has escaped. Stop him, stop that Patsy!

(*A wild chase commences. The two* GUARDS *rush madly down either side to intercept him at the back of the house.* KILROY *wheels about at the top of the center aisle, and runs back down it, panting, gasping out questions and entreaties to various persons occupying aisle seats, such as*)

KILROY How do I git out? Which way do I go, which way do I get out? Where's the Greyhound depot? Hey, do you know where the Greyhound bus depot is? What's the best way out, if there is any way out? I got to find one. I had enough of this place. I had too much of this place. I'm free. I'm a free man with equal rights in this world! You better believe it because that's news for you and you had better believe it! Kilroy's a free man with equal rights in this world! All right, now, help me, somebody, help me find a way out, I got to find one, I don't like this place! It's not for me and I am not buying any! Oh! Over there! I see a sign that says EXIT. That's a sweet word to me, man, that's a lovely word, EXIT! That's the entrance to paradise for Kilroy! Exit, I'm coming, Exit, I'm coming!

(*The Street People have gathered along the forestage to watch the chase.* ESMERALDA, *barefooted, wearing only a slip, bursts out of the* GYPSY'S *establishment like an animal broken out of a cage, darts among the Street People to the front of the Crowd which is shouting like the spectators at the climax of a corrida. Behind her,* NURSIE *appears, a male actor, wigged and dressed austerely as a duenna, crying out in both languages*)

NURSIE Esmeralda! Esmeralda!

GYPSY Police!

NURSIE Come back here, Esmeralda!

GYPSY Catch her, idiot!

NURSIE Where is my lady bird, where is my precious treasure?

GYPSY Idiot! I told you to keep her door locked!

NURSIE She jimmied the lock, Esmeralda!

(*These shouts are mostly lost in the general rhubarb of the chase and the shouting Street People.* ESMERALDA *crouches on the forestage, screaming encouragement in*

Spanish to the fugitive. ABDULLAH *catches sight of her, seizes her wrist, shouting)*

ABDULLAH Here she is! I got her!

(ESMERALDA *fights savagely. She nearly breaks loose, but* NURSIE *and the* GYPSY *close upon her, too, and she is overwhelmed and dragged back, fighting all the way, toward the door from which she escaped. Meanwhile—timed with the above action—shots are fired in the air by* KILROY'S *Pursuers. He dashes, panting, into the boxes of the theatre, darting from one box to another, shouting incoherently, now, sobbing for breath, crying out)*

KILROY *Mary, help a Christian! Help a Christian, Mary!*

ESMERALDA *Yankee! Yankee, jump! (The* OFFICERS *close upon him in the box nearest the stage. A dazzling spot of light is thrown on him. He lifts a little gilded chair to defend himself. The chair is torn from his grasp. He leaps upon the ledge of the box)* Jump! Jump, Yankee!

(The GYPSY *is dragging the girl back by her hair)*

KILROY *Watch out down there! Geronimo!*

(He leaps onto the stage and crumples up with a twisted ankle. ESMERALDA *screams demoniacally, breaks from her mother's grasp and rushes to him, fighting off his pursuers who have leapt after him from the box.* ABDULLAH, NURSIE *and the* GYPSY *seize her again, just as* KILROY *is seized by his pursuers. The* OFFICERS *beat him to his knees. Each time he is struck,* ESMERALDA *screams as if she received the blow herself. As his cries subside into sobbing, so do hers, and at the end, when he is quite helpless, she is also overcome by her captors and as they drag her back to the* GYPSY'S *she cries to him)*

ESMERALDA *They've got you! They've got me! (Her mother slaps her fiercely)* Caught! Caught! We're caught!

(She is dragged inside. The door is slammed shut on her continuing outcries. For a moment nothing is heard but KILROY'S *hoarse panting and sobbing.* GUTMAN *takes*

command of the situation, thrusting his way through the crowd to face KILROY *who is pinioned by two* GUARDS)

GUTMAN (*Smiling serenely*) Well, well, how do you do! I understand that you're seeking employment here. We need a Patsy and the job is yours for the asking!

KILROY I don't. Accept. This job. I been. Shanghied!

(KILROY *dons Patsy outfit*)

GUTMAN Hush! The Patsy doesn't talk. He lights his nose, that's all!

GUARD Press the little button at the end of the cord.

GUTMAN That's right. Just press the little button at the end of the cord!

(KILROY *lights his nose. Everybody laughs*)

GUTMAN Again, ha ha! Again, ha ha! Again!

(*The nose goes off and on like a firefly as the stage dims out. The curtain falls. There is a short intermission*)

BLOCK SEVEN

THE DREAMER *is singing with mandolin, "Noche de Ronde." The Guests murmur, "cool—cool . . ."* GUTMAN *stands on the podiumlike elevation downstage right, smoking a long thin cigar, signing an occasional tab from the bar or café. He is standing in an amber spot. The rest of the stage is filled with blue dusk. At the signal the song fades to a whisper and* GUTMAN *speaks.*

GUTMAN Block Seven on the Camino Real—I like this hour. (*He gives the audience a tender gold-toothed smile*) The fire's gone out of the day but the light of it lingers . . . In Rome the continual fountains are bathing stone heroes with silver, in Copenhagen the Tivoli gardens are lighted, they're selling the lottery on San Juan de Latrene . . .

(THE DREAMER *advances a little, playing the mandolin softly*)

LA MADRECITA (*Holding up glass beads and shell necklaces*) Recuerdos, recuerdos?

GUTMAN And these are the moments when we look into ourselves and ask with a wonder which never is lost altogether: "Can this be all? Is there nothing more? Is this what the glittering wheels of the heavens turn for?" (*He leans forward as if conveying a secret*) —Ask the Gypsy! Un poco dinero will tickle the Gypsy's palm and give her visions!

(ABDULLAH *emerges with a silver tray, calling*)

ABDULLAH Letter for Signor Casanova, letter for Signor Casanova!

(JACQUES *springs up but stands rigid*)

GUTMAN Casanova, you have received a letter. Perhaps it's the letter with the remittance check in it!

JACQUES (*In a hoarse, exalted voice*) Yes! It is! The letter! With the remittance check in it!

GUTMAN Then why don't you take it so you can maintain your residence at the Siete Mares and so avoid the more somber attractions of the "Ritz Men Only"?

JACQUES My hand is—

GUTMAN Your hand is paralyzed? . . . By what? *Anxiety? Apprehension?* . . . Put the letter in Signor Casanova's pocket so he can open it when he recovers the use of his digital extremities. Then give him a shot of brandy on the house before he falls on his face!

(JACQUES *has stepped down into the plaza. He looks down at* KILROY *crouched to the right of him and wildly blinking his nose*)

JACQUES Yes. I know the Morse code. (KILROY'S *nose again blinks on and off*) Thank you, brother. (*This is said as if acknowledging a message*) I knew without asking the Gypsy that something of this sort would happen to you. You have a spark of anarchy in your spirit and that's not to be tolerated. Nothing wild or honest is tolerated here! It has to be extinguished or used only to light up your nose for Mr. Gutman's amusement . . . (JACQUES *saunters around* KILROY *whistling "La Golondrina." Then satisfied that no one is suspicious of this encounter . . .*) Before the final block we'll find some way out of here! Meanwhile, patience and courage, little brother! (JACQUES *feeling he's been there too long starts away giving* KILROY *a reassuring pat on the shoulder and saying*) Patience! . . . Courage!

LADY MULLIGAN (*From the* MULLIGANS' *table*) Mr. Gutman!

GUTMAN Lady Mulligan! And how are you this evening, Lord Mulligan?

LADY MULLIGAN (*Interrupting* LORD MULLIGAN'S *rumblings*) He's not at all well. This . . . climate is so enervating!

LORD MULLIGAN I was so weak this morning . . . I couldn't screw the lid on my tooth paste!

LADY MULLIGAN Raymond, tell Mr. Gutman about those two impertinent workmen in the square! . . . These two idiots pushing a white barrel! Pop up every time we step outside the hotel!

LORD MULLIGAN —point and giggle at me!

LADY MULLIGAN Can't they be discharged?

GUTMAN They can't be discharged, disciplined nor bribed! All you can do is pretend to ignore them.

LADY MULLIGAN I can't eat! . . . Raymond, stop stuffing!

LORD MULLIGAN *Shut up!*

GUTMAN (*To the audience*) When the big wheels crack on this street it's like the fall of a capital city, the destruction of Carthage, the sack of Rome by the white-eyed giants from the North! I've seen them fall! I've seen the destruction of them! Adventurers suddenly frightened of a dark room! Gamblers unable to choose between odd and even! Con men and pitchmen and plume-hatted cavaliers turned baby-soft at one note of the Streetcleaners' pipes! When I observe this change, I say to myself: "Could it happen to ME?"—The answer is "YES!" And that's what curdles my blood like milk on the doorstep of someone gone for the summer!

(*A Hunchback Mummer somersaults through his hoop of silver bells, springs up and shakes it excitedly toward a downstage arch which begins to flicker with a diamond-blue radiance; this marks the advent of each legendary character in the play. The music follows: a waltz from the time of Camille in Paris*)

GUTMAN (*Downstage to the audience*) Ah, there's the music of another legend, one that everyone knows, the legend of the sentimental whore, the courtesan who made the mistake of love. But now you see her coming into this plaza not as she was when she burned with a fever that cast a thin light over Paris, but changed, yes, faded as lanterns and legends fade when they burn into day! (*He turns and shouts*) Rosita, sell her a flower!

(MARGUERITE *has entered the plaza. A beautiful woman of indefinite age. The Street People cluster about her with wheedling cries, holding up glass beads, shell necklaces and so forth. She seems confused, lost, half-awake.* JACQUES *has sprung up at her entrance but has difficulty making his way through the cluster of vendors.* ROSITA *has snatched up a tray of flowers and cries out*)

ROSITA Camellias, camellias! Pink or white, whichever a lady finds suitable to the moon!

GUTMAN That's the ticket!

MARGUERITE Yes, I would like a camellia.

ROSITA (*In a bad French accent*) Rouge ou blanc ce soir?

MARGUERITE It's always a white one, now . . . but there used to be five evenings out of the month when a pink camellia, instead of the usual white one, let my admirers know that the moon those nights was unfavorable to pleasure, and so they called me—Camille . . .

JACQUES Mia cara! (*Imperiously, very proud to be with her, he pushes the Street People aside with his cane*) Out of the way, make way, let us through, please!

MARGUERITE Don't push them with your cane.

JACQUES If they get close enough they'll snatch your purse. (MARGUERITE *utters a low, shocked cry*) What is it?

MARGUERITE *My purse is gone! It's lost! My papers were in it!*

JACQUES Your passport was in it?

MARGUERITE My passport and my permiso de residencia! (*She leans faint against the arch during the following scene.* ABDULLAH *turns to run.* JACQUES *catches him*)

JACQUES (*Seizing* ABDULLAH'S *wrist*) Where did you take her?

ABDULLAH Oww!—P'tit Zoco.

JACQUES The Souks?

ABDULLAH The Souks!

JACQUES Which cafés did she go to?

ABDULLAH Ahmed's, she went to—

JACQUES Did she smoke at Ahmed's?

ABDULLAH Two kif pipes!

JACQUES Who was it took her purse? Was it *you?* We'll see!

(*He strips off the boy's burnoose. He crouches whimpering, shivering in a ragged slip*)

MARGUERITE Jacques, let the boy go, he didn't take it!

JACQUES He doesn't have it on him but knows who does!

ABDULLAH No, no, I don't know!

JACQUES You little son of a Gypsy! Senta! . . . You know who I am? I am Jacques Casanova! I belong to the Secret Order of the Rose-colored Cross! . . . Run back to Ahmed's. Contact the spiv that took the lady's purse. Tell him to keep it but give her back her papers! There'll be a large reward.

(*He thumps his can on the ground to release* ABDULLAH *from the spell. The boy dashes off.* JACQUES *laughs and turns triumphantly to* MARGUERITE)

LADY MULLIGAN Waiter! That adventurer and his mistress must not be seated next to Lord Mulligan's table!

JACQUES (*Loudly enough for* LADY MULLIGAN *to hear*) This hotel has become a mecca for black marketeers and their expensively kept women!

LADY MULLIGAN Mr. Gutman!

MARGUERITE Let's have dinner upstairs!

WAITER (*Directing them to terrace table*) *This* way, M'sieur.

JACQUES We'll take our usual table.

(*He indicates one*)

MARGUERITE Please!

WAITER (*Overlapping* MARGUERITE'S *"please!"*) This table is reserved for Lord Byron!

JACQUES (*Masterfully*) This table is always our table.

MARGUERITE I'm not hungry.

JACQUES Hold out the lady's chair, cretino!

GUTMAN (*Darting over to* MARGUERITE'S *chair*) Permit me!

(JACQUES *bows with mock gallantry to* LADY MULLIGAN *as he turns to his chair during seating of* MARGUERITE)

LADY MULLIGAN We'll move to *that* table!

JACQUES —You must learn how to carry the banner of Bohemia into the enemy camp.

(*A screen is put up around them*)

MARGUERITE Bohemia has no banner. It survives by discretion.

JACQUES I'm glad that you value discretion. *Wine list!* Was it discretion that led you through the bazaars this afternoon wearing your cabochon sapphire and diamond ear-drops? You were fortunate that you lost only your purse and papers!

MARGUERITE Take the wine list.

JACQUES Still or sparkling?

MARGUERITE Sparkling.

GUTMAN May I make a suggestion, Signor Casanova?

JACQUES Please do.

GUTMAN It's a very cold and dry wine from only ten metres below the snowline in the mountains. The name is Quando!—meaning when! Such as "When are remittances going to be received?" "When are accounts to be settled?" Ha ha ha! Bring Signor Casanova a bottle of Quando with the compliments of the house!

JACQUES I'm sorry this had to happen in—your presence . . .

MARGUERITE That doesn't matter, my dear. But why don't you *tell* me when you are short of money?

JACQUES I thought the fact was apparent. It is to everyone else.

MARGUERITE The letter you were expecting, it still hasn't come?

JACQUES (*Removing it from his pocket*) It came this afternoon—Here it is!

MARGUERITE You haven't opened the letter!

JACQUES I haven't had the nerve to! I've had so many unpleasant surprises that I've lost faith in my luck.

MARGUERITE Give the letter to me. Let me open it for you.

JACQUES Later, a little bit later, after the—wine . . .

MARGUERITE Old hawk, anxious old hawk!

(*She clasps his hand on the table: he leans toward her: she kisses her fingertips and places them on his lips*)

JACQUES Do you call that a kiss?

MARGUERITE I call it the ghost of a kiss. It will have to do for now.

(*She leans back, her blue-tinted eyelids closed*)

JACQUES Are you tired? Are you tired, Marguerite? You know you should have rested this afternoon.

MARGUERITE I looked at silver and rested.

JACQUES You looked at silver at Ahmed's?

MARGUERITE No, I rested at Ahmed's, and had mint-tea.

(THE DREAMER *accompanies their speech with his guitar. The duologue should have the style of an antiphonal poem, the cues picked up so that there is scarcely a separation between the speeches, and the tempo quick and the voices edged*)

JACQUES You had mint-tea downstairs?

MARGUERITE No, upstairs.

JACQUES Upstairs where they burn the poppy?

MARGUERITE Upstairs where it's cool and there's music and the haggling of the bazaar is soft as the mummur of pigeons.

JACQUES That sounds restful. Reclining among silk pillows on a divan, in a curtained and perfumed alcove above the bazaar?

MARGUERITE Forgetting for a while where I am, or that I don't know where I am . . .

JACQUES Forgetting alone or forgetting with some young companion who plays the lute or the flute or who had silver to show you? Yes. That sounds very restful. And yet you do seem tired.

MARGUERITE If I seem tired, it's your insulting solicitude that I'm tired of!

JACQUES Is it insulting to feel concern for your safety in this place?

MARGUERITE Yes, it is. The implication is.

JACQUES What is the implication?

MARGUERITE You know what it is: that I am one of those *aging—voluptuaries*—who used to be paid for pleasure but now have to pay!—Jacques, I won't be followed, I've gone too far to be followed!—*What is it?*

(*The* WAITER *has presented an envelope on a salver*)

WAITER A letter for the lady.

MARGUERITE How strange to receive a letter in a place where nobody knows I'm staying! Will you open it for me? (*The* WAITER *withdraws.* JACQUES *takes the letter and opens it*) Well! What is it?

JACQUES Nothing important. An illustrated brochure from some resort in the mountains.

MARGUERITE What is it called?

JACQUES Bide-a-While. (*A chafing dish bursts into startling blue flame at the Mulligans' table.* LADY MULLIGAN *clasps her hands and exclaims with affected delight, the* WAITER *and* MR. GUTMAN *laugh agreeably.* MARGUERITE *springs up and moves out upon the forestage.* JACQUES *goes to her*) Do you know this resort in the mountains?

MARGUERITE Yes. I stayed there once. It's one of those places with open sleeping verandahs, surrounded by snowy pine woods. It has rows and rows of narrow white iron beds as regular as tombstones. The invalids smile at each other when axes flash across valleys, ring, flash, ring again! Young voices shout across valleys Hola! And mail is delivered. The friend that used to write you ten-page letters contents himself now with a postcard bluebird that tells you to "Get well Quick!" (JACQUES *throws the brochure away*) —And when the last bleeding comes, not much later nor earlier than expected, you're wheeled discreetly into a little tent of white gauze, and the last thing you know of this world, of which you've known so little and yet so much, is the smell of an empty ice box.

(*The blue flame expires in the chafing dish.* GUTMAN *picks up the brochure and hands it to the* WAITER, *whispering something*)

JACQUES You won't go back to that place.

(*The* WAITER *places the brochure on the salver again and approaches behind them*)

MARGUERITE I wasn't released. I left without permission. They sent me this to remind me.

WAITER (*Presenting the salver*) You dropped this.

JACQUES We threw it away!

WAITER Excuse me.

JACQUES Now, from now on, Marguerite, you must take better care of yourself. Do you hear me?

MARGUERITE I hear you. No more distractions for me? No more entertainers in curtained and perfumed alcoves above the bazaar, no more young men that a pinch of white powder or a puff of gray smoke can almost turn to someone devoutly remembered?

JACQUES No, from now on—

MARGUERITE What "from now on," old hawk?

JACQUES Rest. Peace.

MARGUERITE Rest in peace is that final bit of advice they carve on gravestones, and I'm not ready for it! Are you? Are *you* ready for it? (*She returns to the table. He fol-*

lows her) Oh, Jacques, when are we going to leave here, how are we going to leave here, you've got to tell me!

JACQUES I've told you all I know.

MARGUERITE Nothing, you've given up hope!

JACQUES I haven't, that's not true.

(GUTMAN *has brought out the white cockatoo which he shows to* LADY MULLIGAN *at her table*)

GUTMAN (*His voice rising above the murmur*) Her name is Aurora.

LADY MULLIGAN Why do you call her Aurora?

GUTMAN She cries at daybreak.

LADY MULLIGAN Only at daybreak?

GUTMAN Yes, at daybreak only.

(*Their voices and laughter fade under*)

MARGUERITE How long is it since you've been to the travel agencies?

JACQUES This morning I made the usual round of Cook's, American Express, Wagon-lits Universal, and it was the same story. There are no flights out of here till further orders from someone higher up.

MARGUERITE Nothing, nothing at all?

JACQUES Oh, there's a rumor of something called the Fugitivo, but—

MARGUERITE The What!!! ?

JACQUES The Fugitivo. It's one of those non-scheduled things that—

MARGUERITE When, when, when?

JACQUES I told you it was non-scheduled. Non-scheduled means it comes and goes at no predictable—

MARGUERITE Don't give me the dictionary! I want to know how does one get on it? Did you bribe them? Did you offer them money? No. Of course you didn't! And I know why! You really don't want to leave here. You *think* you don't want to go because you're brave as an old hawk. But the truth of the matter—the real not the royal truth—is that you're terrified of the Terra Incognita outside that wall.

JACQUES You've hit upon the truth. I'm terrified of the unknown country inside or outside this wall or any place on earth without you with me! The only country, known or unknown that I can breathe in, or care to, is the country in which we breathe together, as we are now at this table. And later, a little while later, even closer than this, the sole inhabitants of a tiny world whose limits are those of the light from a rose-colored lamp—beside the sweetly, completely known country of your cool bed!

MARGUERITE The little comfort of love?

JACQUES Is that comfort so little?

MARGUERITE Caged birds accept each other but flight is what they long for.

JACQUES I want to stay here with you and love you and guard you until the time or way comes that we both can leave with honor.

MARGUERITE "Leave with honor"? Your vocabulary is almost as out-of-date as your cape and your cane. How could anyone quit this field with honor, this place where there's nothing but the gradual wasting away of everything decent in us . . . the sort of desperation that comes after even desperation has been worn out through long wear! . . . Why have they put these screens around the table?

(*She springs up and knocks one of them over*)

LADY MULLIGAN There! You see? I don't understand why you let such people stay here.

GUTMAN They pay the price of admission the same as you.

LADY MULLIGAN What price is that?

GUTMAN Desperation!—With cash here! (*He indicates the Siete Mares*) Without cash there! (*He indicates Skid Row*) Block Eight on the Camino Real!

BLOCK EIGHT

There is the sound of loud desert wind and a flamenco cry followed by a dramatic phrase of music.

A flickering diamond blue radiance floods the hotel entrance. The crouching, grimacing Hunchback shakes his hoop of bells which is the convention for the appearance of each legendary figure.

LORD BYRON *appears in the doorway readied for departure.* GUTMAN *raises his hand for silence.*

GUTMAN You're leaving us, Lord Byron?

BYRON Yes, I'm leaving you, Mr. Gutman.

GUTMAN What a pity! But this is a port of entry and departure. There are no permanent guests. Possibly you are getting a little restless?

BYRON The luxuries of this place have made me soft. The metal point's gone from my pen, there's nothing left but the feather.

GUTMAN That may be true. But what can you do about it?

BYRON Make a departure!

GUTMAN From yourself?

BYRON From my present self to myself as I used to be!

GUTMAN *That's* the *furthest* departure a man could make! I guess you're sailing to Athens? There's another war there and like all wars since the beginning of time it can be interpreted as a—struggle for *what?*

BYRON —For *freedom!* You may laugh at it, but it still means something to *me!*

GUTMAN Of course it does! I'm not laughing a bit, I'm beaming with admiration.

BYRON I've allowed myself many distractions.

GUTMAN Yes, indeed!

BYRON But I've never altogether forgotten my old devotion to the—

GUTMAN —To the *what,* Lord Byron? (BYRON *passes nervous fingers through his hair*) You can't remember the object of your one-time devotion?

(*There is a pause.* BYRON *limps away from the terrace and goes toward the fountain*)

BYRON When Shelley's corpse was recovered from the sea . . . (GUTMAN *beckons* THE DREAMER *who approaches and accompanies* BYRON'S *speech*) —It was burned on the beach at Viareggio.—I watched the spectacle from my carriage because the stench was revolting . . . Then it—fascinated me! I got out of my carriage. Went nearer, holding a handkerchief to my nostrils!—I saw that the front of the skull had broken away in the flames, and there— (*He advances out upon the stage apron, followed by* ABDULLAH *with the pine torch or lantern*) And there was the brain of Shelley, indistinguishable from a cooking stew!—*boiling, bubbling, hissing!*—in the *blackening—cracked—pot*—of his skull! (MARGUERITE *rises abruptly.* JACQUES *supports her*) —Trelawney, his friend, Trelawney, threw salt and oil and frankincense in the flames and finally the almost intolerable stench— (ABDULLAH *giggles.* GUTMAN *slaps him*) —was *gone* and the burning was *pure!*—as a man's burning should be . . . A man's burning *ought* to be pure!—*not* like mine—(a crepe suzette—burned in brandy . . .) *Shelley's* burning was finally very *pure!* But the body, the corpse, split open like a grilled pig! (ABDULLAH *giggles irrepressibly again.* GUTMAN *grips the back of his neck and he stands up stiff and assumes an expression of exaggerated solemnity*) —And then

Trelawney—as the ribs of the corpse unlocked—reached into them as a baker reaches quickly into an oven! (ABDULLAH *almost goes into another convulsion*) —And snatched out—as a baker would a biscuit!—the *heart* of Shelley! Snatched the heart of Shelley out of the blistering corpse!—Out of the purifying—blue-flame . . . (MARGUERITE *resumes her seat;* JACQUES *his*) —And it was *over!*—I thought— (*He turns slightly from the audience and crosses upstage from the apron. He faces* JACQUES *and* MARGUERITE) —I thought it was a disgusting thing to do, to snatch a man's heart from his body! What can one can do with another man's heart? (JACQUES *rises and strikes the stage with his cane*)

JACQUES (*Passionately*) He can do this with it! (*He seizes a loaf of bread on his table, and descends from the terrace*) *He can twist it like this!* (*He twists the loaf*) *He can tear it like this!* (*He tears the loaf in two*) *He can crush it under his foot!* (*He drops the bread and stamps on it*) *—And kick it away—like this!* (*He kicks the bread off the terrace.* LORD BYRON *turns away from him and limps again out upon the stage apron and speaks to the audience*)

BYRON That's very true, Señor. But a poet's vocation, which used to be my vocation, is to influence the heart in a gentler fashion than you have made your mark on that loaf of bread. He ought to purify it and lift it above its ordinary level. For what is the heart but a sort of— (*He makes a high, groping gesture in the air*) —A sort of—*instrument!*—that translates *noise* into *music,* chaos into—*order* . . . (ABDULLAH *ducks almost to the earth in an effort to stifle his mirth.* GUTMAN *coughs to cover his own amusement*) *—a mysterious order!* (*He raises his voice till it fills the plaza*) —That was my vocation once upon a time, before it was obscured by vulgar plaudits!—Little by little it was lost among gondolas and palazzos!—masked balls, glittering salons, huge shadowy courts and torch-lit entrances!—Baroque façades, canopies and carpets, candelabra and gold plate among snowy damask, ladies with throats as slender as flower-stems, bending and breathing toward me their fragrant breath— —Exposing their breasts to me! Whispering, half-smiling!—And everywhere marble, the visible grandeur of marble, pink and gray marble, veined and tinted as flayed corrupting flesh,—all these provided agreeable distractions from the rather frightening solitude of a poet. Oh, I wrote many cantos in Venice and Constantinople and in Ravenna and Rome, on all of those Latin and Levantine excursions that my twisted foot led me into—but I wonder about them a little. They seem to improve as the wine in the bottle—dwindles . . . *There is a passion for declivity in this world!* And lately I've found myself listening to hired musicians behind a row of artificial palm trees—instead of the single—pure-stringed instrument of my heart . . . Well, then, it's time to leave here! (*He turns back to the stage*) —There is a time for departure even when there's no certain place to go! I'm going to look for one, now. I'm sailing to Athens. At least I can look up at the Acropolis, I can stand at the foot of it and look up at broken columns on the crest of a hill—if not purity, at least its recollection . . . I can sit quietly looking for a long, long time in absolute silence, and possibly, yes, *still* possibly—The old pure music will come to me again. Of course on the other hand I may hear only the little noise of insects in the grass . . . But I am sailing to Athens! *Make voyages!—Attempt them!*—there's nothing else . . .

MARGUERITE (*Excitedly*) *Watch where he goes!* (LORD BYRON *limps across the plaza with his head bowed, making slight, apologetic gestures to the wheedling Beggars who shuffle about him. There is music. He crosses toward the steep Alleyway Out. The following is played with a quiet intensity so it will be in a lower key than the later Fugitivo Scene)* Watch him, watch him, see which way he goes. Maybe he knows of a way that we haven't found out.

JACQUES Yes, I'm watching him, Cara.

(LORD *and* LADY MULLIGAN *half rise, staring anxiously through monocle and lorgnon)*

MARGUERITE Oh, my God, I believe he's going up that alley.

JACQUES Yes, he is. He has.

LORD and LADY MULLIGAN Oh, the fool, the idiot, he's going under the arch!

MARGUERITE Jacques, run after him, warn him, tell him about the desert he has to cross.

JACQUES I think he knows what he's doing.

MARGUERITE I can't look!

(She turns to the audience, throwing back her head and closing her eyes. The desert wind sings loudly as BYRON *climbs to the top of the steps)*

BRYON *(To several porters carrying luggage—which is mainly caged birds)* THIS WAY!

(He exits. KILROY *starts to follow. He stops at the steps, cringing and looking at* GUTMAN. GUTMAN *motions him to go ahead.* KILROY *rushes up the stairs. He looks out, loses his nerve and sits—blinking his nose.* GUTMAN *laughs as he announces—)*

GUTMAN Block Nine on the Camino Real!

(He goes into the hotel)

BLOCK NINE

ABDULLAH *runs back to the hotel with the billowing flambeau. A faint and far away humming sound becomes audible . . .* MARGUERITE *opens her eyes with a startled look. She searches the sky for something. A very low percussion begins with the humming sound, as if excited hearts are beating.*

MARGUERITE Jacques! I hear something in the sky!

JACQUES I think what you hear is—

MARGUERITE (*With rising excitement*) —*No, it's a plane, a great one, I see the lights of it, now!*

JACQUES Some kind of fireworks, Cara.

MARGUERITE Hush! LISTEN! (*She blows out the candle to see better above it. She rises, peering into the sky*) *I see it! I see it! There! It's circling over us!*

LADY MULLIGAN Raymond, Raymond, sit down, your face is flushed!

HOTEL GUESTS (*Overlapping*) —What is it?
—The FUGITIVO!
—THE FUGITIVO! THE FUGITIVO!
—Quick, get my jewelry from the hotel safe!
—Cash a check!
—Throw some things in a bag! I'll wait here!
—Never mind luggage, we have our money and papers!
—Where is it now?
—There, there!
—It's turning to land!
—To go like this?
—Yes, go anyhow, just go anyhow, just go!

—Raymond! Please!
—Oh, it's rising again!
—Oh it's—*SHH! MR. GUTMAN!*

(GUTMAN *appears in the doorway. He raises a hand in a commanding gesture*)

GUTMAN Signs in the sky should not be mistaken for wonders! (*The Voices modulate quickly*) Ladies, gentlemen, please resume your seats! (*Places are resumed at tables, and silver is shakily lifted. Glasses are raised to lips, but the noise of concerted panting of excitement fills the stage and a low percussion echoes frantic heart beats.*

(GUTMAN *descends to the plaza, shouting furiously to the Officer*) Why wasn't I told the Fugitivo was coming?

(*Everyone, almost as a man, rushes into the hotel and reappears almost at once with hastily collected possessions.* MARGUERITE *rises but appears stunned. There is a great whistling and screeching sound as the aerial transport halts somewhere close by, accompanied by rainbow splashes of light and cries like children's on a roller-coaster. Some incoming Passengers approach the stage down an aisle of the theatre, preceded by Redcaps with luggage*)

PASSENGERS —What a heavenly trip!
—The scenery was thrilling!
—It's so quick!
—The only way to travel! Etc., etc.

(*A uniformed man, the* PILOT, *enters the plaza with a megaphone*)

PILOT (*Through the megaphone*) Fugitivo now loading for departure! Fugitivo loading immediately for departure! Northwest corner of the plaza!

MARGUERITE Jacques, it's the Fugitivo, it's the non-scheduled thing you heard of this afternoon!

PILOT All out-going passengers on the Fugitivo are requested to present their tickets and papers immediately at this station.

MARGUERITE He said "out-going passengers"!

PILOT Out-going passengers on the Fugitivo report immediately at this station for customs inspection.

MARGUERITE (*With a forced smile*) Why are you just standing there?

JACQUES (*With an Italian gesture*) Che cosa possa fare!

MARGUERITE Move, move, do something!

JACQUES *What!*

MARGUERITE Go to them, ask, find out!

JACQUES I have no idea what the damned thing is!

MARGUERITE I do, I'll tell you! It's a way to escape from this abominable place!

JACQUES Forse, forse, non so!

MARGUERITE It's a way *out* and *I'm* not going to miss it!

PILOT Ici la Douane! Customs inspection here!

MARGUERITE Customs. That means luggage. Run to my room! Here! Key! Throw a few things in a bag, my jewels, my furs, but hurry! Vite, vite, vite! I don't believe there's much time! No, everybody is— (*Outgoing Passengers storm the desk and table*) —Clamoring for tickets! There must be limited space! Why don't you do what I tell you? (*She rushes to a man with a rubber stamp and a roll of tickets*) Monsieur! Señor! Pardonnez-moi! I'm going, I'm going out! I want my ticket!

PILOT (*Coldly*) Name, please.

MARGUERITE Mademoiselle—Gautier—but I—

PILOT Gautier? Gautier? We have no Gautier listed.

MARGUERITE I'm—*not* listed! I mean I'm—traveling under another name.

TRAVEL AGENT What name are you traveling under?

(PRUDENCE *and* OLYMPE *rush out of the hotel half dressed, dragging their furs. Meanwhile* KILROY *is trying to make a fast buck or two as a Redcap. The scene gathers wild momentum, is punctuated by crashes of per-*

cussion. Grotesque mummers act as demon custom inspectors and immigration authorities, etc. Baggage is tossed about, ripped open, smuggled goods seized, arrests made, all amid the wildest importunities, protests, threats, bribes, entreaties; it is a scene for improvisation)

PRUDENCE Thank God I woke up!

OLYMPE Thank God I wasn't asleep!

PRUDENCE I knew it was non-scheduled but I *did* think they'd give you time to get in your girdle.

OLYMPE Look who's trying to crash it! I know damned well *she* don't have a reservation!

PILOT (*To* MARGUERITE) What name did you say, Mademoiselle? Please! People are waiting, you're holding up the line!

MARGUERITE I'm so confused! Jacques! What name did you make my reservation under!

OLYMPE She has no reservation!

PRUDENCE *I have, I got mine!*

OLYMPE *I got mine!*

PRUDENCE *I'm* next!

OLYMPE Don't push *me,* you old bag!

MARGUERITE I was here first! I was here before anybody Jacques, quick! Get my money from the hotel safe!

(JACQUES *exits*)

AGENT *Stay in line!*

(*There is a loud warning whistle*)

PILOT Five minutes. The Fugitivo leaves in five minutes. Five, five minutes only!

(*At this announcement the scene becomes riotous*)

TRAVEL AGENT *Four minutes! The Fugitivo leaves in four minutes!* (PRUDENCE *and* OLYMPE *are shrieking at him in French. The warning whistle blasts again*) *Three minutes, the Fugitivo leaves in three minutes!*

MARGUERITE (*Topping the turmoil*) Monsieur! Please! I was here first, I was here before anybody! Look! (JACQUES *returns with her money*) I have thousands of francs! Take whatever you want! Take all of it, it's yours!

PILOT Payment is only accepted in pounds sterling or dollars. Next, please.

MARGUERITE You don't accept francs? They do at the hotel! They accept my francs at the Siete Mares!

PILOT Lady, don't argue with me, I don't make the rules!

MARGUERITE (*Beating her forehead with her fist*) Oh, God, Jacques! Take these back to the cashier! (*She thrusts the bills at him*) Get them changed to dollars or—*Hurry! Tout de suite!* I'm—going to faint . . .

JACQUES But Marguerite—

MARGUERITE *Go! Go! Please!*

PILOT Closing, we're closing now! The Fugitivo leaves in two minutes!

(LORD *and* LADY MULLIGAN *rush forward*)

LADY MULLIGAN Let Lord Mulligan through.

PILOT (*To* MARGUERITE) You're standing in the way.

(OLYMPE *screams as the Customs Inspector dumps her jewels on the ground. She and* PRUDENCE *butt heads as they dive for the gems: the fight is renewed*)

MARGUERITE (*Detaining the* PILOT) Oh, look, Monsieur! Regardez ça! My diamond, a solitaire—two carats! Take that as security!

PILOT Let me go. The Loan Shark's across the plaza!

(*There is another warning blast.* PRUDENCE *and* OLYMPE *seize hat boxes and rush toward the whistle*)

MARGUERITE (*Clinging desperately to the* PILOT) You don't understand! Señor Casanova has gone to change money! He'll be here in a second. And I'll pay five, ten, twenty times the price of—*JACQUES! JACQUES! WHERE ARE YOU?*

VOICE (*Back of auditorium*) We're closing the gate!

MARGUERITE You can't close the gate!

PILOT Move, Madame!

MARGUERITE I won't move!

LADY MULLIGAN I tell you, Lord Mulligan is the Iron &

Steel man from Cobh! Raymond! They're closing the gate!

LORD MULLIGAN I can't seem to get through!

GUTMAN Hold the gate for Lord Mulligan!

PILOT (*To* MARGUERITE) Madame, stand back or I will have to use force!

MARGUERITE Jacques! Jacques!

LADY MULLIGAN Let us through! We're clear!

PILOT Madame! Stand back and let these passengers through!

MARGUERITE No, No! I'm first! I'm next!

LORD MULLIGAN Get her out of our way! That woman's a whore!

LADY MULLIGAN How dare you stand in our way?

PILOT Officer, take this woman!

LADY MULLIGAN Come on, Raymond!

MARGUERITE (*As the* OFFICER *pulls her away*) Jacques! Jacques! Jacques! (JACQUES *returns with changed money*) Here! Here is the money!

PILOT All right, give me your papers.

MARGUERITE —My papers? Did you say my papers?

PILOT Hurry, hurry, your pasport!

MARGUERITE —Jacques! He wants my papers! Give him my papers, Jacques!

JACQUES —The lady's papers are lost!

MARGUERITE (*Wildly*) No, no, no, THAT IS NOT TRUE! HE WANTS TO KEEP ME HERE! HE'S LYING ABOUT IT!

JACQUES Have you forgotten that your papers were stolen?

MARGUERITE I gave you my papers, I gave you my papers to keep, you've got my papers.

(*Screaming,* LADY MULLIGAN *breaks past her and descends the stairs*)

LADY MULLIGAN Raymond! Hurry!

LORD MULLIGAN (*Staggering on the top step*) I'm sick! I'm sick!

(*The Streetcleaners disguised as expensive morticians in swallowtail coats come rapidly up the aisle of the theatre and wait at the foot of the stairway for the tottering tycoon*)

LADY MULLIGAN You cannot be sick till we get on the Fugitivo!

LORD MULLIGAN Forward all cables to Guaranty Trust in Paris.

LADY MULLIGAN Place de la Concorde.

LORD MULLIGAN Thank you! All purchases C.O.D. to Mulligan Iron & Steel Works in Cobh—Thank you!

LADY MULLIGAN Raymond! Raymond! Who are these men?

LORD MULLIGAN I know these men! I recognize their faces!

LADY MULLIGAN Raymond! They're the Streetcleaners! (*She screams and runs up the aisle screaming repeatedly, stopping half-way to look back. The Two Streetcleaners seize* LORD MULLIGAN *by either arm as he crumples*) Pack Lord Mulligan's body in dry ice! Ship Air Express to Cobh care of Mulligan Iron & Steel Works, in Cobh! (*She runs sobbing out of the back of the auditorium as the whistle blows repeatedly and a Voice shouts*) I'm coming! I'm coming!

MARGUERITE Jacques! Jacques! Oh, God!

PILOT The Fugitivo is leaving, all aboard! (*He starts toward the steps.* MARGUERITE *clutches his arm*) Let go of me!

MARGUERITE You can't go without me!

PILOT Officer, hold this woman!

JACQUES Marguerite, let him go!

(*She releases the* PILOT'S *arm and turns savagely on* JACQUES. *She tears his coat open, seizes a large envelope of papers and rushes after the* PILOT *who has started down the steps over the orchestra pit and into a center aisle of the house. Timpani build up as she starts down the steps, screaming—)*

MARGUERITE Here! I have them here! Wait! I have my papers now, I have my papers!

(The PILOT *runs cursing up the center aisle as the Fugitivo whistle gives repeated short, shrill blasts; timpani and dissonant brass are heard. Outgoing Passengers burst into hysterical song, laughter, shouts of farewell. These can come over a loudspeaker at the back of the house)*

VOICE IN DISTANCE Going! Going! Going!

MARGUERITE *(Attempting as if half-paralyzed to descend the steps)* NOT WITHOUT ME, NO, NO, NOT WITHOUT ME!

(Her figure is caught in the dazzling glacial light of the follow-spot. It blinds her. She makes violent, crazed gestures, clinging to the railing of the steps; her breath is loud and hoarse as a dying person's, she holds a blood-stained handkerchief to her lips. There is a prolonged, gradually fading, rocketlike roar as the Fugitivo takes off. Shrill cries of joy from departing passengers; something radiant passes above the stage and streams of confetti and tinsel fall into the plaza. Then there is a great calm, the ship's receding roar diminished to the hum of an insect)

GUTMAN *(Somewhat compassionately)* Block Ten on the Camino Real.

BLOCK TEN

There is something about the desolation of the plaza that suggests a city devastated by bombardment. Reddish lights flicker here and there as if ruins were smoldering and wisps of smoke rise from them.

LA MADRECITA (*Almost inaudibly*) Donde?

THE DREAMER Aquí. Aquí, Madrecita.

MARGUERITE Lost! Lost! Lost! Lost!

(*She is still clinging brokenly to the railing of the steps.* JACQUES *descends to her and helps her back up the steps*)

JACQUES Lean against me, Cara. Breathe quietly, now.

MARGUERITE Lost!

JACQUES Breathe quietly, quietly, and look up at the sky.

MARGUERITE Lost . . .

JACQUES These tropical nights are so clear. There's the Southern Cross. Do you see the Southern Cross, Marguerite? (*He points through the proscenium. They are now on the bench before the fountain; she is resting in his arms*) And there, over there, is Orion, like a fat, golden fish swimming North in the deep clear water, and we are together, breathing quietly together, leaning together, quietly, quietly together, completely, sweetly together, not frightened, now, not alone, but completely quietly together . . . (LA MADRECITA, *led into the center of the plaza by her son, has begun to sing very softly; the reddish flares dim out and the smoke disappears*) All of us have a desperate bird in our hearts, a memory of—some distant mother with—wings . . .

MARGUERITE I would have—left—without you . . .

JACQUES I know, I know!

MARGUERITE Then how can you—still—?

JACQUES Hold you? (MARGUERITE *nods slightly*) Because you've taught me that part of love which is tender. I never knew it before. Oh, I had—mistresses that circled me like moons! I scrambled from one bed-chamber to another bed-chamber with shirttails always aflame, from girl to girl, like buckets of coal-oil poured on a conflagration! But never loved until now with the part of love that's tender . . .

MARGUERITE —We're used to each other. That's what you think is love . . . You'd better leave me now, you'd better go and let me go because there's a cold wind blowing out of the mountains and over the desert and into my heart, and if you stay with me now, I'll say cruel things, I'll wound your vanity, I'll taunt you with the decline of your male vigor!

JACQUES Why does disappointment make people unkind to each other?

MARGUERITE Each of us is very much alone.

JACQUES Only if we distrust each other.

MARGUERITE We have to distrust each other. It is our only defense against betrayal.

JACQUES I think our defense is love.

MARGUERITE Oh, Jacques, we're used to each other, we're a pair of captive hawks caught in the same cage, and so we've grown used to each other. That's what passes for love at this dim, shadowy end of the Camino Real . . . What are we sure of? Not even of our existence, dear comforting friend! And whom can we ask the questions that torment us? "What is this place?" "Where are we?" —a fat old man who gives sly hints that only bewilder us more, a fake of a Gypsy squinting at cards and tea-leaves. What else are we offered? The never-broken procession of little events that assure us that we and strangers about us are still going on! Where? Why? and the perch that we hold is unstable! We're threatened with eviction, for this is a port of entry and departure, there are no permanent guests! And where else have we to go when we leave here? Bide-a-While? "Ritz Men Only"? Or under that ominous arch into Terra Incognita? We're lonely. We're frightened. We hear the Streetcleaners' piping not far away. So now and then, although we've wounded each other time and again—we stretch out hands to each other in the dark that we can't escape from—we huddle together for some dim-communal comfort—and that's what passes for love on this terminal stretch of the road that used to be royal. What is it, this feeling between us? When you feel my exhausted weight against your shoulder—when I clasp your anxious old hawk's head to my breast, what is it we feel in whatever is left of our hearts? Something, yes, something—delicate, unreal, bloodless! The sort of violets that could grow on the moon, or in the crevices of those far away mountains, fertilized by the droppings of carrion birds. Those birds are familiar to us. Their shadows inhabit the plaza. I've heard them flapping their wings like old charwomen beating worn-out carpets with gray brooms . . . But tenderness, the violets in the mountains—can't break the rocks!

JACQUES The violets in the mountains can break the rocks if you believe in them and allow them to grow!

(*The plaza has resumed its usual aspect. Abdullah enters through one of the downstage arches*)

ABDULLAH Get your carnival hats and noisemakers here! Tonight the moon will restore the virginity of my sister!

MARGUERITE (*Almost tenderly touching his face*) Don't you know that tonight I am going to betray you?

JACQUES —Why would you do that?

MARGUERITE Because I've out-lived the tenderness of my heart. Abdullah, come here! I have an errand for you! Go to Ahmed's and deliver a message!

ABDULLAH I'm working for Mama, making the Yankee dollar! Get your carnival hats and—

MARGUERITE *Here, boy!*

(*She snatches a ring off her finger and offers it to him*)

JACQUES —Your cabochon sapphire?

MARGUERITE Yes, my cabochon sapphire!

JACQUES Are you mad?

MARGUERITE Yes, I'm mad, or nearly! The specter of lunacy's at my heels tonight! (JACQUES *drives* ABDULLAH *back with his cane*) Catch, boy! The other side of the fountain! Quick! (*The guitar is heard molto vivace. She tosses the ring across the fountain.* JACQUES *attempts to hold the boy back with his cane.* ABDULLAH *dodges in and out like a little terrier, laughing.* MARGUERITE *shouts encouragement in French. When the boy is driven back from the ring, she snatches it up and tosses it to him again, shouting*) *Catch, boy! Run to Ahmed's!* Tell the charming young man that the French lady's bored with her company tonight! Say that the French lady missed the Fugitivo and wants to forget she missed it! Oh, and reserve a room with a balcony so I can watch your sister appear on the roof when the moonrise makes her a virgin! (ABDULLAH *skips shouting out of the plaza.* JACQUES *strikes the stage with his cane. She says, without looking at him*) Time betrays us and we betray each other.

JACQUES Wait, Marguerite.

MARGUERITE No! I can't! The wind from the desert is sweeping me away!

(*A loud singing wind sweeps her toward the terrace, away from him. She looks back once or twice as if for some gesture of leave-taking but he only stares at her fiercely, striking the stage at intervals with his cane, like a death-march.* GUTMAN *watches, smiling, from the terrace, bows to* MARGUERITE *as she passes into the hotel. The drum of* JACQUES' *cane is taken up by other percus-*

sive instruments, and almost unnoticeably at first, weird-looking celebrants or carnival mummers creep into the plaza, silently as spiders descending a wall. A sheet of scarlet and yellow rice paper bearing some cryptic device is lowered from the center of the plaza. The percussive effects become gradually louder. JACQUES *is oblivious to the scene behind him, standing in front of the plaza, his eyes closed)*

GUTMAN Block Eleven on the Camino Real.

BLOCK ELEVEN

GUTMAN The Fiesta has started. The first event is the coronation of the King of Cuckolds.

(*Blinding shafts of light are suddenly cast upon* CASANOVA *on the forestage. He shields his face, startled, as the crowd closes about him. The blinding shafts of light seem to strike him like savage blows and he falls to his knees as—The Hunchback scuttles out of the* GYPSY'S *stall with a crown of gilded antlers on a velvet pillow. He places it on* JACQUES' *head. The celebrants form a circle about him chanting*)

JACQUES What is this?—a crown—

GUTMAN A crown of horns!

CROWD Cornudo! Cornudo! Cornudo! Cornudo! Cornudo!

GUTMAN Hail, all hail, the King of Cuckolds on the Camino Real!

(JACQUES *springs up, first striking out at them with his cane. Then all at once he abandons self-defense, throws off his cape, casts away his cane, and fills the plaza with a roar of defiance and self-derision*)

JACQUES Si, si, sono cornudo! Cornudo! Cornudo! Casanova is the King of Cuckolds on the Camino Real! Show me crowned to the world! Announce the honor! Tell the world of the honor bestowed on Casanova, Chevalier de Seingalt! Knight of the Golden Spur by the Grace of His Holiness the Pope . . . Famous adventurer! Con man Extraordinary! Gambler! Pitch-man par excellence! Shill! Pimp! Spiv! *And—great—lover . . .* (*The Crowd howls with applause and laughter but his voice rises above them with sobbing intensity*) Yes, I said GREAT LOVER!

The greatest lover wears the longest horns on the Camino! GREAT! LOVER!

GUTMAN Attention! Silence! The moon is rising! The restoration is about to occur!

(*A white radiance is appearing over the ancient wall of the town. The mountains become luminous. There is music. Everyone, with breathless attention, faces the light.* KILROY *crosses to* JACQUES *and beckons him out behind the crowd. There he snatches off the antlers and returns him his fedora.* JACQUES *reciprocates by removing* KILROY'S *fright wig and electric nose. They embrace as brothers. In a Chaplinesque dumb-play,* KILROY *points to the wildly flickering three brass balls of the* LOAN SHARK *and to his golden gloves: then with a terrible grimace he removes the gloves from about his neck, smiles at* JACQUES *and indicates that the two of them together will take flight over the wall.* JACQUES *shakes his head sadly, pointing to his heart and then to the Siete Mares.* KILROY *nods with regretful understanding of a human and manly folly. A Guard has been silently approaching them in a soft shoe dance.* JACQUES *whistles "La Golondrina."* KILROY *assumes a very nonchalant pose. The Guard picks up curiously the discarded fright wig and electric nose. Then glancing suspiciously at the pair, he advances.* KILROY *makes a run for it. He does a baseball slide into the* LOAN SHARK'S *welcoming doorway. The door slams. The Cop is about to crash it when a gong sounds and* GUTMAN *shouts*)

GUTMAN SILENCE! ATTENTION! THE GYPSY!

GYPSY (*Appearing on the roof with a gong*) The moon has restored the virginity of my daughter Esmeralda!

(*The gong sounds*)

STREET PEOPLE Ahh!

GYPSY The moon in its plenitude has made her a virgin!

(*The gong sounds*)

STREET PEOPLE Ahh!

GYPSY Praise her, celebrate her, give her suitable homage!
(*The gong sounds*)

STREET PEOPLE Ahh!

GYPSY Summon her to the roof! (*She shouts*) ESMERALDA! (*Dancers shout the name in rhythm*) RISE WITH THE MOON, MY DAUGHTER! CHOOSE THE HERO!

(ESMERALDA *appears on the roof in dazzling light. She seems to be dressed in jewels. She raises her jeweled arms with a harsh flamenco cry*)

ESMERALDA OLE!

DANCERS OLE!

(*The details of the Carnival are a problem for director and choreographer but it has already been indicated in the script that the Fiesta is a sort of serio-comic, grotesque-lyric "Rites of Fertility" with roots in various pagan cultures. It should not be over-elaborated or allowed to occupy much time. It should not be more than three minutes from the appearance of* ESMERALDA *on the* GYPSY'S *roof till the return of* KILROY *from the* LOAN SHARK'S. KILROY *emerges from the Pawn Shop in grotesque disguise, a turban, dark glasses, a burnoose and an umbrella or sunshade*)

KILROY (*To* JACQUES) So long, pal, I wish you could come with me.

(JACQUES *clasps his cross in* KILROY'S *hands*)

ESMERALDA Yankee!

KILROY (*To the audience*) So long, everybody. Good luck to you all on the Camino! I hocked my golden gloves to finance this expedition. I'm going. Hasta luega. I'm going. I'm gone!

ESMERALDA Yankee!

(*He has no sooner entered the plaza than the riotous women strip off everything but the dungarees and skivvy which he first appeared in*)

KILROY (*To the women*) Let me go. Let go of me! Watch out for my equipment!

ESMERALDA Yankee! Yankee!

(*He breaks away from them and plunges up the stairs of the ancient wall. He is half-way up them when* GUTMAN *shouts out*)

GUTMAN Follow-spot on that gringo, light the stairs!

(*The light catches* KILROY. *At the same instant* ESMERALDA *cries out to him*)

ESMERALDA *Yankee! Yankee!*

GYPSY What's goin' on down there?

(*She rushes into the plaza*)

KILROY Oh, no, I'm on my way out!

ESMERALDA Espere un momento!

(*The* GYPSY *calls the police, but is ignored in the crowd*)

KILROY Don't tempt me, baby! I hocked my golden gloves to finance this expedition!

ESMERALDA Querido!

KILROY Querido means sweetheart, a word which is hard to resist but I must resist it.

ESMERALDA Champ!

KILROY I used to be Champ but why remind me of it?

ESMERALDA Be champ again! Contend in the contest! Compete in the competition!

GYPSY (*Shouting*) *Naw, naw, not eligible!*

ESMERALDA *Pl-eeeeeeze!*

GYPSY Slap her, Nursie, she's flippin'.

(ESMERALDA *slaps* NURSIE *instead*)

ESMERALDA Hero! Champ!

KILROY I'm not in condition!

ESMERALDA You're still the Champ, the undefeated Champ of the golden gloves!

KILROY Nobody's called me that in a long, long time!

ESMERALDA Champ!

KILROY My resistance is crumbling!

ESMERALDA Champ!

KILROY It's crumbled!

ESMERALDA Hero!

KILROY GERONIMO! (*He takes a flying leap from the stairs into the center of the plaza. He turns toward* ESMERALDA *and cries*) DOLL!!

(KILROY *surrounded by cheering Street People goes into a triumphant eccentric dance which reviews his history as fighter, traveler and lover. At finish of the dance, the music is cut off, as* KILROY *lunges, arm uplifted towards* ESMERALDA, *and cries*)

KILROY *Kilroy the Champ!*

ESMERALDA *KILROY the Champ!*

(*She snatches a bunch of red roses from the stunned* NURSIE *and tosses them to* KILROY)

CROWD (*Sharply*) OLE!

(*The* GYPSY, *at the same instant, hurls her gong down, creating a resounding noise.* KILROY *turns and comes down towards the audience, saying to them*)

KILROY *Y'see?*

(*Cheering Street People surge towards him and lift him in the air. The lights fade as the curtain descends*)

CROWD (*In a sustained yell*) *OLE!*

(*The curtain falls. There is a short intermission*)

BLOCK TWELVE

The stage is in darkness except for a spotlight which picks out ESMERALDA *on the* GYPSY'S *roof.*

ESMERALDA Mama, what happened?—Mama, the lights went out!—Mama, where are you? It's so dark I'm scared!—MAMA!

(*The lights are turned on displaying a deserted plaza. The* GYPSY *is seated at a small table before her stall*)

GYPSY Come on downstairs, Doll. The mischief is done. You've chosen your hero!

GUTMAN (*From the balcony of the Siete Mares*) Block Twelve on the Camino Real.

NURSIE (*At the fountain*) Gypsy, the fountain is still dry!

GYPSY What d'yuh expect? There's nobody left to uphold the old traditions! You raise a girl. She watches television. Plays be-bop. Reads *Screen Secrets.* Comes the Big Fiesta. The moonrise makes her a virgin—which is the neatest trick of the week! And what does she do? Chooses a Fugitive Patsy for the Chosen Hero! Well, show him in! Admit the joker and get the virgin ready!

NURSIE You're going through with it?

GYPSY Look, Nursie! I'm operating a legitimate joint! This joker'll get the same treatment he'd get if he breezed down the Camino in a blizzard of G-notes! Trot, girl! Lubricate your means of locomotion!

(NURSIE *goes into the* GYPSY'S *stall. The* GYPSY *rubs her hands together and blows on the crystal ball, spits on it and gives it the old one-two with a "shammy" rag . . . She mutters "Crystal ball, tell me all . . . crystal ball tell me all" . . . as* KILROY *bounds into the plaza from her stall . . . a rose between his teeth*)

GYPSY Siente se, por favor.

KILROY No comprendo the lingo.

GYPSY Put it down!

NURSIE (*Offstage*) Hey, Gypsy!

GYPSY Address me as Madam!

NURSIE (*Entering*) *Madam!* Winchell has scooped you!

GYPSY In a pig's eye!

NURSIE The Fugitivo has "*fftt . . .*"!

GYPSY In Elizabeth, New Jersey . . . ten fifty seven P.M. . . . Eastern Standard Time—while you were putting them kiss-me-quicks in your hair-do! Furthermore, my second exclusive is that the solar system is drifting towards the constellation of Hercules: *Skiddoo!* (NURSIE *exits. Stamping is heard offstage*) *Quiet, back there! God damn it!*

NURSIE (*Offstage*) She's out of control!

GYPSY Give her a double-bromide! (*To* KILROY) Well, how does it feel to be the Chosen Hero?

KILROY I better explain something to you.

GYPSY Save your breath. You'll need it.

KILROY I want to level with you. Can I level with you?

GYPSY (*Rapidly stamping some papers*) How could you help but level with the Gypsy?

KILROY I don't know what the hero is chosen for

(ESMERALDA *and* NURSIE *shriek offstage*)

GYPSY Time will brief you . . . Aw, I hate paper work! . . . NURSEHH! (NURSIE *comes out and stands by the table*) This filing system is screwed up six ways from Next Sunday . . . File this crap under crap!— (*To* KILROY) The smoking lamp is lit. Have a stick on me! (*She offers him a cigarette*)

KILROY No thanks.

GYPSY Come on, indulge yourself. You got nothing to lose that won't be lost.

KILROY If that's a professional opinion, I don't respect it.

GYPSY Resume your seat and give me your full name.

KILROY Kilroy.

GYPSY (*Writing all this down*) Date of birth and place of that disaster?

KILROY Both unknown.

GYPSY Address?

KILROY Traveler.

GYPSY Parents?

KILROY Anonymous.

GYPSY Who brought you up?

KILROY I was brought up and down by an eccentric old aunt in Dallas.

GYPSY Raise both hands simultaneously and swear that you have not come here for the purpose of committing an immoral act.

ESMERALDA (*From offstage*) Hey, Chico!

GYPSY *QUIET!* Childhood diseases?

KILROY Whooping cough, measles and mumps.

GYPSY Likes and dislikes?

KILROY I like situations I can get out of. I don't like cops and—

GYPSY Immaterial! Here! Signature on this!
(*She hands him a blank*)

KILROY What is it?

GYPSY You always sign something, don't you?

KILROY Not till I know what it is.

GYPSY It's just a little formality to give a tone to the establishment and make an impression on our out-of-town trade. Roll up your sleeve.

KILROY What for?

GYPSY A shot of some kind.

KILROY What kind?

GYPSY Any kind. Don't they always give you some kind of a shot?

KILROY "They"?

GYPSY Brass-hats, Americanos!
(*She injects a hypo*)

KILROY I am no guinea pig!

GYPSY Don't kid yourself. We're all of us guinea pigs in the laboratory of God. Humanity is just a work in progress.

KILROY I don't make it out.

GYPSY Who does? The Camino Real is a funny paper read backwards! (*There is weird piping outside.* KILROY *shifts on his seat. The* GYPSY *grins*) Tired? The altitude makes you sleepy?

KILROY It makes me nervous.

GYPSY I'll show you how to take a slug of tequila! It dilates the capillaries. First you sprinkle salt on the back of your hand. Then lick it off with your tongue. Now then you toss the shot down! (*She demonstrates*) —And then you bite into the lemon. That way it goes down easy, but what a bang!—You're next.

KILROY No, thanks, I'm on the wagon.

GYPSY There's an old Chinese proverb that says, "When your goose is cooked you might as well have it cooked with plenty of gravy." (*She laughs*) Get up, baby. Let's have a look at yuh!—You're not a bad-looking boy. Sometimes working for the Yankee dollar isn't a painful profession. Have you ever been attracted by older women?

KILROY Frankly, no, ma'am.

GYPSY Well, there's a first time for everything.

KILROY That is a subject I cannot agree with you on.

GYPSY You think I'm an old bag? (KILROY *laughs awkwardly. The* GYPSY *slaps his face*) Will you take the cards or the crystal?

KILROY It's immaterial.

GYPSY All right, we'll begin with the cards. (*She shuffles and deals*) Ask me a question.

KILROY Has my luck run out?

GYPSY Baby, your luck ran out the day you were born. Another question.

KILROY Ought I to leave this town?

GYPSY It don't look to me like you've got much choice in the matter . . . Take a card.

(KILROY *takes one*)

GYPSY Ace?

KILROY Yes, ma'am.

GYPSY What color?

KILROY Black.

GYPSY Oh, oh—That does it. How big is your heart?

KILROY As big as the head of a baby.

GYPSY It's going to break.

KILROY That's what I was afraid of.

GYPSY The Streetcleaners are waiting for you outside the door.

KILROY Which door, the front one? I'll slip out the back!

GYPSY Leave us face it frankly, your number is up! You must've known a long time that the name of Kilroy was on the Streetcleaners' list.

KILROY Sure. But not on top of it!

GYPSY It's always a bit of a shock. Wait a minute! Here's good news. The Queen of Hearts has turned up in proper position.

KILROY What's that mean?

GYPSY Love, Baby!

KILROY Love?

GYPSY The Booby Prize!—Esmeralda!

(*She rises and hits a gong. A divan is carried out. The* GYPSY'S *Daughter is seated in a reclining position, like an odalisque, on this low divan. A spangled veil covers her face. From this veil to the girdle below her navel, that supports her diaphanous bifurcated skirt, she is nude except for a pair of glittering emerald snakes coiled over her breasts.* KILROY'S *head moves in a dizzy circle and a canary warbles inside it*)

KILROY WHAT'S—WHAT'S *HER* SPECIALTY?—Tea-leaves?

(*The* GYPSY *wags a finger*)

GYPSY You know what curiosity did to the tom cat!—Nursie, give me my glamour wig and my forty-five. I'm hitting the street! I gotta go down to Walgreen's for change.

KILROY What change?

GYPSY The change from that ten-spot you're about to give me.

NURSIE Don't argue with her. She has a will of iron.

KILROY I'm not arguing! (*He reluctantly produces the money*) But let's be *fair* about this! I hocked my golden gloves for this saw-buck!

NURSIE All of them Yankee bastids want something for nothing!

KILROY I want a receipt for this bill.

NURSIE No one is gypped at the Gypsy's!

KILROY That's wonderful! How do I know it?

GYPSY It's in the cards, it's in the crystal ball, it's in the tea-leaves! Absolutely no one is gypped at the Gypsy's! (*She snatches the bill. The wind howls*) Such changeable weather! I'll slip on my summer furs! Nursie, break out my summer furs!

NURSIE (*Leering grotesquely*) *Mink or sable?*

GYPSY *Ha ha, that's a doll!* Here! Clock him! (NURSIE *tosses her a greasy blanket, and the* GYPSY *tosses* NURSIE *an alarm clock. The* GYPSY *rushes through the beaded string curtains*) *Adios!* Ha ha!!

(*She is hardly offstage when two shots ring out.* KILROY *starts*)

ESMERALDA (*Plaintively*) Mother has such an awful time on the street.

KILROY You mean that she is insulted on the street?

ESMERALDA By strangers.

KILROY (*To the audience*) I shouldn't think acquaintances

would do it. (*She curls up on the low divan.* KILROY *licks his lips*) —You seem very different from—this afternoon . . .

ESMERALDA This afternoon?

KILROY Yes, in the plaza when I was being roughed up by them gorillas and you was being dragged in the house by your Mama! (ESMERALDA *stares at him blankly*) You don't remember?

ESMERALDA I never remember what happened before the moonrise makes me a virgin.

KILROY —That—comes as a shock to you, huh?

ESMERALDA Yes. It comes as a shock.

KILROY (*Smiling*) You have a little temporary amnesia they call it!

ESMERALDA Yankee . . .

KILROY Huh?

ESMERALDA I'm glad I chose you. I'm glad that you were chosen. (*Her voice trails off*) I'm glad. I'm very glad . . .

NURSIE Doll!

ESMERALDA —What is it, Nursie?

NURSIE How are things progressing?

ESMERALDA Slowly, Nursie—

(NURSIE *comes lumbering in*)

NURSIE I want some light reading matter.

ESMERALDA He's sitting on *Screen Secrets.*

KILROY (*Jumping up*) Aw. Here. (*He hands her the fan magazine. She lumbers back out, coyly*) —I—I feel——self-conscious . . . (*He suddenly jerks out a silver-framed photo*) —D'you—like pictures?

ESMERALDA Moving pictures?

KILROY No, a—motionless—snapshot!

ESMERALDA Of you?

KILROY Of my—real—true woman . . . She was a platinum blonde the same as Jean Harlow. Do you remember Jean Harlow? No, you wouldn't remember Jean Harlow.

It shows you are getting old when you remember Jean Harlow. (*He puts the snapshot away*) . . . They say that Jean Harlow's ashes are kept in a little private cathedral in Forest Lawn . . . Wouldn't it be wonderful if you could sprinkle them ashes over the ground like seeds, and out of each one would spring another Jean Harlow? And when spring comes you could just walk out and pick them off the bush! . . . You don't talk much.

ESMERALDA You want me to *talk?*

KILROY Well, that's the way we do things in the States. A little vino, some records on the victrola, some quiet conversation—and then if both parties are in a mood for romance . . . Romance—

ESMERALDA Music! (*She rises and pours some wine from a slender crystal decanter as music is heard*) They say that the monetary system has got to be stabilized all over the world.

KILROY (*Taking the glass*) Repeat that, please. My radar was not wide open.

ESMERALDA I said that *they* said that—uh, skip it! But we couldn't care less as long as we keep on getting the Yankee dollar . . . plus federal tax!

KILROY That's for surely!

ESMERALDA How do you feel about the class struggle? Do you take sides in that?

KILROY Not that I—

ESMERALDA Neither do we because of the dialectics.

KILROY Who! Which?

ESMERALDA Languages with accents, I suppose. But Mama don't care as long as they don't bring the Pope over here and put him in the White House.

KILROY Who would do that?

ESMERALDA Oh, the Bolsheviskies, those nasty old things with whiskers! *Whiskers scratch!* But little moustaches tickle . . .

(*She giggles*)

KILROY I always got a smooth shave . . .

ESMERALDA And how do you feel about the Mumbo Jumbo? Do you think they've got the Old Man in the bag yet?

KILROY The Old Man?

ESMERALDA God. We don't thing so. We think there has been so much of the Mumbo Jumbo it's put Him to sleep!

(KILROY *jumps up impatiently*)

KILROY This is not what I mean by a quiet conversation. I mean this is no where! *No where!*

ESMERALDA What sort of talk do you want?

KILROY Something more—intimate sort of! You know, like—

ESMERALDA —Where did you get those eyes?

KILROY *PERSONAL! Yeah* . . .

ESMERALDA Well,—where did you get those eyes?

KILROY Out of a dead cod-fish!

NURSIE (*Shouting offstage*) DOLL!

(KILROY *springs up, pounding his left palm with his right fist*)

ESMERALDA What?

NURSIE Fifteen minutes!

KILROY I'm no hot-rod mechanic. (*To the audience*) I bet she's out there holding a stop watch to see that I don't over-stay my time in this place!

ESMERALDA (*Calling through the string curtains*) *Nursie, go to bed, Nursie!*

KILROY (*In a fierce whisper*) That's right, go to bed, Nursie!!

(*There is a loud crash offstage*)

ESMERALDA —Nursie has gone to bed . . .

(*She drops the string curtains and returns to the alcove*)

KILROY (*With vast relief*) —Ahhhhhhhhhh . . .

ESMERALDA What've you got your eyes on?

KILROY Those green snakes on you—what do you wear them for?

ESMERALDA Supposedly for protection, but really for fun. (*He crosses to the divan*) What are you going to do?

KILROY I'm about to establish a beach-head on that sofa. (*He sits down*) How about—lifting your veil?

ESMERALDA I can't lift it.

KILROY Why not?

ESMERALDA I promised Mother I wouldn't.

KILROY I thought your mother was the broadminded type.

ESMERALDA Oh, she is, but you know how mothers are. You can lift it for me, if you say pretty please.

KILROY Aww——

ESMERALDA Go on, say it! Say pretty please!

KILROY No!!

ESMERALDA Why not?

KILROY It's silly.

ESMERALDA Then you can't lift my veil!

KILROY Oh, all right. Pretty please.

ESMERALDA Say it again!

KILROY Pretty please.

ESMERALDA Now say it once more like you meant it. (*He jumps up. She grabs his hand*) Don't go away.

KILROY You're making a fool out of me.

ESMERALDA I was just teasing a little. Because you're so cute. Sit down again, please—*pretty* please! (*He falls on the couch*)

KILROY What is that wonderful perfume you've got on?

ESMERALDA Guess!

KILROY Chanel Number Five?

ESMERALDA No.

KILROY Tabu?

ESMERALDA No.

KILROY I give up

ESMERALDA It's *Noche en Acapulco!* I'm just dying to go to Acapulco. I wish that you would take me to Acapulco. (*He sits up*) What's the matter?

KILROY You gypsies' daughters are invariably reminded of something without which you cannot do—just when it looks like everything has been fixed.

ESMERALDA That isn't nice at all. I'm not the gold-digger type. Some girls see themselves in silver foxes. I only see myself in Acapulco!

KILROY At Todd's Place?

ESMERALDA Oh, no, at the Mirador! Watching those pretty boys dive off the Quebrada!

KILROY Look again, Baby. Maybe you'll see yourself in Paramount Pictures or having a Singapore Sling at a Statler bar!

ESMERALDA You're being sarcastic?

KILROY Nope. Just realistic. All of you gypsies' daughters have hearts of stone, and I'm not whistling "Dixie"! But just the same, the night before a man dies, he says, "Pretty please—will you let me lift your veil?"—while the Streetcleaners wait for him right outside the door!—Because to be warm for a little longer is life. And love?—that's a four-letter word which is sometimes no better than one you see printed on fences by kids playing hooky from school!—Oh, well—what's the use of complaining? You gypsies' daughters have ears that only catch sounds like the snap of a gold cigarette case! Or, pretty please, Baby,—we're going to Acapulco!

ESMERALDA *Are* we?

KILROY See what I mean? (*To the audience*) Didn't I tell you?! (*To* ESMERALDA) Yes! In the morning!

ESMERALDA Ohhhh! I'm dizzy with joy! My little heart is going pitty-pat!

KILROY My big heart is going boom-boom! Can I lift your veil now?

ESMERALDA If you will be gentle.

KILROY I would not hurt a fly unless it had on leather mittens.

(*He touches a corner of her spangled veil*)

ESMERALDA Ohhh . . .

KILROY What?

ESMERALDA Ohhhhhh!!

KILROY Why! What's the matter?

ESMERALDA You are not being gentle!

KILROY I *am* being gentle.

ESMERALDA You are *not* being gentle.

KILROY What was I being, then?

ESMERALDA Rough!

KILROY I am *not* being rough.

ESMERALDA Yes, you *are* being rough. You have to be gentle with me because you're the first.

KILROY Are you kidding?

ESMERALDA No.

KILROY How about all of those other fiestas you've been to?

ESMERALDA Each one's the first one. That is the wonderful thing about gypsies' daughters!

KILROY You can say that again!

ESMERALDA I don't like you when you're like that.

KILROY Like what?

ESMERALDA Cynical and sarcastic.

KILROY I am sincere.

ESMERALDA Lots of boys aren't sincere.

KILROY Maybe they aren't but I am.

ESMERALDA Everyone says he's sincere, but everyone isn't sincere. If everyone was sincere who says he's sincere there wouldn't be half so many insincere ones in the world and there would be lots, lots, lots more really sincere ones!

KILROY I think you have got something there. But how about gypsies' daughters?

ESMERALDA Huh?

KILROY Are they one hundred percent in the really sincere category?

ESMERALDA Well, yes, and no, mostly no! But some of them are for a while if their sweethearts are gentle.

KILROY Would you believe I am sincere and gentle?

ESMERALDA I would believe that you believe that you are . . . For a while . . .

KILROY Everything's for a while. For a while is the stuff that dreams are made of, Baby! Now?—Now?

ESMERALDA Yes, now, but be gentle!—*gentle* . . .

(*He delicately lifts a corner of her veil. She utters a soft cry. He lifts it further. She cries out again. A bit further . . . He turns the spangled veil all the way up from her face*)

KILROY I am sincere.

ESMERALDA I am sincere.

KILROY I am sincere.

ESMERALDA I am sincere.

KILROY I am sincere.

ESMERALDA I am sincere.

KILROY I am sincere.

ESMERALDA I am sincere. (KILROY *leans back, removing his hand from her veil. She opens her eyes*) Is that all?

KILROY I am tired.

ESMERALDA —Already?

(*He rises and goes down the steps from the alcove*)

KILROY I am tired, and full of regret . . .

ESMERALDA Oh!

KILROY It wasn't much to give my golden gloves for.

ESMERALDA You pity yourself?

KILROY That's right, I pity myself and everybody that goes to the Gypsy's daughter. I pity the world and I pity the God who made it.

(*He sits down*)

ESMERALDA It's always like that as soon as the veil is

lifted. They're all so ashamed of having degraded themselves, and their hearts have more regret than a heart can hold!

KILROY Even a heart that's as big as the head of a baby!

ESMERALDA You don't even notice how pretty my face is, do you?

KILROY You look like all gypsies' daughters, no better, no worse. But as long as you get to go to Acapulco, your cup runneth over with ordinary contentment.

ESMERALDA —I've never been so insulted in all my life!

KILROY Oh, yes, you have, Baby. And you'll be insulted worse if you stay in this racket. You'll be insulted so much that it will get to be like water off *a duck's back!* (*The door slams. Curtains are drawn apart on the* GYPSY. ESMERALDA *lowers her veil hastily.* KILROY *pretends not to notice the* GYPSY'S *entrance. She picks up a little bell and rings it over his head*) Okay, Mamacita! I am aware of your presence!

GYPSY Ha-ha! I was followed three blocks by some awful man!

KILROY Then you caught him.

GYPSY Naw, he ducked into a subway! I waited fifteen minutes outside the men's room and he never came out!

KILROY Then you went in?

GYPSY No! I got myself a sailor!—The streets are brilliant! . . . Have you all been good children? (ESMERALDA *makes a whimpering sound*) The pussy will play while the old mother cat is away?

KILROY Your sense of humor is wonderful, but how about my change, Mamacita?

GYPSY What change are you talking about?

KILROY Are you boxed out of your mind? The change from that ten-spot you trotted over to Walgreen's?

GYPSY Ohhhhh—

KILROY *Oh, what?*

GYPSY (*Counting on her fingers*) Five for the works, one

dollar luxury tax, two for the house percentage and two more pour la service!—makes ten! Didn't I tell you?

KILROY —What kind of a deal is this?

GYPSY (*Whipping out a revolver*) A rugged one, Baby!

ESMERALDA Mama, don't be unkind!

GYPSY Honey, the gentleman's friends are waiting outside the door and it wouldn't be nice to detain him! Come on —Get going—Vamoose!

KILROY Okay, Mamacita! Me voy! (*He crosses to the beaded string curtains: turns to look back at the* GYPSY *and her daughter. The piping of the Streetcleaners is heard outside*) Sincere?—Sure! That's the wonderful thing about gypsies' daughters!

(*He goes out.* ESMERALDA *raises a wondering fingertip to one eye. Then she cries out*)

ESMERALDA Look, Mama! Look, Mama! A tear!

GYPSY You have been watching television too much . . .

(*She gathers the cards and turns off the crystal ball as light fades out on the phony paradise of the* GYPSY'S)

GUTMAN Block Thirteen on the Camino Real.

(*He exits*)

BLOCK THIRTEEN

In the blackout the Streetcleaners place a barrel in the center and then hide in the Pit.

KILROY, *who enters from the right, is followed by a spotlight. He sees the barrel and the menacing Streetcleaners and then runs to the closed door of the Siete Mares and rings the bell. No one answers. He backs up so he can see the balcony and calls:*

KILROY Mr. Gutman! Just gimme a cot in the lobby. I'll do odd jobs in the morning. I'll be the Patsy again. I'll light my nose sixty times a minute. I'll take prat-falls and assume the position for anybody that drops a dime on the street . . . Have a heart! Have just a LITTLE heart. Please!

(*There is no response from* GUTMAN'S *balcony.* JACQUES *enters. He pounds his cane once on the pavement*)

JACQUES Gutman! Open the door!—*GUTMAN! GUTMAN!*

(EVA, *a beautiful woman, apparently nude, appears on the balcony*)

GUTMAN (*From inside*) Eva darling, you're exposing yourself!

(*He appears on the balcony with a portmanteau*)

JACQUES What are you doing with my portmanteau?

GUTMAN Haven't you come for your luggage?

JACQUES Certainly not! I haven't checked out of here!

GUTMAN Very few do . . . but residences are frequently terminated.

JACQUES Open the door!

GUTMAN Open the letter with the remittance check in it!

JACQUES In the morning!

GUTMAN Tonight!

JACQUES Upstairs in my room!

GUTMAN Downstairs at the entrance!

JACQUES I won't be intimidated!

GUTMAN (*Raising the portmanteau over his head*) What?!

JACQUES Wait!—(*He takes the letter out of his pocket*) Give me some light. (KILROY *strikes a match and holds it over* JACQUES' *shoulder*) Thank you. What does it say?

GUTMAN —Remittances?

KILROY (*Reading the letter over* JACQUES' *shoulder*) *—discontinued . . .*

(GUTMAN *raises the portmanteau again*)

JACQUES Careful, I have— (*The portmanteau lands with a crash. The* BUM *comes to the window at the crash.* A. RATT *comes out to his doorway at the same time*) —fragile—mementoes . . . (*He crosses slowly down to the portmanteau and kneels as . . .* GUTMAN *laughs and slams the balcony door.* JACQUES *turns to* KILROY. *He smiles at the young adventurer*) —"And so at last it has come, the distinguished thing!"

(A. RATT *speaks as* JACQUES *touches the portmanteau*)

A. RATT Hey, Dad—Vacancy here! A bed at the "Ritz Men Only." A little white ship to sail the dangerous night in.

JACQUES Single or double?

A. RATT There's only singles in this pad.

JACQUES (*To* KILROY) Match you for it.

KILROY What the hell, we're buddies, we can sleep spoons! If we can't sleep, we'll push the wash stand against the door and sing old popular songs till the crack of dawn! . . . "Heart of my heart, I love that melody!" . . . You bet your life I do. (JACQUES *takes out a pocket hand-*

kerchief and starts to grasp the portmanteau handle) —It looks to me like you could use a Redcap and my rates are non-union! (*He picks up the portmanteau and starts to cross towards the "Ritz Men Only." He stops at right center*) Sorry, buddy. Can't make it! The altitude on this block has affected my ticker! And in the distance which is nearer than further, I hear—the Streetcleaners' —piping!

(*Piping is heard*)

JACQUES COME ALONG!

(*He lifts the portmanteau and starts on*)

KILROY NO. Tonight! I prefer! To sleep! Out! Under! The stars!

JACQUES (*Gently*) I understand, Brother!

KILROY (*To* JACQUES *as he continues toward the "Ritz Men Only"*) Bon Voyage! I hope that you sail the dangerous night to the sweet golden port of morning!

JACQUES (*Exiting*) Thanks, Brother!

KILROY Excuse the *corn!* I'm sincere!

BUM Show me the way to go home! . . .

GUTMAN (*Appearing on the balcony with white parakeet*) Block Fourteen on the Camino Real.

BLOCK FOURTEEN

At opening, the BUM *is still at the window.*

The Streetcleaners' piping continues a little louder. KILROY *climbs, breathing heavily, to the top of the stairs and stands looking out at Terra Incognita as . . .*

MARGUERITE *enters the plaza through alleyway at right. She is accompanied by a silent* YOUNG MAN *who wears a domino.*

MARGUERITE Don't come any further with me. I'll have to wake the night porter. Thank you for giving me safe conduct through the Medina. (*She has offered her hand. He grips it with a tightness that makes her wince*) Ohhhh . . . I'm not sure which is more provocative in you, your ominous silence or your glittering smile or— (*He's looking at her purse*) What do you want? . . . Oh! (*She starts to open the purse. He snatches it. She gasps as he suddenly strips her cloak off her. Then he snatches off her pearl necklace. With each successive despoilment, she gasps and retreats but makes no resistance. Her eyes are closed. He continues to smile. Finally, he rips her dress and runs his hands over her body as if to see if she had anything else of value concealed on her*) —What else do I have that you want?

THE YOUNG MAN (*Contemptuously*) Nothing.

(THE YOUNG MAN *exits through the cantina, examining his loot. The* BUM *leans out his window, draws a deep breath and says*)

BUM Lonely.

MARGUERITE (*To herself*) Lonely . . .

KILROY (*On the steps*) Lonely . . .

(*The Streetcleaners' piping is heard.* MARGUERITE *runs to the Siete Mares and rings the bell. Nobody answers. She crosses to the terrace.* KILROY, *meanwhile, has descended the stairs*)

MARGUERITE Jacques!

(*Piping is heard*)

KILROY Lady?

MARGUERITE What?

KILROY *—I'm—safe* . . .

MARGUERITE I wasn't expecting that music tonight, were you?

(*Piping*)

KILROY It's them Streetcleaners.

MARGUERITE I know.

(*Piping*)

KILROY You better go on in, lady.

MARGUERITE No.

KILROY GO ON IN!

MARGUERITE NO! I want to stay out here and I do what I want to do! (KILROY *looks at her for the first time*) Sit down with me please.

KILROY They're coming for me. The Gypsy told me I'm on top of their list. Thanks for. Taking my. Hand.

(*Piping is heard*)

MARGUERITE Thanks for taking mine.

(*Piping*)

KILROY Do me one more favor. Take out of my pocket a picture. My fingers are. Stiff.

MARGUERITE This one?

KILROY My one. True. Woman.

MARGUERITE A silver-framed photo! Was she really so fair?

KILROY She was so fair and much fairer than they could tint that picture!

MARGUERITE Then you have been on the street when the street was royal.

KILROY Yeah . . . when the street was royal!

(*Piping is heard.* KILROY *rises*)

MARGUERITE Don't get up, don't leave me!

KILROY I want to be on my feet when the Streetcleaners come for me!

MARGUERITE Sit back down again and tell me about your girl.

(*He sits*)

KILROY Y'know what it is you miss most? When you're separated. From someone. You lived. With. And loved? It's waking up in the night! With that—warmness beside you!

MARGUERITE Yes, that *warmness* beside you!

KILROY Once you get used to that. *Warmness!* It's a hell of a lonely feeling to wake up without it! Specially in some dollar-a-night hotel room on Skid! A hot-water bottle won't do. And a stranger. Won't do. It has to be some one you're used to. And that you. *KNOW LOVES* you! (*Piping is heard*) Can you see them?

MARGUERITE I see no one but you.

KILROY I looked at my wife one night when she was sleeping and that was the night that the medics wouldn't okay me for no more fights . . . Well . . . My wife was sleeping with a smile like a child's. I kissed her. She didn't wake up. I took a pencil and paper. I wrote her. Good-bye!

MARGUERITE That was the night she would have loved you the most!

KILROY Yeah, *that* night, but what about *after* that night? Oh, Lady . . . Why should a beautiful girl tie up with a broken-down champ?—The earth still turning and her obliged to turn with it, not out—of dark into light but out of light into dark? Naw, naw, naw, naw!—Washed up!—Finished! (*Piping*) . . . that ain't a word that a man can't look at . . . There ain't no words in the language a man can't look at . . . and know just what they mean. And be. And act. And *go!* (*He turns to the waiting Streetcleaners*) Come on! . . . Come on! . . . COME ON, YOU SONS OF BITCHES! KILROY IS HERE! HE'S READY!

(*A gong sounds.* KILROY *swings at the Streetcleaners. They circle about him out of reach, turning him by each of their movements. The swings grow wilder like a boxer. He falls to his knees still swinging and finally collapses flat on his face. The Streetcleaners pounce but* LA MADRECITA *throws herself protectingly over the body and covers it with her shawl. Blackout*)

MARGUERITE Jacques!

GUTMAN (*On balcony*) Block Fifteen on the Camino Real.

BLOCK FIFTEEN

LA MADRECITA *is seated: across her knees is the body of* KILROY. *Up center, a low table on wheels bears a sheeted figure. Beside the table stands a* MEDICAL INSTRUCTOR *addressing Students and Nurses, all in white surgical outfits*

INSTRUCTOR This is the body of an unidentified vagrant.

LA MADRECITA This was thy son, America—and now mine.

INSTRUCTOR He was found in an alley along the Camino Real.

LA MADRECITA Think of him, now, as he was before his luck failed him. Remember his time of greatness, when he was not faded, not frightened.

INSTRUCTOR More light, please!

LA MADRECITA More light!

INSTRUCTOR Can everyone see clearly!

LA MADRECITA Everyone must see clearly!

INSTRUCTOR There is no external evidence of disease.

LA MADRECITA He had clear eyes and the body of a champion boxer.

INSTRUCTOR There are no marks of violence on the body.

LA MADRECITA He had the soft voice of the South and a pair of golden gloves.

INSTRUCTOR His death was apparently due to natural causes.

(*The Students make notes. There are keening voices*)

LA MADRECITA Yes, blow wind where night thins! He had many admirers!

INSTRUCTOR There are no legal claimants.

LA MADRECITA He stood as a planet among the moons of their longing, haughty with youth, a champion of the prize-ring!

INSTRUCTOR No friends or relatives having identified him—

LA MADRECITA You should have seen the lovely monogrammed robe in which he strode the aisles of the Colosseums!

INSTRUCTOR After the elapse of a certain number of days, his body becomes the property of the State—

LA MADRECITA Yes, blow wind where night thins—for laurel is not everlasting . . .

INSTRUCTOR And now is transferred to our hands for the nominal sum of five dollars.

LA MADRECITA This was thy son,—and now mine . . .

INSTRUCTOR We will now proceed with the dissection. Knife, please!

LA MADRECITA Blow wind! (*Keening is heard off stage*) Yes, blow wind where night thins! You are his passing bell and his lamentation. (*More keening is heard*) Keen for him, all maimed creatures, deformed and mutilated—his homeless ghost is your own!

INSTRUCTOR First we will open up the chest cavity and examine the heart for evidence of coronary occlusion.

LA MADRECITA His heart was pure gold and as big as the head of a baby.

INSTRUCTOR We will make an incision along the vertical line.

LA MADRECITA Rise, ghost! Go! Go bird! "Humankind cannot bear very much reality."

(*At the touch of her flowers,* KILROY *stirs and pushes himself up slowly from her lap. On his feet again, he rubs his eyes and looks around him*)

VOICES (*Crying offstage*) Olé! Olé! Olé!

KILROY Hey! Hey, somebody! Where am I?

(*He notices the dissection room and approaches*)

INSTRUCTOR (*Removing a glittering sphere from a dummy corpse*) Look at this heart. It's as big as the head of a baby.

KILROY My heart!

INSTRUCTOR Wash it off so we can look for the pathological lesions.

KILROY Yes, siree, that's my heart!

GUTMAN Block Sixteen!

(KILROY *pauses just outside the dissection area as a Student takes the heart and dips it into a basin on the stand beside the table. The Student suddenly cries out and holds aloft a glittering gold sphere*)

INSTRUCTOR Look! This heart's solid gold!

BLOCK SIXTEEN

KILROY (*Rushing forward*) That's mine, you bastards!

(*He snatches the golden sphere from the* MEDICAL INSTRUCTOR. *The autopsy proceeds as if nothing had happened as the spot of light on the table fades out, but for* KILROY *a ghostly chase commences, a dreamlike re-enactment of the chase that occurred at the end of Block Six.* GUTMAN *shouts from his balcony*)

GUTMAN Stop, thief, stop, corpse! That gold heart is the property of the State! Catch him, catch the golden-heart robber!

(KILROY *dashes offstage into an aisle of the theatre. There is the wail of a siren: the air is filled with calls and whistles, roar of motors, screeching brakes, pistol-shots, thundering footsteps. The dimness of the auditorium is transected by searching rays of light—but there are no visible pursuers*)

KILROY (*As he runs panting up the aisle*) This is my heart! It don't belong to no State, not even the U.S.A. Which way is out? Where's the Greyhound depot? Nobody's going to put my heart in a bottle in a museum and charge admission to support the rotten police! Where are they? Which way are they going? Or coming? Hey, somebody, help me get out of here! Which way do I—which way—which way do I—*go! go! go! go! go!* (*He has now arrived in the balcony*) *Gee, I'm lost! I don't know where I am!* I'm all turned around, I'm *confused,* I don't understand—what's—happened, it like a—*dream,* it's—just like a—dream . . . *Mary! Oh, Mary! Mary!* (*He has entered the box from which he leapt in Act One. A clear shaft of light falls on him. He looks up into it, crying) Mary, help a Christian!! Help a Christian, Mary!*—It's like a dream . . .

(ESMERALDA *appears in a childish nightgown beside her gauze-tented bed on the* GYPSY'S *roof. Her Mother appears with a cup of some sedative drink, cooing . . .*

GYPSY Beddy-bye, beddy-bye, darling. It's sleepy-time down South and up North, too, and also East and West!

KILROY (*Softly*) Yes, it's—like a—dream . . .

(*He leans panting over the ledge of the box, holding his heart like a football, watching* ESMERALDA)

GYPSY Drink your Ovaltine, Ducks, and the sandman will come on tip-toe with a bag full of dreams . . .

ESMERALDA I want to dream of the Chosen Hero, Mummy.

GYPSY Which one, the one that's coming or the one that is gone?

ESMERALDA The *only* one, *Kilroy! He was sincere!*

KILROY That's *right! I was,* for a while!

GYPSY How do you know that Kilroy was sincere?

ESMERALDA He said so.

KILROY That's the truth, I *was!*

GYPSY When did he say that?

ESMERALDA When he lifted my veil.

GYPSY Baby, they're always sincere when they lift your veil; it's one of those natural reflexes that don't mean a thing.

KILROY (*Aside*) What a cynical old bitch that Gypsy mama is!

GYPSY And there's going to be lots of other fiestas for you, baby doll, and lots of other chosen heroes to lift your little veil when Mamacita and Nursie are out of the room.

ESMERALDA No, Mummy, never, I mean it!

KILROY I *believe* she means it!

GYPSY Finish your Ovaltine and say your Now-I-Lay-Me.

(ESMERALDA *sips the drink and hands her the cup*)

KILROY (*With a catch in his voice*) I had one true woman, which I can't go back to, but now I've found another.

(*He leaps onto the stage from the box*)

ESMERALDA (*Dropping to her knees*) Now I lay me down to sleep, I pray the Lord my soul to keep. If I should die before I wake, I pray the Lord my soul to take.

GYPSY God bless Mummy!

ESMERALDA And the crystal ball and the tea-leaves.

KILROY *Pssst!*

ESMERALDA What's that?

GYPSY A tom-cat in the plaza.

ESMERALDA God bless all cats without pads in the plaza tonight.

KILROY Amen!

(*He falls to his knees in the empty plaza*)

ESMERALDA God bless all con men and hustlers and pitchmen who hawk their hearts on the street, all two-time losers who're likely to lose once more, the courtesan who made the mistake of love, the greatest of lovers crowned with the longest horns, the poet who wandered far from his heart's green country and possibly will and possibly won't be able to find his way back, look down with a smile tonight on the last cavaliers, the ones with the rusty armor and soiled white plumes, and visit with understanding and something that's almost tender those fading legends that come and go in this plaza like songs not clearly remembered, oh, sometime and somewhere, let there be something to mean the word *honor* again!

QUIXOTE (*Hoarsely and loudly, stirring slightly among his verminous rags*) Amen!

KILROY Amen . . .

GYPSY (*Disturbed*) —That will do, now.

ESMERALDA *And, oh, God, let me dream tonight of the Chosen Hero!*

GYPSY Now, sleep. Fly away on the magic carpet of dreams!

(ESMERALDA *crawls into the gauze-tented cot. The* GYPSY *descends from the roof*)

KILROY *Esmeralda! My little Gypsy sweetheart!*

ESMERALDA (*Sleepily*) Go away, cat.

(*The light behind the gauze is gradually dimming*)

KILROY This is no cat. This is the chosen hero of the big fiesta, Kilroy, the champion of the golden gloves with his gold heart cut from his chest and in his hands to give you!

ESMERALDA Go away. Let me dream of the Chosen Hero.

KILROY What a hassle! Mistook for a cat! What can I do to convince this doll I'm real? (*Three brass balls wink brilliantly*) —Another transaction seems to be indicated! (*He rushes to the* LOAN SHARK'S. *The entrance immediately lights up*) My heart is gold! What will you give me for it? (*Jewels, furs, sequined gowns, etc., are tossed to his feet. He throws his heart like a basketball to the* LOAN SHARK, *snatches up the loot and rushes back to the* GYPSY'S) *Doll! Behold this loot! I gave my golden heart for it!*

ESMERALDA Go away, cat . . .

(*She falls asleep.* KILROY *bangs his forehead with his fist, then rushes to the* GYPSY'S *door, pounds it with both fists. The door is thrown open and the sordid contents of a large jar are thrown at him. He falls back gasping, spluttering, retching. He retreats and finally assumes an exaggerated attitude of despair*)

KILROY Had for a button! Stewed, screwed and tattooed on the Camino Real! Baptized, finally, with the contents of a slop-jar!—Did anybody say the deal was rugged?!

(QUIXOTE *stirs against the wall of Skid Row. He hawks and spits and staggers to his feet*)

GUTMAN Why, the old knight's awake, his dream is over!

QUIXOTE (*To* KILROY) Hello! Is that a fountain?

KILROY —Yeah, but—

QUIXOTE I've got a mouthful of old chicken feathers . . .

(*He approaches the fountain. It begins to flow.* KILROY *falls back in amazement as the Old Knight rinses his mouth and drinks and removes his jacket to bathe, handing the tattered garment to* KILROY)

QUIXOTE (*As he bathes*) Qué passa, mi amigo?

KILROY The deal is rugged. D'you know what I mean?

QUIXOTE Who knows better than I what a rugged deal is! (*He produces a tooth brush and brushes his teeth*) —Will you take some advice?

KILROY Brother, at this point on the Camino I will take anything which is offered!

QUIXOTE *Don't! Pity! Your! Self!* (*He takes out a pocket mirror and grooms his beard and moustache*) The wounds of the vanity, the many offenses our egos have to endure, being housed in bodies that age and hearts that grow tired, are better accepted with a tolerant smile —like *this!*—You *see?*

(*He cracks his face in two with an enormous grin*)

GUTMAN Follow-spot on the face of the ancient knight!

QUIXOTE Otherwise what you become is a bag full of curdled cream—*leche mala,* we call it!—attractive to nobody, least of all to yourself! (*He passes the comb and pocket mirror to* KILROY) Have you got any plans?

KILROY (*A bit uncertainly, wistfully*) Well, I was thinking of—going *on* from—*here!*

QUIXOTE Good! Come with me.

KILROY (*To the audience*) Crazy old bastard. (*Then to the Knight*) Donde?

QUIXOTE (*Starting for the stairs*) Quien sabe!

(*The fountain is now flowing loudly and sweetly. The Street People are moving toward it with murmurs of wonder.* MARGUERITE *comes out upon the terrace*)

KILROY Hey, there's—!

QUIXOTE Shhh! Listen!

(*They pause on the stairs*)

MARGUERITE Abdullah!

(GUTMAN *has descended to the terrace*)

GUTMAN Mademoiselle, allow me to deliver the message for you. It would be in bad form if I didn't take some final part in the pageant. (*He crosses the plaza to the opposite façade and shouts "Casanova!" under the window of the "Ritz Men Only." Meanwhile* KILROY *scratches out the verb "is" and prints the correction "was" in the inscription on the ancient wall*) Casanova! Great lover and King of Cuckolds on the Camino Real! The last of your ladies has guaranteed your tabs and is expecting you for breakfast on the terrace!

(CASANOVA *looks first out of the practical window of the flophouse, then emerges from its scabrous doorway, haggard, unshaven, crumpled in dress but bearing himself as erectly as ever. He blinks and glares fiercely into the brilliant morning light.* MARGUERITE *cannot return his look, she averts her face with a look for which anguish would not be too strong a term, but at the same time she extends a pleading hand toward him. After some hesitation, he begins to move toward her, striking the pavement in measured cadence with his cane, glancing once, as he crosses, out at the audience with a wry smile that makes admissions that would be embarrassing to a vainer man than* CASANOVA *now is. When he reaches* MARGUERITE *she gropes for his hand, seizes it with a low cry and presses it spasmodically to her lips while he draws her into his arms and looks above her sobbing, dyed-golden head with the serene, clouded gaze of someone mortally ill as the mercy of a narcotic laps over his pain.* QUIXOTE *raises his lance in a formal gesture and cries out hoarsely, powerfully from the stairs*)

QUIXOTE *The violets in the mountains have broken the rocks!*

(QUIXOTE *goes through the arch with* KILROY)

GUTMAN (*To the audience*) The Curtain Line has been spoken! (*To the wings*) Bring it down!

(*He bows with a fat man's grace as—The curtain falls*)

William Inge

The Dark at the Top of the Stairs

FOR TENNESSEE WILLIAMS

Manufactured in the United States of America by H. Wolff

INTRODUCTION

If the writing is honest it cannot be separated from the man who wrote it. It isn't so much his mirror as it is the distillation, the essence, of what is strongest and purest in his nature, whether that be gentleness or anger, serenity or torment, light or dark. This makes it deeper than the surface likeness of a mirror and that much more truthful.

I think the man William Inge is faithfully portrayed in the work of William Inge the dramatist. The perceptive and tender humanity that shines in *The Dark at the Top of the Stairs* is a dominant trait of Bill Inge as I have known him these past fourteen years. Now the American theatre public has begun to know him. When they enter The Music Box theatre of Forty-fifth Street, west of Broadway, it is like going next door to call on a well-liked neighbor. There is warmth and courtesy in their reception. There is an atmosphere of serenity in his presence, there is understanding in it, and the kindness of wisdom and the wisdom of kindness. They enter and take comfortable seats by the fireside without anxiety, for there is no air of recent or incipient disorder on the premises. No bloodstained ax has been kicked under the sofa. If the lady of the house is absent, she has really gone to baby-sit for her sister, her corpse is not stuffed hastily back of the coalbin. If the TV is turned on it will not break into the panicky report of unidentified aircraft of strange design over the rooftops. In other words, they are given to believe that nothing at all disturbing or indecorous is going to happen to them in the course of their visit. But they are in for a surprise, not a violent one but a considerable one, for William Inge the playwright, like

William Inge the gentleman from Kansas via St. Louis, uses his good manners for their proper dramatic purpose, which is to clothe a reality which is far from surface. It is done, as they say, with mirrors, but the mirrors may all of a sudden turn into x-ray photos, and it is done so quietly and deftly that you hardly know the moment when the mirrors stop being mirrors and the more penetrating exposures begin to appear on the stage before you. All of a sudden, but without any startling explosion, it happens, and you're not sure just when and how. This nice, well-bred next-door neighbor, with the accent that belongs to no region except the region of good manners, has begun to uncover a world within a world, and it is not the world that his welcome prepared you to meet, it's a secret world that exists behind the screen of neighborly decorum. And that's when and where you meet the talent of William Inge, the true and wonderful talent which is for offering, first, the genial surface of common American life, and then not ripping but quietly dropping the veil that keeps you from seeing yourself as you are. Somehow he does it in such a way that you are not offended or startled by it. It's just what you are, and why should you be ashamed of it? We are what we are, and why should we be ashamed of it more than enough to want to improve it a little? That's what Bill Inge tells you, in his quiet, gently modulated voice that belongs to no region but the region of sincerity and understanding. No, don't be ashamed of it, but see it and know it and make whatever corrections you feel able to make, and they are bound to be good ones.

X-ray photos, coming out of mirrors, may reveal the ravages of tissues turning malignant or of arteries beginning to be obstructed by deposits of calcium or fat. This is God's or the devil's way of removing us to make room for our descendants. Do they work together, God and the devil? I sometimes suspect that there's a sort of understanding between them, which we won't understand until Doomsday.

But Inge reveals the operations of both these powerful mysteries in our lives if you will meet him halfway, and therein lies his very peculiar talent. You hardly know the revelation has happened until you have parted from him and started home, to your house next door to the Music Box on Forty-fifth Street.

This has a great deal to do with the fact that the very handsome and outwardly serene face of William Inge, the gentleman-playwright, looks a bit older than his forty years.

Take fourteen from forty-four years and you are left with thirty, which was Bill's age when I met him in St. Louis in January, 1945. This was just a few weeks after Laurette Taylor had started breaking the ice of a Chicago winter with her performance, there, of my first success, *The Glass Menagerie*. I had returned to my parents' home in St. Louis as a refugee from the shock of sudden fame, but the flight was not far enough to serve its purpose. I had been home hardly a day when my mother interrupted my work in the basement of our rented suburban home—we had recently ascended from the city-apartment level of economy—to tell me the drama critic of the St. Louis *Star-Times* was on the phone. Bill Inge told me that he also did feature stories on theatrical folk passing through St. Louis and he would like to do a sort of "Home Town Boy Makes Good" article on me. He also wondered, sympathetically, if I would not enjoy a little social diversion other than that provided by family friends in St. Louis, since my own small group of past associates in the city had scattered far and wide, by this time, like fugitives from a sanguinary overthrow of state. He gave me his address and a time to come there. He was living in a housing project, way downtown in a raffish part of the city, but when he opened the door I saw over his shoulder a reproduction of my favorite

Picasso and knew that the interview would be as painless as it turned out to be.

After I had gone back to Chicago to finish out the break-in run of *Menagerie*, Bill came up one week end to see the play. I didn't know until then that Bill wanted to be a playwright. After the show, we walked back to my hotel in the Loop of Chicago, and on the way he suddenly confided to me, with characteristic simplicity and directness, that being a successful playwright was what he most wanted in the world for himself. This confession struck me, at the time, as being just a politeness, an effort to dispel the unreasonable gloom that had come over me at a time when I should have been most elated, an ominous letdown of spirit that followed me like my shadow wherever I went. I talked to him a little about this reaction, but I didn't feel that he was listening to me. I think Bill Inge had already made up his mind to invoke this same shadow and to suffuse it with light: and that, of course, is exactly what he has done.

The history of his rise in our theatre is deceptively smooth in its surface appearance, for back of it lies the personal Odyssey of Bill Inge, and in the Odyssey, which I know and which has amazed and inspired me, is a drama as fine and admirable as any of the ones he has given, one after another—an unbroken succession of distinguished and successful plays—to the American Theatre, and someday I hope that he will make a play of it, his personal Iliad and Odyssey, a truly Homeric drama, but one in which the stairs rise from dark to light through something remarkably fine and gallant in his own nature.

TENNESSEE WILLIAMS

Key West
January, 1958

The Dark at the Top of the Stairs was first presented by Saint Subber and Elia Kazan at The Music Box, New York City, on December 5, 1957, with the following cast:

CAST
(In order of appearance)

CORA FLOOD, *a young housewife*	Theresa Wright
RUBIN FLOOD, *her husband*	Pat Hingle
SONNY FLOOD, *the ten-year-old son*	Charles Saari
BOY OUTSIDE	Jonathan Shawn
REENIE FLOOD, *the sixteen-year-old daughter*	Judith Robinson
FLIRT CONROY, *a flapper friend of Reenie's*	Evans Evans
MORRIS LACEY, *Cora's brother-in-law*	Frank Overton
LOTTIE LACEY, *Cora's older sister*	Eileen Heckart
PUNKY GIVENS, *Flirt's boy friend*	Carl Reindel
SAMMY GOLDENBAUM, *Punky's friend*	Timmy Everett
CHAUFFEUR	Anthony Ray

DIRECTED BY Elia Kazan
SETTING BY Ben Edwards
COSTUMES BY Lucinda Ballard
LIGHTING BY Jean Rosenthal

The home of Rubin Flood, his wife and two children, in a small Oklahoma town close to Oklahoma City. The time is the early 1920's.

ACT ONE

A Monday afternoon in early spring.

ACT TWO

After dinner, the following Friday.

ACT THREE

The next day, late afternoon.

ACT ONE

Scene: The setting for the entire play is the home of RUBIN FLOOD *and his wife and two children, in a small Oklahoma town close to Oklahoma City. The time is the early 1920's, during an oil boom in the area. The house is comfortable and commodious, with probably eight or nine rooms. It is one of those square, frame houses built earlier in the century, that stand secure as blocks, symbols of respectability and material comfort.*

All we see of the FLOODS' *house is the living room, where the action of the play takes place. There is a flight of stairs at the far left. At the top of them is the upstairs hallway, which is not accessible to windows and sunlight. During the daytime scenes, this small area is in semidarkness, and at night it is black. When the hallway is lighted, we can see the feet of the characters who happen to be there. We are conscious of this area throughout the play, as though it holds some possible threat to the characters.*

On the far right, downstairs, is the outside entrance, with a small hallway one must go through before coming into the living room.

In the middle of the living room is a wicker table and two comfortable wicker chairs, placed one on each side. Upstage center are sliding doors leading into the parlor, where we see a player piano. To the left of these doors and under the stairway, is a swinging door leading into the dining room. Extreme downstage left is a fireplace and a large comfortable leather chair. This area is considered RUBIN'S. *In the rest of the room are book shelves, a desk, a few small tables and portraits of* CORA FLOOD'S *mother and father. Through a large window at the back, we see part of the front porch to the house, and can see characters coming and going.*

As for the atmosphere of the room, despite the moodiness of shadowy corners and Victorian (more or less) furnishings, there is an implied comfort and hospitality.

When the curtain goes up, it is a late Monday afternoon in the early spring, about five o'clock. Outside, the sun is setting, but the room is still filled with soft, warm light.

The stage is empty when the curtain rises. CORA *and* RUBIN *are both upstairs, he preparing to leave on a business trip.*

CORA (*Off*) Rubin!

RUBIN (*Off*) Yah!

CORA (*Off*) How many times do I have to tell you to rinse your hands before you dry them on a towel? You leave the bathroom looking like a wild horse had been using it. (RUBIN *laughs*) I can smell the bay rum clear over here. My! You're certainly getting spruced up!

RUBIN (*Starting downstairs, carrying a suitcase. He is quite a good-looking man of thirty-six, still robust, dressed in Western clothes—a big Stetson, boots, narrow trousers, colorful shirt and string tie*) I gotta look good for my customers.

CORA (*Calling down to him*) How long will you be gone this time?

RUBIN I oughta be home end of the week. Saturday.

CORA (*Calling down*) That's better than you usually do. Where will you be?

RUBIN (*Goes to his corner, where he keeps his business*

paraphernalia) I've made out my route for ya. I've left it on the mantel.

NEWSBOY (*Calling into house from outside*) Hey, Mr. Flood. Jonsey says your tire's ready at the garage.

RUBIN O.K., Ed, I'll be down to get it.

CORA (*Coming downstairs*) Rubin, you've waited this long to go, why don't you wait now until morning? Here it is almost suppertime. You won't be able to see any customers tonight, no matter where you go. Wait until morning. I'll get up early and fix you breakfast. I'll fix you biscuits, Rubin.

RUBIN I shoulda been out first thing this mornin'. Monday, and I'm just gettin' away. I can make it to Muskogee tonight and be there first thing in the mornin'. I can finish up by noon and then get on to Chicasha.

CORA I wish you were home more, Rubin.

RUBIN I gotta make a livin'.

CORA Other men make a living without traveling all over the country selling harness.

RUBIN The way other men make a livin' is *their* business. I gotta make mine the best way I know how. I can't be no schoolmaster like your old man was when he brung you all out here from Pennsylvania. I can't be no dentist like your brother-in-law Morris. I was raised on a ranch and thought I'd spend my life on it. Sellin' harness is about all I'm prepared for . . . as long as there's any harness to sell.

CORA (*With a trace of self-pity*) I envy women who have their husbands with them all the time. I never have anyone to take me any place. I live like a widow.

RUBIN What do you want me to do? Give up my job and stay home here to pleasure you every day?

CORA (*She is often disturbed by his language*) Rubin! Don't say that.

RUBIN Jesus Christ, ya talk like a man had nothin' else to do but stay home and entertain you.

CORA Rubin! It's not just myself I'm thinking of. It's the children. We have a daughter sixteen years old now. Do you realize that? Yes. Reenie's sixteen. And Sonny's ten. Sometimes they act like they didn't have a father.

RUBIN (*Sits at table to sharpen his knife*) You're always tellin' me how good they do at school. The girl plays the piano, don't she? And the boy does somethin', too. Gets up and speaks pieces, or somethin' like that?

(*In* CORA'S *sewing basket he finds a sock on which to wipe his knife*)

CORA (*Again she is shocked*) Rubin! Not on a clean sock!

RUBIN Seems to me you all get along all right without me.

CORA Rubin, I worry about them. Reenie's so shy of people her own age, I don't know what to make of her. She's got no confidence at all. And I don't know how to give her any, but you could. Her eyes light up like candles every time you go near her.

RUBIN (*A little embarrassed*) Come on now, Cora.

CORA It's true . . . and the boy. Other boys tease him and call him names, Rubin. He doesn't know how to get along with them.

RUBIN He oughta beat the tar outa the other boys.

CORA He's not like you, Rubin. He's not like anyone I ever knew. He needs a father, Rubin. So does Reenie. Kids need a father when they're growing up, same as they need a mother.

RUBIN You din allus talk like that. God almighty, when those kids was born, you hugged 'em so close to ya, ya made me think they was your own personal property, and I din have nothin' to do with 'em at all.

CORA Rubin, that's not so.

RUBIN The hell it ain't. Ya pampered 'em so much and coddled 'em, they thought I was just bein' mean if I tried to drill some sense into their heads.

CORA Rubin. Don't say that.

RUBIN You're always kissin' and makin' over the boy until I sometimes wonder who's top man around here.

CORA Rubin!

RUBIN I just said I wonder.

CORA If I kept the kids too close to me, it's only because you weren't there, and I had to have *someone* close to me. I had to have *some*one.

RUBIN You're like an old mare Pa used to have on the ranch. Never wanted to give up her colts. By God, she'd keep 'em locked inside her and make all us men dig inside her with our hands to get 'em out. She never wanted to let 'em go.

CORA (*A little repelled by the comparison*) Rubin, I don't like what you just said.

RUBIN Well, she was a good mare in every other way.

CORA You talk shamefully at times.

RUBIN Well . . . I got my own way of sayin' things and it's pretty hard to change.

CORA (*Watching him primp before the mirror*) You like being out on the road, don't you? You like to pretend you're still a young cowboy.

RUBIN It wasn't a bad life.

CORA Rubin, there are ever so many things you could do in town. Mr. Binny down here on the corner makes a very good living just selling groceries to the neighborhood people. We could find a store like that, Rubin, and the kids and I could help you, too. You'd be happier doing something like that, Rubin. I know you would.

RUBIN Don't tell me how t'be happy. I told you over and over, I ain't gonna spend my life cooped up in no store.

CORA Or a filling station, Rubin. You could run a filling station or a garage . . .

RUBIN God damn it, Cora. I don't mean to have that kinda life. I just wasn't cut out for it. Now, quit pickin' at me. We been married seventeen years now. It seems t'me, you'd be ready t'accept me the way I am, or start lookin' for a new man.

CORA I don't want a new man. You know that.

RUBIN Then start tryin' to put up with the one you got.

CORA I do try.

RUBIN 'Cause he ain't gonna change. Kiss me g'bye. (*Playfully rough with her*) You come here and kiss me. (*He grabs her in a fast embrace, and they kiss*)

CORA (*Cautiously*) Rubin, you've got to leave me some money.

RUBIN How much you gonna need?

CORA Uh . . . could you let me have maybe twenty-five dollars?

RUBIN (*Hitting the ceiling*) Twenty-five dollars? I'm only gonna be gone till Saturday.

CORA I have a lot of expenses this week, and . . .

RUBIN *I* pay the bills.

CORA I take care of the utilities, Rubin. And we have a big gas bill this month, last month was so cold. And Reenie's invited to a big birthday party out at the country club. The Ralston girl, and Reenie has to take her a present.

RUBIN Me? Buy presents for Harry Ralston's girl when he owns half this town?

CORA I don't often ask for this much.

RUBIN (*Taking a bill from his wallet*) Twenty's the best I can do.

CORA Thank you, Rubin. The Ralstons are giving Mary Jane a big dance. (*Finding a button loose on his coat*) Here, let me fix that.

RUBIN Cora, that'll be all right.

CORA It'll only take a minute, sit down. (*They sit, and* CORA *takes needle and thread from her sewing basket*) They're having a dance orchestra from Oklahoma City.

RUBIN Harry and Peg Ralston puttin' on the dog now, are they?

CORA Oh, yes. I hardly ever see Peg any more.

RUBIN I guess they don't have time for any of their old friends, now that they've got so much money.

CORA Anyway, they've asked Reenie to the party, I'm thankful for that.

RUBIN The country club, huh? By God, I'd die in the poorhouse 'fore I'd ever do what Harry Ralston done.

CORA Now, Rubin . . .

RUBIN I mean it. He shot hisself in the foot to collect enough insurance money to make his first investment in oil.

CORA Do you believe all those stories?

RUBIN Hell, yes, I believe it. I know it for a fact. He shot hisself in the foot. He oughta be in jail now. Instead, he's a social leader, givin' parties out at the country club. And I'm supposed to feel real proud he invited my daughter. Hurry up.

CORA I ran into Peg downtown during the winter. My, she was wearing a beautiful fur coat. Gray squirrel. And she was wearing a lot of lovely jewelry, too.

RUBIN She's spendin' his money as fast as old Harry makes it.

CORA Why shouldn't she have a few nice things?

RUBIN They tell me they both started drinkin' now. They go out to those country club parties and get drunk as lords.

CORA Peg didn't used to be like that.

RUBIN They're all like that now. The town's gone oil-boom crazy. Chamber of Commerce says we're the wealthiest town per capita in all the Southwest. I guess they're not exaggeratin' much, either, with all this oil money, those damned Indians ridin' around in their limosines, gettin' all that money from the government, millions of dollars. Millions of dollars, and nobody knows what to do with it. Come on, hurry up now . . .

CORA (*Finishing with the button*) Rubin, if you want to

make an investment, if you should hear of something absolutely sure, you can take that money Mama left me when she died. Two thousand dollars, Rubin. You can make an investment with that.

RUBIN There ain't no such thing as a *sure thing* in the oil business.

CORA Isn't there?

RUBIN No. Ya can make a million dollars or lose your ass overnight.

CORA Rubin, you don't have to use words like that.

RUBIN I do a good job supportin' ya, don't I?

CORA Of course.

RUBIN Then let's let well enough alone.

CORA I was only thinking, it makes you feel kind of left out to be poor these days.

(*Suddenly, from outside, we hear the sounds of young boys' jeering voices*)

BOY'S VOICES

Sonny Flood! His name is mud!
Sonny runs home to Mama!
Sonny plays with paper dolls!
Sonny Flood, his name is mud!

CORA See, there! (*She jumps up nervously and runs outside to face her son's accosters*) You boys run along. My Sonny hasn't done anything to hurt you. You go home now or I'll call your mothers, every last one of you. You should be ashamed of yourselves, picking on a boy who's smaller than you are.

(SONNY *comes running into the house now. It is hard to discern his feelings*)

RUBIN (*Follows* CORA *out to the porch*) Cora, cut it out.

CORA I can't stand quietly by while they're picking on my boy!

RUBIN It's *his* battle. He's gotta fight it out for hisself.

CORA If they touch one hair of that boy's head I'll destroy them.

VOICE (*One last heckler*) Sonny Flood, his name is mud!

CORA I'll destroy them.

(CORA *re-enters the house*)

VOICE Sonny Flood, his name is mud.

RUBIN (*Still on the porch*) Hey, come here, you fat butterball.

BOY Hi, Mr. Flood.

RUBIN How you doin', Jonathan? Let me see how you're growin'. (*He lifts the boy up*) Gettin' fat as a pig. Say hello to your pa for me.

(*The boy runs off and* RUBIN *comes back inside*)

CORA Sonny, did they hurt you?

SONNY No.

CORA What started it this time?

SONNY I don't know.

CORA Did you say anything to make them mad?

SONNY No.

CORA They're just jealous because you make better grades than they do. They're just jealous, the little beasts.

RUBIN Son!

SONNY Huh?

RUBIN Want me to teach you how to put up a good fight?

SONNY (*Turning away from his father*) I don't think so.

RUBIN (*To* CORA) What else can I do? Buy him a shotgun?

CORA There should be *something* we can do. *Something.*

RUBIN Everybody's gotta figure out his own way of handlin' things, Cora. Whether he fights or whether he runs.

CORA I hate for anything to make me feel so helpless.

RUBIN I gotta be goin'.

CORA Say good-bye to your father, Sonny.

RUBIN (*Making a point of being friendly*) Good-bye, son.

SONNY (*Diffidently*) G'bye.

RUBIN (*Giving up*) Oh, hell.

CORA Isn't there anything you can say to him?

RUBIN Cora, if that boy wants me to help him, he's gotta

come to me and tell me how. I never know what's on his mind.

CORA You're just not interested.

RUBIN Oh, hell, I give up. I plain give up.

(*Exasperated,* RUBIN *bolts outside,* CORA *anxiously following him to the door*)

CORA Rubin . . . Rubin . . . (*We hear* RUBIN'S *car drive off.* CORA *comes back inside*) Why don't you listen to your father, Sonny? Why don't you let him help you?

SONNY Where's Reenie?

CORA She's downtown. Your father isn't here very often. Why don't you try and get along with him when he is?

SONNY (*Wanting to evade the issue*) I don't know.

CORA Most boys your age *worship* their fathers.

SONNY I like him, all right. Where are my movie stars?

CORA Forget your movie stars for a minute. You have a father to be proud of, Sonny. He and his family were pioneers. They fought Indians and buffalo, and they settled this country when it was just a wilderness. Why, if there was a movie about them, you couldn't wait to see it.

SONNY Mom, it just makes it worse when you come out and tell those boys you're going to call their mothers.

CORA You just won't listen to me, will you? You just won't listen to anyone. You're so set in your ways.

SONNY I want my movie stars.

CORA I put them in the book shelves when I was straightening up this morning. The only pastime you have is coming home here and playing with those pictures of movie stars.

(SONNY *gets out his scrapbook and spreads it on the floor*)

SONNY I like them.

CORA That's all the friends you have. Not real friends at all. Just *pictures* of all the lovely friends you'd *like* to have. There's a mighty big difference between pictures of people and the way people really are.

SONNY I like pictures.

CORA Maybe you should get out and play with the other boys more often, Sonny.

SONNY They play stupid games.

CORA People distrust you if you don't play the same games they do, Sonny. It's the same after you grow up.

SONNY I'm not going to play games just to make them like me.

CORA (*Suddenly warm and affectionate*) Come to me, Sonny. I wish I understood you better, boy.

SONNY I don't see why.

CORA (*Caressing him*) No, I don't suppose you do. You're a speckled egg, and the old hen that laid you can't help wondering how you got in the nest. But I love you, Sonny. More than anything else in the world.

SONNY Mom, can I go to a movie tonight?

CORA You know the rules. One movie a week, on Friday night.

SONNY Please, Mom. It's a real special movie tonight. Honest, I just *got* to see it.

CORA Oh, I bet. It's always something special and you've just got to see it like your very life depended on it. No. You're supposed to study on week nights. Now, stay home and study.

SONNY I've already got all my lessons.

CORA You have to speak at Mrs. Stanford's tea party next Saturday. Why don't you memorize a new recitation?

SONNY I can't find anything I like.

CORA Oh! I found a cute little poem in the Oklahoma City paper this morning. It's about a little boy who hates to take castor oil. It starts off:
"Of all the nasty things, gee whiz!
I think the very worst there is . . ."

SONNY (*Obviously bored*) I want to do something serious.

CORA Serious! Like what?

SONNY I dunno.

CORA Goodness, it seems to me we've got enough serious things in the world without you getting up to recite sad pieces.

(*Outside the window, we see* FLIRT *and* REENIE *come onto the porch, giggling*)

SONNY I'm tired of all those stupid pieces you cut out of the papers.

CORA My goodness! Aren't we getting superior! Oh, here's your sister, Sonny. Be a little gentleman and open the door for her.

REENIE (*Sticking her head in through the door, asking cautiously*) Is Daddy gone, Mom?

CORA Yes, he's gone. The coast is clear.

REENIE (*Runs to* CORA *excitedly. She is a plain girl with no conscious desire to be anything else*) Oh, Mom, it's the prettiest dress I ever had.

CORA Bring it in.

REENIE Come on in, Flirt.

FLIRT (*Enters carrying a large dress box. She is a vivacious young flapper of the era*) Hello, Mrs. Flood.

CORA Hello, Flirt.

(FLIRT *opens the box*)

REENIE And they took up the hem and took in the waist so that it fits me just perfectly now.

FLIRT I think it's simply scrumptious, Mrs. Flood.

CORA Thank you, Flirt. Hold it up, Reenie.

FLIRT Yes, hold it up.

REENIE (*Holding the dress before her*) Is Dad going to be awfully mad, Mom?

CORA I told you, he's not going to know anything about it for a while, Reenie. He gave me some money before he left, enough for me to make a small down payment. My, I bet Flirt thinks we're terrible, plotting this way.

FLIRT Shucks, no. Mama and I do the same thing.

REENIE Oh, Mom. You should see the dress Flirt got.

FLIRT It's all red, with spangles on it, and a real short skirt. It's just darling. Daddy says he feels like disowning me in it.

CORA Did you buy your dress at Delman's, too, Flirt?

FLIRT (*She can't help boasting an advantage*) No. Mama takes me into Oklahoma City to buy all my clothes.

CORA Oh!

SONNY (*Feeling the dress*) Look, it's got stars.

REENIE (*Snapping angrily*) Sonny, take your dirty hands off my new dress.

SONNY (*Ready to start a fight any time* REENIE *is*) My hands are *not* dirty! So there.

REENIE You make me mad. Why don't you go outdoors and play ball instead of staying in the house all the time, spying on everything I do. Mother, why don't you make him go out and play?

SONNY It's my house as much as it's yours, and I've got as much right to be here as you do. So there!

CORA (*Always distressed by their fighting*) Reenie. He only wanted to touch the dress. He likes pretty things, too.

FLIRT Gee whiz, he hasn't done anything, Reenie.

CORA Of course he hasn't. You kids are just antagonistic to each other. You scrap all the time.

SONNY I hate you.

REENIE I hate you, too.

CORA Now stop that. Is that any way for a brother and sister to talk? I'm not going to have any more of it. Flirt, are you taking the Ralston girl a birthday present?

FLIRT Mama got me a compact to give her. It's the only thing we could think of. She already has everything under the sun.

CORA Yes, I suppose so. Her parents are so wealthy now. Well, I'll have to shop for something for Reenie to take her.

FLIRT You know, my folks knew the Ralstons before he made all his money. Mama says Mrs. Ralston used to clerk in a millinery store downtown.

CORA Yes, I knew her then.

FLIRT And my daddy says that Mr. Ralston was so crazy to make money in oil that he shot himself in the foot. Isn't that awful?

SONNY Why did he do that?

(REENIE *goes into the parlor to try on her dress.* SONNY *sits at the table.* FLIRT *fascinates him*)

FLIRT So he could collect enough insurance money to make his first investment in oil. Did you hear that story, too, Mrs. Flood?

CORA Oh, yes . . . you hear all kinds of stories about the Ralstons now.

FLIRT And you know, some of the women out at the country club didn't want to give Mr. Ralston a membership because they disapproved of *her*.

CORA Is that so?

FLIRT But when you've got as much money as the Ralstons do, I guess you can be a member of *any*thing. I just hate Mary Jane Ralston. Some of the boys at school think she's pretty but I think she's a *cow*. I'm not being jealous, either. I guess if I had as much money to spend on clothes as she does, I'd have been voted the prettiest girl in school, too. Anyway, I'm absolutely positive she peroxides her hair.

CORA Really?

REENIE (*Poking her head out between the sliding doors*) Are you sure?

FLIRT Yes. Because she and I play on the same volley ball team in gym class, and her locker is right next to mine, and . . .

CORA (*Reminding her of* SONNY'S *presence*) Flirt!

FLIRT Isn't it terrible for me to say all these things, when I'm going to her birthday party? But I don't care. She just invited me because she had to. Because my daddy's her daddy's lawyer.

SONNY (*As* REENIE *comes out of parlor wearing her new dress, he makes a grotesque face and props his feet on the table*) Ugh . . . .

CORA Oh, Reenie! it's lovely. Sonny, take your feet down. Let me see! Oh, Reenie. He did a fine job. Flirt! tell me more about the young man who's taking Reenie to the party.

FLIRT He's a Jew, Mrs. Flood.

CORA Oh, he is?

REENIE Do you think it's all right for me to go out with a Jew, Mom?

CORA Why, of course, dear, if he's a nice boy.

FLIRT His name is Sammy Goldenbaum, and he comes from Hollywood, California, and his mother's a moving-picture actress.

CORA Really?

REENIE Flirt just found that out, Mom. I didn't know it before.

SONNY (*All ears*) A moving-picture actress!

FLIRT Yes, but she just plays itsy-bitsy parts in pictures. I saw her once. She played a real stuck-up society woman, and she was Gloria Swanson's rival. You see, they were in love with the same man, Thomas Meighan, and she told all these lies about Gloria Swanson to make people think Gloria Swanson wasn't nice, so she could marry Thomas Meighan herself. But Thomas Meighan found out all about it, finally, and . . .

REENIE Mom, what's a Jewish person like?

CORA Well, I never knew many Jewish people, Reenie, but . . .

FLIRT I've heard that some of them can be awful fast with girls.

CORA I'm sure they're just like any other people.

FLIRT (*Dancing coquettishly about room*) They don't believe in Christianity.

CORA Most of them don't.

REENIE But do they act different?

CORA (*Not really knowing*) Well . . .

FLIRT My daddy says they always try to get the best of you in business.

CORA There are lots of very nice Jewish people, Reenie.

FLIRT Oh, sure! Gee whiz, of course.

REENIE I don't know what to expect.

FLIRT Kid, he's a *boy*. That's all you have to know.

CORA There are Jewish families over in Oklahoma City, but I guess there aren't any here in town.

FLIRT Oh, yes there are, Mrs. Flood. The Lewises are Jewish, only they changed their name from Levin so no one would know.

CORA I guess I did hear that some place.

REENIE Mom, I feel sort of scared to go out with someone so different.

FLIRT (*She never seems aware of her casual offensiveness*) Oh, you're crazy, Reenie. Gee whiz, I'd never go steady with a Jewish boy, but I'd sure take a date with one—if I didn't have any other way of going.

CORA Now, Reenie, I'm sure that any friend of the Givens boy is nice, whether he's Jewish or not. And besides, his mother's a movie actress. Think of that.

FLIRT Yes, but not a famous one.

CORA (*To* REENIE) Now, you have a nice date to the party, and a lovely new dress to wear. You can be sure you'll have a good time.

FLIRT Gosh, yes! After all, a party's a party. And it's out at the country club, and they're having a swell dance orchestra from Oklahoma City, and they're giving favors. I can't wait. Fix your hair real cute and you'll look all right. (*Looks at her wrist watch*) Oh, heck! I've got to go home.

CORA Do you want to stay here for supper, Flirt?

FLIRT No. It's my night to fix supper for the folks. My mother makes me fix supper once a week, cook's night out. She says it's good for me to learn something about homemaking. Isn't that crazy? The only thing I know how to cook is salmon loaf. I learned how to make it in domestic science class. I've made salmon loaf every Monday night now for the whole year. Kid, can you help me study for that stupid old civics test we're having next week?

REENIE I guess so.

FLIRT Civics! Why can't they teach us something in that old school that'd do us some good?

CORA Good-bye, Flirt.

FLIRT Good-bye, Mrs. Flood, good-bye, Reenie. Oh, Sonny, you come over to *my* house and play sometime. I know how to be nice to little boys.

CORA Good-bye! (FLIRT *exits*) Sonny, you've got to go to the store now if we're going to have anything for supper tonight.

SONNY Mom! Can I get a candy bar?

CORA Wouldn't you rather have the nickel to put in your piggy bank?

SONNY No—I want a candy bar.

CORA All right. If you promise not to eat it before supper.

REENIE I want one, too. I want a nut Hershey.

CORA Bring one for Reenie, too.

SONNY She can get her own candy bar.

REENIE He's mean, Mom.

SONNY I don't care. She makes me mad, and I don't like her.

CORA Sonny, she's your sister.

SONNY I don't care. I don't like her.

(*He exits*)

CORA Oh, God, some day you kids are going to be sorry. When you can't even get along with people in your own family, how can you expect to get along with people out in the world? (*Goes to the window and looks out, protectively*) Poor Sonny, every time he leaves the house, those neighborhood bullies pick on him. I guess they've all gone home now.

(REENIE *takes off her new dress and throws it on a chair*)

REENIE I don't know if I like Flirt or not.

CORA (*Comes away from the window*) Why, what's the matter?

REENIE The only reason she likes me is because I help her with her studies.

(REENIE *goes into the parlor, gets her daytime clothes, and comes back into the living room to put them on*)

CORA Why do you say that?

REENIE I just do.

CORA You don't think *anyone* likes you, do you?

REENIE Mom, maybe we shouldn't have bought the dress.

CORA What?

REENIE I mean it, Mom. Dad'd be awful mad if he knew.

CORA I told you, he's not going to know.

REENIE Won't he be here the night of the party?

CORA No. And even if he were, he wouldn't notice the dress was new unless you told him about it.

REENIE Just the same, Mom, I don't feel right about it.

CORA Why don't you feel right?

REENIE Because . . . the dress cost so much, and what good is it going to do me? I never have a good time at those dances, anyway. No one ever dances with me.

CORA This time it's going to be different. You've got a new dress, and you've got a nice young man coming here all the way from California to be your escort. Think of it. Why, most young girls would be too excited to breathe.

REENIE It's just a *blind* date.

CORA What are you talking about?

REENIE They give blind dates to all the girls in town that nobody else wants to take.

CORA Daughter, I'm sure that's not so.

REENIE Oh, Mom, you just don't know.

CORA I do too.

REENIE Besides, he's Jewish. I never knew a Jewish boy before. I'm scared.

CORA Daughter, you're just looking for excuses. You just don't want to go, do you? Reenie, don't you want to have friends?

REENIE Yes, but . . .

CORA You're not going to make friends just staying home playing the piano, or going to the library studying your lessons. I'm glad you're studious and talented, but those things aren't enough just in themselves.

REENIE I don't want to talk about it any more.

CORA You're going to have to talk about these things someday. Where are you going?

REENIE To practice the piano.

(*She goes into the parlor and starts playing scales*)

CORA (*Angrily impatient*) That's where you spend half your life, *practicing* at the piano. (REENIE *bangs on piano exasperatedly and exits to dining room*) But will you get up and play for people so they'll know how talented you are? No. You hide your light under a bushel. You stay home and play behind closed doors, where no one can hear you except your own family. All you do is *pity* yourself at the piano. That's all. You go in there and pity yourself, playing all those sad pieces.

(REENIE *comes out of dining room, and calms herself by watering her plants*)

REENIE Mom, I just couldn't get up before an audience and play. I just couldn't.

CORA Why couldn't you? What good is it for your father to have bought the piano? What use is it? (REENIE *begins to sob*) Now, don't cry, Reenie. I'm sorry. (REENIE *goes into parlor and resumes her monotonous scales.* CORA *goes to telephone*) Long distance? Give me three-six-oh-seven-J in Oklahoma City, please. (*There is a wait of several moments*) Hello, Lottie. . . . Lottie, can you and Morris come over to dinner Friday night? I haven't seen you for so long, I want to talk with you, Lottie. I've just got to see some of my own flesh and blood. (*We hear* RUBIN'S *car slam to a stop outside; the car door slams and then he comes stomping up to the front porch*) Reenie's going to a big party out at the country club, and I thought I'd have a nice dinner first. . . . Rubin won't be here and I'll want company. Please come. Oh, I'm so glad. I'll be looking forward to seeing you.

RUBIN (*Bursting into the house*) What the hell's been goin' on behind my back? (*Sees the innocent dress lying on a chair*) There it is!

CORA (*Her phone call over*) Rubin!

RUBIN (*Displaying the dress as evidence*) So this is what ya wanted the extra money for. Fine feathers! Fine feathers! And ya buy 'em when my back is turned.

CORA Rubin, we were going to tell you. . . .

RUBIN A man has t'go downtown and talk with some of his pals before he knows what's goin' on in his own family.

CORA Who told you?

RUBIN That's all right who told me. I got my own ways a findin' out what goes on when my back is turned.

CORA You didn't leave town at all. You've been down to that dirty old pool hall.

RUBIN I got a right to go to the pool hall whenever I damn please.

CORA I thought you were in such a hurry to get out of town. Oh, yes, you had to get to Muskogee tonight.

RUBIN I can still make it to Muskogee. (*Finds the price*

tag on the dress) Nineteen seventy-five! Lord have mercy! Nineteen seventy-five.

CORA Did Loren Delman come into the pool hall while you were there? Did he? Did he tell you? If he did I'll never buy anything in that store again.

RUBIN That'd suit me just fine.

CORA Oh, why couldn't he have kept his mouth shut? I was going to pay for the dress a little at a time, and . . .

RUBIN "The finest dress I had in the store," he says, walkin' into the Arcade with a big cigar stuck in his mouth, wearin' a suit of fine tailored clothes. "I just sold your wife the finest dress I had in the store."

CORA Oh, that makes me furious.

RUBIN Jesus Christ, woman, whatta you take me for, one a those millionaire oil men? Is that what you think you're married to?

REENIE (*Pokes her head in through parlor door, speaking with tears and anxiety*) I told you he'd be mad, Mom. Let's take the dress back, Mom. I don't want to go to the party anyhow.

CORA (*Angrily impatient*) Get back in that parlor, Reenie, and don't come in here until I tell you to.

(CORA *slams the parlor doors shut*)

RUBIN See there! That girl don't even want the dress. It's *you,* puttin' all these high-fallutin' ideas in her head about parties, and dresses and nonsense.

CORA Rubin, of course Reenie doesn't want to go to the party. She never wants to go any place. All she wants to do is lock herself in the parlor and practice at the piano, or go to the library and hide her nose in a book. After all, she's going to want to get married one of these days, isn't she? And where's she going to look for a husband? In the public library?

(RUBIN *goes to his corner, sits in his big leather chair, and draws a pint of whiskey out of his desk drawer*)

RUBIN I bought her a fine dress . . . just a little while back.

CORA Oh, you did?

RUBIN Yes, I did.

CORA That's news to me. When?

RUBIN Just a few months ago. Sure I did.

CORA I certainly never saw it. What'd it look like?

RUBIN It was white.

CORA Rubin Flood, that was the dress you bought her three years ago when she graduated from the eighth grade. And she hasn't had a new dress since then, except for a few school clothes.

RUBIN Why couldn't she wear the white dress to the party?

CORA Because she's grown three inches since you got her that dress, and besides I cut it up two years ago and dyed it black and made her a skirt out of it to wear with a middy.

RUBIN Just the same, I ain't got money to throw away on no party togs. I just ain't got it.

CORA Oh, no. You don't have money when we need something here at home, do you?

RUBIN I'm tellin' ya, right now I don't.

CORA But you always have money for a bottle of bootleg whiskey when you want it, don't you? And I daresay you've got money for a few other things, too, that I needn't mention just at present.

RUBIN What're ya talkin' about?

CORA *You* know what I'm talking about.

RUBIN The hell I do.

CORA I know what goes on when you go out on the road. You may tell me you spruce up for your customers, but I happen to know better. Do you think I'm a fool?

RUBIN I don't know what you're talkin' about.

CORA I happen to have friends, decent, self-respecting

people, who tell me a few things that happen when you visit Ponca City.

RUBIN You mean the Werpel sisters!

CORA It's all right, who I mean. I have friends over there. That's all I need to say.

RUBIN Those nosy old maids, the Werpel sisters! God damn! Have they been runnin' to you with stories?

CORA Maybe you don't have money to buy your daughter a new dress, but it seems you have money to take Mavis Pruitt to dinner whenever you're over there, and to a movie afterwards, and give her presents.

RUBIN I've known Mavis . . . Pruitt ever since I was a boy! What harm is there if I take her to a movie?

CORA You're always too tired to take *me* to a movie when you come home.

RUBIN Life's different out on the road.

CORA I bet it is.

RUBIN Besides, I din ask her. She come into the Gibson House one night when I was havin' my dinner. What could I do but let her join me?

CORA She went to the Gibson House because she knew *you* were there. I know what kind of woman she is.

RUBIN She's not as bad as she's painted. That poor woman's had a hard time of it, too.

CORA Oh, she has!

RUBIN Yes, she has. I feel sorry for her.

CORA Oh, you do!

RUBIN Yes, I do. Is there any law that says I can't feel sorry for Mavis Pruitt?

CORA She's had her eye on you ever since I can remember.

RUBIN Oh, shoot!

CORA What happened to the man she left town with after we were married?

RUBIN He run off and left her.

CORA For good reason, too, I bet. I also heard that she was seen sporting a pair of black-bottom hose shortly after you left town, and that you were seen buying such a pair of hose at the Globe Dry Goods Store.

RUBIN By God, you got yourself a real detective service goin', haven't you?

CORA I don't ask people to tell me these things. I wish to God they didn't.

RUBIN All right. I bought her a pair of hose. I admit it. It was her birthday. The hose cost me sixty-eight cents. They made that poor woman happy. After all, I've known her ever since I was a boy. Besides, I was a li'l more flush then.

CORA How do you think it makes me feel when people tell me things like that?

RUBIN Ya oughtn'ta listen.

CORA How can I help it?

RUBIN (*He has to stop to remember to call Mavis Pruitt by her full name, to keep* CORA *from suspecting too much familiarity between them*) There's nothin' 'tween me and Mavis . . . Pruit . . . Mavis Pruitt, nothin' for you to worry about.

CORA There's probably a woman like her in every town you visit. That's why you want to get out of town, to go frisking over the country like a young stallion.

RUBIN You just hush your mouth. The daughter'll hear you.

CORA (*Indulging in a little self-pity*) A lot you care about your daughter. A lot you care about any of us.

RUBIN You don't think I care for ya unless I set ya on my knee and nuzzle ya.

CORA What you need for a wife is a squaw. Why didn't you marry one of those Indian women out on the reservation? Yes. She'd make you rich now, too, wouldn't she? And you wouldn't have to pay any attention to her at all.

(SONNY *is seen coming onto porch*)

RUBIN All right. Maybe that's what I *shoulda* done.

CORA Oh. So you want to throw it up to me!

RUBIN Throw what?

(SONNY *quietly enters the room, carrying a sack of groceries.* CORA *and* RUBIN *are too far into battle to notice him*)

CORA You know what, Rubin Flood.

RUBIN I don't know nothin'.

CORA You never *wanted* to marry me.

RUBIN I never said that.

CORA It's true, isn't it?

RUBIN I'm tellin' ya, it ain't.

CORA It is. I've felt it all these years.

(SONNY *crosses and goes through the parlor into the dining room, still unobserved by* RUBIN *and* CORA)

RUBIN All right. If you're so determined to think it, then go ahead. I admit, in some ways I din wanna marry nobody. Can't ya understand how a man feels, givin' up his freedom?

CORA And how does a woman feel, knowing her husband married her only because . . . because he . . . (CORA *now spots* REENIE *spying between the parlor doors. She screams at her*) Reenie, get away from there!

RUBIN None of this is what we was arguin' about in the first place. We was arguin' about the dress. Ya gotta take it back.

CORA *I won't.*

RUBIN *Ya will.*

CORA Reenie's going to wear her new dress to the party, or you'll have to bury me.

RUBIN You'll take that dress back to Loren Delman, or I'm leavin' this house for good and never comin' back.

CORA Go on. You're only home half the time as it is. We can get along without you the rest of the time.

RUBIN Then that's what you're gonna do. There'll be ice-cream parlors in hell before I come back to this place and listen to your jaw.

(*He bolts into the hallway*)

CORA Get out! Get out and go to Ponca City. Mavis Pruitt is waiting. She's probably getting lonesome without you.

(SONNY *quietly enters from the dining room, and watches*)

RUBIN By God, Cora, it's all I can do to keep from hittin' you when you talk like that.

CORA (*Following him into hallway, taunting him. Here they are both unseen by audience*) Go on and hit me! You wouldn't dare! (*But he does dare. We hear the sound of his blow, which sends* CORA *reeling back into parlor*) Rubin! (REENIE *watches from the parlor.* SONNY *is still in the living room*)

RUBIN I'll go to Ponca City, and drink booze and take Mavis to the movies, and raise every kind of hell I can think of. T'hell with you!

(*He bolts outside*)

CORA (*Running to the door*) Don't you ever set foot in this house again, Rubin Flood. I'll never forget what you've said. Never! Don't you ever come back inside this house again!

(*We hear* RUBIN'S *car drive off now.* CORA *returns to the living room, still too dazed to be sure what has happened*)

SONNY Gee, Mom. That was the worst fight you ever had, wasn't it?

CORA How long have you been standing there, Sonny?

SONNY Since he hit you.

REENIE (*Coming forth*) Did he mean it about not coming back? Oh, Mom, why did you have to say all those things? I love Daddy. Why do you say those things to him?

CORA Oh, God, I hate for you kids to see us fight this way.

SONNY What did he mean, he didn't want to marry you?

CORA You're not old enough to understand these things, Sonny.

SONNY Did he hurt you, Mom. Did he?

CORA I'm still too mad to know whether he did or not.

REENIE I don't think he'll ever come back. What'll we do, Mom?

CORA Now, don't worry, Reenie.

REENIE Will we have to go to the poorhouse?

CORA No, of course not. Now, quit worrying.

REENIE But if Daddy doesn't come back?

CORA I still have the money my mother left me, haven't I? And if worst comes to worst we can always go to Oklahoma City and move in with your Aunt Lottie and Uncle Morris.

SONNY (*Jumping up and down in glee*) Goody, goody, goody. I wanta move to Oklahoma City.

REENIE Listen to him, Mom. He's *glad* Daddy's gone. He's *glad*.

SONNY I don't care. I wanta move to Oklahoma City.

REENIE I don't. *This* is home. *This* is. And I don't want to move.

CORA Now, children!

REENIE I hate you.

SONNY I hate you, too. So there! Oklahoma City! Oklahoma City! I wanta move to Oklahoma City!

CORA Stop it! There's been enough fighting in this house for one night. Reenie, take your dress upstairs and hang it in the closet.

REENIE I hate the old dress now. It's the cause of all the trouble. I hate it.

CORA You do what I tell you. You take that dress upstairs and hang it in the closet. You're going to go to that party if I have to take you there myself. (REENIE *starts upstairs*) The next time you're invited to a party, I'll let you go in a hand-me-down.

SONNY (*With the joy of discovering a new continent*) Oklahoma City.

CORA (*Wearily*) I'll go out and fix supper, although I don't imagine any of us will feel like eating.

SONNY I do. I'm hungry.

CORA (*A little amused*) Are you? Good. Come to me, Sonny! (*With a sudden need for affection*) Do you love me, boy? Do you love your old mom?

SONNY More than all the world with a fence around it.

CORA (*Clasping him to her*) Oh, God, what would I do without you kids? I hope you'll always love me, Sonny. I hope you always will. (REENIE *comes downstairs*) Where are you going, daughter?

(REENIE *looks disdainfully at them, and marches into the parlor, where, in a moment, we hear her playing a lovely Chopin nocturne*)

SONNY Mom, I'm going to sell my autographed photograph of Fatty Arbuckle. Millicent Dalrymple said she'd give me fifteen cents for it. And Fatty Arbuckle isn't one of my favorites any more. If I sold the photograph, I'd have enough to go to the movie tonight and buy a sack of popcorn, besides.

CORA (*Lying on the floor beside him*) If the world was falling to pieces all about you, you'd still want to go to the movies, wouldn't you?

SONNY I don't see why not.

CORA Your mother's unhappy, Sonny. Doesn't that mean anything to you?

SONNY Well . . . I'm sorry.

CORA I want you kids near me tonight. Can't you understand? Oh, God, wouldn't it be nice if life were as sweet as music! (*For a moment, mother and son lie together in each other's arms. Then* CORA *stands, as though fearing her own indulgence, and takes* SONNY *by the hand*) Come! Help me set the table, Sonny.

CURTAIN

ACT TWO

Scene: At rise of curtain, we hear a banging rendition of "Smiles" coming from the parlor, where LOTTIE *is at the piano,* SONNY *by her side, both singing in hearty voices.* REENIE *stands listlessly watching, drying a dish.* MORRIS *sits in* RUBIN'S *chair, working one of those baffling little hand puzzles, which has got the best of him.* LOTTIE *proves to be a big, fleshy woman, a few years older than* CORA. *She wears a gaudy dress and lots of costume jewelry.* MORRIS *is a big defeated-looking man of wrecked virility.*

LOTTIE and SONNY (*Singing*) "There are smiles that make us happy . . ."

CORA (*Coming into living room from kitchen*) I won't need you to help me with the dishes, Reenie. I want you to go upstairs now and get ready for your party. (*Calls into parlor*) Sonny! Sonny!

MORRIS Sure was a good dinner, Cora.

CORA What, Morris?

MORRIS (*Trying to make himself heard above the piano*) I said, it sure was a good dinner.

CORA Thank you, Morris. Now go and get dressed, Reenie. (REENIE *reluctantly goes upstairs*) Sonny! Sonny! Lottie, will you please stop that racket. A body can't hear himself think.

(LOTTIE *and* SONNY *finish the chorus*)

CORA Sonny, I said you've got to help me in the kitchen.

SONNY Why can't Reenie?

CORA She cleared the table for me, and now she has to bathe and get ready for her party.

SONNY I have to do everything around here.

LOTTIE (*In the voice one uses to indulge a child*) I think it's a shame. (SONNY *and* CORA *exit into the dining room.* LOTTIE *comes into the living room. To* MORRIS) Cora always was jealous because I could play the piano and she couldn't. (*Looks to see if* CORA *is out of hearing distance*) Do I have something to tell you! Do you know why she asked us over here?
(*She hurries over to* MORRIS)

MORRIS For dinner.

LOTTIE No! She and Rubin have had another fight. She told me all about it while I was in the kitchen helping her get dinner on the table.

MORRIS What about, this time?

LOTTIE About a new dress she bought for Reenie. But what difference does that make? They could fight about anything. Only this time he hit her.

MORRIS He did?

LOTTIE Don't tell her I told you. Poor Cora. I guess maybe she has a hard time with Rubin.

MORRIS Has Rubin walked out again?

LOTTIE You guessed it. Do you know what she wants to do now, honey? She wants to bring the kids over to Oklahoma City to live *with us?* She says I suggested they do that some time ago. I guess maybe I did, but my God, I never thought they'd do it. We'd be perfectly miserable with her and the two kids living with us, wouldn't we, Morris? With only one extra bedroom, one of 'em would have to sleep on the davenport in the living room, and then what would happen when your patients started coming in the morning?

MORRIS Yah. It wouldn't work out very well.

LOTTIE No. Oh, my! The way she pampers those kids, Morris. If she had her way, she'd spoil 'em rotten.

MORRIS What did you tell her, honey?

LOTTIE Well, I haven't told her anything yet. I was so

flabbergasted when she asked me, I just hemmed . . . (SONNY *enters the parlor to put away a big vase that* CORA *has just washed.* LOTTIE *sees him*) Hi! Honey.

SONNY They got me working again.

LOTTIE I think it's terrible.

(SONNY *exits into the dining room*)

LOTTIE . . . and hawed until I could think of something to say. Oh, Morris, put away that puzzle and listen to me. She's going to come to you sometime this evening and ask you about it, and all you need to say is, "I'm leaving all that in Lottie's hands, Cora." Can you remember that? Just say it real nice, like it was none of your business.

MORRIS I'll remember.

LOTTIE You say you will, but will you?

MORRIS Yes, honey.

LOTTIE I don't know. You're so afraid of hurting people's feelings.

MORRIS That's not so.

LOTTIE Oh, it is too. Don't I know! You had to go to see some psychologist over in Oklahoma City because you were so afraid of hurting your patients when you drilled their teeth. Now, confess it. It was actually making you sick, that you had to drill your patients' teeth and hurt them.

MORRIS Honey, I wasn't really *sick* about it.

LOTTIE You were too. Now remember what I say. Don't get *soft-hearted* at the last minute and tell Cora to bring the kids and come on over. My God, Morris, we'd be in the loony bin in less than two days with them in the house. Cora may be my own flesh and blood but I couldn't live with her to save my life. And I love those kids of hers. I do, Morris. But I couldn't live with them. They'd drive me crazy. You, too. You know they would.

CORA (*Enters the parlor to put napkins in the sideboard*) Almost finished.

LOTTIE You shoulda let me help you. (*But* CORA *has re-*

turned to the kitchen) Cora said something to me about her getting a job at one of the big department stores over in Oklahoma City. Can you see her doin' a thing like that? I can't. "Cora," I said, "you wouldn't last two days at that kind of work, on your feet all day, taking people's sass." Well, I don't know if I convinced her or not, but I gave her something to think about. (*Sneaks back to parlor door to see if* CORA *is within earshot, then comes back to* MORRIS, *speaking in a very confidential voice*) Morris? Do you think Rubin still plays around with Mavis Pruitt over in Ponca City?

MORRIS (*Clamming up*) I don't know, honey.

LOTTIE You do too.

MORRIS I'm telling you, I don't.

LOTTIE You men, you tell each other everything, but you all want to protect each other. And wild horses and screaming ravens couldn't get you to talk.

MORRIS Well, whatever Rubin does . . . like that . . . is *his* business.

LOTTIE My! Don't we sound righteous all of a sudden! Well, I bet anything he still sees her.

MORRIS Well, don't you let on to Cora.

LOTTIE I won't. Did I ever tell you about the first time she met Rubin?

MORRIS Yes, honey.

LOTTIE I did not! Cora and I were coming out of the five-and-ten. She'd wanted to buy a little lace to put on a dress. And here comes Rubin, like a picture of Sin, riding down the street on a shiny black horse. My God, he was handsome. Neither of us knew who he was. But he looked at Cora and smiled, and Cora began to get all nervous and fluttery. And do you know what? He came by the house that very night and wanted to see her. Mama and Papa didn't know what to do. They stood around like they were afraid of Rubin. But Cora went out riding with him. He'd brought a buggy with him. And six weeks later they were married. Mama and Papa were worried sick. Rubin's people were all right, but they were ranchers. Kind of wild. And Cora only seventeen, not out of high school. I think that's the reason Papa had his stroke, don't you, Morris?

MORRIS Maybe . . .

LOTTIE I do. They just felt like Cora might as well be dead as married to a man like Rubin. But Cora was always a determined creature. Mama and Papa were no match for her when she wanted her own way.

MORRIS Well, I like Rubin.

LOTTIE I do, too, honey. I'm not saying anything against him. And he's made a lot better husband than I ever thought he would. But I'm glad *I'm* not married to him. I'd be worried to death all the time. Im glad I'm married to a nice man I can trust.

(MORRIS *does not know how to respond to this endearment. He crosses the room troubledly*)

MORRIS What'll Cora do if Rubin doesn't come back?

LOTTIE Well, that's not our problem, honey.

MORRIS Yes, but just the same, I . . .

LOTTIE Listen, she's got a nice big house here, hasn't she? She can take in roomers if she has to. And Mama left her two thousand dollars when she died, didn't she? Yes, Cora was the baby, so Mama left the money to her. I'm not going to worry.

REENIE (*Upstairs*) Aunt Lottie!

MORRIS All right. I was just wondering.

LOTTIE Now, remember. All you've got to say is, "I'm leaving all that to Lottie, Cora."

MORRIS Yes, honey.

(REENIE *comes downstairs looking somewhat wan and frightened*)

LOTTIE Shhhh! (*Now she turns to* REENIE *with a prepared smile*) Well, honey, aren't you getting ready for your party? Morris and I are dying to see your new dress.

REENIE I don't feel well. I wish I didn't have to go.

LOTTIE (*Alarmed*) You don't feel well? Did you tell your mother?

REENIE Yes. But she won't believe me. I wish you'd tell her, Aunt Lottie.

LOTTIE (*Rushes excitedly into dining room, where we hear her speaking to* CORA) Cora! Reenie says she isn't feeling well. Cora, I think maybe she shouldn't go to the party. She says she doesn't want to go. Cora, what do you think is wrong?

CORA (*Enters living room from dining room—followed by* LOTTIE) There's nothing wrong with the child, Lottie.

LOTTIE But she says she isn't feeling well, Cora. (*Turns to* REENIE) Come here, honey, let me see if you've got a temperature. No. Not a sign of temperature. Stick out your tongue. Are you sick at your stomach?

REENIE Kind of.

LOTTIE My God, Cora. Her little hands are like ice.

CORA (*Quite calm and wise*) There's nothing wrong with the child, Lottie. She gets to feeling like this every time she goes to a party.

LOTTIE She's not going to have a very good time if she doesn't feel well.

CORA It's something she's got to get over, Lottie. Plans are already made now. I got her the dress and she's got a date with a boy who's come here all the way from California. Now, I'm not going to let her play sick and not go. The Ralston girl would never invite Reenie to another party as long as she lived if she backed out now. (*Her strategy defeated,* REENIE *goes back up the stairs*)

LOTTIE It's awful funny when a young girl doesn't want to go to a party, don't you think so, Morris? (*She watches* REENIE'S *departure, puzzledly*) I just thought of something. I've got a bottle of perfume I'm going to give her. It's Coty's L'Origan. Finest perfume made. One of the big drugstores in Oklahoma City was having an anniversary sale. With each box of Coty's face powder, they gave you a little bottle of perfume, stuck right on top of the box. Morris, run out to the car and get me that package. It's on the back seat. I'll take it upstairs to Reenie. It'll make her feel good, don't you think?

CORA That's very thoughtful of you, Lottie.

MORRIS (*On his way to door*) You'll have her smelling like a fancy woman.

LOTTIE (*With a sudden bite*) How do *you* know what a fancy woman smells like?

MORRIS I can make a joke, can't I?

(MORRIS *exits.* CORA *and* LOTTIE *sit on either side of the table*)

LOTTIE It was a wonderful dinner, Cora.

CORA I'm glad you thought so. It all tasted like ashes to me.

LOTTIE Oh, now, Cora, quit taking on.

CORA Seventeen years we've been married, Lottie, and we still can't get along.

LOTTIE What are you talking about? Why, I've known times when you got along just fine . . . for months at a time.

CORA When Rubin was gone.

LOTTIE Cora, that's not so.

CORA Lottie, it's not good for kids to see their parents fighting.

LOTTIE Cora, you've got the two nicest kids in the whole world. Why, they're wonderful children, Cora.

CORA I worry about them, Lottie . . . You saw Reenie just now. Here she is, sick because she's going to a party, when most girls her age would be tickled to death. And the other boys tease Sonny so.

LOTTIE Oh, Reenie'll get over that. So will Sonny.

CORA Kids don't just "get over" these things, in some magic way. These troubles stay with kids sometimes, and affect their lives when they grow up.

MORRIS (*Returns with a small package*) This what you want?

LOTTIE Yes. Reenie—I've got something for you, Reenie. I've got something here to make you smell good. Real French perfume. Morris says it'll make you smell like a fancy woman.

(*She goes running upstairs, exuding her own brand of warmth and affection*)

CORA Lottie's awful good-hearted, Morris.

MORRIS She thinks an awful lot of your kids, Cora.

CORA I know she does. Morris, I've been thinking, wouldn't it be nice if Sonny and Reenie could go to those big schools you have in Oklahoma City? I mean . . .

LOTTIE (*Hurrying back downstairs*) Cora, I wish you'd let me curl Reenie's hair for her. I could have her looking like a real baby doll. I'm an artist at it. Last week, Morris took me to a party at the Shrine, and everybody told me I had the prettiest head of hair at the whole party.

CORA Go on and do it.

LOTTIE I can't right now. She's in the bathtub. When are you going to get your hair bobbed, Cora?

CORA Rubin doesn't like bobbed hair.

LOTTIE Oh, he doesn't! You like my bobbed hair, don't you, Morris?

MORRIS It's all right, honey.

LOTTIE I'll be darned if I'd let any man tell me whether I could bob my hair or not. Why, I wouldn't go back to long hair now for anything. Morris says maybe I should take up smoking cigarettes now. Would you believe it, Cora? Women all over Oklahoma City are smoking cigarettes now. Isn't that disgraceful? What in God's name are we all coming to?

CORA (*There is too much on her mind for her to partake now of* LOTTIE'S *small talk*) I . . . I'd better finish up in the kitchen.

(*She exits through the dining-room door*)

LOTTIE Morris, I don't know what to do. I just can't bear to see little Cora so unhappy.

MORRIS After all, it's not your worry, honey.

LOTTIE Oh, I know, but in a way it *is* my worry. I mean, I've always looked after Cora, ever since we were girls. I took her to her teacher the first day of school. I gave up the wishbone for her every time we had fried chicken. She was the baby of the family, and I guess we all felt we had to pamper her.

MORRIS Honey, if you want to take in her and the kids, it's up to you. We'd manage somehow.

LOTTIE Oh, God, Morris! Life'd be miserable.

SONNY (*Enters through parlor*) Wanta see my movie stars, Aunt Lottie?

LOTTIE I guess so, honey. (SONNY *goes into parlor to get scrapbooks as* LOTTIE *turns to* MORRIS *with a private voice*) Every time we come over here we've got to look at his movie stars.

MORRIS Got any of Norma Talmadge?

SONNY (*Spreading the scrapbook on the floor before them*) Sure.

LOTTIE Norma Talmadge, Norma Talmadge! That's all you ever think about is Norma Talmadge. I don't know what you see in her. Besides, she's a Catholic.

MORRIS Honey, you've just got a bug about the Catholics.

LOTTIE Oh I do, do I! Maybe you'd like to marry Norma Talmadge someday and then let the Pope tell you what to do the rest of your life, making you swear to leave all your money to the church, and bring up all your children Catholic, and then join the Knights of Columbus and take an oath to go out and kill all the nice Protestant women when the day comes for the Catholics to take over the world.

(CORA *enters the parlor on her way to the sideboard, then wanders into the living room*)

MORRIS Honey, where do you pick up these stories?

LOTTIE Well, it's the truth. Marietta Flagmeyer told me. Cora, Marietta has this very close friend who used to be a Catholic but isn't any more. She even joined a convent, but she ran away because she found out all those things and wouldn't stand for them. This friend told Marietta that the Catholics keep the basements of their churches filled with guns and all kinds of ammunition . . .

CORA (*She has heard* LOTTIE'S *rantings before*) Lottie! (*She shakes her head hopelessly and returns to the parlor, on her way to the kitchen*)

LOTTIE . . . because some day they plan to rise and take over the world, and kill off all the rest of us who don't want to be Catholics. I believe every word of it, too.

MORRIS Well . . . I still like Norma Talmadge. Got any of Bebe Daniels?

SONNY Yes.

(*He hands* MORRIS *a picture, which* LOTTIE *snaps up first for an approving look*)

LOTTIE I don't know what you see in her.

(*She now passes the picture on to* MORRIS)

MORRIS You don't like any of the women stars, honey.

LOTTIE I guess I don't. I hear they're all a bunch of trollops. (*To* SONNY) Honey, when is your daddy coming home?

SONNY Oh, he's not coming back at all. He and Mom had a fight. Here's one of your favorites, Aunt Lottie.

(*He hands her a picture*)

LOTTIE Who? Rudolph Valentino. He's not one of my favorites at all.

MORRIS You saw *The Sheik* four times.

LOTTIE That's just because Marietta Flagmeyer wanted me to keep her company.

MORRIS Rudolph Valentino must be a Catholic, too. He's an Eyetalian.

LOTTIE But he's not a Catholic. Marietta's friend has a

book that lists all the people in Hollywood who are Catholics. (*She studies the picture very intently*) You know, it scares me a little to look at him. Those eyes, that seem to be laughing at you, and all those white teeth. I think it's a sin for a man to be as pretty as he is. Why, I'd be scared to death to let a man like him touch me. (CORA *returns now, without her apron; she is carrying a paper bag*) But you know, they say he's really a very nice man. Cora, do you know there's this woman over in Oklahoma City who worships Rudolph Valentino? That's the truth. Marietta knows her. She's made a little shrine to him down in her basement, and she keeps the room filled with candles and she goes down there every day and says a little prayer for him.

CORA I thought you were going to fix Reenie's hair.

LOTTIE Oh, yes. I guess she's out of the bathtub now.

CORA (*Puts the bag on the table*) There's a lot of fried chicken left, Lottie. I brought you some to take home with you.

LOTTIE Won't you and the kids want it?

CORA They won't eat anything but the breast.

LOTTIE Thanks, Cora.

CORA Sonny, I don't want your pictures all over the floor when the young people come by for Reenie.

SONNY All right.

MORRIS (*As* LOTTIE *takes a drumstick out of the bag*) Honey, you just ate.

LOTTIE Don't scold me, Daddy. (*She whispers boldly to him before starting upstairs*) Remember what I told you, Morris. (*Now she goes hurrying up the stairs*) Reenie! I'm coming up to fix your hair. I'm going to turn you into a real baby doll.

REENIE (*Upstairs*) I'm in here, Aunt Lottie.

(MORRIS *draws over to the door, as though hoping to evade* CORA)

CORA Morris . . . Morris! I suppose Lottie told you what's happened.

MORRIS Well, uh . . . yes, Cora . . . she said something about it.

CORA I guess now that maybe my folks were right, Morris. I shouldn't have married Rubin.

MORRIS You're going to forget all this squabble after a while, Cora. So's Rubin.

CORA I don't think we *should* forget it. I don't think we should *try* to come back together. I think I've failed.

MORRIS Now, Cora, I think you're exaggerating things in your own mind.

CORA Morris, I'm only thirty-four. That's still young. I thought I'd like to take the kids to Oklahoma City and put them in school there, and get myself a job in one of the department stores. I know I've never done work like that, but I think I'd like it, and . . . it seems to me that I've got to, Morris. I've got to.

MORRIS Well, Cora . . . maybe . . .

LOTTIE (*Upstairs we see her feet treading the hallway*) Let's go into the bathroom, Reenie, where the light's better.

MORRIS It's awful hard, Cora, being on your feet all day.

CORA But I'd get used to it.

MORRIS Well . . . it's hard for me to advise you, Cora.

CORA Morris, I was wondering if maybe the kids and I could come and live with you and Lottie for a while. Just for a while. Until we got used to the city. Until I got myself a job and we felt more or less at home.

MORRIS Well, I . . . uh . . .

CORA I promise we wouldn't be any bother. I mean, I'd keep things straightened up after the kids, and do as much of the cooking as Lottie wanted me to do.

MORRIS Well, I . . . uh . . .

CORA I just don't know what else the kids and I can do, Morris.

MORRIS Yes. Well . . . Cora, I don't know just what to say.

CORA Would we be too much in the way, Morris?

MORRIS Oh, no. Of course not, Cora. *But* . . .

CORA (*Hopefully*) I think we could manage. And I'd pay our share of the bills. I'd insist on that.

(FLIRT, PUNKY *and* SAMMY *are seen through the window, coming onto the porch*)

MORRIS Well, Cora, I . . .

LOTTIE (*Comes hurtling halfway down the stairs, full of anxiety*) Cora, Reenie's sick. She's vomiting all over the bathroom.

(*She bustles back upstairs as* CORA *starts to follow*)

CORA Oh, my God! (*The doorbell rings, catching* CORA *for a moment*) Oh, dear! It's the young people after Reenie. Sonny, put on your manners and answer the door. (SONNY *runs to the door, stopping to turn on the porch light before opening it. We see the three young people on the porch outside*—FLIRT *in dazzling party dress, and the two boys in uniforms from a nearby military academy. One boy,* PUNKY GIVENS, *is seen drinking from a flask, preparing himself to meet people. Inside,* CORA *starts upstairs in worried concern*) Oh, dear! What could be wrong with the child? Morris, try to entertain the young people until I get back.

(CORA *goes off.* SONNY *swings open the door*)

SONNY Won't you come in?

FLIRT (*Comes dancing into the hallway, bringing the atmosphere of a chilly spring night with her*) Hi, Sonny! Is your sister ready?

SONNY Not yet.

FLIRT Oh, shucks! (*Sticks her head out the door*) Come on in, fellows. We're going to have to wait. (PUNKY GIVENS *and* SAMMY GOLDENBAUM *make a colorful entrance. Both are dressed in uniforms of lustrous blue, which fit them like smooth upholstery.* FLIRT *begins the introductions*) Sammy, this is Sonny Flood, Reenie's little brother.

(SAMMY GOLDENBAUM *steps forth correctly, his plumed headgear in his hand. He is a darkly beautiful young man of seventeen, with lustrous black hair, black eyes and a captivating smile. Yet, something about him seems a little foreign, at least in comparison with the Midwestern company in which he now finds himself. He could be a Persian prince, strayed from his native kingdom. But he has become adept over the years in adapting himself, and he shows an eagerness to make friends and to be liked*)

SAMMY Hi, Sonny!

SONNY (*Shaking hands*) Hi!

FLIRT (*Bringing* PUNKY *up from the rear*) And this is Punky Givens. (*She all but drags him from the dark corner of the hallway to face the lighted room full of people. For* PUNKY *is a disappointment as a human being. The military academy has done nothing as yet for his posture, and he wears his uniform as though embarrassed by its splendor. He offers a limp hand when being introduced, mumbles some incoherent greeting, and then retires in hopes that no one will notice him. These introductions made,* FLIRT *now notices* MORRIS) Oh, hello! I'm Flirt Conroy. How're you?

MORRIS How d'ya do? I'm Morris Lacey. Reenie's uncle. From Oklahoma City.

FLIRT Oh, yes, I've heard her speak about you. Fellows, this is Dr. Lacey. He's Reenie's uncle. From Oklahoma City.

SAMMY (*Crossing the room to present himself to* MORRIS, *he is brisk and alert, even though his speech betrays a slight stammer*) How do you do, sir? My name is G-Goldenbaum. Sammy, they call me.

MORRIS Glad to know you, Sammy.

FLIRT And this is Punky Givens. (*Nudging him*) Stand up straight, Punky.

MORRIS Glad to know you, Punky. (PUNKY *mumbles.* MORRIS *now feels the burden of his responsibility as temporary host*) Uh . . . anyone care for a Life Saver? (*He offers a pack from his pocket, but no one is interested.* LOTTIE *comes bustling down the stairs, eager to take over the situation, exuberantly babbling inconsequentials all the way down*)

LOTTIE Hello, everyone! I'm Lottie Lacey, Reenie's aunt. I'm Cora Flood's sister. From Oklahoma City. Oklahoma City's a great big town now. People say in another ten years it's going to be the biggest city in the whole United States, bigger even than New York or Chicago. You're the little Conroy girl, aren't you? I've heard my sister speak of you. My! What a pretty red dress. Have you all met my husband? Dr. Lacey. He's a dentist. Come over to Oklahoma City and he'll pull all your teeth. (*She laughs heartily, and then her eyes slowly widen at the magnificent uniforms*) My goodness! Aren't those handsome getups?

SAMMY (*Stepping forth*) How do you do, ma'am? I'm Sammy Goldenbaum. From California.

LOTTIE Oh, yes. Cora told me about the young man from California. He's from Hollywood, Morris. His mother's in the movies. Has she played in anything I might have seen?

SAMMY She was in T-Thomas Meighan's last picture. Her name is Gertrude Vanderhof. It was a very small part. She isn't a star or anything.

LOTTIE Gertrude Vanderhof! Did we see Thomas Meighan's last picture, Morris? I don't believe so. I like Thomas Meighan, but we don't have time to see *all* the movies. Do you think you ever saw Gertrude Vanderhof in anything, Morris?

(LOTTIE *seems to refer to her husband on every topic without waiting for his judgment. Nevertheless,* MORRIS *mulls over this last query as* FLIRT *interrupts*)

FLIRT Mrs. Lacey, have you met Punky Givens?

LOTTIE How do you do? I've heard my sister speak of you. Your people are very prominent in town, aren't they? Yes, I've heard Cora speak of them. (PUNKY *offers a hand and mumbles*) What did you say? (*He repeats his mumble.* LOTTIE *is still at sea but makes the best of things*) Thank you very much.

(*At the top of the stairs, we see* REENIE'S *feet trying to get up the courage to bring her down, and we hear* CORA *coaxing her*)

CORA (*Off*) Go on, Reenie.

(*But* REENIE *can't make it yet. The feet go scurrying back to safety*)

LOTTIE (*Trying to avoid embarrassment*) Well, I'm afraid you're all going to have to wait a few minutes. Reenie isn't quite ready.

CORA (*Upstairs*) Reenie, not another word.

LOTTIE Cora's upstairs now, helping her. I guess you'll have to entertain yourselves a while. Do any of you play mahjong?

(*She notices the bag of fried chicken, and hides it under the table*)

FLIRT I want to play some music. Got any new piano rolls, Sonny?

SONNY A few.

(*They run into the parlor, to the piano*)

FLIRT Gee, I wish you had a Victrola like we do.

LOTTIE (*Sitting, turning her attention to* SAMMY) My, you're a long way from home, aren't you?

SAMMY Yes, ma'am.

LOTTIE Morris and I went to California once. A Shriners' convention. Oh, we thought it was perfectly wonderful, all those oranges and things. Didn't we, Morris? I should think you'd want to go home on your spring vacation.

SAMMY Well, I . . . I guess I don't really have a home . . . Mrs. Lacey.

(SONNY *wanders back from the parlor.* SAMMY *fills him with curiosity and fascination*)

LOTTIE Did you tell me your mother lived out there?

SAMMY Yes, but, you see, she's pretty busy in moving pictures, and . . . Oh, she feels awfully bad that she doesn't have more time for me. Really she does. But she doesn't have a place where I could stay right now . . . and . . . But, it's not *her* fault.

LOTTIE Where's your father?

SAMMY Oh, I never knew him.

LOTTIE You never knew your father?

SAMMY No. You see, he died before I was born. My mother has been married . . . a few times since then. But I never met any of her husbands . . . although they were all very fine gentlemen.

LOTTIE Well—I just never knew anyone who didn't have a home. Do you spend your whole life in military academies?

SAMMY Just about. I bet I've been in almost every military academy in the whole country. Well, I take that back. There's some I didn't go to. I mean . . . there's some that wouldn't take me.

SONNY (*Out of the innocent blue*) My mother says you're a Jew.

LOTTIE (*Aghast*) Sonny!

SAMMY Well . . . yes, Sonny. I guess I am.

LOTTIE (*Consolingly*) That's perfectly all right. Why, we don't think a thing about a person's being Jewish, do we, Morris?

MORRIS No. Of course not.

SAMMY My father was Jewish. Mother told me. Mother isn't Jewish at all. Oh, my mother has the most beautiful blond hair. I guess I take after my father . . . in looks, anyhow. He was an actor, too, but he got killed in an automobile accident.

LOTTIE That's too bad. Sonny, I think you should apologize.

SONNY Did I say something bad?

SAMMY Oh, that's all right. It doesn't bother me that I'm Jewish. Not any more. I guess it used to a little . . . Yes, it did used to a little.

LOTTIE (*Who must find a remedy for everything*) You know what you ought to do? You ought to join the Christian Science church. Now, I'm not a member myself, but I know this Jewish woman over in Oklahoma City, and she was very, very unhappy, wasn't she, Morris? But she joined the Christian Science church and has been perfectly happy ever since.

SONNY I didn't mean to say anything wrong.

SAMMY You didn't say anything wrong, Sonny.

(*The piano begins playing "The Sheik of Araby" with precise, automatic rhythm.* FLIRT *dances in from the parlor*)

FLIRT Come on, Punky, let's dance. (*She sings*) The Sheik of Araby—boom—boom—boom—his heart belongs to me. Come *on,* Punky.

SAMMY (*Always courteous, to* LOTTIE) Would you care to dance, ma'am?

LOTTIE Me? Good heavens, no. I haven't danced since I was a girl. But I certainly appreciate your asking. Isn't he respectful, Morris?

(LOTTIE *exits to dining room*)

SAMMY Wanta wild West ride, Sonny?

(*He kneels on the floor, permitting* SONNY *to straddle his back. Then* SAMMY *kicks his feet in the air like a wild colt, as* SONNY *holds to him tight*)

FLIRT (*At the back of the room, instructs* PUNKY *in the intricacies of a new step*) No, Punky. That's not it. You take one step to the left and then *dip.* See? Oh, it's a wonderful step, and all the kids are doing it.

LOTTIE (*Enters from kitchen with a plate of cookies, which she offers to* SAMMY *and* SONNY) Would you like a cookie?

SAMMY (*Getting to his feet, the ride over*) Gee, that gets to be pretty strenuous.

(FLIRT *and* PUNKY *now retire to the parlor where they indulge in a little private lovemaking*)

SONNY Where did you get those clothes?

SAMMY They gave them to me at the academy, Sonny.

FLIRT (*Protesting* PUNKY'S *advances*) Punky, *don't.*

(LOTTIE *observes this little intimacy, having just started into the parlor with the plate of cookies. It rouses some of her righteousness*)

SAMMY No. I take that back. They didn't *give* them to me. They never give you anything at that place. I paid for them. Plenty!

SONNY Why do you wear a sword?

SAMMY (*Pulls the sword from its sheath, like a buccaneer, and goes charging about the room in search of imagined villains*) I wear a sword to protect myself! See! To kill off all the villains in the world. (*He frightens* LOTTIE) Oh, don't worry, ma'am. It's not sharp. I couldn't hurt anyone with it, even if I wanted to. We just wear them for show.

SONNY (*Jumping up and down*) Can I have a sword? I want a sword.

SAMMY Do you, Sonny? Do you want a sword? Here, Sonny, I'll give you *my* sword, for all the good it'll do you.

LOTTIE (*To* MORRIS) Cora will probably buy Sonny a sword now. (*Now* SONNY *takes the sword and imitates the actions of* SAMMY. LOTTIE *is apprehensive*) Now, you be careful, Sonny.

SAMMY What do you want a sword for, Sonny?

SONNY (*With a lunge*) To *show* people.

LOTTIE Sonny! Be careful with that thing.

SAMMY And what do you want to show people, Sonny?

SONNY I just want to *show* 'em.

(*He places the sword between his arm and his chest, then drops to the floor, the sword rising far above his body, giving the appearance that he is impaled.* LOTTIE *is horrified*)

LOTTIE Oh, darling—put it down. Sonny, please don't play with that nasty thing any more.

(SONNY *rises now and laughs with* SAMMY. LOTTIE *puts the sword away in the parlor, where she again comes upon* FLIRT *and* PUNKY, *now engaged in more serious necking. Morally outraged, she runs up the stairs to inform* CORA)

SAMMY (*Kneeling beside* SONNY, *as though to make himself a physical equal*) What'll we do now, Sonny? Are there any games you want to play? Do you want to fight Indians? or set bear traps? or go flying over volcanoes? or climb the Alps?

SONNY (*Eagerly*) Yes . . . yes.

SAMMY Gee, so do I, Sonny. But we can't. Not tonight anyway. What else can we do?

SONNY I can show you my movie stars.

SAMMY I've had enough of movie stars. What else?

SONNY I can speak a piece.

SAMMY You can? (*Jumps to his feet*) Hey, everyone! Stop the music. Sonny's going to speak a piece.

(SAMMY *stops the piano, which* FLIRT *finds quite annoying*)

LOTTIE (*Hurrying downstairs*) Did you hear that, Morris? Sonny's going to speak a piece.

FLIRT (*To* SAMMY) Hey, what are you doing?

SAMMY (*To* SONNY) Where do you want to stand, sir?

LOTTIE He's got a little platform in the parlor where he practices.

SAMMY (*Having taken over as impresario*) Into the parlor, everyone. Into the parlor to hear Sonny speak his piece.

FLIRT (*Pulling* PUNKY'S *arm*) Come on, Punky. Come on. We *have* to listen, don't we?

SAMMY Quiet, everyone. Quiet!

(*All enter the parlor, except* MORRIS, *who crosses toward the door, as though he hoped to escape, as* SONNY *begins the famous soliloquy with boyish fervor.* MORRIS *looks as though he might share some of Hamlet's woes. After* SONNY *begins,* CORA *starts down the stairs with* REENIE)

SONNY

"To be, or not to be: that is the question:
Whether 'tis nobler in the mind to suffer
The slings and arrows of outrageous fortune,
Or to take arms against a sea of troubles,
And by opposing end them? To die: to sleep;
No more; and, by a sleep to say we end
The heart-ache and the thousand natural shocks
That flesh is heir to, 'tis a consummation
Devoutly to be wish'd. To die, to sleep;
To sleep: perchance to dream: ay, there's the rub,
For in that sleep of death what dreams may come
When we have shuffled off this mortal coil,
Must give us pause. . . ."

CORA (*While* SONNY *is reciting*) Oh, Sonny's reciting. Why, he's reciting Shakespeare. He must have gotten out that dusty volume of Shakespeare over in the bookcase, and memorized that speech all on his own. (*Points to* SAMMY *in the parlor*) Reenie, there's your young man. Isn't he handsome? Now you're going to have a good time. I can feel it in my bones.

(SONNY *and* CORA *finish speaking at the same time. There is immediate loud acclaim for* SONNY)

SAMMY That was *won*derful, Sonny.

(*All come into the living room now,* SAMMY *carrying* SONNY *on his shoulders like a triumphant hero*)

LOTTIE He's a second Jackie Coogan.

FLIRT That was just wonderful, Sonny.

LOTTIE Cora, you should have been here. Sonny recited Shakespeare. It was just wonderful.

CORA Yes. I heard him.

SAMMY Sonny's a genius. I'm going to take you to Hollywood, Sonny, and put you in the movies. You'll be the greatest actor out there, Sonny.

FLIRT Oh, I think Shakespeare's just wonderful. I'm going to read him sometime, really I am.

CORA (*Going to* SAMMY) Good evening, young man. I'm Mrs. Flood.

SAMMY (*Putting* SONNY *down*) Beg your pardon, ma'am. I'm Sammy Goldenbaum.

CORA Welcome. I see my son's been entertaining you.

SAMMY He sure has, ma'am.

CORA He started speaking pieces about a year ago. Just picked it up. Some people think he's talented.

SAMMY I think so, too, ma'am. Very.

CORA (*Brings* REENIE *forth*) Reenie! Sammy, this is my daughter Reenie.

SAMMY Good evening, Reenie.

REENIE (*Reluctantly*) Good evening.

SAMMY You certainly look nice. That's a very beautiful dress.

FLIRT Isn't it cute! I helped her pick it out. (CORA *quietly grabs* FLIRT'S *arm and prevents her from taking over*) Ouch!

SAMMY Gee! I didn't expect you to be . . . like you are. I mean . . . well, Punky told me you were a friend of Flirt's, so I just naturally thought you'd be . . . well, kind of like Flirt is. Although Flirt is a very nice girl. I didn't mean to imply anything against her. But . . . *you're* very nice, too, in a different way.

REENIE (*Still a little distrustful*) Thank you . . .

SAMMY Would you call me *Sammy?*

REENIE Sammy.

SAMMY And may I call you Reenie?

REENIE I guess so.

SAMMY It's awfully nice of you to let me take you to the party. I know just how a girl feels, going out with some crazy guy she doesn't even know.

REENIE Oh . . . that's all right. After all, you don't know anything about me, either.

SAMMY You know, I've never been to many parties, have you?

REENIE Not many.

SAMMY I always worry that maybe people aren't going to like me, when I go to a party. Isn't that crazy? Do you ever get kind of a sick feeling in the pit of your stomach when you dread things? Gee, I wouldn't want to miss a party for anything. But every time I go to one, I have to reason with myself to keep from feeling that the whole world's against me. See, I've spent almost my whole life in military academies. My mother doesn't have a place for me, where she lives. She . . . she just doesn't know what else to do with me. But you mustn't misunderstand about my mother. She's really a very lovely person. I guess every boy thinks his mother is very beautiful, but my mother really is. She tells me in every letter she writes how sorry she is that we can't be together more, but she has to think of her work. One time we were together, though. She met me in San Francisco once, and we were together for two whole days. She let me take her to dinner and to a show and to dance. Just like we were sweethearts. It was the most wonderful time I ever had. And then I had to go back to the old military academy. Every time I walk into the barracks, I get kind of a depressed feeling. It's got hard stone walls. Pictures of generals hanging all over . . . oh, they're very fine gentlemen, but they all look so kind of hard-boiled and stern . . . you know what I mean. (CORA *and* LOTTIE *stand together, listening to* SAMMY'S *speech with motherly expressions.* FLIRT *is bored.* PUNKY *is half asleep, and now he gives a sudden, audible yawn that startles everyone)* Well, gee! I guess I've bored you enough, telling you about myself.

CORA *and* LOTTIE Oh, no. You haven't either.

FLIRT *(Impatient to get to the party)* Come on, kids. Let's hurry.

SAMMY *(Tenderly, to* REENIE*)* Are you ready?

CORA *(As though fearing* REENIE *might bolt and run)* Reenie?

REENIE Yes.

SAMMY May I help you into your wrap?

(The word "wrap" *is a false glorification of her Sunday coat, which he offers her, helping her into it)*

REENIE Thank you.

CORA *(Whispering to* LOTTIE*)* I wish I could have bought her one of those little fur jackets like Flirt is wearing.

FLIRT Stand up straight, Punky, and say good night to everyone.

(PUNKY *tries again, but remains inarticulate)*

CORA *(Assuming that* PUNKY *said good night)* Good night, Punky. Tell your mother hello for me.

FLIRT Very pleased to have met you, Mr. and Mrs. Lacey. Good night, Mrs. Flood.

CORA Good night, Flirt.

LOTTIE *and* MORRIS Good night.

SONNY *(Pulling at* SAMMY'S *coat tails)* Do you have to go?

SAMMY I'm afraid I do, Sonny.

SONNY Can I go, too? Please? Can I go, too?

SAMMY Gee, I don't know. *(He thinks a moment and then consults* FLIRT *and* PUNKY*)* Hey, is there any reason Sonny can't come along? I promise to look after him. Think what a great time he'd have.

(FLIRT *and* PUNKY *look dubious)*

SONNY *(Takes his welcome immediately for granted and*

dances about the room joyously) Goody, goody! I'm going to the party. I'm going to the party.

REENIE (*Running to* CORA'S *side*) Mother, I'm not going if Sonny goes too. Other girls don't have to be bothered by their little brothers.

CORA I agree with you, daughter.

FLIRT (*She loves to lash out when she has a victim*) No. It's not a kids' party, Sammy. That was a stupid idea. I think you should mind your own business.

CORA (*Trying to cool* FLIRT'S *temper*) Now, Flirt.

FLIRT (*To* REENIE) He's always trying to boss everyone.

CORA (*To* SAMMY) I guess Sonny'd better not go.

SONNY (*Crying, jumping in protest*) I want to go to the party. I want to go to the party.

SAMMY (*Trying to be consoling*) I guess it was a pretty dumb idea, Sonny.

SONNY I WANT TO GO TO THE PARTY! I WANT TO GO TO THE PARTY!

(SONNY *flies into a real tantrum now, throws himself on the floor, pounding the floor with his fists and kicking it with his toes, his face red with rage.* CORA *and* LOTTIE *flutter about him like nervous hens*)

CORA Sonny! Sonny! Stop it this instant. Sonny, I'll not let you go to another movie for a whole month if you don't stop.

LOTTIE Oh, what'll I do? Oh, here, Sonny, do you want a little cookie, sweetheart?

FLIRT Now we'll never get there.

CORA I never can do a thing with him when he throws one of these tantrums.

SAMMY (*Quietly goes to* SONNY'S *side and speaks in a voice that is firm with authority, yet still thoughtful and considerate*) Sonny, that's no way to behave.

SONNY (*Suddenly quiet*) Isn't it?

SAMMY No, Sonny. You mustn't ever act like that.

SONNY (*More reasonable now*) But I want to go to the party.

SAMMY But if you act that way, no one's *ever* going to ask you to a party.

SONNY Aren't they?

SAMMY No, Sonny. You have to be a good boy before people ask you to parties. Even then, they don't always ask you.

SONNY I love parties more than anything else in the world.

SAMMY So do I, Sonny. I love parties, too. But there's lots of parties I can't go to.

SONNY Honest?

SAMMY Honest. It was wrong of me to suggest that you go to the party tonight. You're not old enough yet. You'll be old enough someday though, and then you can go to all the parties you like.

SONNY Can I?

SAMMY Sure. Now, I tell you what I'll do. I'll gather up all the favors I can find at the party. Want me to? And I'll give them to your sister to bring home to you. And then you can have a party here all by yourself. Would you like that? You can throw a big party in Sammy's honor, without any old grownups around to interfere. Will that make you happy?

SONNY Yes, yes.

SAMMY O.K. Are we still buddies?

SONNY Yes.

SAMMY Forever and ever?

SONNY Forever and ever.

(SONNY *impulsively hugs him*)

SAMMY Gee! I love kids.

CORA (*Awed as though by a miracle*) You're the first person in the entire world who's ever been able to do a thing with the boy when he goes into one of his tantrums.

SAMMY You know, it's funny, but . . . I always seem to know just how kids feel.

FLIRT (*Still impatient*) Come on, Sammy.

(FLIRT *and* PUNKY *exit*)

CORA Good night, Sammy. I hope you'll be able to come back sometime.

SAMMY Thank you, ma'am. It's very nice to feel welcome.

LOTTIE *and* MORRIS Good night. Come over to see us sometime in Oklahoma City. It's a big town. You can stay in the extra bedroom. I hope you like cats.

CORA (*While* LOTTIE *and* MORRIS *are speaking*) Oh, Reenie, don't forget your present. You're feeling better now, aren't you?

REENIE Yes, Mom.

SAMMY (*Breaking away from* LOTTIE *and* MORRIS) Excuse me.

(SAMMY *offers* REENIE *his arm now, and together they walk proudly out*)

CORA (*After they exit*) Why, that's the nicest young man I ever met.

LOTTIE I thought so, too, Cora. And my goodness, he was handsome. Morris says he felt sorry for him, though.

CORA Sorry? Oh, Morris.

LOTTIE He seemed like a perfectly happy boy to me. But Morris says he looked like a very unhappy boy to him. What makes you think that, Morris?

MORRIS Oh . . . I don't know.

CORA Unhappy? Why, he made himself right at home, didn't he?

LOTTIE I should say he did. He was laughing and enjoying himself. But Morris says sometimes the people who act the happiest are really the saddest.

CORA Oh, Morris.

LOTTIE Morris, I think you make these things up. Ever since you went to that psychologist, you've gone around imagining everyone's unhappy. (MORRIS *quietly gets up and walks to the door, leaving* LOTTIE *to wonder if she has said anything wrong*) Where are you going, Morris?

MORRIS Thought I'd go out for a little walk, honey.
(MORRIS *exits*)

LOTTIE (*Following him to the door*) Oh. Well, don't be gone long. We've got to get started back soon.

CORA Oh, please don't talk about going.

LOTTIE My God, Cora, we can't stay here all night. (*She peers out the window now, wondering about* MORRIS) Morris is funny, Cora. Sometimes he just gets up like that and walks away. I never know why. Sometimes he's gone for hours at a time. He says the walk helps his digestion, but I think it's because he just wants to get away from me at times. Did you ever notice how he is with people? Like tonight. He sat there when all the young people were here, and he didn't say hardly a word. His mind was a thousand miles away. Like he was thinking about something. He seems to be always thinking about something.

CORA Morris is nice to you. You've got no right to complain.

LOTTIE He's nice to me . . . in *some* ways.

CORA Good heavens, Lottie! He gave you those red patent-leather slippers, and that fox neckpiece . . . you should be grateful.

LOTTIE I know, but . . . there's *some* things he hasn't given me.

CORA Lottie! That's not his fault. You've got no right to hold that against him!

LOTTIE Oh, it's just fine for you to talk. You've got two nice kids to keep you company. What have I got but a house full of cats?

CORA Lottie, you always claimed you never wanted children.

LOTTIE Well . . . what else can I say to people?

CORA (*This is something of a revelation to her*) I just never knew.

LOTTIE (*Having suddenly decided to say it*) Cora . . . I can't let you and the kids come over and live with us.

CORA (*This is a blow to her*) Oh . . . Lottie.

LOTTIE I'm sorry, Cora. I just can't do it.

CORA Lottie, I was depending on you . . .

LOTTIE Maybe you've depended on me too much. Ever since you were a baby, you've run to me with your problems, and now I've got problems of my own.

CORA What am I going to do, Lottie.

LOTTIE Call up Rubin and ask him to come back. Beg him to come back, if you have to get down on your knees.

CORA I mustn't do that, Lottie.

LOTTIE Why not?

CORA Because we just can't keep from fighting, Lottie. You know that. I just don't think it's right, our still going on that way.

LOTTIE Do you still love him?

CORA Oh . . . don't ask me, Lottie.

LOTTIE Do you?

CORA Oh . . . yes.

LOTTIE Cora, I don't think you should listen to the stories those old Werpel sisters tell you.

CORA He's as good as admitted it, Lottie.

LOTTIE Well, Cora, I don't think it means he likes you any the less, because he's seen Mavis Pruitt a few times.

CORA No . . . I know he loves me.

LOTTIE (*Asking very cautiously*) Does he still want to be intimate?

CORA That's only animal, Lottie. I couldn't indulge myself that way if I didn't feel he was being honorable.

LOTTIE (*Breaks into a sudden raucous laugh*) My God, a big handsome buck like Rubin! Who cares if he's honorable?

CORA (*A little shocked*) Lottie!

LOTTIE (*We see now a sudden lewdness in* LOTTIE *that has*

not been discernible before) Cora, did you hear what the old maid said to the burglar? You see, the burglar came walking into her bedroom with this big, long billy club and . . .

CORA Lottie!

LOTTIE (*Laughing so hard she can hardly finish the story*) And the old maid . . . she was so green she didn't know what was happening to her, she said . . .

CORA Lottie! That's enough. That's enough.

LOTTIE (*Shamed now*) Shucks, Cora. I don't see what's wrong in having a little fun just telling stories.

CORA Sometimes you talk shamefully, Lottie, and when I think of the way Mama and Papa brought us up . . .

LOTTIE Oh, Mama and Papa, Mama and Papa! Maybe they didn't know as much as we gave them credit for.

CORA You're changed since you were a girl, Lottie.

LOTTIE What if I am!

CORA I never heard such talk.

LOTTIE Well, that's all it is. It's only talk. Talk, talk, talk.

CORA Lottie, are you sure you can't take us in?

LOTTIE It'd mean the end of my marriage too, Cora. You don't understand Morris. He's always nice and quiet around people, so afraid of hurting people's feelings. But he's the most nervous man around the house you ever saw. He'd try to make the best of it if you and the kids came over, but he'd go to pieces. I know he would.

CORA Honest?

LOTTIE I'm not joking, Cora. My God, you're not the only one who has problems. Don't think that for a minute.

CORA A few moments ago, you said *you* had problems, Lottie . . .

LOTTIE Problems enough.

CORA Tell me, Lottie.

LOTTIE Oh, why should I?

CORA Doesn't Morris ever make love to you any more?

LOTTIE (*It takes her several moments to admit it*) . . . No. It's been over three years since he even touched me . . . that way.

CORA (*Another revelation*) Lottie!

LOTTIE It's the God's truth, Cora.

CORA Lottie! What's wrong?

LOTTIE How do I know what's wrong? How does anyone ever know what's wrong with anyone else?

CORA I mean . . . is there another woman?

LOTTIE Not unless she visits him from the spirit world. (*This releases her humor again and she is diverted by another story*) Oh, say, Cora, did I tell you about this woman over in Oklahoma City who's been holding séances? Well, Marietta went to her and . . . (*But suddenly, again, she loses her humor and makes another sad admission*) Oh, no, there isn't another woman. Sometimes I wish there was.

CORA Lottie, you don't mean that.

LOTTIE How the hell do *you* know what I mean? He's around the house all day long, now that he's got his dental office in the dining room. Day and night, day and night. Sometimes I get tired of looking at him.

CORA Oh, Lottie . . . I'd always felt you and Morris were so devoted to each other. I've always felt you had an almost perfect marriage.

LOTTIE Oh, we're still devoted, still call each other "honey," just like we did on our honeymoon.

CORA But what happened? Something must have happened to . . .

LOTTIE Did you notice the way Morris got up out of his chair suddenly and just walked away, with no explanation at all? Well, something inside Morris did the same thing several years ago. Something inside him just got up and went for a walk, and never came back.

CORA I . . . just don't understand.

LOTTIE Sometimes I wonder if maybe I've been too bossy. Could be. But then I always supposed that Morris *liked* me because I was bossy.

CORA I always envied you, having a husband you could boss.

LOTTIE Yes, I can boss Morris because he just isn't there any more to fight back. He doesn't care any more if I boss him or not.

CORA Just the same, he never hit you.

LOTTIE I wish he would.

CORA Lottie!

LOTTIE I do. I wish to God someone *loved* me enough to hit me. You and Rubin fight. Oh, God I'd like a good fight. Anything'd be better than this *nothing*. Morris and I go around always being so sweet to each other, but sometimes I wonder maybe he'd like to kill me.

CORA Lottie, you don't mean it.

LOTTIE Do you remember how Mama and Papa used to caution us about men, Cora?

CORA Yes, I remember.

LOTTIE My God, they had me so afraid of ever giving in to a man, I was petrified.

CORA So was I.

LOTTIE Yes, you were until Rubin came along and practically raped you.

CORA Lottie! I don't want Sonny to hear talk like that.

LOTTIE Why not? Let him hear!

CORA (*Newly aghast at her sister's boldness*) Lottie!

LOTTIE Why do we feel we always have to protect kids?

CORA Keep your voice down. Rubin never did anything like that.

LOTTIE Didn't he?

CORA Of course not!

LOTTIE My God, Cora, he had you pregnant inside of two weeks after he started seeing you.

CORA Sssh.

LOTTIE I never told. I never even told Morris. My God, do you remember how Mama and Papa carried on when they found out?

CORA I remember.

LOTTIE And Papa had his stroke just a month after you were married. Oh, I just thought Rubin was the wickedest man alive.

CORA I never blamed Rubin for that. I was crazy in love with him. He just swept me off my feet and made all my objections seem kinda silly. He even made Mama and Papa seem silly.

LOTTIE Maybe I shoulda married a man like that. I don't know. Maybe it was as much my fault as Morris'. Maybe I didn't . . . respond right . . . from the very first.

CORA What do you mean, Lottie?

LOTTIE Cora, I'll tell you something. Something I've never told another living soul. I never did enjoy it the way some women . . . say they do.

CORA Lottie! You?

LOTTIE Why do you say *me* like that? Because I talk kinda dirty at times? But that's all it is, is talk. I talk all the time just to convince myself that I'm alive. And I stuff myself with victuals just to feel I've got something inside me. And I'm full of all kinds of crazy curiosity about . . . all the things in life I seem to have missed out on. Now I'm telling you the truth, Cora. Nothing ever really happened to me while it was going on.

CORA Lottie . . .

LOTTIE That first night Morris and I were together, right after we were married, when we were in bed together for the first time, after it was all over, and he had fallen asleep, I lay there in bed wondering what in the world all the cautioning had been about. Nothing had happened to me at all, and I thought Mama and Papa musta been makin' things up.

CORA Oh, Lottie!

LOTTIE So, don't come to me for sympathy, Cora. I'm not the person to give it to you.

(*Outside there is a low rumble of thunder.* SONNY *enters from the dining room with a cup of flour paste and his scrapbook.* MORRIS *returns from his walk, his face mysterious and grave*)

MORRIS We'd better be starting back now, honey. It looks like rain.

CORA Oh, don't talk about leaving. Can't you and Lottie stay all night? I'd get up early and fix your breakfast. I'll fix you biscuits.

MORRIS I can't, Cora. I got patients coming first thing in the morning.

LOTTIE And I have to go home to let out the cats.

MORRIS It was a wonderful dinner, Cora.

CORA Thank you, Morris.

LOTTIE (*On a sudden impulse, she springs to her feet, hoists her skirt to her waist, and begins wrestling with her corset*) My God, I'm gonna take off this corset and ride back home in comfort.

CORA (*Runs protectively to* SONNY, *and stands between him and* LOTTIE, *to prevent his seeing this display*) Sonny! Turn your head.

LOTTIE My God! That feels good. (*She rolls the corset under her arm and rubs the flesh on her stomach in appreciation of its new freedom. Then she reaches for the bag of fried chicken*) Thanks for the fried chicken, Cora, Oh, good! A gizzard. (*She brings out a gizzard to gnaw on*) It was a wonderful dinner. You're a better cook than I am.

CORA That's not so.

LOTTIE Kiss me good-bye, Sonny.

SONNY Good-bye, Aunt Lottie.

LOTTIE (*Hugging him close*) Good night, darling.

MORRIS That was a fine recitation, Edwin Booth.

SONNY Thank you, Uncle Morris.

LOTTIE (*Facing her husband with a bright smile, as though nothing but happiness had ever passed between them*) I'm ready, Daddy.

MORRIS All right, Mama. Good of you to have us, Cora.

CORA Glad you could come, Morris.

LOTTIE (*At the door, thinks of one last piece of news she must impart to her sister before leaving*) Oh, Cora! I forgot to tell you. Mamie Keeler's in the hospital.

MORRIS (*Goes out on the porch now*) Looks like it's gonna rain any minute now.

CORA What's wrong?

LOTTIE Some kind of female trouble.

CORA Oh . . . that's too bad.

(*But* LOTTIE *can tell by the sound of* CORA'S *voice that she is too preoccupied now with her own worries to care about Mamie Keeler*)

LOTTIE Oh, God, Cora . . . I just can't go off and leave you this way.

CORA I'll be all right, Lottie.

LOTTIE Look, Cora . . . if you and the kids wanta come over and stay with us . . . we'll manage somehow . . .

CORA Oh, thank you, Lottie. (*They embrace as though recognizing the bond of their blood*) But I'm going to work this out for myself, Lottie.

LOTTIE Good-bye, Cora.

MORRIS (*From outside*) It's beginning to rain, honey.

LOTTIE (*Hurrying out the door*) Hold your horses, Morris. I'm coming. Don't be impatient now.

(*They exit. Now* CORA *returns to the center of the room, feeling somehow deserted*)

SONNY It's always so quiet after company leaves, isn't it?

CORA Hush, Sonny. I'm trying to think.

(*From outside, we hear the sound of* MORRIS' *car driving off, and then the sound of the rain and the wind*)

SONNY Let's move to California, Mom. Please, let's move to California.

(*But* CORA *has made a sudden decision. She rushes to the telephone*)

CORA Long distance. (*A moment's wait*) This is Mrs. Flood, three-two-one. I want to talk to Mr. Rubin Flood at the Hotel Boomerang in Blackwell . . . Yes, I'll wait.

SONNY (*In an innocent voice*) I bet he isn't there. I bet anything.

CORA Hello? He isn't? Would you ask them if he's been there this week? (*A moment's wait*) He hasn't! Oh . . . Well, please tell him, if he does come, to call his family immediately. It's very important.

(*A fallen expression on her face, she sits for a moment, wondering what next move to make. Then she hears a car approaching from the distance. She jumps up and runs to the window*)

SONNY It isn't Dad. I can always tell the sound of his car.

(CORA *comes back to the middle of the room*)

CORA Run along to bed now, Sonny. It's late. I have to go out and empty the pan under the ice box.

(CORA *goes out through the dining-room door.* SONNY *walks slowly, hesitantly, to the foot of the stairs and stands there, looking up at the blackness at the top. He stands there several moments, unable to force himself to go further. From the kitchen we hear* CORA'S *muffled sobs.* SONNY *cries out in fear*)

SONNY Mom!

(CORA *returns now, not wanting* SONNY *to know she has been crying*)

CORA Sonny, I thought I told you to go upstairs. (*She looks at him now and sees his embarrassed fear*) Sonny, why are you so afraid of the dark?

SONNY 'Cause . . . you can't see what's in front of you. And it might be something awful.

CORA You're the man of the house now, Sonny. You mustn't be afraid.

SONNY I'm not afraid . . . if someone's with me.

(CORA *walks over to him and takes his hand*)

CORA Come, boy. We'll go up together.

(*They start up the stairs to face the darkness hovering there like an omen*)

CURTAIN

ACT THREE

Scene: It is the next day, late afternoon. Outside, there is a drizzling rain that has continued through the day. REENIE *has not dressed all day. She sits by the fire in her robe, rubbing her freshly shampooed hair with a towel.* CORA *enters from the dining room, wearing a comfortable old kimono. She looks at the tray by* REENIE'S *side.*

CORA Reenie! Is that all you feel like eating?

REENIE Yes.

CORA But that's all you've had all day, Reenie. You don't eat enough to keep a bird alive.

REENIE I . . . I'm not hungry, Mom.

CORA Now quit feeling sorry for yourself, just because you didn't have a good time last night.

REENIE Mom, is Dad coming back?

CORA I don't know. I tried to call him last night but couldn't get him.

REENIE Aren't you mad at him any more?

CORA No . . . I'm not mad.

REENIE Even though he hit you?

CORA Even though he hit me. I was defying him to do it . . . and he did. I can't blame him now.

REENIE Do you think he *will* be back, Mom?

CORA This is the day he was supposed to come back. It's almost suppertime and he still isn't here.

REENIE But it's been raining, Mom. I'll bet the roads are bad.

CORA You love your father, don't you?

REENIE Yes.

CORA Well, I'm glad. The people we love aren't always perfect, are they? But if we love them, we have to take them as they are. After all, I guess I'm not perfect, either.

REENIE You are too, Mom. You're absolutely perfect, in every way.

CORA No, I'm not, Reenie. I . . . I have my own score to settle for. I've always accused your father of neglecting you kids, but maybe I've hurt you more with pampering. You . . . and Sonny, too.

REENIE What do you mean, Mom?

CORA Oh, nothing. I can't say anything more about it right now. Forget it. (*For some reason we don't yet know, she tries to change the subject*) Are you feeling a little better now?

REENIE I guess so.

CORA Well, the world isn't going to end just because your young man went off and left you.

REENIE Oh, Mom. It was the most humiliating thing that ever happened to me.

CORA Where do you think Sammy went?

REENIE He went out to the cars at intermission time with some other girl.

CORA To spoon?

REENIE They call it *necking.*

CORA Are you sure of this?

REENIE Mom, that's what all the boys do at intermission time. They take girls and go out to the cars. Some of them don't even come back for the rest of the dance.

CORA But are you sure Sammy did that? Did you see him?

REENIE No, Mom. I just know that's what he did.

CORA Wouldn't *you* have gone out to one of the cars with him?

REENIE (*With self-disparagement*) Oh. Mom.

CORA What makes you say "Oh, Mom" that way?

REENIE He wouldn't have liked *me* that way.

CORA But why? Why not?

REENIE I'm just not *hot stuff* like the other girls.

CORA Reenie, what an expression! You're pretty. You're every bit as pretty as Flirt or Mary Jane. Half a woman's beauty is in her confidence.

REENIE Oh, Mom.

CORA Reenie, I've tried to raise you proper, but . . . you're sixteen now. It's perfectly natural if a boy wants to kiss you, and you let him. It's all right if you *like* the boy.

REENIE (*A hesitant admission*) Oh . . . Sammy kissed me.

CORA (*Quite surprised*) He did?

REENIE On the way out to the party, in Punky's car. Flirt and Punky were in the front seat, Sammy and I in the back. Punky had a flask . . .

CORA The little devil!

REENIE Mom, most of those wealthy boys who go away to school are kind of wild.

CORA Go on.

REENIE Well, Punky and Flirt started necking, very first thing. Flirt, I don't mean to be tattling, but she *is* kind of fast.

CORA I guessed as much. You aren't tattling.

REENIE Well, Sammy and I felt kind of embarrassed, with no one else to talk to, and so he took my hand. Oh, he was very nice about it, Mom. And then he put an arm around me, and said . . . "May I kiss you, Reenie?" And I was so surprised, I said yes before I knew *what* I was saying. And he kissed me. Was it all right, Mom?

CORA Did you like the young man? That's the important thing.

REENIE Yes, I . . . I liked him . . . very much. (*She sobs helplessly*) Oh, Mom.

CORA There, there, Reenie dear. If he's the kind of young man who goes around kissing all the girls, you don't want to worry about him any more. You did right to leave the party!

REENIE Did I, Mom?

CORA Of course you did. I'm very disappointed in Sammy. I thought he was such a nice boy. But I guess appearances can be deceiving.

REENIE Oh Mom!

CORA There, there, dear. There are plenty of other young men in the world. You're young. You're not going to have to worry.

REENIE (*Struggling to her feet*) Mom, I don't think I ever want to get married.

CORA Reenie!

REENIE I mean it, Mom.

CORA You're too young to make a decision like that.

REENIE I'm serious.

CORA What makes you say such a thing? Tell me.

REENIE I don't want to fight with anyone, like you and Daddy.

CORA Oh, God.

REENIE Every time you and Daddy fight, I just feel that the whole house is going to cave in all around me.

CORA Then I *am* to blame.

REENIE And I think I'd be lots happier, just by myself, teaching school, or working in an office building.

CORA No, daughter. You need someone after you grow up. You need someone.

REENIE But I don't want to. I don't *want* to need anyone, ever in my life. It's a horrible feeling to need someone.

CORA (*Disturbed*) Daughter!

REENIE Anyway, the only times I'm really happy are when I'm alone, practicing at the piano or studying in the library.

CORA Weren't you happy last night when Sammy kissed you?

REENIE I guess you can't count on happiness like that.

CORA Daughter, when you start getting older, you'll find yourself getting lonely and you'll want someone; someone who'll hear you if you get sick and cry out in the night; and someone to give you love and let you give your love back to him in return. Oh, I'd hate to see any child of mine miss that in life. (*There is a moment of quiet realization between them. Then we hear the sound of a car drawing up to the house.* CORA *running to the window, is as excited as a girl*) That must be your father! No, it's Sonny. In a big limousine. He's getting out of the car as if he owned it. Mrs. Stanford must have sent him home with her chauffeur.

(*She gives "chauffeur" its American pronunciation.* SONNY, *in his Sunday suit, bursts into the house waving a five-dollar bill in his mother's face*)

SONNY Mom. Look, Mom! Mrs. Stanford gave me five dollars for speaking my piece. See? Five whole dollars. She said I was the most talented little boy she ever saw. See, Mom? Then she got out her pocketbook and gave me five whole dollars. See?

CORA I declare. Why, Sonny, I'm proud of you, boy. That's the very first money you ever earned, and I'm very proud.

SONNY And Mrs. Stanford sent me home with her chauffeur, too, Mom. (*He gives the word its French pronunciation*) That's the way you're supposed to pronounce it, chauf*feur*. It's French.

CORA If you spend any more time at Mrs. Stanford's, you'll be getting too high-hat to come home. (*She notices* REENIE *starting upstairs*) We'll talk later, Reenie. (REENIE *exits.* CORA *again turns her attention to* SONNY) Did you have anything to eat?

SONNY Oh, Mom, it was just delicious. She had all kinds of little sandwiches. Gee, they were good. And cocoa, too, Mom, with lots of whipped cream on top, in little white cups with gold edges. Gee, they were pretty. And lots of little cakes, too, with pink frosting and green. And ice cream, too. I just ate and ate and ate.

CORA Good. That means I won't have to get you any supper.

SONNY No. I don't want any supper. I'm going to the movies tonight. And to the Royal Candy Kitchen afterwards, to buy myself a great big sundae with chocolate and marshmallow and cherries and . . .

CORA Now, wait a minute, Sonny. This is the first money you've ever earned in your life, and I think you should save it.

SONNY Oh, Mom!

CORA I mean it. Five dollars is a lot of money, and I'm not going to let you squander it on movies and sundaes. You'll thank me for this some day.

(*She takes his piggy bank from the bookcase*)

SONNY I will not. I will not thank you!

CORA Sonny.

(*She takes the bill from him and drops it into the bank.* SONNY *is wild at the injustice*)

SONNY Look what you've done. I hate you! I wanta see the movie. I've just gotta see the movie. If I can't see the movie, I'll kill myself.

CORA Such foolish talk!

SONNY I mean it. I'll kill myself.

CORA Now, be quiet, Sonny, I want to have a little talk.

SONNY Can I sell the milk bottles for money?

CORA No! Now quit pestering me about the movies. You've already talked me into letting you see one movie this week. I have scarcely any money now, and I can't spare a cent. (SONNY *is badly frustrated. He finds the favors that* SAMMY *promised him, displayed on the settee. He throws a handful of confetti recklessly into the air, then dons a paper hat, and blows violently on a paper horn*) Sonny! Stop that racket! You're going to have to clean up that mess.

SONNY You won't let me have any fun at all.

CORA The young man was very thoughtful to have sent you the favors. I wish he had been as thoughtful in other ways.

SONNY Didn't Reenie have a good time at the party last night?

CORA No.

SONNY Serves her right. Serves her right.

CORA Sonny! I'm not going to have any more talk like that. If you and your sister can't get along, you can at least have a little respect for one another. Now, come here, Sonny, I want to talk serious for a little while. (SONNY *taunts her with the horn*) Will you go sit down?

SONNY What's the matter?

(*He sits opposite her at the table*)

CORA Nothing. I just want to talk a while.

SONNY (*Suddenly solemn and apprehensive*) Have I done something bad?

CORA Well, I don't know if you have or if I have. Anyway, we've got to talk about it. Sonny, you mustn't come crawling into my bed any more. I let you do it last night, but I shouldn't have. It was wrong.

SONNY I was scared.

CORA Just the same, that's not to happen again, Sonny. It's not the same when a boy your age comes crawling into bed with his mother. You can't expect me to mean as much to you as when you were a baby. Can you understand, Sonny? (*He looks away from her with unconscious guilt. She studies him*) I think you're older in your feelings than I ever realized. You're a funny mixture, Sonny. In some ways, shy as your sister. In other ways, bold as a pirate.

SONNY I don't like you any more at all.

CORA Sonny!

SONNY I don't care. You make me mad.

CORA (*Going to him*) Oh, God, I've kept you too close to me, Sonny. Too close. I'll take the blame, boy. But don't be mad. Your mother still loves you, Sonny. (*But she sees that they are at an impasse*) Well, we won't talk about it any more. Run along to the store now, before it closes. (*We see* FLIRT'S *face in the door window. She is knocking on the door and calling for* REENIE. CORA *hurries to let her in*) Flirt!

FLIRT (*Rushing inside*) Where's Reenie? Reenie . . . Reenie. Oh, Mrs. Flood, I have the most awful news.

CORA What is it, Flirt?

FLIRT (FLIRT'S *face her whole body are contorted by shock and confused grief*) Oh, it's so awful.

CORA Tell me.

FLIRT Is Reenie here? I've got to tell her, too.

CORA (*Calls upstairs*) Reenie, can you come down? Flirt is here.

REENIE (*Off*) I'm coming.

FLIRT Oh, Mrs. Flood, it's the most awful thing that ever happened in this town. It's the most awful thing I ever heard of happening anywhere.

CORA Did something happen to you, or your family? . . .

FLIRT No, it's Sammy.

CORA Sammy? . . .

REENIE (*Coming downstairs*) What is it, Flirt?

FLIRT Kid! Sammy Goldenbaum . . . killed himself. (*There is a long silence*)

CORA Where did you hear this, Flirt?

FLIRT Mrs. Givens told me. The hotel people over in Oklahoma City called her about it just a little while ago. They found a letter in Sammy's suitcase Mrs. Givens had written him, inviting him to come home with Punky.

CORA Oklahoma City?

FLIRT He went over there last night after he left the

party. He took the midnight train. That's what they figured out, because he registered at the hotel this morning at two o'clock.

CORA How . . . did he do it, Flirt?

FLIRT (*Hides her face in her hands as though hiding from the hideous reality of it*) He . . . Oh, I just can't.

CORA There, there, honey.

FLIRT Oh, I'm such a silly about things. He . . . he jumped out of the window . . . on the fourteenth floor . . . and landed on the pavement below.

CORA Oh, my God.

FLIRT Oh . . . it's really the most terrible thing that ever happened to me. I never did know anyone who killed himself before.

CORA Does anyone have any idea what made him do it?

FLIRT No! Punky says that he used to get kind of moody at times, but Punky never expected him to do anything like *this*.

CORA Why did he go to Oklahoma City in the middle of the night?

FLIRT No one knows that either . . . for sure. But one thing did happen at the party. He was dancing with Mary Jane Ralston . . . that cow . . . just before intermission . . . and Mrs. Ralston . . . she'd had too much to drink . . . comes out in the middle of the floor and stops them.

CORA What for?

FLIRT Well, you know how Mrs. Ralston is. No one takes her very serious even if she does have money. Anyway, she came right out in the middle of the floor and gave Sammy a bawling out . . .

CORA A bawling out? Why?

FLIRT She said she wasn't giving this party for Jews, and she didn't intend for her daughter to dance with a Jew, and besides, Jews weren't allowed in the country club anyway. And that's not so. They are too allowed in the country club. Maybe they're not permitted to be members, but they're certainly allowed as guests. Everyone knows that. (*She turns now to* REENIE, *who has sat numb in a chair since* FLIRT'S *shocking announcement*) Where were you when it all happened?

REENIE I . . . I . . .
(*But she is inarticulate*)

CORA Reenie wasn't feeling well. She left the party and came home.

FLIRT The other kids told me Sammy was looking for you everywhere. He was going around asking everyone, Where's Reenie?

CORA That . . . that's too bad.

FLIRT (*Turning to* CORA) . . . But a thing like that isn't serious enough to make a boy kill himself, is it?

CORA Well . . . he did.

FLIRT An old blabbermouth like Mrs. Ralston?

CORA She was a stranger to Sammy. She probably sounded like the voice of the world.

FLIRT Gee . . . I just don't understand things like that. Do you know something else, Mrs. Flood? They called Sammy's mother way out in California, and told her, and I guess she was terribly sorry and everything, but she told them to go on and have the funeral in Oklahoma City, that she'd pay all the expenses, but she wouldn't be able to come for it because she was working. And she cried over the telephone and asked them please to try and keep her name out of the papers, because she said it wasn't generally known that she had a son.

CORA There won't be anyone Sammy knows at the funeral, will there?

FLIRT Mrs. Givens said Punky and his daddy could drive us over for it. Will you come, Reenie? (REENIE *nods*) Do you wanta come, too, Sonny? (SONNY *nods*) Well . . . it'll be day after tomorrow, in the afternoon. We'll all have to get excused from school. Oh, gee, it all makes me feel so kind of *strange.* Doesn't it *you,* kid? I think I'll go to Sunday School tomorrow. Do you wanta go with me, Reenie? (REENIE *nods yes*) Oh, I feel just terrible.

(FLIRT *bolts out the front door, as though wanting to run away from all that is tragic or sorrowful in life.* CORA *keeps silent for several moments, her eyes on* REENIE)

CORA Where were you when Sammy went off?

REENIE (*Twisting with grief*) Stop it, Mom!

CORA Tell me. Where were you?

REENIE Don't, Mom!

CORA (*Commanding*) *Tell* me.

REENIE I . . . was up in . . . the girls' room.

CORA Where did you leave Sammy?

REENIE As soon as we got to the party, Sammy and I started dancing. He danced three straight dances with me, Mom. Nobody cut in. I didn't think anybody was ever going to cut in, Mom. I got to feeling so humiliated I didn't know what to do. I just couldn't bear for Sammy to think that no one liked me.

CORA Dear God!

REENIE So I told Sammy there was someone at the party I had to talk to. Then I took him over to Mary Jane Ralston and . . . introduced him to her . . . and told him to dance with her.

CORA Reenie!

REENIE I . . . I thought he'd like her.

CORA But you said that *you* liked Sammy. You told me you did.

REENIE But, Mom, I just couldn't *bear* for him to think I was such a wallflower.

CORA You ran off and *hid,* when an ounce of thoughtfulness, one or two kind words, might have saved him.

REENIE I didn't *know.* I didn't *know.*

CORA A nice young man like that, bright and pleasant,

handsome as a prince, caught out here in this sandy soil without a friend to his name and no one to turn to when some thoughtless fool attacks him and he takes it to heart. (REENIE *sobs uncontrollably*) Tears aren't going to do any good now, Reenie. Now, you listen to me. I've heard all I intend to listen to about being so shy and sensitive and afraid of people. I can't respect those feelings any more. They're nothing but selfishness. (REENIE *starts to bolt from the room, just as* FLIRT *did, but* CORA'S *voice holds her*) Reenie! It's a fine thing when we have so little confidence in ourselves, we can't stop to think of the other person.

SONNY (*Who has been a silent listener until now*) I *hate* people.

CORA Sonny!

SONNY I *do.*

CORA Then you're just as bad as Peg Ralston.

SONNY How can you keep from hating?

CORA There are all kinds of people in the world. And you have to live with them all. God never promised us any different. The bad people, you don't hate. You're only sorry they have to be. Now, run along to the store before it closes.

(SONNY *goes out, and finds himself again confronted by the jeers of the neighborhood boys, which sound like the voices that have plagued humanity from the beginning of time*)

BOY'S VOICES Sissy Sonny!

Sonny Flood! His name is mud!

Sonny plays with dolls!

Sonny loves his mama!

(*Hearing the voices,* CORA *runs to the door, but stops herself from going further*)

CORA I guess I can't go through life protecting him from bullies. (*She goes to* REENIE) I'm sorry I spoke so harshly to you, Reenie.

REENIE He asked for *me* . . . for *me*. The only time anyone ever *wanted* me, or *needed* me, in my entire life. And I wasn't there. I didn't stop once to think of . . . Sammy. I've always thought I was the only person in the world who had any feelings at all.

CORA Well . . . you're not, if that's any comfort. Where are you going, dear?

REENIE (*Resignedly*) I haven't done anything to my room all day. I . . . I still have to make my bed.

(REENIE *exits upstairs*)

CORA (*Calling after her*) It's Saturday. Change the linens. I put them in the attic to dry. (CORA *goes into the parlor to pull down the shades.* RUBIN *enters from the dining room. He is in his stocking feet, and is carrying several bags, which he drops onto the floor with a clatter.* CORA *comes running from the parlor*) My God!

RUBIN I scare ya?

CORA Rubin! I hate to be frightened so.

RUBIN I din *mean* to frighten ya.

CORA I didn't hear you drive in.

RUBIN I didn't.

CORA Where's the car?

RUBIN It ain't runnin' right. Left it downtown at the garage. I walked home.

CORA Why did you come in the back way?

RUBIN Cora, what difference does it make if I come in the back way or the front way, or down the chimney? My boots was covered with mud. So I left 'em out on the back porch. I din wanta track up your nice, clean house. Now, wasn't that thoughtful of me?

CORA Did you get my message?

RUBIN What message?

CORA (*A little haughty*) Oh . . . nothing.

RUBIN What message you talkin' about?

CORA The route you left me said you'd be in Blackwell

last night. I called you there, but . . . Well, I suppose you had better places to be.

RUBIN That's right. I did. What'd ya call me for?

CORA (*Hurt*) I don't know now. You'll be wanting a hot bath. I'll go turn on the water tank. (CORA *exits through dining-room door.* RUBIN *sits in his big chair and drops his face into his hands with a look of sad discouragement. Then he begins to unpack one of the bags, taking out small pieces of harness and tossing them on the floor. In a few moments,* CORA *returns*) What made you decide to come back?

RUBIN I lost my job.

CORA What?

RUBIN I said I lost my job.

CORA Rubin! You've always sold more harness for the company than any of the other salesmen.

RUBIN Yah. The on'y trouble is, *no* one's selling much harness today because no one's buyin' it. People are buyin' automobiles. Harness salesmen are . . . things of the past.

CORA Do you mean . . . your company's going out of business?

RUBIN That's it! You won the kewpie doll.

CORA Oh, Rubin!

RUBIN So that's why ya couldn't get me in Blackwell last night. I went somewhere else, regardless of what you were thinkin', lookin' for a job.

CORA (*A little embarrassed with regret*) Oh . . . I apologize, Rubin.

RUBIN Oh, that's all right. You have to get in your li'l digs ev'ry once in a while. I'm used to 'em.

CORA I'm really awfully sorry. Believe me.

RUBIN I was in Tulsa, talkin' to some men at the Southwest Supply Company. They're hirin' lotsa new men to go out in the fields and sell their equipment.

CORA (*Seizing her opportunity*) Rubin Flood, now that you've lost one traveling job, I'm not going to let you take another. You go downtown the first thing Monday morning and talk to John Fraser. He's bought out all the Curley Cue markets in town, and he needs men to manage them. He'd give you a job in a minute. Now, you do what I say, Rubin.

RUBIN (*He looks at her for several moments before getting to his feet*) God damn! I come home here t'apologize to you for hittin' ya. I been feelin' all week like the meanest critter alive, because I took a sock at a woman. My wife, at that. I walked in here ready to *beg* ya to forgive me. Now I feel like doin' it all over again. Don't you realize you can't talk to a man like that? Don't you realize that every time you talk that way, I just gotta go out and raise more hell, just to prove to myself I'm a free man? Don't you know that when you talk to a man like that, you're not givin' him credit for havin' any brains, or any guts, or a spine, or . . . or a few other body parts that are pretty important, too? All these years we been married, you never once really admitted to yourself what kinda man I am. No, ya keep talkin' to me like I was the kinda man you think I *oughta* be. (*He grabs her by the shoulders*) Look at me. Don't you know who I am? Don't you know who I am?

CORA Rubin, you're hurting me.

RUBIN I'm takin' the job if I can get it. It's a damn good job, pays good money.

CORA I don't care about money.

RUBIN No, you don't! Not until you see Peg Ralston come waltzin' down the street in a new fur coat, and then you start wonderin' why old Rubin don't shoot hisself in the foot to make a lot of money.

CORA Rubin, I promise you I'll never envy Peg Ralston another thing, as long as I live.

RUBIN Did it ever occur to you that maybe I feel like a

cheapskate because I can't buy you no fur coat? Did you ever stop to think maybe I'd like to be able to send my kids away to a fine college?

CORA All I'm asking is for you to give them something of *yourself*.

RUBIN God damn it! What have *I* got to give 'em? In this day and age, what's a man like me got to give? With the whole world so all-fired crazy about makin' money, how can *any* man, unless he's got a million dollars stuck in his pocket, feel he's got anything else to give that's very important?

CORA Rubin!

RUBIN I mean it, Cora.

CORA I never realized you had such doubts.

RUBIN The new job is work I've never done. Work I never even thought of doin'. Learnin' about all that goddamn machinery, and how to get out there and demonstrate it. Working with different kinds of men, that's smarter than I am, that think fast and talk sharp and mean all business. Men I can't sit around and chew tobacco with and joke with like I did m'old customers. I . . . I don't like 'em. I don't know if I'm *gonna* like them.

CORA But you just said you wanted the job.

RUBIN I don't like them, but I'm gonna join them. A fellow's gotta get into the swim. There's nothing else to do. But I'm scared. I don't know how I'll make out. I . . . I'm scared.

CORA I never supposed you had it *in* you to fear.

RUBIN I s'pose all this time you been thinkin' you was married to one a them movin'-pitcher fellas that jump off bridges and hold up trains and shoot Indians, and are never scared a nothin'. Times are changin', Cora, and I dunno where they're goin'. When I was a boy, there wasn't much more to this town than a post office. I on'y had six years a schoolin' cause that's all the Old Man thought I'd ever need. Now look at things. School buildin's, churches, fine stores, movie theatres, a country club. Men becomin' millionaires overnight, drivin' down the street in big limousines, goin' out to the country club and gettin' drunk, acting like they was the lords of creation. I dunno what to think of things now, Cora. I'm a stranger in the very land I was born in.

CORA (*Trying to restore his pride*) Your folks pioneered this country.

RUBIN Sometimes I wonder if it's not a lot easier to pioneer a country than it is to settle down in it. I look at the town now and don't recognize anything in it. I come home here, and I still have to get used to the piano, and the telephone, and the gas stove, and the lace curtains at the windows, the carpets on the floor. All these things are still *new* to me. I dunno what to make of 'em. How can *I* feel I've got anything to give to my children when the world's as strange to me as it is to them?

CORA (*With a new awareness of him*) Rubin!

RUBIN I'm doin' the best I can, Cora. Can't ya understand that? I'm doin' the best I can.

CORA Yes, Rubin. I know you are.

RUBIN Now, there's a few more things I gotta say . . . I wanna apologize. I'm sorry I hit ya, Cora. I'm awful sorry.

CORA I know I provoked you, Rubin.

RUBIN You provoked me, but . . . I still shouldn'ta hit ya. It wasn't manly.

CORA I'm not holding it against you, Rubin.

RUBIN And I'm sorry I made such a fuss about you gettin' the girl a new dress. But I was awful worried about losin' my job then, and I din have much money left in the bank.

CORA Rubin, if I'd known that, I wouldn't have *thought* of buying the dress. You should have told me, Rubin.

RUBIN I din wanta make you worry, too.

CORA But that's what I'm for.

RUBIN That's all I gotta say, Cora, except that . . . I love ya. You're a good woman and I couldn't git along without you.

CORA I love you, too, Rubin. And I couldn't get along without you another day.

RUBIN You're clean, and dainty. Give a man a feeling of decency . . . and order . . . and respect.

CORA Thank you, Rubin.

RUBIN Just don't get the idea you can rearrange *me* like ya do the house, whenever ya wanta put it in order.

CORA I'll remember. (*There is a short silence between them now, filled with new understanding*) When you have fears about things, please tell me, Rubin.

RUBIN It's hard for a man t'admit his fears, even to hisself.

CORA Why? Why?

RUBIN He's always afraid of endin' up like . . . like your brother-in-law Morris.

CORA Oh!

(CORA *has a new appreciation of him. She runs to him, throwing her arms about him in a fast embrace. A glow of satisfaction radiates from* RUBIN, *to have his woman back in his arms*)

RUBIN Oh, my goodness. (RUBIN *carries* CORA *center, where they sit like honeymooners, she on his lap; and he kisses her.* SONNY *returns now with a sack of groceries, and stands staring at his parents until they become aware of him*) H'lo, son.

SONNY Hi!

CORA Take the groceries to the kitchen, Sonny. (*Obediently,* SONNY *starts for the dining-room door*) Rubin, Mrs. Stanford paid Sonny five dollars this afternoon for speaking a piece at her tea party.

RUBIN I'll be damned. He'll be makin' more money than his Old Man.

(SONNY *exits now through dining-room door*)

CORA Be nice to him, Rubin. Show him you want to be his friend.

RUBIN I'm nice to that boy, ain't I?

CORA Sometimes you do talk awfully rough and bad-natured.

RUBIN Well . . . *life's* rough. *Life's* bad-natured.

CORA I know. And I keep trying to pretend it isn't.

RUBIN I'll remind ya.

CORA Every time I see the kids go out of the house, I worry . . . like I was watching them go out into life, and they seem so young and helpless.

RUBIN But ya gotta let 'em go, Cora. Ya can't hold 'em.

CORA I've always felt I could give them life like a present, all wrapped in white, with every promise of happiness inside.

RUBIN That ain't the way it works.

CORA No. All I can promise them is life itself. (*With this realization, she gets off* RUBIN'S *lap*) I'd better go to the kitchen and put the groceries away.

RUBIN (*Grabs her to him, not willing to let her go*) T'hell with the groceries!

CORA (*A maidenly protest*) Rubin!

RUBIN (*Caressing her*) Is there any chance of us bein' alone t'night?

CORA (*Secretively*) I think Reenie plans to go to the library. If you give Sonny a dime, I'm sure he'll go to the movies.

RUBIN It's a deal.

(*He tries again to re-engage her in lovemaking*)

CORA Now, Rubin, be patient.

(*She exits through the dining-room door as* REENIE *comes running downstairs*)

REENIE Did I hear Daddy?

RUBIN Hello, daughter.

REENIE (*She runs into his arms and he lifts her high in the air*) Oh, Daddy!

RUBIN Well, how's my girl?

REENIE I feel better now that you're home, Daddy.

RUBIN Thank ya, daughter.

REENIE I've been practicing a new piece, Daddy. It's Chopin. Do you want me to play it for you?

RUBIN Sure. I like sweet music same as anyone.

REENIE I can't play it quite perfect yet, but almost.

(REENIE *goes into parlor and in a moment we hear another wistful piece by Chopin*)

RUBIN That's all right. (SONNY *now returns and stands far right.* RUBIN, *center, faces him. They look at each other with wonder and just a little resentment. But* RUBIN *goes to* SONNY, *making the effort to offer himself*) Son, your mom tells me you do real well, goin' around speaking pieces, gettin' to be a reg'lar Jackie Coogan. I got a customer has a daughter does real well at that kinda thing. Gets up before people and whistles.

SONNY Whistles?

RUBIN Yah! Like birds. Every kinda bird ya ever heard of. Maybe you'd like to meet her sometime.

SONNY Oh, maybe.

(RUBIN *feels himself on uncertain ground with his son*)

RUBIN Your mom said maybe you'd like to go to the movie tonight. I guess I could spare you the money. (*He digs into his pocket*)

SONNY I've changed my mind. I don't want to now.

(SONNY *turns from his father*)

RUBIN (*Looks at his son as though realizing sadly the breech between them. With a feeling of failure, he puts a warm hand on* SONNY'S *shoulder*) Oh! Well, I ain't gonna argue. (*He walks out, and as he passes the parlor, he speaks to* REENIE) That's real purty, daughter.

REENIE Thank you, Daddy.

RUBIN (*Opens dining-room door and speaks to* CORA) Cora, those kids ain't goin' to the movies. Come on now.

CORA (*Off*) I'll be up in a minute, Rubin.

RUBIN (*Closing the door behind him, speaking to* REENIE *and* SONNY) I'm goin' upstairs now, and have my bath.

(REENIE *and* SONNY *watch him all the way as he goes upstairs*)

SONNY They always want to be alone.

REENIE All married people do, crazy.

(SONNY *impulsively sticks out his tongue at her. But she ignores him, picking up one of the favors, a reminder of* SAMMY, *and fondling it tenderly.* SONNY *begins to feel regret*)

SONNY I'm sorry I made a face at you, Reenie.

REENIE (*Sobbing softly*) Go on and make as many faces as you like. I'm not going to fight with you any more.

SONNY Don't cry, Reenie.

REENIE I didn't know Sammy had even remembered the favors until I started to go. Then I went to find my coat, and there they were, sticking out of my pocket. At the very moment he was putting them there . . . he must have had in mind doing what he did.

SONNY (*With a burst of new generosity*) *You! You* keep the favors, Reenie.

REENIE He promised them to *you*.

SONNY Just the same . . . *you* keep them, Reenie.

REENIE Do you mean it?

SONNY Yes.

REENIE You never were thoughtful like this . . . before.

(CORA *comes through the dining-room door now, hears the children's plans, and stands unobserved, listening*)

SONNY Reenie, do you want to go to the movie tonight? It's Mae Murray in *Fascination*, and there's an *Our Gang Comedy* first.

REENIE I don't feel I should.

SONNY When I feel bad, I just *have* to go to the movies. I just *have* to.

REENIE I was supposed to go to the library tonight.

SONNY Please go with me, Reenie. Please.

REENIE Do you really want me?

SONNY Yes, Reenie. Yes.

REENIE Where would you get the money to take *me,* Sonny? I have to pay adult admission. It's thirty-five cents.

SONNY I've got all the money we'll need.

(*He runs for his piggy bank as* CORA *makes a quick return to the dining room*)

REENIE Sonny! Mother told you you had to save that money.

SONNY I don't care. She's not going to boss me for the rest of my life. It's *my* money, and I've got a right to spend it. (*With a heroic gesture of defiance, he throws the piggy bank smashing against the fireplace, its pieces scattering on the floor*)

REENIE Sonny!

SONNY (*Finding his five-dollar bill in the rubble*) And we'll have enough for popcorn, too, and for ice cream afterwards at the Royal Candy Kitchen.

(*Now we see* CORA *in the parlor again, a silent witness*)

REENIE I feel very proud to be treated by my little brother.

SONNY Let's hurry. The comedy starts at seven o'clock and I don't want to miss it.

REENIE We can stay for the second show if we miss the comedy.

SONNY Oh, I want to stay for the second show, anyway. I always see the comedy twice.

CORA (*Coming forth now*) Are you children going some place?

REENIE We're going to the movie, Mom.

CORA Together?

REENIE Yes.

CORA Well . . . that's nice.

REENIE Darn it. I left my rubbers out on the porch.

(*She exits*)

RUBIN (*From upstairs*) Cora!

CORA I'll be up in a minute, Rubin. (*She turns thoughtfully to her son*) Have you forgiven your mother, Sonny?

SONNY (*Inscrutable*) Oh . . . maybe.

CORA Your mother still loves you, Sonny.

(*She puts an arm around him but he avoids her embrace*)

SONNY Don't, Mom.

CORA All right. I understand.

RUBIN (*Upstairs, growing more impatient*) Cora! Come on, honey!

CORA (*Calling back to him*) I'll be up in a minute, Rubin. (SONNY *looks at her with accusing eyes*) Good Bye, Sonny!

(REENIE *sticks her head in the door from outside*)

REENIE Hurry up, Sonny!

RUBIN Come on, Cora!

(CORA *starts up the stairs to her husband, stopping for one final look at her departing son. And* SONNY, *just before going out the door, stops for one final look at his mother, his face full of confused understanding. Then he hurries out to* REENIE, *and* CORA, *like a shy maiden, starts up the stairs, where we see* RUBIN'S *naked feet standing in the warm light at the top*)

CORA I'm coming, Rubin. I'm coming.

CURTAIN

Dore Schary

Sunrise at Campobello

FOR MY BEST FRIEND MIRIAM

Manufactured in the United States of America by H. Wolff

FOREWORD

Last January I made up my mind to write *Sunrise at Campobello*. I had read everything that had been written about Franklin D. Roosevelt since his death and I had on numerous occasions felt that there was a moving and dramatic tale to be told concerning the years of his illness, but I had not yet applied either my energy or my time to truly study the material as a source for a play. Now I had the time and, hopefully, the energy.

I went to work and almost immediately determined that the final image in the play was to be the figure of FDR standing at the podium in Madison Square Garden on the afternoon of June 26, 1924, when he nominated Alfred E. Smith as the Presidential candidate for the Democratic Party. It was that dramatic appearance which changed the course of FDR's life, and consequently, the lives of so many Americans. On that day in his speech he delivered the famous "Happy Warrior" phrase (a quote from a poem by William Wordsworth and suggested by Joseph Proskauer), and in one stroke disabused his party of the notion that he was incapable of public service and became, in the opinion of political columnists of that era, the most attractive political personality of his time.

Only thirty-four months before his dynamic renascence, he had been stricken with infantile paralysis and suffered permanent crippling of his legs. The story of those thirty-four months would, I felt, tell a story of challenge and response, of defeat and despair, turned into victory and confidence.

The characters were almost fiction-like in their dramaturgical potential. FDR, rising from the crucible of pain to become, eventually, a four-time President of the United States; his wife Eleanor, an awkward and shy young woman, who in these months was forged by circumstances which ultimately made her the First Lady of the world; Louis McHenry Howe, a homely man, an eccentric asthmatic who maintained a vigil of devotion and lived to see his prophecy (made in 1912, that FDR would become President) come true. There was a house full of children. Also, there was the matriarchal Sara Delano Roosevelt, who had contempt for politics and who, deeply anxious for her son during his illness, strongly urged him to retire to Hyde Park and the life of a country squire. Finally, there was the rich and saucy character of Alfred E. Smith and the part he played in the climax of these three years.

The incidents were considerable. There was a magnificent bibliography, the Hyde Park Library bursting with details and records, and, finally, the personal recollections of the Roosevelt family.

I had the final scene first. The initial scene in the play came next to mind. That would be the day he took ill at Campobello, August 10, 1921. The title (in Thornton Wilder's figure of speech) came down my arm to the pencil—*Sunrise at Campobello.* All I needed was three acts of playwrighting.

I made some obvious decisions early in the game. Al Smith would never say "raddio" and he wouldn't wear a brown derby. FDR would not say "My friends." But I still had three acts to write.

The material was sifted and selected. Relationships were probed and studied. Significant quotes were placed in chronological sequence. I charted the details: the day and manner in which he was carried from Campobello; the first day he wore his leg braces and when he started on his crutches; the clothes he wore and his favorite poems and readings; the fears he had and his faith in God; his conflicts with his mother; his business ventures and his wrong guesses (such as his conviction that Herbert Hoover would be the Democratic candidate in 1924); the way he crawled; and the exact dimensions of the kitchen chairs he reconstructed into wheel chairs.

I culled the letters that might be used and the fragments of remembered dialogue that might cue me to the way he talked in private conversation during that period. I came to know his choice colors and those of Mrs. Roosevelt. I learned about Louis Howe's favorite cigarettes. (Sweet Caporals); FDR's indignation because of the bigotry so nakedly exposed against Al Smith; FDR's explanations of his illness to his children so that they would have no unspoken fears of it; Eleanor's first plunge into public speaking at the blunt prodding of Louis Howe; and I became familiar with scads of names, dates and events.

But I was still three acts away from a play.

One day in May, I was ready for that frightening yet tremendously exciting moment when you sit down and write tentatively and hopefully—Act One, Scene 1.

The characters and happenings began to slip into place. The dialogue moved me into the era of some thirty-seven years ago, and I was on the way.

What has been written is true. Dramatic needs forced me to compress and to edit some of the events, but if the play has force and emotion it is because the real people lived these days with force and emotion.

In March, 1957, I wrote Mrs. Roosevelt asking for permission to do this play. My letter read in part, "What I propose to tell is the story of a man and the people around him who, after an ordeal, emerged strong and triumphant. I hope to write a tribute that will do justice to a phase of his life. I pledge my devotion and whatever skill I may have to do the task."

I hope, with all my heart, that the task is well done.

January 14, 1958 DORE SCHARY

I take this opportunity to acknowledge the invaluable aid received from personal recollections and comments by Mrs. Eleanor Roosevelt, Mrs. James Halsted, Congressman James Roosevelt and Mr. Franklin D. Roosevelt, Jr.

I also extend deep appreciation to the authors of the vast bibliography concerning the life, times and works of Franklin D. Roosevelt.

Finally, my sincere thanks to Dr. Herman Kahn, director of the Hyde Park Memorial Library, and to his assistant, Raymond Corry, and to the entire staff of the Library for their constant guidance and aid.

Sunrise at Campobello was first presented by The Theatre Guild and Dore Schary at the Cort Theatre, New York City, on January 30, 1958, with the following cast:

(*In order of appearance*)

ANNA ROOSEVELT	Roni Dengel
ELEANOR ROOSEVELT	Mary Fickett
FRANKLIN D. ROOSEVELT, JR.	Kenneth Kakos
JAMES ROOSEVELT	James Bonnet
ELLIOTT ROOSEVELT	Perry Skaar
EDWARD	James Earl Jones
FRANKLIN DELANO ROOSEVELT	Ralph Bellamy
JOHN ROOSEVELT	Jeffrey Rowland
MARIE	Ethel Everett
LOUIS MCHENRY HOWE	Henry Jones
MRS. SARA DELANO ROOSEVELT	Anne Seymour
MISS MARGUERITE (MISSY) LEHAND	Mary Welch
DOCTOR BENNET	James Reese
FRANKLIN CALDER	William Fort
STRETCHER BEARERS	Edwin Phillips, Vincent Dowling, Floyd Curtis
MR. BRIMMER	Clifford Carpenter
MR. LASSITER	Richard Robbins
GOVERNOR ALFRED E. SMITH	Alan Bunce
DALY	Jerry Crews
POLICEMAN	Floyd Curtis
SENATOR WALSH	Vincent Dowling
A SPEAKER	Edwin Phillips

DIRECTED BY Vincent J. Donehue
PRODUCTION DESIGNED AND LIGHTED BY Ralph Alswang
COSTUMES BY Virginia Volland

ACT ONE

Scene 1. The living room of the Franklin D. Roosevelt home at Campobello, New Brunswick, Canada, August 10, 1921.

Scene 2. The same, September 1, 1921.

Scene 3. The same, September 13, 1921.

ACT TWO

Scene 1. The living room of the Franklin D. Roosevelt home in New York, May, 1922.

Scene 2. The same, January, 1923.

ACT THREE

Scene 1. The same, May, 1924.

Scene 2. Madison Square Garden (an anteroom), June 26, 1924.

Scene 3. The platform, moments later.

ACT ONE

Scene One

Scene: It is August 10, 1921. We are in the large living room of the FRANKLIN DELANO ROOSEVELT *summer home at Campobello, New Brunswick, Canada. It is a homey, sprawling summer lodge. Picture windows reveal the firs and pines of the forest and allow us to view part of the bay. The sky is pink with the coming dusk. A porch runs along outside the house and we can see some of it. The entire atmosphere is woodsy and comfortable, not elegant or fancy, but rather, a house that has seen hard wear by an energetic and healthy family. There are no electric lights. At night the house is illuminated by kerosene lamps, many of which are placed about the room.*

At rise: The stage is empty. Then ANNA ROOSEVELT, *wearing a bathing suit and carrying a picnic basket, can be glimpsed coming across the porch.*

ANNA (*As she comes into the house*) Mother! (*Then louder*) Mother!

(MRS. ELEANOR ROOSEVELT *appears on the steps leading down into the room. She is a tall, stately and willowy young woman of thirty-six. She is dressed in a white flannel skirt and blue sweater and wears white sneakers. She looks warm and a bit disheveled*)

ELEANOR Yes, Anna.

ANNA Mother, you missed all the fun. After sailing, we went swimming in the lagoon and then we trotted across the spit and dove into the bay.

ELEANOR It sounds very strenuous. I am delighted that I never learned how to swim. (*She motions* ANNA *upstairs.* ANNA *smiles and starts up the steps*) If you're through with the picnic I'd better take the basket.

(ANNA *smiles, hands* ELEANOR *the basket and continues up the steps.* FRANKLIN JR., *wearing a bathing suit, storms in and throws his towel and his sweater down near the clothes rack*)

FRANKLIN JR. (*Wearily*) Hello, Mother.

ELEANOR Hello, young Franklin. (*He crosses to the couch and collapses*) Franklin, I know that you're on the verge of exhaustion, but you are to get up from that couch and put your towel and sweater where they be-long.

FRANKLIN JR. (*Questioningly*) Now?

ELEANOR Now.

(FRANKLIN JR. *groans his way from the couch, picks up the sweater and towel, puts them on the rack, and then staggers back in the direction of the couch.* ELEANOR *looks at him and crosses stage right to the study off the living room.* JIMMY *and* ELLIOTT *now enter from the porch. Both of them are also wearing bathing suits. They too toss their towels and sweaters more or less in the di-rection of the clothes rack*)

JIMMY (*To* ELLIOTT) You paddle your way along like a polliwog. Your hands have to hit the water clean— (*He illustrates*) That's the only way to get pull into your stroke—like this when you come back.

ELLIOTT You aren't exactly champion of the world, you know.

JIMMY I'm only telling you what Pa told me. He told it to all of us, but you don't listen. Elliott, you never listen.

(*By now* ELLIOTT *has become aware of* FRANKLIN JR., *stretched out on the couch, and he silently indicates to* JIMMY *that they do something about this.* JIMMY *and* ELLIOTT *begin to tiptoe toward the couch.* FRANKLIN JR., *though his back is to both of them, senses that he is about to be attacked*)

FRANKLIN JR. You leave me alone. (ELLIOTT *and* JIMMY *rush* FRANKLIN JR. *and wrestle him off the couch.* FRANKLIN JR. *calls out*) That's a rotten thing to do. (*He is now on the floor, and repeats earnestly*) A real rotten thing to do.

(ELEANOR *appears from the study door*)

ELEANOR Hello, Jimmy—Elliott.

JIMMY Mother, you missed the real fun. We finished up swimming—

ELEANOR Anna told me all about it.

ELLIOTT It was freezing—absolutely freezing.

(*The boys begin picking up their suits and towels*)

ELEANOR Where's Johnny?

JIMMY He's with Father on the dock. (ELEANOR *crosses over to a cardboard megaphone that hangs near the door.* JIMMY *calls out with mock alarm*) Oh, no, Mother.

ELEANOR It's time they were home. (ELLIOTT *and* FRANKLIN JR., *off to a side, are silently hand-wrestling, unperceived by* ELEANOR, *who crosses to the screen door, opens it and calls out*) Franklin! Johnny! (*Then, even louder*) Franklin! Johnny!!

JIMMY Mother, I hate to say this, but your voice coming through there sounds like the call to judgment.

ELEANOR That's enough from you, Mr. James Roosevelt. Now, upstairs. All of you—upstairs.

(*She points her finger to the upper floor. The boys nod and then form a group. They hide their right fists behind their backs and then, at a nod of* JIMMY'S *head, extend their hands with fingers outstretched. After they do this,* JIMMY *and* ELLIOTT *appear to be disgusted*)

FRANKLIN JR. (*Preening*) This time I win.

ELEANOR (*Smiles at them and then turns to the door and lifts up her megaphone and calls*) Franklin! Johnny!

(JIMMY *and* ELLIOTT *make a seat for* FRANKLIN JR. *with*

their hands, and then carry him up the steps, groaning loudly at his weight)

ELLIOTT (*As they go up*) He's stuffed with lead—all lead.

(ELEANOR *hangs up the megaphone as* EDWARD *enters with a slip of paper and pencil. He is a young colored man, about twenty*)

EDWARD Mrs. McGowan says she needs all this from town, Mrs. Roosevelt.

(ELEANOR *takes the list and studies it*)

ELEANOR (*Nodding*) We'll pick up everything tomorrow, Edward. (*She returns the list to* EDWARD) And please add some hard candy and chocolate. Also, some cigarettes for Mr. Roosevelt.

(EDWARD *nods as he makes a notation.* ANNA, *now dressed in casual clothes, comes down the steps. She carries a book*)

ANNA Mother, I don't know why you picked *Julius Caesar* for us to read tonight. All the good parts are for men.

ELEANOR You and I, like all the others, will double up in the parts.

ANNA I'd like to read Brutus.

ELEANOR Your father makes the final decisions on casting. (*She turns to* EDWARD) Please tell Mrs. McGowan that we're going sailing and picnicking again tomorrow. I'll talk with her later about the lunch.

EDWARD Yes, Mrs. Roosevelt.

(*He exits*)

ANNA Mother, we'd all appreciate it if we could get something other than fried chicken and hard-boiled eggs.

ELEANOR (*She nods her head*) Then tomorrow perhaps we'll try fried eggs and hard-boiled chicken.

(ANNA *looks at her, aghast. Glimpsed coming up the porch is* FDR. *He is about forty at this time, muscular, tall and graceful. He is wearing a white cap, a bathing suit and a robe*)

FDR (*Calling from porch*) Eleanor, they heard you all the way across to Eastport.

ELEANOR (*To* ANNA) Stand by, the Captain's home.

(FDR *opens the door*)

FDR Hello, Eleanor. Sis. (*To someone offstage*) Come on, small fry.

(FDR *lifts* JOHNNY *through the bay window and into the room*)

ANNA Last again—the runt.

JOHNNY Don't call me runt. I'm Johnny.

FDR (*Rumpling* JOHNNY'S *hair*) You tell her, son. Eleanor, you missed all the fun.

ELEANOR (*Wearily*) So Anna, James, Elliott and Franklin Jr. have told me.

(MARIE *enters from upstairs*)

MARIE Ah, there you are, my friend Johnny.

JOHNNY Marie, I don't want to go upstairs.

ELEANOR Yes you do.

JOHNNY (*To* FDR, *who has crossed to the couch*) Father?

(FDR *shakes his head*)

MARIE Johnny, *il faut t'habiller pour diner.*

JOHNNY *Un moment, s'il vous plait.* Papa, *comment va tu?*

FDR *Ca va bien.* Come on, I'll make your journey upstairs a pleasant one.

(FDR *sweeps* JOHNNY *up on his back and races up the steps with him*)

JOHNNY Giddyup-giddyap.

MARIE *Voila,* Johnny! Dinner as usual, Mrs. Roosevelt? (*She starts up the stairs*)

ELEANOR Yes, Marie. Six-thirty.

(*We hear the voices of the boys as they greet their father as he arrives upstairs with* JOHNNY *on his back*)

JIMMY'S VOICE Hello, Father. Why don't you do that for me?

ELLIOTT'S VOICE I don't want to read Cassius.

FRANKLIN JR.'S VOICE I don't think I like Shakespeare at all.

ANNA (*To* ELEANOR, *as she hears the loud voices*) Boys are so loud and noisy. Mother, how you put up with the four of them. I don't know.

ELEANOR The four boys are easy. (*She points to* ANNA) It's the one girl.

ANNA (*Rather proud*) Do you think I'm difficult?

ELEANOR I think you feel surrounded by the men in the family.

ANNA (*Not at all perturbed*) Before Granny went to Europe she told me she thinks you're too severe with me.

ELEANOR I'm aware of your chats with Granny.

ANNA (*Confidentially*) Actually, Granny spoils us. The boys can talk her out of anything—all they have to do is speak a little French or agree with her.

ELEANOR And what about you?

ANNA Oh, of course, so can I.

(FDR *has just started down the stairs*)

FDR (*To* ANNA) So can you what?

ANNA (*Puzzled*) What?

FDR I heard you say "so can I."

ANNA Oh—talk Granny out of anything I want—just like the boys. Especially if I agree with her when she says something about Mr. Howe.

(JIMMY *comes down dressed. He carries a copy of* Julius Caesar)

JIMMY Oh, Father, is Mr. Howe coming back here?

FDR No. He's going to be tied up in Washington.

ELEANOR (*Suspiciously*) Jimmy, why do you ask?

JIMMY Nothing.

FDR Why do you ask—nothing? What kind of English is that? (*Then slowly, looking at* JIMMY) Why do you ask?

JIMMY For no reason.

FDR That's better.

ELEANOR But you had a reason, Jimmy. I want you to tell me.

JIMMY Well, usually he rooms next to me, and that coughing and— (*He illustrates, wheezes*) wheezing he does so much keeps me up at night. And if he burns that incense to stop the coughing—that's worse than anything.

FDR You never appear to be suffering from a lack of sleep.

JIMMY Father, I'm serious—

FDR (*Cutting in*) Jimmy—I'm serious, too. I want no criticism of or complaints about Mr. Louie Howe from you or anyone else. Is that understood?

JIMMY Understood.

ANNA Granny always says that Mr. Howe—

FDR (*Cutting in*) I know all about Granny's opinions of Mr. Howe and I don't want them repeated by you. (*Then, closing the door to discussion*) And I would appreciate it if you and Jimmy would do some rehearsing for tonight's reading. (*He indicates the side door.* JIMMY *and* ANNA *know when to answer back and when not to. They go out the side door.* FDR *looks up at* ELEANOR) Babs, how about a hard drink? I feel rather tired and achy. That's the first swim I've had in years that didn't refresh me.

ELEANOR You should be more careful.

FDR Eleanor, I am not catching another cold and I am not becoming an alcoholic.

ELEANOR I just want you to get out of that wet suit.

FDR In a few minutes. (ELEANOR *goes to the cabinet underneath the stairway and prepares* FDR'S *drink.* FDR *glances at a newspaper*) It's a pleasure to open a paper and see my name out of it. This is a tidy item. Almost six million unemployed and Harding playing his tuba. (*He tosses his cap on the window seat and walks toward the couch.* ELEANOR *hands him a drink*) Thanks, Babs.

Good—that will take the chill out of my bones. (*He refers again to the paper*) I often think of something Woodrow Wilson said to me. "It is only once in a generation that a people can be lifted above material things. That is why conservative government is in the saddle for two-thirds of the time."

ELEANOR Louie insists that you can reverse the trend.

FDR Yes, I know. He doesn't like my staying in this Wall Street job. Says it's hardly the place for a dedicated progressive.

ELEANOR Well, Franklin, is it?

FDR Babs, it's five hundred a week. And confidentially, Mrs. R., the light on my political horizon appears rather dim and dark. There is nothing as unattractive to a party as a defeated candidate.

ELEANOR I hardly think you will be held responsible for the defeat of the Democratic Party. After all, Cox was the presidential candidate, not you.

FDR Babs, I've weathered battles with Tammany Hall, seven years in the Navy Department, and Ma*ma's* massive objections to politics—which she rates one step higher than garbage collecting. I am quite sure that Wall Street will not corrupt my political convictions.

ELEANOR That's a comfort.

(FDR *goes toward her, teasingly*)

FDR Babs, if I get into deep water, keep an eye on me.

ELEANOR "God takes man into deep water not to drown him but to cleanse him."

FDR Helpful hint from helpful wife. Thank you, ma'am. Thank you kindly.

(ELLIOTT *and* FRANKLIN JR. *come downstairs*)

ELLIOTT Ma, we're hungry.

ELEANOR It'll only be a few moments now.

FDR (*Picking up a letter*) From Ma*ma.*

FRANKLIN JR. What does Granny say?

(ANNA *and* JIMMY *come in from the side room*)

ANNA Father, we have to decide about who's going to read what.

(JOHNNY *comes down the steps, followed by* MARIE)

FDR As you know, we'll all have to play a variety of roles. However, the main assignments are as follows: Your mother will read Calpurnia—Anna, you shall read Portia— (*He eyes her*) And Cinna the Poet, and Octavius. You, Jimmy, shall be Brutus.

JIMMY I've been studying Antony.

FDR I shall read Marc Antony. You are Brutus. Elliott, you will make a fine Cassius. You, Franklin, have the round look of Casca. And you, Johnny, will be the mobs, the citizens and the sounds of battle. (JOHNNY *nods, pleased*) And you, Marie, you will be Julius Caesar.

MARIE *Merci.*

(FDR *looks archly at the others*)

FDR Probably my greatest stroke of casting.

ELLIOTT What's in Granny's letter?

ANNA Please tell us, Father.

(FDR *picks up the letter from Ma*ma)

FDR Well, let's see. Granny has moved to London to see Cousin Muriel, whose slight operation apparently was successful. Though Ma*ma* doesn't have a high opinion of British medicine. (*He laughs, then reads silently a moment*) Granny doesn't approve of Muriel's bed. Too hard.

JIMMY She says my bed's too soft.

FDR Granny believes in hard beds for men—soft beds for women. (*He resumes reading*) Now—Granny may sail on the twenty-fourth, which would get her home on the thirty-first—or maybe a week later, which would bring her home September the seventh. (*He laughs*) She may stay. She loves the hotel. "Much love to the precious children. I expect to find a French family on my return. Devotedly, Mama." (*He puts the letter down and looks at the children*) That means Granny expects you all to be speaking perfect French. (*He continues to look at them*) So you had better be speaking perfect French. *Ici on parle français.*

(EDWARD *now enters*)

EDWARD Mrs. Roosevelt, dinner's ready.

ELEANOR Thank you, Edward.

ELLIOTT What has Mrs. McGowan got to eat tonight?

ELEANOR Whatever Mrs. McGowan has to eat you will enjoy.

ELLIOTT I'm sure of that, Mother. I just wanted to know.

ELEANOR Let life surprise you, Elliott. It's more fun that way.

JIMMY (*Sitting down next to* FDR) How's your arm, Father?

ELEANOR (*Protesting*) Franklin.

FDR This will only take a minute, Babs. (*He puts his arm on the table opposite* JIMMY. *They clasp hands. The children group around.* JIMMY *is already straining every muscle*) Ready?

JIMMY Ready.

(FDR puts JIMMY's *arm down, rolling him to the floor at the same time*)

FDR Undefeated and still champion. (*The children cheer and move out toward the dining room.* FDR *saunters over to the bay window*) This time of day is always the best. It's as if the sun were standing still for a last glimpse—a long lingering look before saying good night.

ELEANOR It's a nice quiet time.

FDR I wish I could stay till after Labor Day.

(*Suddenly* FDR *stumbles and grabs his back. He recovers.* ELEANOR *sees the grimace of pain and crosses to him*)

ELEANOR Why, Franklin!

FDR Must be a spot of lumbago— (ELEANOR *puts her hand to his brow*) No, I don't feel feverish. Just suddenly— (*He snaps his* fingers) Like that—

ELEANOR You get into bed. I'll bring you a tray.

FDR (*Half a smile*) I hoped you'd say that.

(ELEANOR *goes toward the kitchen. Just as* FDR *hits the steps, the sound of the children in the dining room can be heard. Both* ELEANOR *and* FDR *stop as we hear the voices of the children, offstage*)

VOICES Two!—Four!—Six!—Eight!—Who do we appreciate?—Mrs. McGowan! Mrs. McGowan! Mrs. McGowan! Yaaay!

(*Sounds of handclapping and yells.* ELEANOR *exits.* FDR, *amused, pauses and listens, then continues slowly up the steps, as*

THE CURTAIN FALLS

Scene Two

Scene: The scene is the same. It is September 1, 1921. It is night. The kerosene lights dimly illuminate the room.

At rise: LOUIS HOWE *enters from the kitchen with a tray covered with a white napkin. He is a small and homely man. He wears, as he does at all times, a badly wrinkled suit and vest, along with a high stiff collar. His ties and handkerchiefs are garish. He is a chain smoker and an asthmatic. He is never without a cigarette in his mouth or in his hand. He hurries upstairs.*

ELEANOR'S VOICE (*Offstage*) Louie—

HOWE Be right there.

ELEANOR'S VOICE (*Offstage*) Thank you, Louie.

HOWE Call me if you need anything. (*He comes down the steps and sees* JIMMY. *During the above,* JIMMY *has crossed to the bottom of the stairs, wearing pajamas and bathrobe*) Hello, Jim. What's wrong?

JIMMY Nothing, Mr. Howe.

HOWE Then why aren't you asleep?

JIMMY I couldn't sleep. How's my father?

HOWE Having a fairly good night.

JIMMY Can I see him tonight?

HOWE No—in a couple of days.

JIMMY We're all a little scared.

HOWE (*In a reprimanding tone*) Well your father isn't and he wouldn't want you to be, Jim.

JIMMY I'll try. I'd feel better if I knew what was going on, but I don't want to bother Mother.

HOWE That's right. She's had enough to do for the past three weeks.

JIMMY But—

HOWE But what?

JIMMY Sometimes I get frightened. So does Anna.

HOWE Well, stop being frightened. Those germs never ran into anybody as tough as your father. They'll be yelling for help by the time he gets through with them.

JIMMY He's strong, all right.

HOWE (*Now placatingly*) He's a strong and big man in many ways. Jimmy, when I first got up here I was scared, too. I was worried about your father being so sick. But now he's beginning to fight back—and when he fights—well, sir, you know the first time I saw him was in Albany in nineteen eleven. He was fighting a tough battle with Tammany Hall. Believe me, they can fight like roughnecks. Well, he won that one going away—like what Dempsey did to Carpentier. And, Jimmy, he's going to win this one.

JIMMY (*Relieved*) I hope you're right.

HOWE I've never been wrong in my life. Only once, when I figured the ice on the pond in Saratoga was thick enough to skate on. Well, sir, it took three days to wring me out.

(ELEANOR, *carrying a tray, appears on the stairs.* JIMMY *and* HOWE *turn as she appears*)

ELEANOR (*As she sees* JIMMY) Jimmy.

JIMMY I was just up for a glass of water, Mother.

(JIMMY *takes the tray and exits to the kitchen*)

HOWE All right?

(ELEANOR *nods as she takes off her apron.* JIMMY *returns from the kitchen*)

ELEANOR All right, dear. Now you go in and get some sleep.

JIMMY I will. And you'd better get some rest, too, Mother. (ELEANOR *nods*) 'Night.

ELEANOR Good night, James.

JIMMY Good night, Mr. Howe.

(JIMMY *exits into the side room*)

HOWE Eleanor, why the hell can't we get some electric lights in here?

ELEANOR You know we can't. Louie, what's bothering you?

HOWE Where's Mrs. Roosevelt?

ELEANOR Ma*ma's* in her room. She'll probably be down in a few minutes. Louie, be understanding. It's been a desperately unhappy day for her.

HOWE I am understanding, Eleanor. I like the old lady. She fascinates me. Monumental and impregnable as the Rock of Gibraltar.

ELEANOR I know the problem that you have with Ma*ma.*

HOWE It's no problem. She just hates the sight of me. She considers me the ward-heeler in Franklin's life.

ELEANOR Louie, don't quarrel with her.

HOWE Eleanor—I promise to shinny on my side if she shinnies on hers. (*A pause*) It's going to be rough, but you're going to have to tell her the truth.

ELEANOR (*Wearily*) Louie, if we can only get him well enough to move him into New York. Each day with him here is like— (*Controlling herself*) He should be in a hospital, getting the best care, the most modern treatment.

HOWE Now you just remember this—nobody could have done more than you, or done it better.

(*At this moment,* MRS. SARA DELANO ROOSEVELT *comes down the steps. At this time she is in her middle sixties, a strong, dominant, vibrant figure of a woman. She is dressed in expensive and elegant clothes. She is at all times the Lady of the Manor. She guards her emotions in stoical form. While everyone knows exactly what she thinks, the only one she ever quarrels with openly and nakedly is* FDR)

SARA Eleanor? Franklin sleeping?

ELEANOR Yes—he's been resting for over two hours.

SARA Has the pain eased?

ELEANOR A bit. His legs are less sensitive to touch. A cup of tea, Ma*ma?*

SARA I would like a cup.

ELEANOR It will only be a moment, dear.

(*As* ELEANOR *exits,* SARA *recognizes the presence of* HOWE. *He puts his suit jacket on. Aware that he is now permitted to speak, he does so*)

HOWE How are you feeling, Mrs. Roosevelt?

SARA Oh, Mr. Howe. A little tired—but a good night's rest will pick me up, I'm sure. I came directly from New York after the boat docked. The crossing was rather rough—and seemed endless.

HOWE Yes, so Eleanor said.

SARA How is your wife?

HOWE Why, Grace is fine, thank you. She took my son Hartley home with her yesterday.

(SARA *nods, then takes note of the smoky atmosphere*)

SARA The air is rather stuffy, don't you think?

HOWE (*Casually*) We had the door open, but it's damn cold outside.

SARA (*After a polite pause*) Have you been here all the time since Franklin's illness?

HOWE I arrived a couple of days after he took ill. Been here since—and plan to stay till we take him back.

SARA Do the doctors know when that will be?

HOWE They hope in a couple of weeks.

SARA I admire the way all of you are behaving. (ELEANOR *has entered with the tea; she places it before* SARA. *To* ELEANOR) Thank you, dear.

ELEANOR Louie—tea?

HOWE No, thanks.

SARA Eleanor dear, if you're not too worn out—I'm so anxious to hear as much as I can about everything.

ELEANOR Yes, Ma*ma.*

HOWE Mrs. Roosevelt, this girl has worked like a squad of trained nurses. Dr. Lovett was amazed at how well she had done it all.

SARA (*To* ELEANOR) Couldn't you get any nurses, dear?

ELEANOR We tried, but none were available. Campobello is quite remote.

SARA If you don't mind—this is the first opportunity we've had to talk.

ELEANOR Of course, Ma*ma.* Franklin was taken ill on August tenth—just three weeks ago. At first it seemed to be a heavy cold. Finally Dr. Bennet called in a specialist, who diagnosed it as a clot on the spinal cord.

SARA He couldn't have been a good specialist.

ELEANOR We thought he was. But Franklin didn't respond to the treatment. About a week ago Uncle Fred reached me by telephone—we have to go into town for that.

SARA I always thought it was absurd to be so cut off.

ELEANOR You know that Franklin never wanted a phone here.

SARA Go ahead, dear.

ELEANOR Uncle Fred had talked to some other doctors, who began to suspect it was infantile paralysis. So he arranged for Dr. Lovett of Boston to come up. He diagnosed it almost immediately. And we're doing as he suggested ever since.

SARA And what does he think—how severe is the paralysis?

ELEANOR He believes it to be a mild attack—and feels that Franklin will recover almost completely.

SARA (*Slowly*) Almost?—

ELEANOR Well, Ma*ma*—at first Franklin lost control even of his hands. He couldn't write—or hold a spoon. Now his arms and hands are almost all well. We still don't know about his legs—or—his back.

SARA (*Slowly*) He can't sit up?

ELEANOR No, dear, not yet.

(SARA *puts down her cup, takes a handkerchief and puts it to her lips, stifling a desire to cry*)

HOWE The doctors feel sure his back muscles will be all right.

SARA His legs—those wonderful legs—what about them?

ELEANOR The doctors don't know.

SARA (*Shaking her head*) It's too much—I can't believe it. (*Sobbing*) My poor boy—my poor boy—

ELEANOR Ma*ma*—perhaps we shouldn't talk any more—you're exhausted.

SARA (*Stopping her tears*) No—I couldn't sleep right now. The children? Is it safe for them to be here?

ELEANOR Dr. Lovett said having already been exposed to the illness there is no point moving them.

SARA I can certainly help with the children.

ELEANOR That would be wonderful.

(*She passes her hand over her tired eyes*)

HOWE (*Seeing the gesture*) Eleanor—you have to get some rest. We all do. (*Seeing that no one picks up the hint*) I think I'll turn in myself. Will you excuse me?

SARA Good night, Mr. Howe.

ELEANOR Rest well, Louie.

HOWE 'Night. (*He exits up steps—wheezing and cough-*

ing and smoking. Suddenly he trips on the dimly lit steps) I don't know why the hell they can't put some electric lights in here.

(HOWE *is out of sight*)

SARA (*After a pause*) He's a vulgar little man.

ELEANOR He's a very dear little man.

SARA I find him very difficult.

ELEANOR You make that quite clear.

SARA I'm not skillful at hiding my true feelings, Eleanor.

ELEANOR That may not be a virtue, Ma*ma*. You should know as soon as Louie heard of Franklin's illness, he gave up a lucrative job in Washington to rush here and help out. There's nothing in life more important to him than Franklin.

SARA Nor to any of us.

ELEANOR Then, that's something we can share with Louie, isn't it?

SARA (*A weary sigh*) It has been a grueling day. I'm tired.

ELEANOR Ma*ma*, there's something very special in the relationship between Louie and Franklin.

SARA I've never quite understood it. It's possible Mr. Howe merely enjoys riding along on Franklin's coattails.

(HOWE *has been coming down the steps and has heard* SARA'S *last remark. He covers his anger*)

HOWE Eleanor—

ELEANOR (*Quickly rising*) Yes, Louie?

HOWE Franklin needs you a minute.

(ELEANOR *goes up the steps quickly*)

SARA Eleanor!

HOWE It's nothing alarming, Mrs. Roosevelt.

SARA (*Determined to be polite*) You suffer a great deal from asthma, don't you?

HOWE (*As he lights a cigarette*) A great deal. I'd be lonesome without it.

SARA You know that smoking isn't very good for you—you know that.

HOWE I do.

(*He puffs deliberately in defiance of* SARA'S *advice*)

SARA What are the plans for Franklin after they take him to New York?

HOWE First he goes to the hospital—and then, well, I guess it depends on how all that goes.

SARA You say that he will be able to be moved in two or three weeks.

HOWE We hope so.

SARA As soon as he's able to leave the hospital I want him to go to Hyde Park. Everything he loves is there. It's home to him. Always has been. It's large enough for the entire family and that's where he can be made most comfortable.

HOWE Well, I'm sure that as soon as Franklin's well enough he and Eleanor will decide where he would like to recuperate.

SARA If Franklin's to have any permanent injury, the best place for him is Hyde Park. We can make a full life for him there. He can write, take care of the estate, raise his family as he was raised, and there will be enough to keep him active without overtaxing him or spending his energy.

HOWE Mrs. Roosevelt, I've heard Franklin say that in public service a man must be prepared to spend and be spent. He may not be willing to accept a sedentary life in the country.

SARA Mr. Howe, we must do everything that is possible to discourage him from remaining active in politics.

HOWE Mrs. Roosevelt, Hyde Park or Timbuktu, Franklin's policital future is ordained. That sounds mystical, I know. But I feel it as sure as I feel my heart beating.

SARA (*The politeness is wearing thin*) Believe me, Mr.

Howe, I respect your devotion, but Franklin is more to me than a prospective candidate for public office. He's my son.

HOWE He is also Eleanor's husband, the father of five children and my dearest friend.

SARA (*The hard fist*) Then he is blessed indeed to be the subject of so much affection.

HOWE (*Losing his temper*) But he is, above all, himself, Mrs. Roosevelt, and he happens to be the best damned progressive in the country.

SARA (*Closing the iron door*) My only interest is in his getting well—not his status as a politician. I am grateful for the care and devotion you have given Franklin. I am less grateful for your untimely and grandiose schemes.

HOWE Mrs. Roosevelt, for the next few months Franklin may have need for some grandiose schemes. So may we all.

(SARA *gives him a cold and penetrating glance*)

SARA Good night, Mr. Howe.

(*She turns and walks up the steps as*

THE CURTAIN FALLS

Scene Three

Scene: We are in the living room again. There is some luggage stacked around. It is a sunny morning, September 13, 1921.

At rise: MISSY LEHAND *is stage right, typing from some notes. She is* FDR'S *private secretary. She is a handsome woman, with auburn hair and a strong and sure manner.* EDWARD *comes into the living room and takes out some of the baggage.* JOHNNY, *carrying a bow and arrow and wearing a simple Indian headdress, follows behind* EDWARD. *As he comes in, he lets out an Indian war whoop.*

EDWARD Mr. Johnny, I'm busy. I can't play Indians any more.

JOHNNY Let me help you carry the bags.

EDWARD It's not your work. Now you go about your business and let me go about mine.

(EDWARD *now has three of the suitcases and out he goes*)

MISSY How, Big Chief! Need anything?

JOHNNY Just Anna. Jimmy sent me in for her. He orders us around like we were in the Navy. (*Calling out*) Anna!

MISSY Ssh.

JOHNNY (*In a hoarse whisper*) Sorry. Anna!

ANNA (*From upstairs*) Ssh. (*She appears, holding her suitcase. She is dressed for departure*) Stop yelling like a wild Indian.

JOHNNY Jimmy says—

ANNA What Jimmy says doesn't interest me in the slightest.

JOHNNY We're supposed to wait outside.

ANNA I know—like—children.

JOHNNY I enjoy being a boy.

ANNA I'm going to have some breakfast and go out the back way.

(*She exits to kitchen*)

JOHNNY Miss LeHand, are they gonna carry Father out on a stretcher?

MISSY Well, that's the plan.

JOHNNY Why can't Jimmy, Elliott, Franklin and I do it?

MISSY (*Smiling, but sensitive to* JOHNNY'S *ambitions*) That's a wonderful idea. But, you see, your father has made other plans, and it's too late to change.

(LOUIE HOWE, *carrying a suitcase, comes down the steps from above*)

JOHNNY Okay. I'd better go before Jimmy sends Elliott for me. (*He looks at* HOWE) Good morning, Mr. Howe.

(HOWE *waves an airy good morning.* JOHNNY *exits*)

MISSY He's a cute one.

HOWE They're all cute. But there sure are a helluva lot of them. How's it going, Missy?

MISSY Now that Anna is downstairs, the kids are all packed and waiting for the Robert E. Lee.

HOWE Ma*ma?*

MISSY Upstairs with the Boss and Mrs. R. Doc Bennet, too.

HOWE We've got about a half an hour.

MISSY This is going to be a rough trip for Mr. R.

HOWE Once we get him across the bay and into Eastport —the rough time's over.

MISSY (*Putting papers into a briefcase*) You're going to have a lot of angry newspapermen breathing down your collar. They all want to see Mr. R.

HOWE They'll see him—after he's on the train all propped up in his berth—a grin on his face. Once we get to Eastport—I'll flash the other dock, tell the newspapermen to come over, and explain there was a change of plans due to the tide or currents or something.

MISSY (*Glancing at some notes before she packs them*) When do we break the news that the Boss has infantile?

HOWE Later. When we get to New York. Some time tomorrow. (*Reading from a release*) "After thorough examinations, doctors today revealed Franklin D. Roosevelt recently suffered a mild attack of infantile paralysis. His legs have been temporarily affected, but it is anticipated he will have a complete recovery."

MISSY (*Glumly*) Well, that's a gay little news item.

HOWE Missy—where are those usual radiantly hopeful thoughts?

MISSY Louie—I've been here for two weeks taking dictation and trying to act as he does—as if nothing is the matter. Sometimes it seems a sad and foolish game. He lies there, rattling on with plans for business conferences and meetings. Overhaul the Democratic Party—select the candidates for twenty-two and twenty-four—organize this charity and reorganize that. I listen with wonder and I want to cry.

HOWE Missy—maybe he doesn't mean one word of what he's planning or trying to do—but he wants us to believe it—so, Missy, believe. (EDWARD *enters*) Edward, my stuff goes into the boat headed to Eastport.

EDWARD Yes sir, I know. (*Turns to* MISSY) What about your things, Miss LeHand?

MISSY To the first boat. Thanks.

(EDWARD *by now has the next to the last load, and exits. As he starts out,* DR. BENNET *comes down from upstairs*)

BENNET Our patient's about ready to be moved. I'll send the men in with the stretcher. When they bring Mr. Roosevelt down, we'll give him a short rest in here and then take him to the boat.

MISSY Doctor—

BENNET Yes?

MISSY How is he today?

BENNET About the same. He's in pain, but I've given him something to help that. He's running a fever—but he refuses to take it seriously. Body of a bull—disposition of a lamb.

(*He crosses to the door and goes out to the porch as* SARA *comes in. She is dressed for travel*)

HOWE Good morning, Mrs. Roosevelt.

SARA Good morning. Are the children all ready, Miss LeHand?

MISSY Yes, they're all outside.

SARA I don't think they should see their father carried on a stretcher.

HOWE Well—I'm afraid that will be unavoidable.

MISSY Certainly the least excitement for Mr. Roosevelt, the better.

(EDWARD *returns for the last few pieces of luggage.* DR. BENNET *and four men enter. The men are villagers and are dressed in dungarees, sweaters and clothing typical of coastal towns. They are neighbors and friends. The stretcher they carry ishomemade, crude but serviceable*)

HOWE Good morning, men.

FRANKLIN CALDER (*The leader of the group*) Morning. (*Glancing at* SARA *and* MISSY) Ma'am. Ma'am.

SARA Good morning, Captain.

(*The others nod as they remove their hats*)

MISSY Morning.

HOWE I want to thank all of you sincerely for what you have done and are doing.

CALDER No thanks expected, Mr. Howe.

BENNET Look at the stretcher they made. They've even fixed up a back rest.

HOWE Wonderful—really.

(*The men nod their acknowledgment of* HOWE'S *compliment*)

BENNET We'd better move.

(*As the men are directed upstairs by* DR. BENNET, *who precedes them,* EDWARD *exits.* SARA *looks upstairs apprehensively.* HOWE *is sympathetic to her feelings.* ELEANOR *comes down from upstairs. She carries her large handbag, an extra blanket, and a soft felt hat of* FDR'S. *She is tired, and, like the others, tense but contained*)

MEN (*Passing* ELEANOR) Good morning, ma'am.

ELEANOR Good morning. Good morning, Captain Calder. (*Handing* MISSY *an envelope*) Missy—these are some get-well letters which came in before you arrived. I've had no time to answer.

MISSY (*With a smile*) Small wonder.

(*She puts the envelope in her briefcase*)

ELEANOR (*Turns to* MISSY) Are the children all ready?

MISSY Yes. Mademoiselle is with them—near the dock.
SARA Do you think the children should see this?
ELEANOR They may have to learn to see a lot of things.
SARA Perhaps. But it may be a shock, particularly to the younger ones.
HOWE They'll get older.
SARA (*To* HOWE, *shocked*) Mr. Howe.
HOWE I didn't mean that the way it sounded. But I think Eleanor's right.
SARA I believe you and I have varying opinions of what is right and wrong.
ELEANOR Frankly, I suppose the children are excited by it. They'd probably love to be carried to a boat on a stretcher.
SARA Furthermore, Franklin's arrival at Eastport should not be handled as a circus.
ELEANOR Ma*ma,* Franklin is a man of some reputation. We can't give an imperial order and ask the crowds to disperse.
HOWE I think you must agree, Mrs. Roosevelt, that it is far better to have the ubiquitous press first find Franklin sitting in his berth in the train, rather than see him carried on a stretcher.
SARA Franklin's day of departure could have been kept secret.
HOWE No, it could not, Mrs. Roosevelt. The newspapermen have been eying Campobello since the day Franklin took ill.

(SARA'S *eyes go to the stair landing*)

ELEANOR (*Crossing to* SARA) Ma*ma,* I too have seen him walk up and down those steps many times.
SARA I do not approve of Franklin being placed on exhibition.
ELEANOR This is not a pleasant time for any of us—particularly Franklin.

(*As* SARA *considers this, the stretcher appears, borne by the four men.* DR. BENNET *guides the men. On the stretcher is* FDR. *He wears a plain dark-blue robe over pajamas and is partly covered by blankets*)

BENNET (*Instructing*) Lift your side—right—that's it. Lower the other side. That's fine. Over the post—

FDR Men, it's a lot easier going down than up. Be grateful for small favors. (SARA, ELEANOR, HOWE *and* MISSY *watch. Their emotions, of course, are guarded, but we sense by their tenseness and reaction what they feel.* SARA *grips her pocketbook,* MISSY *stands tense, and* ELEANOR, *holding the brim of* FDR'S *hat, fingers it nervously. The men bring the stretcher down safely and set it on the floor. It is clear* FDR *is still a sick man but trying to cover his condition by good humor*) Thank you, gentlemen. The journey was a pleasant one. Where's my missus?

ELEANOR Here, darling.

FDR How about a look around, Doc?

BENNET Yes indeed.

(*With* ELEANOR *and* FRANKLIN CALDER, DR. BENNET *props the back of the stretcher up so that* FDR, *sitting up, can look around. By now, the others in the room are relaxed and cover their nervousness.* DR. BENNET *ushers the men out, indicating that he will call them when ready*)

FDR I tell you there's no other way to travel. (*He digs into his robe, produces a pack of cigarettes and his holder. He peers around*) The place hasn't changed in the month I've been away. (HOWE, *stepping over to him, lights the cigarette for* FDR) Thanks, Louie, my boy. How have you planned the logistics?

HOWE (*Knowing* FDR *loves these shenanigans*) First, the children, Missy, your mother and Eleanor take off for the main dock. That's where the sightseers and the press have congregated. A goodly crowd has gathered and waits eagerly. (*Going into a heavy Dutch burlesque accent*) But, *mein herr,* vhile all der peepuls is vatching da von boat coming on der vater—vee go avay in da odder boat for Eastport und get on der train. *Gut? Nicht wahr?*

FDR Ah, a diversionary tactic.

HOWE Precisely, *mein herr.*

FDR As Assistant Secretary of the Navy I used to rate a seventeen-gun salute. Have you arranged for that?

HOWE You're just an ex-assistant—no guns. You're lucky we got water.

FDR Eleanor, you'd better give me that hat before you tear it to ribbons. (ELEANOR *hands him his hat, which he puts on his head*) How do I look—snappy?

SARA Never better.

FDR Louie, I approve of your plan.

HOWE It's about time. I've been waiting breathlessly.

FDR (*To the others*) He's not fooling. Louie's first love was the theatre. He loves applause.

(LOUIE *executes a neat time-step. The others, in the spirit of it, applaud*)

HOWE (*Looks at his watch*) I hate to break up the party but I think it's about time boat number one got on its way.

MISSY That's me.

FDR Missy, plan on coming to the hospital Thursday morning. Will you have everything typed by then?

MISSY Of course.

FDR Fine. What's the date of that Boy Scout dinner?

MISSY The seventh of November.

FDR We'd better cancel that. I don't know if I'll feel up to making speeches until after the New Year.

(MISSY *nods as she makes notes*)

MISSY Right.

FDR And bring that list of conferences I've had to cancel out because of this ridiculous child's disease, and we'll plan some new dates.

BENNET That's all, Franklin. They have to get started. You can do all that on the train.

SARA We'll be on the way before they bring you out?

FDR I expect so, Ma*ma*.

SARA I'll tell the children that they'll see you on the train.

(SARA *gives* ELEANOR *a half-glance.* FDR *isn't aware of this by-play, but* HOWE *is, as is* MISSY)

FDR Bon voyage!

SARA (*Gives him a kiss*) Bon voyage!

MISSY See you, Boss.

(FDR *waves a farewell as* SARA *and* MISSY *leave*)

FDR The party is thinning out. (*He removes his hat and rubs his hand through his hair absently*) I think I can say the same for my hair. Where's Duffy?

ELEANOR Outside, waiting for us.

FDR Please bring him in, Babs. Let him ride with me.

BENNET There's no harm in it. I'll get him.

(*He exits and* ELEANOR *follows him to the doorway*)

FDR Well, Louie, I must say you look wretched.

HOWE You know how I hate sea travel.

FDR You could get rid of your asthma if you'd breathe in some good sea air and cut out those cigarettes.

HOWE Look who the hell's talking about cigarettes.

FDR I haven't got asthma.

HOWE *Touché!*

(BENNET *arrives with* DUFFY, *a black Scottie, and* ELEANOR *carries him in and hands him to* FDR)

FDR Hello, Duffy, you old pirate. Say, you're getting fat. One of these days I'll have to take you for a long run in the woods.

(*There is a pause. Does* FDR *mean it? Does he think he will be able to? We don't know. Now* EDWARD *enters*)

EDWARD We're ready to go, Mrs. Roosevelt.

BENNET It's time.

ELEANOR (*She digs into her bag for some keys*) There are the keys, Edward. Now you lock up on the return trip.

EDWARD Yes, ma'am. I'll get everything shipshape.

ELEANOR Drain the pipes.

EDWARD And board up the windows till next season.

HOWE I'll walk you to the boat, Eleanor. See you on the dock, Franklin.

(HOWE *exits*)

EDWARD Good-bye, Mr. Roosevelt—and good luck to you, sir.

FDR Thank you, Edward.

(EDWARD *leaves*)

BENNET I'll be with the men, Franklin.

(*He leaves*)

ELEANOR Franklin, I'm to cross with the children.

FDR How's the sea today?

ELEANOR Choppy.

FDR West wind?

ELEANOR That's right.

FDR Is Calder handling my boat?

ELEANOR Yes.

FDR (*Reassuring her*) He's a good man.

ELEANOR I'll call the men, dear.

(ELEANOR *walks to the door to wave the men in. As she leaves,* FDR *sags back against the stretcher. Suddenly we are aware of what a strain this has been for him. He looks weary and tired. He lowers his head and then looks up and looks around the room as a wave of memories flood his mind. His hands drop in fatigue and pain, and he releases his hat, which he has been holding. It falls out of his reach. As he attempts to retrieve it we see that he cannot move his back. His fingers stretch for it but he cannot touch it. He breathes heavily.* ELEANOR *returns and, realizing what has happened, hands him his hat.* DR. BENNET *returns with the men, and* FDR *pulls himself together*)

ELEANOR Are you sure that you can manage this trip?

FDR I'm going to make a damn good try.

(FDR *puts his hat on and puts his cigarette holder in his*

mouth in that familiar perky fashion. He holds DUFFY *in one arm. The men reach down and lift the stretcher*)

BENNET All right, men—

(*They start out*)

FDR Gentlemen—thank you for the sedan chair. (*As he is carried out*) By gosh—I feel like the Caliph of Bagdad.

THE CURTAIN FALLS

ACT TWO

Scene One

Scene: It is May, 1922. Curtain reveals the downstairs living room of the New York house on Sixty-fifth Street. Like all the Roosevelt homes, it is warm and tasteful and not at all pretentious.

At rise: FDR *is seen stage right, sitting in one of his small kitchen chairs, converted for use as a wheel chair. He is working on some stamps. On the couch is a model of a sail-boat on which* FDR *has been previously working. He drops some of the stamps, then scoots his chair over to a desk on the other side of the room. He picks up from the desk a gadget with an extension arm which when expanded reaches to the floor. He scoots back to the table and, using the gadget, picks up the stamps. He is already quite expert at wheeling his chair. His attitude is far from cheerful. After he works away for a moment or two,* MISSY *enters from the office next to the living room. She carries a sheaf of letters for* FDR *to sign. She, like the others who are close to* FDR, *is sensitive to his moods, and so she is aware* FDR *is having one of his rare bad days.*

MISSY Sorry, Boss, to interrupt, but you wanted to get these off. (FDR *pushes his stamps away and places the letters on the table*) I still have the letters Louie dictated—I hope to finish them before I go tonight.
(FDR *starts to read*)

MISSY In the letter to the Park Commission, I may have

made a mistake. I couldn't remember whether you said *sixty* thousand trees or *sixteen.*

FDR (*Not looking up*) Sixteen.

MISSY Good. That's what I typed in.

FDR My enunciation is usually precise enough to make the distinction between six*teen* and six*ty*.

MISSY No criticism, Mr. R. My hearing must be failing.

FDR (*Handing her a letter*) You'll have to correct this It's *Pine*henge Farm—not *Pin*henge. (MISSY *takes it, looks at it.* FDR *continues, referring to the next letter*) Missy, this rough draft of the letter to Cordell Hull should be triple-spaced.

MISSY (*Ruefully*) I'm having a good day.

FDR Well, if you must know, I'm having a perfectly wretched day.

MISSY I'm sorry.

FDR I can't wear the leg braces because they don't fit—and I don't know why I'm going all the way to Boston to get new ones that also won't fit. And I'm fed up with all those friendly hints that come in the mail—everything from ancient nostrums to brand new gadgets invented by people all the way from Keokuk to Zanzibar.

MISSY They all want to help—not hurt.

FDR Oh, Missy—stop it. No sweetness and light today—please. (*Refers to the letters*) Take them away.

(ELEANOR *comes in. She has been upstairs. She carries books and mail*)

ELEANOR Franklin, I've talked to Regan. He's arranged for the railroad trip to Boston.

FDR (*Almost challengingly*) I may not go to Boston.

(*He wheels over to the desk.* ELEANOR *and* MISSY *exchange a glance.* ELEANOR *gets the message*)

ELEANOR You don't have to go until Friday. You can decide by then. (*She hands the mail to* FDR) There's a cheery letter from Jimmy. And one from Woodrow Wilson.

FDR (*He is reading the letter*) I'm glad to read that Jimmy anticipates good marks. (*Reads on*) Well, that's a relief—he loves Groton. I'm sure Groton is relieved, too. (*He picks up the one from Wilson.* ELEANOR *is putting the books away.* MISSY *glances at the letters she has picked up from* FDR'S *table.* FDR *reads Wilson's letter, his mood changing a bit*) It's an extremely considerate note. (*Reads*) "I am indeed delighted to hear you are getting so well, and so confidently, and I shall try and by generous enough not to envy you. I hope that your generous labors in behalf of the Wilson Foundation have not overtaxed you, and you are certainly to be congratulated on your successful leadership in the complicated and difficult undertaking." That's really quite thoughtful of him.

ELEANOR You have done a lot for the Foundation.

FDR Only because I believe in it. Either we develop some plan for world peace and order or the world will chop itself into bits.

MISSY Excuse me, Boss—may I get on with the rest of these?

FDR (*Cheerire*) On your way, Missy. Later I want to do another draft of that letter to Cordell Hull. What I've got is too obscure. (MISSY *nods and starts to exit*)—Sixteen— (FDR *grins apologetically.* MISSY *understands—exits*) I was apologizing for having lost my temper.

ELEANOR I had a rather tense chore a few minutes ago. I had to let the upstairs maid go. She complained so much about all the work she had to do—most of which she never did anyway.

FDR (*Crossing to her*) Sorry, Babs. You've had a big turnover on maids this year. It's been a busy household.

ELEANOR It's been a nice household.

FDR (*Rolling his chair about the room and putting some of his things away*) I'm getting expert with this chair. It moves easily. See that. (*He executes a sharp turn*)

We have to get a couple like this for Hyde Park. None of those conventional invalid wheel chairs. (*He takes another turn or two in the chair*) This exercise is stimulating—takes some of the loneliness away.

(*He crosses to the couch and picks up a sailboat*)

ELEANOR Loneliness, dear?

FDR Invalidism— (*Quickly*) —even temporary—is very lonely. I remember reading: "A sick man wishes to be where he is not." (*After a moment*) When you're forced to sit a lot—and watch others move about—you feel apart—lonely—because you can't get up and pace around. I find myself irritated when people come in here and parade all over the place. I have to keep exercising self-control to prevent screaming at them to sit down—quiet down—stand still.

ELEANOR I'll remember.

FDR You're quiet and restful.

ELEANOR (*She continues straightening out the room*) I am just tired. Is Louie in his room?

FDR He said he was going out for a feel of the pulse of the city. What he really means—he's going out to buy newspapers. Loves the Teapot Dome stories. Adores political scandals—if they embarrass Republicans.

ELEANOR (*A moment*) Franklin—are there other things I should know that you haven't told me?

FDR (*Lightly*) You mean like about Louie going out to get the papers?

ELEANOR I mean about your—loneliness.

FDR (*Not joking now*) Often when you're alone, certain fears seek you out and hunt for a place in your mind. Well, you know, I've always had a small fear about fire. Since this— (*Indicates his legs*) that fear sometimes overwhelms me. I've nightmares about being trapped and unable to move. I've been practicing crawling so I can be sure that in case of fire I could get to a window by myself—or to a door or a flight of steps.

ELEANOR I didn't know you had been—crawling.

FDR I've been trying—and I can do fairly well—by now. But soon I'll be back on my feet. The back muscles came around—and so will the legs.

ELEANOR Of course they will.

FDR (*Suddenly turns to the ship model and lifts it in one hand*) Do you like her?

ELEANOR She's lovely.

FDR She'll really sail, you know—she's not just a toy. (*He places it back on the couch*) I miss the sea. (*He wheels his chair close to* ELEANOR *and takes her hand as his words come wrenching out of him*) Eleanor, I must say this—once to someone. Those first few days at Campobello when this started, I had despair—deep, sick despair. It wasn't the pain—there was much more of that later on when they straightened the tendons in my legs. No, not the pain—it was the sense that perhaps I'd never get up again. Like a crab lying on its back. I'd look down at my fingers and exert every thought to get them to move. I'd send down orders to my legs and my toes—they didn't obey.

ELEANOR (*As he halts his speech for a moment, she goes to him, her head on his lap*) Darling—

FDR I turned to my faith, Babs—for strength to endure. I feel I have to go through this fire for some reason. Eleanor, it's a hard way to learn humility—but I've been learning by crawling. I know what is meant—you must learn to crawl before you can walk.

(*They embrace. After a moment, the front door is heard slamming and* FDR *straightens as* ANNA'S *voice is heard*)

ANNA'S VOICE Mother—Mother—Mother!

ELEANOR (*Pulls away from* FDR *and sits down, trying to compose herself*) I'm here, Anna—and do quiet down.

ANNA (*Appearing*) Oh—how are you Father?

FDR Sis—

ANNA Mother, I have to talk to you. It's important.

ELEANOR Anna, it will have to wait a little while. I have other important things.

FDR (*Starting out*) This chamber is yours, ladies. *Au revoir.*

ELEANOR (*She starts after him*) Franklin—

FDR Eleanor—I need the exercise. See you later, Sis.

(*He rolls out. After he is gone,* ELEANOR *starts to straighten up the room*)

ANNA Mother, I must talk to you.

ELEANOR Yes, dear. So you told me.

ANNA I can't talk to you on the run.

ELEANOR Anna, you can't make up all the rules. (*Continues to straighten up*) I'm listening.

ANNA It's about my room.

ELEANOR What about your room?

ANNA I cannot understand why I've been moved upstairs into a little cubbyhole—and why Mr. Howe has been given my large room—

ELEANOR That change was made weeks ago—Why has it taken you so long to question it?

ANNA Because I accepted the change without thinking of it.

ELEANOR Oh, you did?

ANNA Yes—but only yesterday—when Granny was here —she asked me the question—direct—and I could not give her a clear answer.

ELEANOR Then, Anna, I suggest you tell Granny to ask me.

(*We hear the sound of the front door being opened*)

ANNA Mother, it seems to me—

ELEANOR It seems to me you're behaving badly.

ANNA I fail to understand why Mr. Howe should—

HOWE'S VOICE (*Offstage*) Hello—

(LOUIE HOWE *enters. He is carrying a stack of newspapers*)

HOWE Ladies. May I recount the happenings on the Appian Way?

ANNA Mother, please—

ELEANOR Anna—I will not discuss this with you now.

HOWE I'm sorry. I'll go.

ANNA (*Her dignity flying high*) There's no need. Mother and I have concluded our conversation, thank you. Excuse me, please.

(*She exits*)

HOWE Marie Antoinette could not have been more noble on her way to the guillotine.

ELEANOR (*Shaking her head*) It's a busy house, Louie, very busy.

HOWE A busy world. (*Rattling through the papers*) There's an item I want you to hear, Eleanor. The Chicago *Tribune*. (*Reading*) "The New York Democratic Party considers Franklin D. Roosevelt its number one choice for Governor."

ELEANOR Oh, Louie, those items you manage to squeeze into the newspapers are good reading but they're pointless.

HOWE They're good for his morale—and mine. (ELEANOR *still has her mind on the previous scene with* ANNA. LOUIE *senses this*) Your morale looks like it's been hit by a Mack Truck.

ELEANOR I have, on occasion, felt far cheerier, Louie.

HOWE You need a good dinner at Mouquin's—I'll take you out tonight. Clear your head with a bottle of vin rosé and some snails.

ELEANOR Perhaps.

HOWE You're probably scared stiff about that speech you have to read. That's what's wearing you down.

ELEANOR Louie, I'll be no good at it. I can't lecture. I giggle at all the wrong times. I can't control my voice—when I shout I think I'm whispering.

HOWE Eleanor, this work has to be done. You are, for

a while, Franklin's eyes, ears—and legs. You must go places he can't go.

ELEANOR I'm certain I'll be awful.

HOWE You are in the hands of Professor Howe—wizard of the spoken word. Seechless mummies given the eloquence of Demosthenes. You don't have to make anything up. Just read it.

ELEANOR I don't like to read a speech.

HOWE Do you think the Gettysburg Address was ad lib?

ELEANOR (*Tired and worn*) I'll try—Leave it at that.

(FDR *suddenly scoots in from the other room*)

FDR (*Seeing* LOUIE) Ah—the pulse taker.

HOWE (*Indicating the papers*) The pulse is good from Maine to California. The nation still endures under Harding. And Teapot Dome is boiling.

FDR (*With finger pointed, as though making a speech*) "Scandals or no scandals—this country will be enduring Republican presidents for a long time unless we rip the barnacles off the Democratic organization and make it a progressive and modern political party." I've just finished writing all that to Cordell Hull.

HOWE Eleanor, that's a good theme for your speech.

FDR My poor retiring Eleanor, being driven into the wilds of the political jungle. Oh, Babs, I invited Marvin and Emmett to dinner—I've got to keep one finger in my lawyer's pie.

ELEANOR We're not very fancy tonight.

FDR My law partners aren't very fussy about their food.

ELEANOR It will be all right.

(*She starts out*)

HOWE Of course it will. I plan to take your wife to Mouquin's tonight for some escargots.

(ELEANOR *is out*)

FDR Eleanor hates rich food. She's too much of a lady to tell you.

HOWE She'll go. It'll do her good to get out of this place

for a while. And now, my friend, we have work to do. (*He searches through desk for a pencil*) I have here a list of your various clubs, organizations, federations, fraternities, unions, societies, associations and groups. You and I are going through this list and do a little job of editing.

FDR (*Instantly on guard—irritated*) What exactly have you in mind?

HOWE The doctors say you're doing too much. I'm merely their obedient servant.

FDR (*Changing the subject*) Let me see the list. (*Looks at it*) You have crossed off almost every organization in which I'm genuinely interested.

HOWE Franklin, you have too many interests. You've got to cut down.

FDR I will not discontinue my work in the Boy Scouts. Their aims are damned important.

HOWE What the hell are you working for—scoutmaster?

FDR I'll decide what goes—and what doesn't.

HOWE All right, Franklin, I'll give you the Boy Scouts—but something else has to go. There's a big breeze blowing and we've got to trim sails—the off-year elections. And you've got to keep your hand in.

FDR I won't be able to move around too much for a while.

HOWE But we can write. We can let people know that a man named Roosevelt has opinions, ideas and convictions.

FDR (*Looks at the list*) All right, we can get rid of some of those.

(MISSY *comes in*)

MISSY Mr. Brimmer is here.

HOWE Who's Mr. Brimmer?

FDR It's a deal I'm working on.

HOWE Another?—Oh!—Franklin!

FDR (*To* MISSY) Send him in.

HOWE Missy, who is this Brimmer?

MISSY (*As she exits*) The Boss will tell you.

HOWE Is this another of your imaginative business deals?

FDR Louie, stop heckling me. Just sit quiet.

HOWE I know how you dislike my pacing about.

(HOWE *takes his perch on the couch and remains motionless until indicated.* MISSY *enters with* MR. BRIMMER, *a husky, well-tailored gentleman.* MISSY *exits through the hall door*)

BRIMMER Good day, Mr. Roosevelt. How are you feeling?

FDR Coming along, Mr. Brimmer. Mr. Howe.

(HOWE *waves a greeting*)

BRIMMER Mr. Howe, it's a pleasure.

FDR I've had a long day, Mr. Brimmer—I wonder if—

(*He leaves off.* BRIMMER *understands*)

BRIMMER I have the full picture ready for presentation. Beginning with the estimates on the construction of the four dirigibles as you requested.

HOWE Dirigibles?

FDR Go ahead, Mr. Brimmer.

(MR. BRIMMER *goes ahead. He is a talker and a walker, and his pacing, it is abvious, gets on* FDR'S *nerves, since he is forced to follow* BRIMMER'S *actions. As he begins to talk, a telephone begins to ring in the office offstage*)

BRIMMER The cost of construction, as you will see, will be cheaper if the dirigibles are built in Germany. Airports and masts could be constructed in suitable locations in Chicago and New York for a daily service, at comparatively low cost. Also included, on this sheet, is the amount of helium gas needed—the cost—the construction—items for storage tanks, et cetera, et cetera, et cetera. Also listed, the approximate cost of personnel to run the ships on a daily basis—the airport crew—ticket agencies—and an advertising allotment, based on minimal efforts until the service catches the public fancy.

FDR (*Trying to stop the flow*) It will catch on.

BRIMMER (*Nothing will stop him*) I agree—absolutely—

I agree. Charted for you are various hours suggested for best air time in connection with commuter trains, auto traffic and accessibility. Also—ideas for campaigns—all to be studied—digested—assimilated and collated—all to be—

(*The phone in the other room has continued to ring since* BRIMMER *started his long speech. This ringing, combined with* BRIMMER'S *walking has made* FDR *edgy.* HOWE, *who has not moved a muscle till now, gets up to answer the phone*)

FDR (*Exploding*) Louie, why the hell are you always moving around?

HOWE (*Stops, surprised, but knowing in an instant*) I'm nervous.

(*He retreats quietly to the corner. The phone in the next room stops ringing*)

FDR Mr. Brimmer—leave all this here with me. I'll study it in detail—and be in touch with you.

BRIMMER We're prepared to seek underwriting—

FDR We can talk of that later. Thank you, Mr. Brimmer. I'm afraid you'll have to excuse me.

BRIMMER Of course, I understand. I'll leave these estimates. (*To* HOWE) It's been a great pleasure, Mr. Howe.

(*Again the airy acknowledgment from* HOWE)

HOWE Thank you, sir.

MR. BRIMMER And good day to you, Mr. Roosevelt.

FDR Good-bye, Mr. Brimmer. (BRIMMER *is out*) Why the devil didn't someone answer the phone?

HOWE I don't know. I also don't know about dirigibles. What's this scheme?

FDR A damn practical one.

HOWE From New York to Chicago?

FDR For a starter. We can build this into a transcontinental line—eventually nonstop, coast to coast.

HOWE Well—

FDR Don't wet-blanket this, Louie. It could mean a fortune. (HOWE *nods—not a word*) And I'm sorry I yelled. Brimmer was driving me mad. Prowling back and forth—like an awkward tiger.

HOWE With a little helium I'll bet he could get to Chicago. (FDR *laughs—breaking his irritation and bad spell.* ELEANOR *enters*)

ELEANOR That must have been a good one.

FDR Louie's a monster.

HOWE Madam, your husband is planning to go into the lighter-than-aircraft business—which proves he has a lighter-than-air head.

FDR Caution, my friend, is the refuge of cowards.

ELEANOR And your refuge, Franklin, is bed. You must rest before dinner.

FDR Very well. (*Hesitates*) Today—I'm going upstairs on my own. (*He wheels to the couch*) Out of this room and up the steps on my own. (*To* HOWE) —Without helium. This is something I've been planning for quite a few days.

(*He pulls himself out of the chair and onto the couch*)

ELEANOR (*Anxiously*) Franklin—perhaps it would be wiser if you waited—

FDR No—now is the time. I can crawl, and I'm going to prove it.

HOWE Franklin, it's been a long day.

FDR I'm going to crawl upstairs to bed. (*He gets on the floor*) Stand back, Louie. Bring the chair. Watch me go. (*Sitting on his haunches and using his hands to move his body, he slides backward on the floor and toward the door. As he does,* ELEANOR *and* HOWE *stand frozen.* FDR *continues speaking*) This method of locomotion I shall call the Roosevelt slide: half waltz, half foxtrot. Easy on the feet, placing all the wear and tear on the derrière. (*He is near the door*) Well, Eleanor? Good?

ELEANOR Wonderful, Franklin, wonderful.

FDR See you later.

(*He is out. After a moment,* LOUIE *wheels the chair out of the room, following* FDR. ELEANOR *stands for a moment, then sinks into a chair. She passes a tired hand over her face. She is about to crack, but manages to hold on as the front door is heard to open*)

SARA'S VOICE (*Offstage*) Good day, everybody—

(*Also heard are* FRANKLIN JR.'S *and* JOHNNY'S *voices*)

FRANKLIN JR.'S VOICE Mummy—Mummy—

(ELEANOR *quickly composes herself.* SARA *enters with* FRANKLIN JR. *and* JOHNNY, *who cross over to* ELEANOR)

ELEANOR Hello, boys. Ma*ma.*

SARA I picked them up at school. Saved Mademoiselle a trip. And I wanted to try out their French.

ELEANOR *Les leçons, comment vont elles?*

JOHNNY *Très bien.*

FRANKLIN JR. *Absolument. Très bien.*

JOHNNY Will you read us the end of yesterday's story?

FRANKLIN JR. You promised.

ELEANOR All right. Wash up and come back. I'll keep my promise.

(*The children go—in a hurry*)

SARA Is Franklin in the study?

ELEANOR No, Ma*ma,* he's upstairs. He went up by himself. Crawling.

SARA (*Shocked*) Crawling?

ELEANOR Yes. It's something he's been practicing by himself. He surprised me today by giving me a demonstration.

SARA But that's too much of a strain. He tries too hard—that's bad for him.

ELEANOR Ma*ma*—how can it be bad for him? It makes him independent.

SARA He can't be seen by the children moving around like that—he can't.

ELEANOR You'll have to discuss that with him. I won't. I can't.

SARA Very well, Eleanor. I will speak to him.

ELEANOR Ma*ma,* please allow Franklin the freedom of his own mind in this matter.

SARA He must not be permitted to place such a strain on his body.

ELEANOR Ma*ma,* he's not a child.

SARA Eleanor, perhaps there are times when a son will speak only to his mother.

(JOHNNY *and* FRANKLIN JR. *come bursting back in*)

JOHNNY Come on, Mummy. Sit down, Granny.

SARA No, darlings, I can't. I have to speak to your father. (*She goes.* ELEANOR *wearily moves to a bookcase, chooses the book she was reading, and sits down.* JOHNNY *and* FRANKLIN JR. *sit near her.* ELEANOR *is tired and the children see it—but of course don't take it seriously*)

FRANKLIN JR. Mommy, you look tired.

ELEANOR (*Searching for her place in the book*) I am a little, darling.

JOHNNY Mommy, who is older—you or Granny?

(ELEANOR *looks at* JOHNNY)

FRANKLIN JR. Granny is—you dummy!

ELEANOR (*Beginning to read—trying to fight her emotions*) "And today being Wednesday, the merry old shoemaker knew that he could only work on the blue shoes which were the only ones that were quiet and still on Wednesday. On all the other days the blue shoes would run and play with all the other brightly colored shoes, but on Wednesday they were still and obedient. 'Oh, my,' said the shoemaker, 'what beautiful blue shoes.' And he thought to himself that he would make them even more beautiful. So he took his hammer and nails and sat down—and merrily began to hammer away. . . ."

(*Suddenly, unexpectedly and uncontrollably,* ELEANOR

begins to cry. She drops the book, turns away from the children and breaks into heartbreaking sobs. The children, stunned, look at her. MISSY *enters—sees the scene and rushes the children out.* ELEANOR, *left alone, continues to cry. After a few moments,* LOUIE HOWE *appears. It is obvious he has been told, because he enters quietly, expecting to see* ELEANOR. *He closes the door behind him)*

HOWE Eleanor, if I can do anything—

ELEANOR (*Shouting through her tears*) No—nothing—and, Louie, I hate Mouquin's and I hate snails and I'm not going.

HOWE Nobody ever lived who is more entitled to a good cry.

(ELEANOR *stops, the well drying. She wipes her eyes—her nose. She straightens her hair)*

ELEANOR I must have terrified the children. (*She gets hold of herself*) I won't ever do that again. Not ever. (*She exits as*

THE CURTAIN FALLS

Scene Two

Scene: We are once again in the New York house living room. In one corner of the room, next to the couch, are a pair of crutches and FDR'S *leg braces. It is January, 1923. Friday. Late afternoon.*

At rise: On the floor are ELLIOTT, FRANKLIN JR. *and* FDR. *A wrestling match which has been in progress, accompanied by yells and groans from the two boys, is finally ended when* FDR, *holding* FRANKLIN JR. *with his powerful right hand and* ELLIOTT *with his equally powerful left, swings them both on their backs and holds them there against their will.*

FDR Say uncle!

ELLIOTT (*Still struggling*) Not me!

FDR (*Applying pressure*) Just for that, you young lout—you will now have to say Uncle—Hiram—Joshua—Lafcadio—Turntable.

ELLIOTT Ouch.

(FRANKLIN JR., *assuming* FDR *is occupied with* ELLIOTT, *has made a move to get away*)

FDR Oh, no, you don't.

(*Now* FDR *applies further pressure on* FRANKLIN JR., *without relaxing any on* ELLIOTT)

FRANKLIN JR. Uncle.

FDR Uncle who?

FRANKLIN JR. Uncle—Hiram—Joshua—Lafcadio—

FDR Turntable.

FRANKLIN JR. Turntable!

(FDR *frees* FRANKLIN JR., *who rises, rubbing his muscles*)

ELLIOTT (*Quickly*) I'm outnumbered. Uncle.

FDR Uncle who?

ELLIOTT Uncle Hiram Joshua Lafcadio Turntable.

FDR (*Releases* ELLIOTT, *then sits up on the floor*) Next time I shall improvise a few more names for our fictitious uncle. (*Extends his arms*) Up we go. (*In a manner indicating this is standard procedure,* FRANKLIN JR. *whips over the wheel chair, turns it into correct position, then he and* ELLIOTT *reach out, grab* FDR'S *legs*) One—two—three. (*They lift.* FDR, *timing the moves, grabs the chair with his hands, and in a moment he is sitting in his chair, smiling and confident*) You two are getting harder to handle. Soon I'll have to draw out my heavy artillery.

ELLIOTT For a minute we almost had you, Pa.

FDR Delusions of grandeur. (ELLIOTT *and* FDR *laugh*)

Boys—today I felt a little more power from my legs. (*Points to his thighs*) Down these heavy frontal muscles—the quadriceps. (*Illustrating on his body*) The bad spots we're still working on are in these thick muscles that run from the hips and buttocks—the gluteus maximus—and then these ham-string muscles on the back of the knees—the gastrocs. Without those I can't get balance or purchase.

FRANKLIN JR. I like the name of those thick muscles.

FDR The gluteus maximus—right there.

FRANKLIN JR. That's it—gluteus maximus.

FDR Once I get them all going at the same time, you'd better start running. (MISSY *enters with the inevitable stack of letters and her notes, together with a framed object*) Enter Missy. Vamoose, sons. Your father is a busy man. I'll give you another lesson tomorrow.

FRANKLIN JR. That's a promise?

FDR That's a promise.

(*They start out*)

ELLIOTT (*To* FRANKLIN JR.) I'll race you upstairs.

(*They dash out.* FDR *by now has rolled his chair to his desk. He is already reading and signing letters* MISSY *has placed there for him.* MISSY *hands* FDR *the framed object*)

MISSY This came in by messenger.

FDR (*Examines the object*) A lovely job of printing. (*He looks up at* MISSY) I sometimes regret having told the newspapers one of my favorite poems was "Invictus."

MISSY This is the fourteenth copy you have received.

FDR (*Examining it*) By all odds the most beautiful. I'd like it hung in my bedroom. (*He hands it back to* MISSY, *who places it on the table*) Missy, these letters to the polio victims. They don't sound stuffy, do they?

MISSY No. They're warm and kind.

FDR (*Laughs as he signs the letter*) McAdoo is so excited over the success of the Democrats in the off-year election, he's already started counting the votes for himself in nineteen twenty-four.

MISSY He can taste the nomination.

FDR He's in for a large and bitter disappointment. It's going to be Al Smith.

(*He proceeds with the other letters.* HOWE *and* ELEANOR *come in.* HOWE *is unwrapping himself from a muffler, heavy coat and gloves.* ELEANOR *is dressed warmly, but not heavily*)

ELEANOR We're home.

FDR Welcome back!

HOWE You wouldn't be so damned cheerful if you had to go out in this weather. (*Looks at* ELEANOR) How the hell she stands it, I don't know.

ELEANOR It's lovely and clear outside.

HOWE (*A groan*) Oh, my God. It's freezing. (*He notices the copy of "Invictus" on the table. He picks it up*) "Invictus." Another rendition of that sticky verse. Franklin, the devotion of your admirers is stifling.

(*He puts it back on the table*)

FDR (*To* ELEANOR) How did it go?

(ELEANOR *points to* HOWE, *indicating he has the answer*)

HOWE Your wife has almost rid herself of those ridiculous giggles, and she even manages to make a point now and then with some measure of effectiveness.

FDR (*Interpreting*) You mean—she was good.

HOWE Adequate.

ELEANOR Thank you, teacher.

MISSY Was it a good turnout, Mrs. R?

ELEANOR Excellent. About three hundred women.

HOWE Five hundred. That's the figure I gave the press.

MISSY Five hundred is a lot of people.

ELEANOR So is three hundred. They listened and signed pledges to work. Oh, Franklin, I read your statement on the League of Nations to the Council and it received genuinely warm applause.

FDR Good. Between your speeches, Howe's shenanigans and my statements, we're keeping my head above water.

HOWE (*Standing up*) Speaking of water—I received a letter this morning from one of your associates in the late lamented lobster business.

FDR (*A wince*) A jarring intrusion, as usual.

HOWE He wishes to know whether you have been permanently discouraged by the stubborn refusal of the lobster market to raise its prices.

FDR Losing twenty-six thousand dollars in a lobster business is hardly a joking matter.

HOWE A bit of a pinch—one might say.

FDR To further add to your merriment—this is a letter from the Montracol Oil Company—

(*He hands the letter to* HOWE)

HOWE Oil company—huh?

FDR Good?

HOWE (*As he reads the letter*) Ah—that's very good. You now have two thousands shares—of gas.

ELEANOR What's this one, Franklin?

FDR This has to do with the investment I made in oil. They didn't strike oil—they found gas. And there's no immediate market in gas.

HOWE Think how you could have combined this gas discovery with the dirigibles. (*Starts to the door*) See you for dinner.

(*He exits, coughing and smoking*)

MISSY He'll probably keep coughing and smoking till he's ninety—but sometimes he worries me.

ELEANOR Franklin, if the incense he burns in his room at night gives him some peace from coughing, why don't you let him burn it here? I wouldn't mind.

FDR I would. He'd have the entire place smelling like a bawdy house.

ELEANOR (*Shocked*) Franklin!

FDR Ma*ma* made remarks about it this morning—not quite as indelicate—but pointed. (*To* MISSY) Let's call it a day, Missy. You're going to the country for the week end?

MISSY That's me. Twenty above zero and I'm off for a holiday.

FDR Have fun.

ELEANOR Good night, Missy. I hope it warms up.

MISSY Thank you. Good night, Boss—Mrs. R.

(FDR *waves her a good night as she exits*)

FDR Really went well?

(ELEANOR *nods, then listens*)

ELEANOR The house is quiet. The children—are they all home?

FDR Can't tell the players without a score card, ma'am. (*Counts on his fingers*) Anna is in her room, reading. Johnny is being read to by Mademoiselle. Jimmy ostensibly is still at Groton. Elliott and Franklin have retired to lick their wounds after a wrestling match.

ELEANOR I can't stop you from doing that—but do be careful. Your legs haven't healed completely from that last fall.

FDR They're coming along fine. (*He wheels over to the couch*) All four of them. I spent some time on those today. Soon it will be canes. First I want to handle those crutches without braces—or vice versa.

ELEANOR Of course.

FDR (*Smiles at her*) Of course, you say. As if you mean it.

(*He pulls himself onto the couch from the chair*)

ELEANOR I do mean it. It's just that I don't want you to rush and do any damage. You've plenty of time, Franklin.

FDR I've been learning something about time. Being unable to rush things along has given me patience. Patience, I think, gives a better sense of when to try for the brass ring—or when to enjoy the ride without grasping for anything.

ELEANOR Oh, yes, Franklin.

FDR Eleanor, when I first took ill I planned and dreamed about a bright future—half believing, half pretending, like a child on a carousel imagining himself a general in command of armies. But for weeks now something has been changing inside of me. I don't know when it began. What minute or day or hour—but today I was suddenly aware that, despite everything, I feel sure-footed.

ELEANOR "A patient man shall bear for a time and afterward joy shall spring up unto him."

FDR Shall spring up unto us. I sometimes wonder how many of your cousins are still confounded that we married. Do you think they still consider me a feather duster?

ELEANOR (*Smiling*) Darling— (*Then, teasing*) There are undoubtedly some of your family who still believe that you didn't get much of a bargain.

FDR I imagine they're reconciled to the truth that I did better than you did. Actually, I think Ma*ma's* only objection to you was that your family said *Rusevelt* while we said *Roosevelt.*

ELEANOR Could not a *Rusevelt* by any other name be just as sweet?

FDR (*Laughing*) Not to Ma*ma*. Thinking back, I can hardly blame some of your relatives. I had a lot to learn, but I didn't want anyone to know it. So the truth is I was an awfully mean cuss in those early days.

ELEANOR Never mean. Perhaps inexperienced.

FDR I was snobbish—haughty. I had the Roosevelt name —the Teddy tradition— (*Imitates Teddy's broad smile*) —sauced in with ambition. (*He pats her hand*) I had to learn something about the human heart. (*He smiles at her*) I've been learning.

ELEANOR You have always known a great deal about my heart.

FDR Cousin—wife—dearest.

ELEANOR (*Holding his hands and looking directly at him*) Franklin, when I was an awkward adolescent I felt unloved and unwanted—with you I have always felt needed—wanted—and that's a blessing for which—

(*The door suddenly opens and* ANNA *comes in*)

ANNA Hello, Mother. How are you, Father.

FDR (*Sharply*) Sis, you've developed an irritating habit of barging into rooms without knocking on doors.

ANNA (*Instantly hurt*) I wanted to put these books back.

FDR Then do it, Sis. (ANNA *is shocked by the harsh greeting and command. She is on the verge of tears. Starting to put the books away, she loses control of them and they clatter to the floor*) That's a stupid, clumsy way to do it.

(ANNA *breaks into tears and runs out of the room.* ELEANOR *and* FDR *exchange a look*)

ELEANOR Rather a sharp attack for a mild offense.

FDR I'll make it up to her later.

ELEANOR I'd best talk to her before she runs to Granny. (*She picks up the books* ANNA *dropped*)

FDR Oh—Ma*ma* is coming for dinner.

ELEANOR Oh—

FDR I do hope she and Louie don't snap at each other. Last time they went as far as the dessert before sharp words.

ELEANOR That's because at the moment Ma*ma* has one objective—Louie, another.

FDR I intend to talk to Ma*ma* about it.

ELEANOR Usually your talks with Ma*ma* last for fifteen minutes—then they become quarrels.

FDR I'll time it. Make sure it's a talk.

(HOWE *enters the room*)

HOWE Change of plans. I spoke to Grace. She's been wondering if I've gotten any uglier. Also, Hartley looked at the postman this morning and wondered if that was Daddy. So I'm going home for dinner. (*He is picking up his muffler, overshoes and hat from where he had left them. He wraps himself up in his clothes, coughing*) Oh, I thought I should report. Anna is seated in the upper hallway, looking as though she has been axed and maced.

ELEANOR I'll try to alleviate the pain. Good night, Louie.

HOWE Good night.

(ELEANOR *leaves.* FDR *looks at* HOWE, *who is huddled in his coat and muffler*)

FDR Can you breathe through all that?

HOWE You know me. If I'm on my feet I assume I'm breathing.

FDR Louie, I'm being reflective.

HOWE Well, that's probably because you're heading for another birthday.

FDR Having made this one, everything after is velvet. (*A moment*) Part of my reflections had to do with you.

HOWE Ah—I'm fired?

FDR (*He takes* HOWE's *hand*) My good friend, as much as you loathe a sentimental moment, thank you for everything.

(HOWE *heads toward the door but pauses at the table on which rests the framed copy of "Invictus." He hesitates, picks up the framed poem, eyes it critically, and looks at* FDR, *who has been watching him all through this.* HOWE *loosens his muffler, takes a mock heroic pose, and then, in a Dutch accent, begins to recite, doing a burlesque rendition*)

HOWE Out of der night that covers me,
Black as der Pit from pole to pole,
I tank whatever Gods may be
For mine unconquerable soul.

In der vell clutch of circumstance
I haf not vinced nor cried aloud.
Under der bludgeonings of chance
Mine head is ploody but unbowed.

(*Slowly, during the next two verses, he drops the accent and begins to recite clearly and beautifully—and we see now that what he has been doing is giving a tribute to* FDR)

Beyond this place of wrath and tears
Looms but the Horror of the shade,
And yet the menace of the years
Finds, and shall find, me unafraid.

It matters not how strait the gate,
How charged with punishments the scroll,
I am the master of my fate:
I am the captain of my soul.

(*As he has finished, he has spoken slowly, movingly.* FDR *looks at him.* HOWE, *when he has finished, looks at* FDR. *There is a pause*) 'Night.

(*He walks out.* ANNA *appears at the doorway, followed by* ELEANOR. ANNA *knocks gently on the door.* FDR *looks up, smiles at her, and then he knocks on the desk in answer*)

ANNA (*Crossing over*) Father.

FDR Hello, Sis. I'm an old grouch.

(*They embrace*)

ANNA Father, I've been selfish.

FDR Now, Sis—no confessionals.

ANNA I have been. (FDR *directs that she bring his wheel chair to him. She does so*) I've been mooning around the house like a child—I felt everybody was keeping me out of rooms. I didn't really understand what you've been going through.

(FDR *pulls himself into the wheel chair*)

ELEANOR I've been to blame for some of that. We should have talked before.

ANNA That's all I ask, Mother. Please talk. Everyone is so occupied—

ELEANOR We'll all try to find more time.

ANNA (*Turning to* FDR) And about my room, Father. I actually prefer it upstairs. (*She smiles*) It's quieter.

FDR Anna dear, most of our blessings come in heavy disguises. (*He moves his chair towards her*) Which, of course, reminds me of a story. 'Way back in the hills of Upstate New York, where a lot of poor tenant farmers live, there was a wise old man whom everybody came to with their troubles. One day a woman came to him with a sad story. She and her husband and four children lived in a one-room cabin and she said it was simply unbearable. The old man asked her if she had any chickens on the farm. When she said she had, he advised her to put the chickens in her house. The next day she came back and said that things were even worse—much worse. Then the old man asked if she owned any cows, and when she said she had two of them, he said: "Put those cows in your house." She did and the next day she came back and said the place was getting to be a horror. So the old man said to her: "You got a horse?" She said she did. "Put the horse into your house." The woman did that, too, and the following day said it was just too much—it was awful. Then the old man said to her, "Well, my dear, now take the horse and those cows and those chickens and get them all out of there—and then come back and tell me how things are." And the next day the woman came back and said: "Thank you, oh, thank you so much. You can't imagine how comfortable we all are at last."

ANNA (*With a warm smile*) Thank you, Father, for not putting the chickens in my room.

FDR (*With a smile*) Sis, in the last two minutes, you've grown ten years wiser.

SARA'S VOICE (*Offstage*) Good evening, everyone—good evening.

ELEANOR We're in here.

SARA'S VOICE (*Offstage*) Franklin, too?

FDR Yes, ma'am. Present.

(SARA *enters, loosening her coat and removing her gloves*)

SARA There you are. Anna, you look lovely. (ANNA *curtsies.* SARA *crosses to* FDR *and kisses him*) It's bitterly cold. Like a frosty night at sea. (*A long look at* FDR) Franklin, you look peaked.

FDR I feel fine.

SARA You're doing too much. I can tell.

FDR (*As a reassuring sign to* ELEANOR, *but talking to* SARA) I won't quarrel with you. If you say I looked peaked—I look peaked.

SARA (*Taking off her things*) Anna, be a darling. (*Hands her gloves and coat and hat and muff to* ANNA) *Tu est très gentille, ma petite.*

ANNA (*Deliberately avoiding any French*) Thank you, Granny.

ELEANOR A cup of tea, Ma*ma?*

SARA I'd love some. (*To* ANNA, *as* ELEANOR *exits*) How are all my darlings?

ANNA (*With a smile*) The boys are as dreadful as ever. And so am I.

SARA Were you outdoors today?

ANNA For a while.

SARA You have to remember to bundle up warm. Overshoes, gloves and something soft and wooly around your neck.

ANNA I know.

SARA Nurse should be very careful with the young ones in weather like this.

ANNA (*After a deep breath*) I heard Mother telling Nurse that this morning.

(*This is possibly the first time* ANNA *has taken this unspoken attitude toward Granny. There is a brief recognition of this by* SARA *and* FDR. *A pause*)

SARA Very sensible.

(ANNA *exits with Granny's things.* ELEANOR *comes in with a tray of tea*)

ELEANOR Cream, Ma*ma?*

SARA Please.

(ELEANOR *pours the tea.* ANNA *returns and stands by*)

ELEANOR Franklin?

FDR No cream—no lemon—four sugars.

SARA Cream is good for you, Franklin.

FDR I don't like cream in my tea.

(ANNA *hands Granny her tea, then hands* FDR *his*)

SARA Thank you, dear.

FDR Sis.

(ELEANOR *hands* ANNA *a cup*)

ANNA Mother, may I have mine upstairs? I want to finish something I've been reading.

ELEANOR Of course.

ANNA Excuse me, Granny, Father—

(*She goes out*)

SARA Anna looks well.

FDR But I look peaked.

SARA Franklin—stop being a tease.

ELEANOR (*Not staying for tea*) I'm afraid I'll have to be excused. I've got to check on the children. We're all eating together tonight and later we're going to read some Shakespeare.

SARA I hope one of the comedies. So much of Shakespeare is too lurid for children.

FDR (*The crier*) Tonight—*As You Like It.*

SARA Lovely.

ELEANOR Excuse me, please.

SARA Of course, dear. (ELEANOR *leaves.* SARA *sips her tea, thinking of the opening gambit. She finds one*) Oh, Franklin, I'm getting some men at Hyde Park to determine how we can electrify the lift. It is, after all, only a large-size dumbwaiter and I—

FDR (*Quickly*) No! (*Perhaps he's been too sharp*) I mean, please don't. The exercise of pulling those ropes is helpful to me. I need it for my arms and shoulders. So, if you're thinking of me—please don't change the dumbwaiter.

SARA I feel you're doing too much, physically.

FDR I wish I could do more. Ma*ma*—it's only my legs that are temporarily bothered. The rest of me is as healthy as ever.

SARA I know that. I know that. I talk to the doctors. They tell me. But sometimes I think that Eleanor, certainly only with motives of deep love, and that ugly little man, push you too rapidly.

FDR I don't think so. Dr. Draper doesn't think so. And please, Ma*ma,* don't refer to Louie Howe any longer with that unpleasant phrase. I've endured it too long as it is.

SARA (*Walking about, genuinely disturbed*) Franklin, your tone of voice is very disturbing to me.

FDR Ma*ma,* if possible, I should like to have a quiet talk with you. I should like not to quarrel. Now, Ma*ma,* I know how upset you've been. This a real wrench for you. But I'm going to get over this—and—if I don't—a big *if* —I shall have to become accustomed to braces and canes and wheel chairs. And so will you.

SARA Oh, Franklin—

FDR Please, let me finish. Louie Howe— (SARA *makes an involuntary grimace*) Ma*ma,* stop that. Louie Howe told me, while I was in the hospital after Campobello, that I had one of two choices. I could lie on my back, be a country squire and write books—*or*—get up and become President of the United States. *Now*—I believe Louie's dreams are far too bright—but I've no intention of retiring to Hyde Park and rusticating.

SARA (*Quietly*) Franklin, when you were a little boy, your dear father took you for a visit to the White House to see President Cleveland.

FDR (*Fidgets*) Mama, I know.

SARA (*Firmly*) Let me finish. And President Cleveland said, "I make a strange wish for you. It is that you may never be President of the United States."

FDR Well, he was playing the odds in wishing that.

SARA Your Cousin Teddy died because of ambitious people around him. Died because he didn't know when to stop—didn't know that you can't make it the same world for all people.

FDR Maybe we can't. But it seems to me that every human has an obligation in his own way to make some little stab at trying.

SARA It's not such a bad world, Franklin—not at all.

FDR I have no personal complaints. I'm lucky. I had rich parents.

SARA Don't be self-conscious about that, Franklin. Advantages of birth should be worn like clothes, with grace and comfort.

FDR (*A familiar tale—and he knows it*) Yes—yes. *Noblesse oblige*. The poor will always be with us. We went through that when I sold the mining stock.

SARA On reflection—you must admit that was a childish gesture.

FDR (*The heat is on*) I would not hang onto stock bringing me an income over the tortured bodies of miners who lived as though they were in the middle ages. These are different times. The attitude of *noblesse oblige* is archaic.

SARA Franklin!

FDR It's another name for indifference.

SARA How dare you! You are talking to your mother.

Even if I were to agree with your romantic political ideas, it would be absurd for you to consider running for public office. The traveling and the speeches would be an enormous strain for you.

FDR At the moment I'm not running for anything—and I won't until I can get around and stand up on my two feet—but that doesn't mean I have to go into hiding.

SARA (*Icily*) I'm not asking you to do that. I'm asking you to be sensible—to take up a permanent residence in Hyde Park where you could be comfortable—where you could use the time for resting and regain your strength.

FDR I love Hyde Park. But I want to use it—not let it bury me.

SARA That's a terrible thing to say.

FDR You know what I mean.

SARA No, Franklin, I do not know what you mean. I only know that your stubbornness is not only your strength but your weakness. And you needn't—

FDR (*Getting angry*) I needn't do a damn thing! I am not going to let myself go down a drain. A bad beating either breaks the stick or the student—Well, I'm not broken. I'm not settling for the life of an ailing invalid. And I will no longer abide implications, innuendos or insinuations that I do so.

SARA I don't want you getting angry. It's not good for you.

FDR (*Heatedly*) It's damn good. For me.

SARA Franklin, I wonder if you truly know what is good for you. You come by your Dutch stubbornness by birth. And, Franklin, some of that Dutch stubbornness is mine —from long association. (*She now becomes firm and dominant*) Franklin, many many years ago, when I was a little girl, I sailed to China with my father on a clipper ship. As we rounded Cape Horn, we headed into a fearful storm. My father, eager and headstrong, urged the Captain to head into the sea—to fight through the storm. But fortunately the Captain of the ship was a better sailor than my father. He wanted to save his ship. He trimmed sails, gave orders to "heave to," rode out the storm safely, and then, when the heavy weather was gone, we were able to sail ahead and nothing was lost—nothing. Be wise, Franklin—ride out the storm. (*A pause.* SARA, *emotionally wrought-up by now, strikes hotter*) Son, let me ask you—what do you believe I want for you—obscurity? Invalidism? Do you believe that this is my ambition for you? Having been a mother for over forty years, do you think this is what I want? Any dream you ever had or could have, I have. All pain you have felt, I have felt. (*By now she is sharp and hard*) I don't want to see you hurt.

FDR That's enough. There'll be no more talking—no more.

(SARA *goes to the side of the room. She is moved and hurt, but genuinely trying to cover her emotions.* FDR *has discarded his pipe and is trying to cover what he feels. At this moment,* ELEANOR *enters. She sees at a glance that there is tension in the room.* SARA *turns her back a moment, then faces* ELEANOR, *contained but cold*)

SARA Eleanor, I cannot have dinner with you tonight.

ELEANOR Ma*ma*—you may have quarreled with Franklin—but not with the rest of the family. (SARA *is mum*) Please?

SARA (*Reluctantly*) Very well—I'll join you. Excuse me.

(ELEANOR *nods.* SARA *looks at* FDR. *He by now is depressed rather than angry.* SARA *leaves.* ELEANOR *watches* FDR, *who sits glumly in his chair for a moment, then whirls around to her*)

ELEANOR Franklin, anything needed?

FDR Nothing.

(ELEANOR *hesitates a moment, then exits.* FDR *sits for a moment. He is low and dispirited. Suddenly he looks up and toward the crutches. He is in his mind challenging his mother and what she has implied. He decides to prove something to himself and to her. He quickly rolls his chair to the crutches. He places them on his knees and then moves to a clearer section of the room. He puts up one crutch, and then the other, attempting to rise off the chair by himself and onto the crutches. He is confident and determined. He is half out of the chair when the crutch slips away from him and he crumples to the floor. He lies there a moment, a look of sickening defeat and humiliation and pain on his face. He rubs his leg. Then, alarmed that perhaps he has been heard, he attempts to get back into his chair. This is not an easy task, but slowly, carefully and painfully, he manages—again almost meeting disaster, but finally overcoming his obstacles, he makes the security and safety of his chair. He pauses, exhausted and in pain. Then he reaches for his crutches, rolls the chair to each crutch successively, and finally by stretching and bending, gets them into his hands and over his knees. He sits now, his head bent forward, a portrait of a man who has lost a battle that seemed so very important. Slowly he leans back, his face now hard and grim, but determined. Then, stubbornly, he places the crutches before him and prepares to try again to rise from the chair. He begins his efforts, but we do not know if he succeeds or not, as*

THE CURTAIN FALLS

ACT THREE

Scene One

Scene: It is May, 1924. We are again in the New York house. Spring flowers are in vases. It is a sunny spring day.

At rise: Seated in the room is MR. LASSITER. *He is a middle-aged man. He is well dressed and carries an air of authority. He looks at his watch, steals a look at the door leading into the room, and then returns his gaze to the outdoors.*

The door opens and FDR, *wheeling his chair, enters the room. Behind him is* HOWE.

FDR How do you do, Mr. Lassiter. Mr. Howe—

LASSITER Mr. Roosevelt.

FDR I regret I had to keep you waiting, because I've been looking forward to this meeting.

LASSITER Mr. Roosevelt, I know that your time is terribly occupied. But what I have to talk to you about is of great importance.

FDR (*With a smile*) I recognized the note of urgency in your telegrams.
(*Wheels his chair near the table.* HOWE *takes his familiar perch on the sofa and* FDR *motions to* LASSITER *to sit down*)

LASSITER You of course know something of the organization I represent.

FDR I do indeed.

LASSITER We have in recent months enlarged the scope of

our work and we hope very shortly to have a national pattern of activity. (FDR *nods*) Your name, Mr. Roosevelt, has stood for something important among the rank and file of our membership.

FDR Please thank the rank and file.

LASSITER I will come directly to the point. Your chairmanship of Governor Smith's campaign for the Presidential nomination has caused much apprehension among many—many of our members.

FDR (*Knowing instantly what the issues are going to be*) That's curious, Mr. Lassiter. What causes this apprehension?

LASSITER Because of our opposition to Governor Smith, we view with alarm your association with and your sponsorship of his cause.

FDR I for one am very flattered at my association with Governor Smith. What is there about him that induces this opposition from your membership, Mr. Lassiter?

LASSITER (*Confidentially*) Mr. Roosevelt, I don't think it necessary for me to dot the i's and cross the t's.

FDR I love to dot the i's and cross the t's.

LASSITER You must certainly be aware of the fears that many Americans have, when they contemplate the election of a Catholic to the Presidency of the United States. The domination of the church over its members is well known. And Governor Smith is a devout Catholic.

HOWE Would he be more acceptable if he were a renegade Catholic?

FDR (*Chidingly, to* HOWE) Louie— (*Then, after a moment's thought*) It occurs to me, Mr. Lassiter, that your members might be satisfied with a personal statement from me that would enlighten them on my views in this matter.

LASSITER (*Hopefully*) I am certain that a statement of the proper kind from you, Mr. Roosevelt, will be of some service.

FDR I have something in mind. (*Wheels his chair to the office door*) Missy—Missy— (*Rolls his chair back.* MISSY *enters*) Would you be good enough to type up a statement. (*Looks at* LASSITER) How many copies would you like, sir?

LASSITER Oh, one or two would be sufficient, Mr. Roosevelt. We would print it and circulate it for the best effect.

FDR And I will see that it gets proper circulation in other quarters. (*He wheels his chair so that he faces* MISSY *more directly. He culls his thoughts and dictates. In his dictation, his voice becomes sharp, and his manner is the manner so associated with him in later years*) "I am not worried that the Roosevelt name will be tarnished by any association with Governor Smith. If a Catholic who has the ability, broadness of view and fine record that entitled him to be considered Presidential timber, cannot be nominated or elected President because of his religion, then we might just as well be consistent and say he cannot be Governor or Congressman or Mayor or hold any other public office or be called upon to serve in the Army or Navy in defense of his country in war." (*He twists his chair around and looks directly at* LASSITER, *who by now is furious*) Is that what you had in mind, Mr. Lassiter?

LASSITER Good day, Mr. Roosevelt.

(*He stalks out of the room*)

FDR Good day.

HOWE I wonder if there is any way of getting the tone of voice you used, in print.

MISSY Unfortunately there are a lot of people who feel exactly like Mr. Lassiter.

FDR The real issue remains. Is Governor Smith best equipped to be the nominee for the Democratic Party and, ultimately, President of the United States? I think he is.

HOWE In this Year of Our Lord, Nineteen Twenty-four,

even if Al Smith were Protestant and "Dry," he couldn't be elected President on the Democratic ticket. If he's the right man, he's running at the wrong time.

MISSY (*Referring to her watch*) Right or wrong, the Governor is about twenty minutes late.

HOWE The Convention isn't till June. We can wait.

FDR (*Glancing at some papers on his desk*) Missy, would you send a note to the Golf Club along with a check for the dues. "I should like my membership changed from active to nonresident." (*There is a pause*) "I can't possibly play golf myself for a year or two." The usual thank you ever and very truly.

MISSY Yes, sir.

FDR (*Taking a brief look at some other papers*) I haven't anything else, Missy. Type up that statement as soon as you can.

MISSY (*Nods and turns to* HOWE *as she starts to exit*) Have anything, Louie?

HOWE Nothing for paper, Missy—just a pocketful of second thoughts.

(FDR *turns to* HOWE *as* MISSY *goes out*)

FDR Second thoughts, Louie? What's worrying you?

HOWE First, breathing. (*He wheezes air into his lungs*) I've been wondering what Al wants to talk to you about this afternoon.

FDR I would suppose it's some genial campaign chatter.

HOWE I think it's something special.

FDR What do your psychic rumblings indicate?

HOWE I haven't yet spelled out all the words on my invisible ouija board.

FDR (*Lightly*) Do you think he regrets his appointment of me as his chairman?

HOWE (*Shaking his head*) He still needs Upstate New York. You're Protestant—Dry—rural. You're the logical cowcatcher. I've been thinking about Burke Cockran.

FDR Why Burke Cockran?

HOWE Ever since Burke died, Smith has been searching for a replacement. He's been trying out speakers to place him in nomination.

FDR If he's finally gotten around to me it must be a reluctant choice.

HOWE Why so?

FDR Oh, Louie, you know that Al has always had a patronizing attitude towards me. (*Imitating* SMITH) "Listen, kid, let me teach you the facts of life in the big city."

HOWE He's one breed of animal. You're another. He made it without a rich family, and he's as good as you are any day.

(FDR *begins to wander about the room in his chair.* HOWE *watches him. A moment*)

FDR It would be odd for a chairman also to nominate. A precedent.

HOWE Would you be up to it?

FDR (*Who has moved from the desk, stops a moment and considers this*) I sometimes wonder if I could stand the gaff of active work. Maybe the aspirations and dreams for public service would disappear in the hard light of practical politics.

HOWE I'm no idle dreamer, Franklin. Working with you is an act of faith. I believe God has an eye on your future.

FDR (*Sharply*) God has an infinite variety of tasks, and I don't believe He's available as a campaign manager.

HOWE Franklin, the problem is this: How to stop a lot of talk from people who say Roosevelt's a nice fellow who once had a fine chance—but isn't it too bad. You might be able to carry the speech off wonderfully and put the party on notice that you're ready for active service. But you could fail and be headed for the political boneyard.

FDR That's a clean picture of the situation.

HOWE Well—

FDR Well, first let's see if Smith begins sizing me up as his nominator.

HOWE And if he does?

FDR Then, Louie, *mein* boy, I'll start sizing him up as my nominee.

(*The door opens and* ELEANOR *enters. She is dressed in afternoon clothes. Her manner is surer and more defined*)

FDR Who's going with you, Eleanor?

ELEANOR I don't need an entourage. I walk in—say my few words—shake a hundred hands, and go on to the next stop.

HOWE (*To* FDR) Why don't you get Eleanor's opinion on what we've been talking about?

FDR Louie has a hunch—and I'm inclined to think he's right—that Al Smith is coming here today to ask me to place him in nomination.

ELEANOR Well, I have heard that he's been shopping around for a speaker.

HOWE (*To* FDR *as he points at* ELEANOR) She hears everything.

FDR (*To* ELEANOR) Well, what do you think?

ELEANOR I think that's a decision that only you can make.

FDR *That's* taking a well-defined position.

ELEANOR I know you'd make a wonderful speech. Whether you're ready to do it is a matter only you can decide.

HOWE What about the risks or advantages politically?

ELEANOR I'm no politician. I have the naïve point of view that in public service one should pursue principles without calculating the consequences.

(FDR *looks at* HOWE *archly*)

HOWE She's right. She's no politician.

(ELEANOR *crosses to* FDR)

ELEANOR Only one point to consider physically. You'd have to stand for almost three-quarters of an hour.

FDR (*Nods*) I would have to go into training for that.

(ELEANOR *crosses to* FDR *and gives him a kiss on the cheek*)

FDR Ummm—I like that cologne.

(ELEANOR *starts out as* MISSY *enters*)

MISSY They're ready, Mr. R.

FDR Oh, Eleanor, take a copy of that, will you. If you find a place to use it this afternoon, rattle it in.

HOWE Hail and farewell!

ELEANOR (*As she exits*) Good-bye.

FDR I think Eleanor is beginning to enjoy this political prowling.

HOWE What's more, she's getting damned good at it. (*The doorbell rings and* HOWE *looks at his watch*) It's late enough. That could be the Governor.

(*We hear sounds from the hallway*)

ELEANOR'S VOICE (*Offstage*) Good afternoon, Governor Smith.

(MISSY *has started out*)

SMITH'S VOICE Hello, Eleanor. And hello, Missy.

MISSY'S VOICE Good afternoon, Governor.

SMITH'S VOICE Why, I've never had a reception from a brace of such beautiful girls. Eleanor, I hear you're getting to be quite a speaker. Glad you're on my side.

ELEANOR'S VOICE The fact that I am makes my speeches sound better.

(FDR *and* HOWE *exchange a look*)

SMITH'S VOICE Hope to see you soon. 'Bye.

MISSY'S VOICE Mr. Roosevelt's in the library, Governor.

(*We hear the sound of the door closing, and in a moment* AL SMITH *enters. He is in his prime—saucy, smart and healthy*)

SMITH Hello, Frank. How're you feeling? Hello, Louie.

FDR Hello, Al.

HOWE Hello, Governor. You're looking fit.

SMITH (*Shakes hands with* FDR) That hand of yours is getting like a vise.

MISSY (*Entering*) Some cold refreshment?

SMITH Why, Missy—there's a law in this country against strong refreshment. An obnoxious law, but nevertheless a law.

MISSY I know. Scotch or rye?

SMITH Scotch, thanks. And don't kill it with soda. (MISSY *exits to mix the drinks*) Frank, I met Eleanor on the way in. She's doing a fine job.

FDR She's been taking her lessons from Professor Howe.

SMITH Louie, you ought to open up a school.

HOWE Any school in practical politics, Governor, would have to have you as the dean.

SMITH Say—I didn't know you could hand out the blarney. (*Turns to* FDR) Frank, I hear you've broken up your law firm with Emmett and Marvin. What's the matter? The work a little too rugged for you?

FDR (*With a smile*) As a matter of fact, Al, it wasn't rugged enough. I did withdraw on the friendliest basis. But their type of work—estates, wills, et cetera—frankly, it bored me to death.

SMITH Certainly keeps you freer to do what you want.

(MISSY *re-enters with the drinks*)

MISSY Your Scotch, Governor. Still alive, I hope.

SMITH (*Trying his drink*) Perfect. Thanks, Missy.

MISSY Yours, Mr. R.

FDR Missy.

MISSY And I brought you a soft drink, Louie.

HOWE Reluctantly—thanks.

MISSY (*As she leaves*) If you need fresh ones, a call will bring you our instant courteous service, available at all hours.

(*She goes out*)

SMITH That girl's a jewel, Frank.

FDR That she is.

(*They sip their drinks*)

SMITH They tell me there's a lot of McAdoo money around town.

HOWE I wish I had some money to bet. Bill isn't going to make it.

SMITH He's coming into town a lot stronger than I thought. You know, Frank, we're putting on a big show here in New York and we can make it look like Smith all through the city, but McAdoo and his organization are coming to this convention with a half-Nelson on all the rules and program machinery. We can get strangled inside Madison Square Garden.

FDR We won't get strangled. Though it's going to be a mighty tough wrestling match.

SMITH I'd like to win this nomination, but there's a good chance it might be a stalemate. (*Takes another sip of his drink*) I was going over the delegate strength with Belle Moscowitz and Joe Proskauer yesterday. (*He looks at* FDR) How do you size it up, Frank?

FDR I don't think you can make it on the first ballot, Al.

SMITH (*With a nod*) That's the way we figured it.

FDR But neither can McAdoo.

SMITH I'll tell you one thing, Frank. If it isn't going to be me, it'll never be McAdoo. I'll fight him with my last breath. Any man who can take the support of an organization like the Ku Klux Klan—he's not my kind of man.

FDR Oh, a letter reached me and I want you to hear part of it.

(*He wheels over to his desk*)

SMITH You handle that chair like a scooter.

FDR Practice makes— (*Imitating* SMITH) —poifect, Al. (*Digs into the pile of mail*) It's from Babe Ruth. I asked him to chairman a committee for you.

SMITH The Babe.

FDR (*Picking up the letter*) "No poor boy can go any too

high in this world to suit me. You know we ball players travel the country a good deal and I hear lots of fellows talking about Al Smith and his chances to be President and I'm telling you that most everybody I talk to is with him."

(*He puts the letter down*)

SMITH (*With a chuckle*) How many ball players are there?

FDR I hope he's as good a prophet as he is a slugger.

SMITH I sure miss Burke Cockran during these days. He had a great instinct in these subtle matters of conventions, nominations and elections. Sort of spooky. I sure miss him. For many reasons.

FDR (*The first probe*) You certainly would have wanted him to nominate you. There was no one better.

SMITH That's a fact. No one better.

FDR He had a magnificent voice and knew how to use it.

SMITH It wasn't just the way he talked, Frank. He had a knack of saying just the right thing.

FDR (*Nodding*) That he did.

SMITH For days now I've been trying to think what Burke would have wanted to say in a nominating speech.

FDR It seems to me he'd have argued for you as a progressive. He certainly would have been aware of the issues—the Klan—the Volstead Act—and the latent issue of your faith. He might have been willing to point out that the obligation above any one candidate was to keep the party together.

SMITH I'm all for party unity, but I don't intend to temporize on the issue of the Klan. And Burke wouldn't have, either.

FDR I agree that it ought to be burned out once and for all. But if we can't get through a resolution condemning the Klan, we still mustn't break up the party.

SMITH Frank, I remember all my early lessons. One of them was that the first objective of a politician is to be elected. Then he can fight for causes. But in the case of the Klan, I'm willing to forget an early lesson.

FDR (*Nods*) There's another issue, Al. Even more important than the Klan. That's the issue of world politics and America's place in it. Burke would have talked of that, perhaps.

SMITH Frank, if you're talking about the League of Nations, that's a dead dodo.

FDR I think if the Democratic Party is going to stand, it has to stand for something big and noble.

SMITH I suppose there's nothing wrong with mankind having a vision of a world organization. But it's only a vision.

FDR Newton Baker wants to submit a resolution to support the League of Nations at the Convention.

SMITH It hasn't got a chance.

FDR Perhaps not. But I think you ought to support it. Woodrow Wilson's in his grave only three months, and I don't think we ought to let his convictions about the League be buried with him.

SMITH (*Grudgingly*) It's all right with me.

HOWE I'll speak to the Program Committee and have Baker put it on the schedule.

SMITH Frank, got any other notions about what Burke Cockran would have to say?

FDR (*With a smile*) Finally, I think he'd make up his own speech, a large part of which would have to do with the fine record of the man he'd be nominating.

SMITH (*Returning the smile*) I suppose a few kind words about me would be in order. Frank, Burke had a theory that no nominating speech ought to run more than thirty to forty minutes.

FDR You can read the Bill of Rights in that time.

SMITH That's a long time for any man to be on his feet.

FDR You certainly can't make an effective speech sitting down.

SMITH You can be sure of that.

FDR After all the months I've spent in this chair, I've come to love the time I spend each day standing on my crutches.

SMITH Uh-huh.

(*There is a pause.* SMITH *looks at his glass, which is empty*)

HOWE Fresh one, Governor?

SMITH No thanks. (*Puts his glass down*) Frank, I'd like you to put me in nomination.

FDR That's a surprise.

(*He looks at* LOUIE)

HOWE Caught me flat-footed.

SMITH Will you do it, Frank?

FDR Certainly.

SMITH I'll want to have a look at what you're going to say, and Joe Proskauer may have an idea or two. He's a good phrase-maker.

FDR I won't mind the addition of a few phrases. But Al, what I say will have to be what I want to say.

SMITH Yes, Frank, you have made that quite clear. (*Looks at his vest-pocket watch*) Say, time runs fast. (*With a wry smile*) I've got some other people I've kept waiting. (*Gets to his feet*) I'm glad you're going to do this, Frank. I appreciate it and won't forget it.

FDR Thank you, Al. I consider it a singular privilege and honor. I'll try to make your choice a good one.

SMITH I'm satisfied you will. Take care, kid.

FDR So long, Al.

SMITH See you, Louie. Say good-bye to Missy.

HOWE I'll take you to the door.

(SMITH *starts to the door, then stops, turns*)

SMITH Frank, did you have an idea I was going to ask you?

FDR A vagrant thought. Why?

SMITH It just occurred to me you were both too surprised to be surprised.

(*He waves his hand and leaves.* HOWE *follows him out.* FDR *scoots to the office door*)

FDR Missy—Missy— (*He rolls back into the room. The front door is heard opening, then closing.* MISSY *enters, just a moment before* HOWE) I'm going to nominate Governor Smith.

MISSY Bravo!

FDR I like him. He's sharp as a blade.

HOWE (*As he enters, it is obvious he is pleased and excited*) I feel like an agent who just had an act booked into the Palace. You have the ball, Franklin. (*Looks at* MISSY) Make him do good, Missy.

MISSY You know me. I write all of Irving Berlin's music and Franklin Roosevelt's speeches.

HOWE Smith will make the announcement tomorrow that you're going to nominate. I'll follow up by flooding him with congratulations.

FDR Louie, ease up. (*He looks at* MISSY) Missy—we have to get a blueprint of that platform at the Garden. I want to know just how far it is from where I'll be sitting to that lectern.

HOWE About ten steps, I'd say, not more.

FDR (*Thinking*) Ten steps. I can do that. I'll take Jimmy with me—he's the biggest. (*Rolls his chair and seems to be measuring*) Ten steps—about twenty feet?

HOWE About.

FDR I'll work on that. We have got to get the exact measurement.

HOWE Work hard, Franklin. (*A pause*) They are liable to be the ten biggest steps you ever took in your life.

(FDR *looks up at* HOWE *questioningly.* MISSY *eyes them both*)

FDR (*Eager to break the solemn mood*) Perhaps—or, to be clinical—I may fall smack on my gluteus maximus.

THE CURTAIN FALLS

Scene Two

Scene: We are in a small room of Madision Square Garden. We are aware of the roaring sound of the Convention hall, which is swarming with delegates. The sound is constant and present in the room, but not loud enough to distract us. It is June 26, 1924, about 11:30 P.M.

At rise: In the room is FDR, *seated in a more conventional wheel chair than the ones he has used in his home. He is bronzed and beaming with vitality.* JAMES, *the eldest son, stands near the back wall, on which his father's crutches lean.* ELEANOR *is seated to the left of* FDR, *knitting.* HOWE *is standing by.* MISSY *is seated to the right of* FDR. *A uniformed* POLICEMAN *is on duty, guarding the door. A screen is in one corner of the room, large enough to cover* FDR *and his wheel chair.* FDR'S *braces are on the desk. A roar goes up outside.* HOWE *looks at his watch.*

HOWE That, very likely, is the finish of Miss Kennedy's address to the brethren.

ELEANOR Now what?

HOWE Now Bill Sweet, to second the nomination of McAdoo—then the roll call—and if Connecticut remembers its cue, it yields to New York—and—
(*He points to* FDR)

FDR Then they get one half-hour of little ol' me.
(DALY, *a young man, dashes in. He is frantic*)

DALY Mr. Roosevelt, I've checked everything again and again—and everything should be all right.

FDR I'm certain it will be, Daly.

DALY You're feeling okay?

FDR (*Nodding*) Fine.

DALY Is there anything I can do for you, sir?

FDR No, thank you.

HOWE (*Noticing* DALY'S *tension*) Say, Daly—

DALY Yes—

HOWE I'd like to make sure that everything is on schedule. Take a look—size up the crowd—get some impressions and then report back. Will you do that?

DALY Of course.

HOWE Thanks. Thanks very much.

(HOWE *motions to* MISSY *to open the door. She does, as* DALY *approaches it. We see the* POLICEMAN *and hear the crowd, louder now.* DALY *goes out, and the door closes*)

FDR Thanks, Louie.

HOWE I wasn't thinking about you. He was driving me crazy. (*He crosses to* FDR) You'd better get ready, Franklin.

FDR Jimmy—

JIMMY I've got them, Father.

(JIMMY *takes the braces from the desk and goes behind the screen with* FDR. HOWE *takes a step toward the screen and calls over*)

HOWE Franklin, I want to take another crack at you about the finish of the speech.

FDR (*Back of the screen*) Louie, not again.

HOWE Yes, again. Listen, Franklin, this phrase of Proskauer's is a rich one, and I think you're murdering it by not using it at the finish.

FDR (*Back of the screen*) It's close enough to the finish.

HOWE I think it ought to be the last thing you say. "I give you—the Happy Warrior of the Political Battlefield —Al Smith." Period. Crash.

FDR (*Back of the screen*) I don't think so. Period. Crash.

HOWE You're wrong. It's a sock phrase and will stick. It ought to be the punch line.

ELEANOR Franklin, may I say a word?

FDR (*Back of the screen*) Certainly. If you're going to agree with me.

ELEANOR Then I've nothing to say.

FDR (*Back of the screen, annoyed*) That's hardly a sign of wifely devotion.

HOWE Your being here and doing this is the most important thing. I only feel you're losing the value of the last minute or two of a good speech.

FDR (*Back of the screen*) Louie—I'm not sold on changing it. I'm sorry.

HOWE Further deponent sayeth not.

(*At that moment* FDR *appears with* JIMMY *from behind the screen*)

JIMMY Did I get it too tight, Father?

FDR I don't think so, Jimmy. No, that's fine.

(*At this moment* SARA ROOSEVELT *enters. The noise is suddenly louder.*)

SARA Franklin, they hardly let me through to you—

FDR Ma*ma,* ever the lady. You came in just at the right time—just as I stepped into my pants.

SARA Oh, Franklin—

FDR Welcome to the smoke-filled back room of politics.

SARA That howling mob outside is frightening.

FDR That howling mob consists of ladies and gentlemen conducting the business of democracy.

SARA How anything of consequence can be accomplished out of such a babble is a miracle.

FDR Ma*ma*—I'm all for noisy congregations. God help us if our conventions ever turn into high school pageants.

SARA Franklin, this is hardly the time to give me lessons in politics. I wanted only a moment to say God bless you.

FDR (*Simply*) He has given me many blessings.

(SARA *kisses him*)

SARA And, Franklin, speak out loudly and clearly.

(SARA *exits*)

HOWE Franklin, if I know Ma*ma,* in a couple of months she'll be working on a political primer. (*He looks at his watch*) I know this is awful—but I'm getting nervous.

ELEANOR And I have dropped three stitches.

FDR Sweet's taking a long time for a seconding speech—

HOWE He's only been on a few minutes. It just seems long.

(*The noise swells as the door bursts open. The* POLICEMAN *is gripping* DALY)

DALY Mr. Howe—Mr. Howe—for God's sake, Miss LeHand, will you tell this man I belong here!

MISSY (*To* POLICEMAN) He does. He does.

(*The* POLICEMAN *unhands* DALY, *who moves into the room, excited*)

DALY Sorry I got panicky. Mr. Howe, you ought to get ready. The crowd is enormous and busting with excitement. Senator Walsh says it's time to get Mr. Roosevelt to the platform.

HOWE Missy—will you check the press handouts. Take Daly here with you for anything you need.

MISSY Right. (*Crosses to* FDR, *shakes his hand*) Boss, I know you'll be tremendous.

FDR Thanks, Missy. For everything.

(MISSY *starts for the door*)

DALY Good luck, Mr. Roosevelt—and to you, Mrs. Roosevelt—and to you, Elliott.

JIMMY James—Jimmy.

DALY Yes—thank you.

HOWE Okay, Daly. Good luck to you.

(DALY *waves and goes out with* MISSY)

FDR Jimmy, are you all set?

JIMMY Yes, Father. In my mind I have gone over it a hundred times. (*He smiles*) You make the speech, and I'll worry about everything else.

FDR (*With a laugh*) That's my son—man of iron. (*Now* FDR *leans over his legs*) Better check the braces. (*He clicks them into place—turns them with his hands and then releases them, leaving his knees limp again.* JIMMY *brings the crutches over*) They should be fine. Jimmy, if I slip, pick me up in a hurry.

(ELEANOR *comes to him and they caress each other*)

FDR (*He takes the crutches from Jimmy*) I'm ready. Jimmy—battle stations!

(JIMMY *starts to push the chair as* DALY *bursts in excitedly*)

DALY Mr. Roosevelt—

THE CURTAIN FALLS

Scene Three

Scene: The scene reveals the platform in Madison Square Garden. We are looking toward the rear platform. Facing us are huge drapes of bunting and pictures of Wilson and Jefferson. Stage front is the speaker's lectern, about twenty feet from the rear, where are grouped FDR *in his wheel chair,* JIMMY, *holding the crutches next to him, the other children,* ELEANOR ROOSEVELT, SARA ROOSEVELT, MISSY, LOUIE HOWE, *and the* POLICEMAN.

At rise: At the lectern is a SPEAKER. *Next to him is* SENATOR WALSH *of Montana, the Chairman. The crowd noise swells, loud and turbulent. It comes from all sides. There is no microphone, and the speakers must yell to be heard. It is bedlam as the* SPEAKER *tries to be heard.*

WALSH (*Banging gavel and screaming*) Ladies and Gentlemen! Please—give the speaker your attention—

(*There is some measure, small but noticeable, of attention*)

SPEAKER (*Also yelling*) There is a good deal of mail accumulating for the delegates in the Convention post office—and we urge you, please, to pick up your mail. It's getting very crowded. Please pick up your mail! Thank you!

(*There is cheering and screaming again.* WALSH *takes the gavel*)

WALSH (*After hammering the audience into some quiet*) We will continue with the calling of the roll. Connecticut!

VOICE (*From the pit*) Connecticut, the Nutmeg State, yields to the great Empire State of New York!

(*An enormous cheer and more yelling*)

WALSH (*Banging for quiet*) Ladies and Gentlemen! (*He hammers away with his gavel and finally gets some attention*) The Chair recognizes the Honorable Franklin D. Roosevelt of the State of New York!

(*As he says this, there is applause.* JIMMY *hands* FDR *the crutches; he gets to his feet and then, proud, smiling and confident, he starts to walk on his crutches to the lectern, as the applause mounts in intensity. Slowly, but strongly and surely,* FDR *walks those ten great steps. The cheering starts—whistles, screams, and rebel yells—and the band plays "Sidewalks of New York."* FDR *reaches the lectern and hands the crutches to* JIMMY, *who takes them and steps down. The screaming crowd continues to sound off.* FDR *stands there, holding the lectern with his left hand. Now he waves his right hand at the crowd in that familiar gesture. He smiles broadly, basking in the warmth of this genuine and whole-hearted tribute to his appearance, his courage and his future. The cheering continues as*

THE CURTAIN FALLS

Lorraine Hansberry

A Raisin in the Sun

What happens to a dream deferred?
Does it dry up
Like a raisin in the sun?
Or fester like a sore—
And then run?
Does it stink like rotten meat?
Or crust and sugar over—
Like a syrupy sweet?

Maybe it just sags
Like a heavy load.

Or does it explode?

—LANGSTON HUGHES

TO MAMA:
IN GRATITUDE FOR THE DREAM

Manufactured in the United States of America by H. Wolff

A Raisin in the Sun was first presented by Philip Rose and David J. Cogan at the Ethel Barrymore Theatre, New York City, March 11, 1959, with the following cast:

(*In order of appearance*)

RUTH YOUNGER	Ruby Dee
TRAVIS YOUNGER	Glyn Turman
WALTER LEE YOUNGER (BROTHER)	Sidney Poitier
BENEATHA YOUNGER	Diana Sands
LENA YOUNGER (MAMA)	Claudia McNeil
JOSEPH ASAGAI	Ivan Dixon
GEORGE MURCHISON	Louis Gossett
KARL LINDNER	John Fiedler
BOBO	Lonne Elder III
MOVING MEN	Ed Hall, Douglas Turner

DIRECTED BY Lloyd Richards
DESIGNED AND LIGHTED BY Ralph Alswang
COSTUMES BY Virginia Volland

The action of the play is set in Chicago's Southside, sometime between World War II and the present.

ACT ONE

Scene 1. Friday morning.
Scene 2. The following morning.

ACT TWO

Scene 1. Later, the same day.
Scene 2. Friday night, a few weeks later.
Scene 3. Moving day, one week later.

ACT THREE

An hour later.

ACT ONE

Scene One

The YOUNGER *living room would be a comfortable and well-ordered room if it were not for a number of indestructible contradictions to this state of being. Its furnishings are typical and undistinguished and their primary feature now is that they have clearly had to accommodate the living of too many people for too many years—and they are tired. Still, we can see that at some time, a time probably no longer remembered by the family (except perhaps for* MAMA*), the furnishings of this room were actually selected with care and love and even hope—and brought to this apartment and arranged with taste and pride.*

That was a long time ago. Now the once loved pattern of the couch upholstery has to fight to show itself from under acres of crocheted doilies and couch covers which have themselves finally come to be more important than the upholstery. And here a table or a chair has been moved to disguise the worn places in the carpet; but the carpet has fought back by showing its weariness, with depressing uniformity, elsewhere on its surface.

Weariness has, in fact, won in this room. Everything has been polished, washed, sat on, used, scrubbed too often. All pretenses but living itself have long since vanished from the very atmosphere of this room.

Moreover, a section of this room, for it is not really a room unto itself, though the landlord's lease would make it seem so, slopes backward to provide a small kitchen area, where the family prepares the meals that are eaten in the living room proper, which must also serve as dining room. The single window that has been provided for these "two" rooms is located in this kitchen area. The sole natural light the family may enjoy in the course of a day is only that which fights its way through this little window.

At left, a door leads to a bedroom which is shared by MAMA *and her daughter,* BENEATHA. *At right, opposite, is a second room (which in the beginning of the life of this apartment was probably a breakfast room) which serves as a bedroom for* WALTER *and his wife,* RUTH.

Time: Sometime between World War II and the present.
Place: Chicago's Southside.

At rise: It is morning dark in the living room. TRAVIS *is asleep on the make-down bed at center. An alarm clock sounds from within the bedroom at right, and presently* RUTH *enters from that room and closes the door behind her. She crosses sleepily toward the window. As she passes her sleeping son she reaches down and shakes him a little. At the window she raises the shade and a dusky Southside morning light comes in feebly. She fills a pot with water and puts it on to boil. She calls to the boy, between yawns, in a slightly muffled voice.*

RUTH *is about thirty. We can see that she was a pretty girl, even exceptionally so, but now it is apparent that life has been little that she expected, and disappointment has already begun to hang in her face. In a few years, before thirty-five even, she will be known among her people as a "settled woman."*

She crosses to her son and gives him a good, final, rousing shake.

RUTH Come on now, boy, it's seven thirty! (*Her son sits up at last, in a stupor of sleepiness*) I say hurry up, Travis! You ain't the only person in the world got to use a bathroom! (*The child, a sturdy, handsome little boy of ten or eleven, drags himself out of the bed and almost blindly takes his towels and "today's clothes" from drawers and a closet and goes out to the bathroom, which is in an outside hall and which is shared by another family or families on the same floor.* RUTH *crosses to the bedroom door at right and opens it and calls in to her husband*) Walter Lee! . . . It's after seven thirty! Lemme see you do some waking up in there now! (*She waits*) You better get up from there, man! It's after seven thirty I tell you. (*She waits again*) All right, you just go ahead and lay there and next thing you know Travis be finished and Mr. Johnson'll be in there and you'll be fussing and cussing round here like a mad man! And be late too! (*She waits, at the end of patience*) *Walter Lee*—it's time for you to get up!

(*She waits another second and then starts to go into the bedroom, but is apparently satisfied that her husband has begun to get up. She stops, pulls the door to, and returns to the kitchen area. She wipes her face with a moist cloth and runs her fingers through her sleep-disheveled hair in a vain effort and ties an apron around her housecoat. The bedroom door at right opens and her husband stands in the doorway in his pajamas, which are rumpled and mismated. He is a lean, intense young man in his middle thirties, inclined to quick nervous movements and erratic speech habits—and always in his voice there is a quality of indictment*)

WALTER Is he out yet?

RUTH What you mean *out?* He ain't hardly got in there good yet.

WALTER (*Wandering in, still more oriented to sleep than to a new day*) Well, what was you doing all that yelling for if I can't even get in there yet? (*Stopping and thinking*) Check coming today?

RUTH They *said* Saturday and this is just Friday and I hopes to God you ain't going to get up here first thing this morning and start talking to me 'bout no money—'cause I 'bout don't want to hear it.

WALTER Something the matter with you this morning?

RUTH No—I'm just sleepy as the devil. What kind of eggs you want?

WALTER Not scrambled. (RUTH *starts to scramble eggs*) Paper come? (RUTH *points impatiently to the rolled up* Tribune *on the table, and he gets it and spreads it out and vaguely reads the front page*) Set off another bomb yesterday.

RUTH (*Maximum indifference*) Did they?

WALTER (*Looking up*) What's the matter with you?

RUTH Ain't nothing the matter with me. And don't keep asking me that this morning.

WALTER Ain't nobody bothering you. (*Reading the news of the day absently again*) Say Colonel McCormick is sick.

RUTH (*Affecting tea-party interest*) Is he now? Poor thing.

WALTER (*Sighing and looking at his watch*) Oh, me. (*He waits*) Now what is that boy doing in that bathroom all this time? He just going to have to start getting up earlier. I can't be being late to work on account of him fooling around in there.

RUTH (*Turning on him*) Oh, no he ain't going to be getting up no earlier no such thing! It ain't his fault that he can't get to bed no earlier nights 'cause he got a bunch of crazy good-for-nothing clowns sitting up running their mouths in what is supposed to be his bedroom after ten o'clock at night . . .

WALTER That's what you mad about, ain't it? The things

I want to talk about with my friends just couldn't be important in your mind, could they?

(*He rises and finds a cigarette in her handbag on the table and crosses to the little window and looks out, smoking and deeply enjoying this first one*)

RUTH (*Almost matter of factly, a complaint too automatic to deserve emphasis*) Why you always got to smoke before you eat in the morning?

WALTER (*At the window*) Just look at 'em down there . . . Running and racing to work . . . (*He turns and faces his wife and watches her a moment at the stove, and then, suddenly*) You look young this morning, baby.

RUTH (*Indifferently*) Yeah?

WALTER Just for a second—stirring them eggs. It's gone now—just for a second it was—you looked real young again. (*Then, drily*) It's gone now—you look like yourself again.

RUTH Man, if you don't shut up and leave me alone.

WALTER (*Looking out to the street again*) First thing a man ought to learn in life is not to make love to no colored woman first thing in the morning. You all some evil people at eight o'clock in the morning.

(TRAVIS *appears in the hall doorway, almost fully dressed and quite wide awake now, his towels and pajamas across his shoulders. He opens the door and signals for his father to make the bathroom in a hurry*)

TRAVIS (*Watching the bathroom*) Daddy, come on!

(WALTER *gets his bathroom utensils and flies out to the bathroom*)

RUTH Sit down and have your breakfast, Travis.

TRAVIS Mama, this is Friday. (*Gleefully*) Check coming tomorrow, huh?

RUTH You get your mind off money and eat your breakfast.

TRAVIS (*Eating*) This is the morning we supposed to bring the fifty cents to school.

RUTH Well, I ain't got no fifty cents this morning.

TRAVIS Teacher say we have to.

RUTH I don't care what teacher say. I ain't got it. Eat your breakfast, Travis.

TRAVIS I *am* eating.

RUTH Hush up now and just eat!

(*The boy gives her an exasperated look for her lack of understanding, and eats grudgingly*)

TRAVIS You think Grandmama would have it?

RUTH No! And I want you to stop asking your grandmother for money, you hear me?

TRAVIS (*Outraged*) Gaaaleee! I don't ask her, she just gimme it sometimes!

RUTH Travis Willard Younger—I got too much on me this morning to be—

TRAVIS Maybe Daddy—

RUTH *Travis!*

(*The boy hushes abruptly. They are both quiet and tense for several seconds*)

TRAVIS (*Presently*) Could I maybe go carry some groceries in front of the supermarket for a little while after school then?

RUTH Just hush, I said. (TRAVIS *jabs his spoon into his cereal bowl viciously, and rests his head in anger upon his fists*) If you through eating, you can get over there and make up your bed.

(*The boy obeys stiffly and crosses the room, almost mechanically, to the bed and more or less carefully folds the covering. He carries the bedding into his mother's room and returns with his books and cap*)

TRAVIS (*Sulking and standing apart from her unnaturally*) I'm gone.

RUTH (*Looking up from the stove to inspect him automatically*) Come here. (*He crosses to her and she studies his head*) If you don't take this comb and fix this here head, you better! (TRAVIS *puts down his books with a great sigh of oppression, and crosses to the mirror. His mother mutters under her breath about his "slubbornness"*) 'Bout to march out of here with that head looking just like chickens slept in it! I just don't know where you get your slubborn ways . . . And get your jacket, too. Looks chilly out this morning.

TRAVIS (*With conspicuously brushed hair and jacket*) I'm gone.

RUTH Get carfare and milk money— (*Waving one finger*) —and not a single penny for no caps, you hear me?

TRAVIS (*With sullen politeness*) Yes'm.

(*He turns in outrage to leave. His mother watches after him as in his frustration he approaches the door almost comically. When she speaks to him, her voice has become a very gentle tease*)

RUTH (*Mocking; as she thinks he would say it*) Oh, Mama makes me so mad sometimes, I don't know what to do! (*She waits and continues to his back as he stands stock-still in front of the door*) I wouldn't kiss that woman good-bye for nothing in this world this morning! (*The boy finally turns around and rolls his eyes at her, knowing the mood has changed and he is vindicated; he does not, however, move toward her yet*) Not for nothing in this world! (*She finally laughs aloud at him and holds out her arms to him and we see that it is a way between them, very old and practiced. He crosses to her and allows her to embrace him warmly but keeps his face fixed with masculine rigidity. She holds him back from her presently and looks at him and runs her fingers over the features of his face. With utter gentleness—*) Now—whose little old angry man are you?

TRAVIS (*The masculinity and gruffness start to fade at last*) Aw gaalee—Mama . . .

RUTH (*Mimicking*) Aw—gaaaaalleeeee, Mama! (*She*

pushes him, with rough playfulness and finality, toward the door) Get on out of here or you going to be late.

TRAVIS (*In the face of love, new aggressiveness*) Mama, could I *please* go carry groceries?

RUTH Honey, it's starting to get so cold evenings.

WALTER (*Coming in from the bathroom and drawing a make-believe gun from a make-believe holster and shooting at his son*) What is it he wants to do?

RUTH Go carry groceries after school at the supermarket.

WALTER Well, let him go . . .

TRAVIS (*Quickly, to the ally*) I *have* to—she won't gimme the fifty cents . . .

WALTER (*To his wife only*) Why not?

RUTH (*Simply, and with flavor*) 'Cause we don't have it.

WALTER (*To* RUTH *only*) What you tell the boy things like that for? (*Reaching down into his pants with a rather important gesture*) Here, son—

(*He hands the boy the coin, but his eyes are directed to his wife's.* TRAVIS *takes the money happily*)

TRAVIS Thanks, Daddy.

(*He starts out.* RUTH *watches both of them with murder in her eyes.* WALTER *stands and stares back at her with defiance, and suddenly reaches into his pocket again on an afterthought*)

WALTER (*Without even looking at his son, still staring hard at his wife*) In fact, here's another fifty cents . . . Buy yourself some fruit today—or take a taxi cab to school or something!

TRAVIS Whoopee—

(*He leaps up and clasps his father around the middle with his legs, and they face each other in mutual appreciation; slowly* WALTER LEE *peeks around the boy to catch the violent rays from his wife's eyes and draws his head back as if shot*)

WALTER You better get down now—and get to school, man.

TRAVIS (*At the door*) O.K. Good-bye.
(*He exits*)

WALTER (*After him, pointing with pride*) That's *my* boy. (*She looks at him in disgust and turns back to her work*) You know what I was thinking 'bout in the bathroom this morning?

RUTH No.

WALTER How come you always try to be so pleasant!

RUTH What is there to be pleasant 'bout!

WALTER You want to know what I was thinking 'bout in the bathroom or not!

RUTH I know what you was thinking 'bout.

WALTER (*Ignoring her*) 'Bout what me and Willy Harris was talking about last night.

RUTH (*Immediately—a refrain*) Willy Harris is a good-for-nothing loud mouth.

WALTER Anybody who talks to me has got to be a good-for-nothing loud mouth, ain't he? And what you know about who is just a good-for-nothing loud mouth? Charlie Atkins was just a "good-for-nothing loud mouth" too, wasn't he! When he wanted me to go in the dry-cleaning business with him. And now—he's grossing a hundred thousand a year. A hundred thousand dollars a year! You still call *him* a loud mouth!

RUTH (*Bitterly*) Oh, Walter Lee . . .
(*She folds her head on her arms over on the table*)

WALTER (*Rising and coming to her and standing over her*) You tired, ain't you? Tired of everything. Me, the boy, the way we live—this beat-up hole—everything. Ain't you? (*She doesn't look up, doesn't answer*) So tired—moaning and groaning all the time, but you wouldn't do nothing to help, would you? You couldn't be on my side that long for nothing, could you?

RUTH Walter, please leave me alone.

WALTER A man needs for a woman to back him up . . .

RUTH Walter—

WALTER Mama would listen to you. You know she listen to you more than she do me and Bennie. She think more of you. All you have to do is just sit down with her when you drinking your coffee one morning and talking 'bout things like you do and— (*He sits down beside her and demonstrates graphically what he thinks her methods and tone should be*) —you just sip your coffee, see, and say easy like that you been thinking 'bout that deal Walter Lee is so interested in, 'bout the store and all, and sip some more coffee, like what you saying ain't really that important to you— And the next thing you know, she be listening good and asking you questions and when I come home—I can tell her the details. This ain't no fly-by-night proposition, baby. I mean we figured it out, me and Willy and Bobo.

RUTH (*With a frown*) Bobo?

WALTER Yeah. You see, this little liquor store we got in mind cost seventy-five thousand and we figured the initial investment on the place be 'bout thirty thousand, see. That be ten thousand each. Course, there's a couple of hundred you got to pay so's you don't spend your life just waiting for them clowns to let your license get approved—

RUTH You mean graft?

WALTER (*Frowning impatiently*) Don't call it that. See there, that just goes to show you what women understand about the world. Baby, don't *nothing* happen for you in this world 'less you pay *somebody* off!

RUTH Walter, leave me alone! (*She raises her head and stares at him vigorously—then says, more quietly*) Eat your eggs, they gonna be cold.

WALTER (*Straightening up from her and looking off*) That's it. There you are. Man say to his woman: I got me a dream. His woman say: Eat your eggs. (*Sadly, but gaining in power*) Man say: I got to take hold of this here world, baby! And a woman will say: Eat your eggs and go to work. (*Passionately now*) Man say: I got to change my life, I'm choking to death, baby! And his woman say— (*In utter anguish as he brings his fists down on his thighs*) —Your eggs is getting cold!

RUTH (*Softly*) Walter, that ain't none of our money.

WALTER (*Not listening at all or even looking at her*) This morning, I was lookin' in the mirror and thinking about it . . . I'm thirty-five years old; I been married eleven years and I got a boy who sleeps in the living room— (*Very, very quietly*) —and all I got to give him is stories about how rich white people live . . .

RUTH Eat your eggs, Walter.

WALTER *Damn my eggs . . . damn all the eggs that ever was!*

RUTH Then go to work.

WALTER (*Looking up at her*) See—I'm trying to talk to you 'bout myself— (*Shaking his head with the repetition*) —and all you can say is eat them eggs and go to work.

RUTH (*Wearily*) Honey, you never say nothing new. I listen to you every day, every night and every morning, and you never say nothing new. (*Shrugging*) So you would rather *be* Mr. Arnold than be his chauffeur. So—I would *rather* be living in Buckingham Palace.

WALTER That is just what is wrong with the colored woman in this world . . . Don't understand about building their men up and making 'em feel like they somebody. Like they can do something.

RUTH (*Drily, but to hurt*) There *are* colored men who do things.

WALTER No thanks to the colored woman.

RUTH Well, being a colored woman, I guess I can't help myself none.

(*She rises and gets the ironing board and sets it up and*

attacks a huge pile of rough-dried clothes, sprinkling them in preparation for the ironing and then rolling them into tight fat balls)

WALTER (*Mumbling*) We one group of men tied to a race of women with small minds.

(*His sister* BENEATHA *enters. She is about twenty, as slim and intense as her brother. She is not as pretty as her sister-in-law, but her lean, almost intellectual face has a handsomeness of its own. She wears a bright-red flannel nightie, and her thick hair stands wildly about her head. Her speech is a mixture of many things; it is different from the rest of the family's insofar as education has permeated her sense of English—and perhaps the Midwest rather than the South has finally—at last—won out in her inflection; but not altogether, because over all of it is a soft slurring and transformed use of vowels which is the decided influence of the Southside. She passes through the room without looking at either* RUTH *or* WALTER *and goes to the outside door and looks, a little blindly, out to the bathroom. She sees that it has been lost to the Johnsons. She closes the door with a sleepy vengeance and crosses to the table and sits down a little defeated*)

BENEATHA I am going to start timing those people.

WALTER You should get up earlier.

BENEATHA (*Her face in her hands. She is still fighting the urge to go back to bed*) Really—would you suggest dawn? Where's the paper?

WALTER (*Pushing the paper across the table to her as he studies her almost clinically, as though he has never seen her before*) You a horrible-looking chick at this hour.

BENEATHA (*Drily*) Good morning, everybody.

WALTER (*Senselessly*) How is school coming?

BENEATHA (*In the same spirit*) Lovely. Lovely. And you know, biology is the greatest. (*Looking up at him*) I dissected something that looked just like you yesterday.

WALTER I just wondered if you've made up your mind and everything.

BENEATHA (*Gaining in sharpness and impatience*) And what did I answer yesterday morning—and the day before that?

RUTH (*From the ironing board, like someone disinterested and old*) Don't be so nasty, Bennie.

BENEATHA (*Still to her brother*) And the day before that and the day before that!

WALTER (*Defensively*) I'm interested in you. Something wrong with that? Ain't many girls who decide—

WALTER *and* BENEATHA (*In unison*) —"to be a doctor."

(*Silence*)

WALTER Have we figured out yet just exactly how much medical school is going to cost?

RUTH Walter Lee, why don't you leave that girl alone and get out of here to work?

BENEATHA (*Exits to the bathroom and bangs on the door*) Come on out of there, please!

(*She comes back into the room*)

WALTER (*Looking at his sister intently*) You know the check is coming tomorrow.

BENEATHA (*Turning on him with a sharpness all her own*) That money belongs to Mama, Walter, and it's for her to decide how she wants to use it. I don't care if she wants to buy a house or a rocket ship or just nail it up somewhere and look at it. It's hers. Not ours—*hers.*

WALTER (*Bitterly*) Now ain't that fine! You just got your mother's interest at heart, ain't you, girl? You such a nice girl—but if Mama got that money she can always take a few thousand and help you through school too—can't she?

BENEATHA I have never asked anyone around here to do anything for me!

WALTER No! And the line between asking and just accepting when the time comes is big and wide—ain't it!

BENEATHA (*With fury*) What do you want from me, Brother—that I quit school or just drop dead, which!

WALTER I don't want nothing but for you to stop acting holy 'round here. Me and Ruth done made some sacrifices for you—why can't you do something for the family?

RUTH Walter, don't be dragging me in it.

WALTER You are in it— Don't you get up and go work in somebody's kitchen for the last three years to help put clothes on her back?

RUTH Oh, Walter—that's not fair . . .

WALTER It ain't that nobody expects you to get on your knees and say thank you, Brother; thank you, Ruth; thank you, Mama—and thank you, Travis, for wearing the same pair of shoes for two semesters—

BENEATHA (*Dropping to her knees*) Well—I *do*—all right?—thank everybody . . . and forgive me for ever wanting to be anything at all . . . forgive me, forgive me!

RUTH Please stop it! Your mama'll hear you.

WALTER Who the hell told you you had to be a doctor? If you so crazy 'bout messing 'round with sick people—then go be a nurse like other women—or just get married and be quiet . . .

BENEATHA Well—you finally got it said . . . It took you three years but you finally got it said. Walter, give up; leave me alone—it's Mama's money.

WALTER *He was my father, too!*

BENEATHA So what? He was mine, too—and Travis' grandfather—but the insurance money belongs to Mama. Picking on me is not going to make her give it to you to invest in any liquor stores— (*Underbreath, dropping into a chair*) —and I for one say, God bless Mama for that!

WALTER (*To* RUTH) See—did you hear? Did you hear!

RUTH Honey, please go to work.

WALTER Nobody in this house is ever going to understand me.

BENEATHA Because you're a nut.

WALTER Who's a nut?

BENEATHA You—you are a nut. Thee is mad, boy.

WALTER (*Looking at his wife and his sister from the door, very sadly*) The world's most backward race of people, and that's a fact.

BENEATHA (*Turning slowly in her chair*) And then there are all those prophets who would lead us out of the wilderness— (WALTER *slams out of the house*) —into the swamps!

RUTH Bennie, why you always gotta be pickin' on your brother? Can't you be a little sweeter sometimes?

(*Door opens.* WALTER *walks in*)

WALTER (*To* RUTH) I need some money for carfare.

RUTH (*Looks at him, then warms; teasing, but tenderly*) Fifty cents? (*She goes to her bag and gets money*) Here, take a taxi.

(WALTER *exits.* MAMA *enters. She is a woman in her early sixties, full-bodied and strong. She is one of those women of a certain grace and beauty who wear it so unobtrusively that it takes a while to notice. Her dark-brown face is surrounded by the total whiteness of her hair, and, being a woman who has adjusted to many things in life and overcome many more, her face is full of strength. She has, we can see, wit and faith of a kind that keep her eyes lit and full of interest and expectancy. She is, in a word, a beautiful woman. Her bearing is perhaps most like the noble bearing of the women of the Hereros of Southwest Africa—rather as if she imagines that as she walks she still bears a basket or a vessel upon her head. Her speech, on the other hand, is as careless as her carriage is precise—she is inclined to slur everything—but her voice is perhaps not so much quiet as simply soft*)

MAMA Who that 'round here slamming doors at this hour? (*She crosses through the room, goes to the window, opens it, and brings in a feeble little plant growing doggedly in a small pot on the window sill. She feels the dirt and puts it back out*)

RUTH That was Walter Lee. He and Bennie was at it again.

MAMA My children and they tempers. Lord, if this little old plant don't get more sun than it's been getting it ain't never going to see spring again. (*She turns from the window*) What's the matter with you this morning, Ruth? You looks right peaked. You aiming to iron all them things? Leave some for me. I'll get to 'em this afternoon. Bennie honey, it's too drafty for you to be sitting 'round half dressed. Where's your robe?

BENEATHA In the cleaners.

MAMA Well, go get mine and put it on.

BENEATHA I'm not cold, Mama, honest.

MAMA I know—but you so thin . . .

BENEATHA (*Irritably*) Mama, I'm not cold.

MAMA (*Seeing the make-down bed as* TRAVIS *has left it*) Lord have mercy, look at that poor bed. Bless his heart —he tries, don't he?

(*She moves to the bed* TRAVIS *has sloppily made up*)

RUTH No—he don't half try at all 'cause he knows you going to come along behind him and fix everything. That's just how come he don't know how to do nothing right now—you done spoiled that boy so.

MAMA Well—he's a little boy. Ain't supposed to know 'bout housekeeping. My baby, that's what he is. What you fix for his breakfast this morning?

RUTH (*Angrily*) I feed my son, Lena!

MAMA I ain't meddling— (*Underbreath; busy-bodyish*) I just noticed all last week he had cold cereal, and when it starts getting this chilly in the fall a child ought to have some hot grits or something when he goes out in the cold—

RUTH (*Furious*) I gave him hot oats—is that all right!

MAMA I ain't meddling. (*Pause*) Put a lot of nice butter on it? (RUTH *shoots her an angry look and does not reply*) He likes lots of butter.

RUTH (*Exasperated*) Lena—

MAMA (*To* BENEATHA. MAMA *is inclined to wander conversationally sometimes*) What was you and your brother fussing 'bout this morning?

BENEATHA It's not important, Mama.

(*She gets up and goes to look out at the bathroom, which is apparently free, and she picks up her towels and rushes out*)

MAMA What was they fighting about?

RUTH Now you know as well as I do.

MAMA (*Shaking her head*) Brother still worrying hisself sick about that money?

RUTH You know he is.

MAMA You had breakfast?

RUTH Some coffee.

MAMA Girl, you better start eating and looking after yourself better. You almost thin as Travis.

RUTH Lena—

MAMA Un-hunh?

RUTH What are you going to do with it?

MAMA Now don't you start, child. It's too early in the morning to be talking about money. It ain't Christian.

RUTH It's just that he got his heart set on that store—

MAMA You mean that liquor store that Willy Harris want him to invest in?

RUTH Yes—

MAMA We ain't no business people, Ruth. We just plain working folks.

RUTH Ain't nobody business people till they go into business. Walter Lee say colored people ain't never going to start getting ahead till they start gambling on some different kinds of things in the world—investments and things.

MAMA What done got into you, girl? Walter Lee done finally sold you on investing.

RUTH No. Mama, something is happening between Walter and me. I don't know what it is—but he needs something—something I can't give him any more. He needs this chance, Lena.

MAMA (*Frowning deeply*) But liquor, honey—

RUTH Well—like Walter say—I spec people going to always be drinking themselves some liquor.

MAMA Well—whether they drinks it or not ain't none of my business. But whether I go into business selling it to 'em *is,* and I don't want that on my ledger this late in life. (*Stopping suddenly and studying her daughter-in-law*) Ruth Younger, what's the matter with you today? You look like you could fall over right there.

RUTH I'm tired.

MAMA Then you better stay home from work today.

RUTH I can't stay home. She'd be calling up the agency and screaming at them, "My girl didn't come in today—send me somebody! My girl didn't come in!" Oh, she just have a fit . . .

MAMA Well, let her have it. I'll just call her up and say you got the flu—

RUTH (*Laughing*) Why the flu?

MAMA 'Cause it sounds respectable to 'em. Something white people get, too. They know 'bout the flu. Otherwise they think you been cut up or something when you tell 'em you sick.

RUTH I got to go in. We need the money.

MAMA Somebody would of thought my children done all but starved to death the way they talk about money here late. Child, we got a great big old check coming tomorrow.

RUTH (*Sincerely, but also self-righteously*) Now that's your money. It ain't got nothing to do with me. We all feel like that—Walter and Bennie and me—even Travis.

MAMA (*Thoughtfully, and suddenly very far away*) Ten thousand dollars—

RUTH Sure is wonderful.

MAMA Ten thousand dollars.

RUTH You know what you should do, Miss Lena? You should take yourself a trip somewhere. To Europe or South America or someplace—

MAMA (*Throwing up her hands at the thought*) Oh, child!

RUTH I'm serious. Just pack up and leave! Go on away and enjoy yourself some. Forget about the family and have yourself a ball for once in your life—

MAMA (*Drily*) You sound like I'm just about ready to die. Who'd go with me? What I look like wandering 'round Europe by myself?

RUTH Shoot—these here rich white women do it all the time. They don't think nothing of packing up their suitcases and piling on one of them big steamships and—swoosh!—they gone, child.

MAMA Something always told me I wasn't no rich white woman.

RUTH Well—what are you going to do with it then?

MAMA I ain't rightly decided. (*Thinking. She speaks now with emphasis*) Some of it got to be put away for Beneatha and her schoolin'—and ain't nothing going to touch that part of it. Nothing. (*She waits several seconds, trying to make up her mind about something, and looks at* RUTH *a little tentatively before going on*) Been thinking that we maybe could meet the notes on a little old two-story somewhere, with a yard where Travis could play in the summertime, if we use part of the insurance for a down payment and everybody kind of pitch in. I could maybe take on a little day work again, few days a week—

RUTH (*Studying her mother-in-law furtively and concentrating on her ironing, anxious to encourage without seeming to*) Well, Lord knows, we've put enough rent into this here rat trap to pay for four houses by now . . .

MAMA (*Looking up at the words "rat trap" and then looking around and leaning back and sighing—in a suddenly reflective mood—*) "Rat trap"—yes, that's all it is. (*Smiling*) I remember just as well the day me and Big Walter moved in here. Hadn't been married but two weeks and wasn't planning on living here no more than a year. (*She shakes her head at the dissolved dream*) We was going to set away, little by little, don't you know, and buy a little place out in Morgan Park. We had even picked out the house. (*Chuckling a little*) Looks right dumpy today. But Lord, child, you should know all the dreams I had 'bout buying that house and fixing it up and making me a little garden in the back— (*She waits and stops smiling*) And didn't none of it happen. (*Dropping her hands in a futile gesture*)

RUTH (*Keeps her head down, ironing*) Yes, life can be a barrel of disappointments, sometimes.

MAMA Honey, Big Walter would come in here some nights back then and slump down on that couch there and just look at the rug, and look at me and look at the rug and then back at me—and I'd know he was down then . . . really down. (*After a second very long and thoughtful pause; she is seeing back to times that only she can see*) And then, Lord, when I lost that baby—little Claude—I almost thought I was going to lose Big Walter too. Oh, that man grieved hisself! He was one man to love his children.

RUTH Ain't nothin' can tear at you like losin' your baby.

MAMA I guess that's how come that man finally worked hisself to death like he done. Like he was fighting his own war with this here world that took his baby from him.

RUTH He sure was a fine man, all right. I always liked Mr. Younger.

MAMA Crazy 'bout his children! God knows there was plenty wrong with Walter Younger—hard-headed, mean, kind of wild with women—plenty wrong with him. But he sure loved his children. Always wanted them to have something—be something. That's where Brother gets all these notions, I reckon. Big Walter used to say, he'd get right wet in the eyes sometimes, lean his head back with the water standing in his eyes and say, "Seem like God didn't see fit to give the black man nothing but dreams —but He did give us children to make them dreams seem worth while." (*She smiles*) He could talk like that, don't you know.

RUTH Yes, he sure could. He was a good man, Mr. Younger.

MAMA Yes, a fine man—just couldn't never catch up with his dreams, that's all.

(BENEATHA *comes in, brushing her hair and looking up to the ceiling, where the sound of a vacuum cleaner has started up*)

BENEATHA What could be so dirty on that woman's rugs that she has to vacuum them every single day?

RUTH I wish certain young women 'round here who I could name would take inspiration about certain rugs in a certain apartment I could also mention.

BENEATHA (*Shrugging*) How much cleaning can a house need, for Christ's sakes.

MAMA (*Not liking the Lord's name used thus*) Bennie!

RUTH Just listen to her—just listen!

BENEATHA Oh, God!

MAMA If you use the Lord's name just one more time—

BENEATHA (*A bit of a whine*) Oh, Mama—

RUTH Fresh—just fresh as salt, this girl!

BENEATHA (*Drily*) Well—if the salt loses its savor—

MAMA Now that will do. I just ain't going to have you

'round here reciting the scriptures in vain—you hear me?

BENEATHA How did I manage to get on everybody's wrong side by just walking into a room?

RUTH If you weren't so fresh—

BENEATHA Ruth, I'm twenty years old.

MAMA What time you be home from school today?

BENEATHA Kind of late. (*With enthusiasm*) Madeline is going to start my guitar lessons today.

(MAMA *and* RUTH *look up with the same expression*)

MAMA Your *what* kind of lessons?

BENEATHA Guitar.

RUTH Oh, Father!

MAMA How come you done taken it in your mind to learn to play the guitar?

BENEATHA I just want to, that's all.

MAMA (*Smiling*) Lord, child, don't you know what to do with yourself? How long it going to be before you get tired of this now—like you got tired of that little play-acting group you joined last year? (*Looking at* RUTH) And what was it the year before that?

RUTH The horseback-riding club for which she bought that fifty-five-dollar riding habit that's been hanging in the closet ever since!

MAMA (*To* BENEATHA) Why you got to flit so from one thing to another, baby?

BENEATHA (*Sharply*) I just want to learn to play the guitar. Is there anything wrong with that?

MAMA Ain't nobody trying to stop you. I just wonders sometimes why you has to flit so from one thing to another all the time. You ain't never done nothing with all that camera equipment you brought home—

BENEATHA I don't flit! I—I experiment with different forms of expression—

RUTH Like riding a horse?

BENEATHA —People have to express themselves one way or another.

MAMA What is it you want to express?

BENEATHA (*Angrily*) Me! (MAMA *and* RUTH *look at each other and burst into raucous laughter*) Don't worry—I don't expect you to understand.

MAMA (*To change the subject*) Who you going out with tomorrow night?

BENEATHA (*With displeasure*) George Murchison again.

MAMA (*Pleased*) Oh—you getting a little sweet on him?

RUTH You ask me, this child ain't sweet on nobody but herself— (*Underbreath*) Express herself!

(*They laugh*)

BENEATHA Oh—I like George all right, Mama. I mean I like him enough to go out with him and stuff, but—

RUTH (*For devilment*) What does *and stuff* mean?

BENEATHA Mind your own business.

MAMA Stop picking at her now, Ruth. (*A thoughtful pause, and then a suspicious sudden look at her daughter as she turns in her chair for emphasis*) What *does* it mean?

BENEATHA (*Wearily*) Oh, I just mean I couldn't ever really be serious about George. He's—he's so shallow.

RUTH Shallow—what do you mean he's shallow? He's *Rich!*

MAMA Hush, Ruth.

BENEATHA I know he's rich. He knows he's rich, too.

RUTH Well—what other qualities a man got to have to satisfy you, little girl?

BENEATHA You wouldn't even begin to understand. Anybody who married Walter could not possibly understand.

MAMA (*Outraged*) What kind of way is that to talk about your brother?

BENEATHA Brother is a flip—let's face it.

MAMA (*To* RUTH, *helplessly*) What's a flip?

RUTH (*Glad to add kindling*) She's saying he's crazy.

BENEATHA Not crazy. Brother isn't really crazy yet—he—he's an elaborate neurotic.

MAMA Hush your mouth!

BENEATHA As for George. Well. George looks good—he's got a beautiful car and he takes me to nice places and, as my sister-in-law says, he is probably the richest boy I will ever get to know and I even like him sometimes—but if the Youngers are sitting around waiting to see if their little Bennie is going to tie up the family with the Murchisons, they are wasting their time.

RUTH You mean you wouldn't marry George Murchison if he asked you someday? That pretty, rich thing? Honey, I knew you was odd—

BENEATHA No I would not marry him if all I felt for him was what I feel now. Besides, George's family wouldn't really like it.

MAMA Why not?

BENEATHA Oh, Mama—the Murchisons are honest-to-God-real-*live*-rich colored people, and the only people in the world who are more snobbish than rich white people are rich colored people. I thought everybody knew that. I've met Mrs. Murchison. She's a scene!

MAMA You must not dislike people 'cause they well off, honey.

BENEATHA Why not? It makes just as much sense as disliking people 'cause they are poor, and lots of people do that.

RUTH (*A wisdom-of-the-ages manner. To* MAMA) Well, she'll get over some of this—

BENEATHA Get over it? What are you talking about, Ruth? Listen, I'm going to be a doctor. I'm not worried about who I'm going to marry yet—if I ever get married.

MAMA *and* RUTH *If!*

MAMA Now, Bennie—

BENEATHA Oh, I probably will . . . but first I'm going to be a doctor, and George, for one, still thinks that's pretty funny. I couldn't be bothered with that. I am going to be a doctor and everybody around here better understand that!

MAMA (*Kindly*) 'Course you going to be a doctor, honey, God willing.

BENEATHA (*Drily*) God hasn't got a thing to do with it.

MAMA Beneatha—that just wasn't necessary.

BENEATHA Well—neither is God. I get sick of hearing about God.

MAMA Beneatha!

BENEATHA I mean it! I'm just tired of hearing about God all the time. What has He got to do with anything? Does he pay tuition?

MAMA You 'bout to get your fresh little jaw slapped!

RUTH That's just what she needs, all right!

BENEATHA Why? Why can't I say what I want to around here, like everybody else?

MAMA It don't sound nice for a young girl to say things like that—you wasn't brought up that way. Me and your father went to trouble to get you and Brother to church every Sunday.

BENEATHA Mama, you don't understand. It's all a matter of ideas, and God is just one idea I don't accept. It's not important. I am not going out and be immoral or commit crimes because I don't believe in God. I don't even think about it. It's just that I get tired of Him getting credit for all the things the human race achieves through its own stubborn effort. There simply is no blasted God —there is only man and it is he who makes miracles!

(MAMA *absorbs this speech, studies her daughter and rises slowly and crosses to* BENEATHA *and slaps her powerfully across the face. After, there is only silence and the daughter drops her eyes from her mother's face, and* MAMA *is very tall before her*)

MAMA Now—you say after me, in my mother's house there is still God. (*There is a long pause and* BENEATHA *stares at the floor wordlessly.* MAMA *repeats the phrase with precision and cool emotion*) In my mother's house there is still God.

BENEATHA In my mother's house there is still God.
(*A long pause*)

MAMA (*Walking away from* BENEATHA, *too disturbed for triumphant posture. Stopping and turning back to her daughter*) There are some ideas we ain't going to have in this house. Not long as I am at the head of this family.

BENEATHA Yes, ma'am.
(MAMA *walks out of the room*)

RUTH (*Almost gently, with profound understanding*) You think you a woman, Bennie—but you still a little girl. What you did was childish—so you got treated like a child.

BENEATHA I see. (*Quietly*) I also see that everybody thinks it's all right for Mama to be a tyrant. But all the tyranny in the world will never put a God in the heavens!
(*She picks up her books and goes out*)

RUTH (*Goes to* MAMA'S *door*) She said she was sorry.

MAMA (*Coming out, going to her plant*) They frightens me, Ruth. My children.

RUTH You got good children, Lena. They just a little off sometimes—but they're good.

MAMA No—there's something come down between me and them that don't let us understand each other and I don't know what it is. One done almost lost his mind thinking 'bout money all the time and the other done commence to talk about things I can't seem to understand in no form or fashion. What is it that's changing, Ruth?

RUTH (*Soothingly, older than her years*) Now . . . you taking it all too seriously. You just got strong-willed children and it takes a strong woman like you to keep 'em in hand.

MAMA (*Looking at her plant and sprinkling a little water on it*) They spirited all right, my children. Got to admit they got spirit—Bennie and Walter. Like this little old plant that ain't never had enough sunshine or nothing—and look at it . . .

(*She has her back to* RUTH, *who has had to stop ironing and lean against something and put the back of her hand to her forehead*)

RUTH (*Trying to keep* MAMA *from noticing*) You . . . sure . . . loves that little old thing, don't you? . . .

MAMA Well, I always wanted me a garden like I used to see sometimes at the back of the houses down home. This plant is close as I ever got to having one. (*She looks out of the window as she replaces the plant*) Lord, ain't nothing as dreary as the view from this window on a dreary day, is there? Why ain't you singing this morning, Ruth? Sing that "No Ways Tired." That song always lifts me up so— (*She turns at last to see that* RUTH *has slipped quietly into a chair, in a state of semiconsciousness*) Ruth! Ruth honey—what's the matter with you . . . Ruth!

CURTAIN

Scene Two

It is the following morning; a Saturday morning, and house cleaning is in progress at the YOUNGERS. *Furniture has been shoved hither and yon and* MAMA *is giving the kitchen-area walls a washing down.* BENEATHA, *in dungarees, with a handkerchief tied around her face, is spraying insecticide into the cracks in the walls. As they work, the radio is on and a Southside disk-jockey program is inappropriately filling the house with a rather exotic saxophone blues.* TRAVIS, *the sole idle one, is leaning on his arms, looking out of the window.*

TRAVIS Grandmama, that stuff Bennie is using smells awful. Can I go downstairs, please?

MAMA Did you get all them chores done already? I ain't seen you doing much.

TRAVIS Yes'm—finished early. Where did Mama go this morning?

MAMA (*Looking at* BENEATHA) She had to go on a little errand.

TRAVIS Where?

MAMA To tend to her business.

TRAVIS Can I go outside then?

MAMA Oh, I guess so. You better stay right in front of the house, though . . . and keep a good lookout for the postman.

TRAVIS Yes'm. (*He starts out and decides to give his* AUNT BENEATHA *a good swat on the legs as he passes her*) Leave them poor little old cockroaches alone, they ain't bothering you none.

(*He runs as she swings the spray gun at him both viciously and playfully.* WALTER *enters from the bedroom and goes to the phone*)

MAMA Look out there, girl, before you be spilling some of that stuff on that child!

TRAVIS (*Teasing*) That's right—look out now!

(*He exits*)

BENEATHA (*Drily*) I can't imagine that it would hurt him —it has never hurt the roaches.

MAMA Well, little boys' hides ain't as tough as Southside roaches.

WALTER (*Into phone*) Hello—let me talk to Willy Harris.

MAMA You better get over there behind the bureau. I seen one marching out of there like Napoleon yesterday.

WALTER Hello, Willy? It ain't come yet. It'll be here in a few minutes. Did the lawyer give you the papers?

BENEATHA There's really only one way to get rid of them, Mama—

MAMA How?

BENEATHA Set fire to this building.

WALTER Good. Good. I'll be right over.

BENEATHA Where did Ruth go, Walter?

WALTER I don't know.

(*He exits abruptly*)

BENEATHA Mama, where did Ruth go?

MAMA (*Looking at her with meaning*) To the doctor, I think.

BENEATHA The doctor? What's the matter? (*They exchange glances*) You don't think—

MAMA (*With her sense of drama*) Now I ain't saying what I think. But I ain't never been wrong 'bout a woman neither.

(*The phone rings*)

BENEATHA (*At the phone*) Hay-lo . . . (*Pause, and a moment of recognition*) Well—when did you get back! . . . And how was it? . . . Of course I've missed you —in my way . . . This morning? No . . . house cleaning and all that and Mama hates it if I let people come over when the house is like this . . . You *have?* Well, that's different . . . What is it— Oh, what the hell, come on over . . . Right, see you then.

(*She hangs up*)

MAMA (*Who has listened vigorously, as is her habit*) Who is that you inviting over here with this house looking like this? You ain't got the pride you was born with!

BENEATHA Asagai doesn't care how houses look, Mama—he's an intellectual.

MAMA *Who?*

BENEATHA Asagai—Joseph Asagai. He's an African boy

I met on campus. He's been studying in Canada all summer.

MAMA What's his name?

BENEATHA Asagai, Joseph. Ah-sah-guy . . . He's from Nigeria.

MAMA Oh, that's the little country that was founded by slaves way back . . .

BENEATHA No, Mama—that's Liberia.

MAMA I don't think I never met no African before.

BENEATHA Well, do me a favor and don't ask him a whole lot of ignorant questions about Africans. I mean, do they wear clothes and all that—

MAMA Well, now, I guess if you think we so ignorant 'round here maybe you shouldn't bring your friends here—

BENEATHA It's just that people ask such crazy things. All anyone seems to know about when it comes to Africa is Tarzan—

MAMA (*Indignantly*) Why should I know anything about Africa?

BENEATHA Why do you give money at church for the missionary work?

MAMA Well, that's to help save people.

BENEATHA You mean save them from *heathenism*—

MAMA (*Innocently*) Yes.

BENEATHA I'm afraid they need more salvation from the British and the French.

(RUTH *comes in forlornly and pulls off her coat with dejection. They both turn to look at her*)

RUTH (*Dispiritedly*) Well, I guess from all the happy faces—everybody knows.

BENEATHA You pregnant?

MAMA Lord have mercy, I sure hope it's a little old girl. Travis ought to have a sister.

(BENEATHA *and* RUTH *give her a hopeless look for this grandmotherly enthusiasm*)

BENEATHA How far along are you?

RUTH Two months.

BENEATHA Did you mean to? I mean did you plan it or was it an accident?

MAMA What do you know about planning or not planning?

BENEATHA Oh, Mama.

RUTH (*Wearily*) She's twenty years old, Lena.

BENEATHA Did you plan it, Ruth?

RUTH Mind your own business.

BENEATHA It is my business—where is he going to live, on the *roof?* (*There is silence following the remark as the three women react to the sense of it*) Gee—I didn't mean that, Ruth, honest. Gee, I don't feel like that at all. I—I think it is wonderful.

RUTH (*Dully*) Wonderful.

BENEATHA Yes—really.

MAMA (*Looking at* RUTH, *worried*) Doctor say everything going to be all right?

RUTH (*Far away*) Yes—she says everything is going to be fine . . .

MAMA (*Immediately suspicious*) "She"— What doctor you went to? (RUTH *folds over, near hysteria.* MAMA *worriedly hovers over her*) Ruth honey—what's the matter with you—you sick?

(RUTH *has her fists clenched on her thighs and is fighting hard to suppress a scream that seems to be rising in her*)

BENEATHA What's the matter with her, Mama?

MAMA (*Working her fingers in* RUTH'S *shoulder to relax her*) She be all right. Women gets right depressed sometimes when they get her way. (*Speaking softly, expertly, rapidly*) Now you just relax. That's right . . . just lean back, don't think 'bout nothing at all . . . nothing at all—

RUTH I'm all right . . .

(*The glassy-eyed look melts and then she collapses into a fit of heavy sobbing. The bell rings*)

BENEATHA Oh, my God—that must be Asagai.

MAMA (*To* RUTH) Come on now, honey. You need to lie down and rest awhile . . . then have some nice hot food.

(*They exit,* RUTH'S *weight on her mother-in-law.* BENEATHA, *herself profoundly disturbed, opens the door to admit a rather dramatic-looking young man with a large package*)

ASAGAI Hello, Alaiyo—

BENEATHA (*Holding the door open and regarding him with pleasure*) Hello . . . (*Long pause*) Well—come in. And please excuse everything. My mother was very upset about my letting anyone come here with the place like this.

ASAGAI (*Coming into the room*) You look disturbed too . . . Is something wrong?

BENEATHA (*Still at the door, absently*) Yes . . . we've all got acute ghetto-itus. (*She smiles and comes toward him, finding a cigarette and sitting*) So—sit down! How was Canada?

ASAGAI (*A sophisticate*) Canadian.

BENEATHA (*Looking at him*) I'm very glad you are back.

ASAGAI (*Looking back at her in turn*) Are you really?

BENEATHA Yes—very.

ASAGAI Why—you were quite glad when I went away. What happened?

BENEATHA You went away.

ASAGAI Ahhhhhhhh.

BENEATHA Before—you wanted to be so serious before there was time.

ASAGAI How much time must there be before one knows what one feels?

BENEATHA (*Stalling this particular conversation. Her hands pressed together, in a deliberately childish gesture*) What did you bring me?

ASAGAI (*Handing her the package*) Open it and see.

BENEATHA (*Eagerly opening the package and drawing out some records and the colorful robes of a Nigerian woman*) Oh, Asagai! . . . You got them for me! . . . How beautiful . . . and the records too!

(*She lifts out the robes and runs to the mirror with them and holds the drapery up in front of herself*)

ASAGAI (*Coming to her at the mirror*) I shall have to teach you how to drape it properly. (*He flings the material about her for the moment and stands back to look at her*) Ah— *Oh-pay-gay-day, oh-gbah-mu-shay*. (*A Yoruba exclamation for admiration*) You wear it well . . . very well . . . mutilated hair and all.

BENEATHA (*Turning suddenly*) My hair—what's wrong with my hair?

ASAGAI (*Shrugging*) Were you born with it like that?

BENEATHA (*Reaching up to touch it*) No . . . of course not.

(*She looks back to the mirror, disturbed*)

ASAGAI (*Smiling*) How then?

BENEATHA You know perfectly well how . . . as crinkly as yours . . . that's how.

ASAGAI And it is ugly to you that way?

BENEATHA (*Quickly*) Oh, no—not ugly . . . (*More slowly, apologetically*) But it's so hard to manage when it's, well—raw.

ASAGAI And so to accommodate that—you mutilate it every week?

BENEATHA It's not mutilation!

ASAGAI (*Laughing aloud at her seriousness*) Oh . . . please! I am only teasing you because you are so very serious about these things. (*He stands back from her and folds his arms across his chest as he watches her pulling at her hair and frowning in the mirror)* Do you remember the first time you met me at school? . . . *(He laughs)* You came up to me and you said—and I thought you were the most serious little thing I had ever seen—you said: *(He imitates her)* "Mr. Asagai—I want very much to talk with you. About Africa. You see, Mr. Asagai, I am looking for my *identity!*" *(He laughs)*

BENEATHA *(Turning to him, not laughing)* Yes— *(Her face is quizzical, profoundly disturbed)*

ASAGAI *(Still teasing and reaching out and taking her face in his hands and turning her profile to him)* Well . . . it is true that this is not so much a profile of a Hollywood queen as perhaps a queen of the Nile— *(A mock dismissal of the importance of the question)* But what does it matter? Assimilationism is so popular in your country.

BENEATHA *(Wheeling, passionately, sharply)* I am not an assimilationist!

ASAGAI *(The protest hangs in the room for a moment and* ASAGAI *studies her, his laughter fading)* Such a serious one. *(There is a pause)* So—you like the robes? You must take excellent care of them—they are from my sister's personal wardrobe.

BENEATHA *(With incredulity)* You—you sent all the way home—for me?

ASAGAI *(With charm)* For you—I would do much more . . . Well, that is what I came for. I must go.

BENEATHA Will you call me Monday?

ASAGAI Yes . . . We have a great deal to talk about. I mean about identity and time and all that.

BENEATHA Time?

ASAGAI Yes. About how much time one needs to know what one feels.

BENEATHA You never understood that there is more than one kind of feeling which can exist between a man and a woman—or, at least, there should be.

ASAGAI (*Shaking his head negatively but gently*) No. Between a man and a woman there need be only one kind of feeling. I have that for you . . . Now even . . . right this moment . . .

BENEATHA I know—and by itself—it won't do. I can find that anywhere.

ASAGAI For a woman it should be enough.

BENEATHA I know—because that's what it says in all the novels that men write. But it isn't. Go ahead and laugh—but I'm not interested in being someone's little episode in America or— (*With feminine vengeance*) —one of them! (ASAGAI *has burst into laughter again*) That's funny as hell, huh!

ASAGAI It's just that every American girl I have known has said that to me. White—black—in this you are all the same. And the same speech, too!

BENEATHA (*Angrily*) Yuk, yuk, yuk!

ASAGAI It's how you can be sure that the world's most liberated women are not liberated at all. You all talk about it too much!

(MAMA *enters and is immediately all social charm because of the presence of a guest*)

BENEATHA Oh—Mama—this is Mr. Asagai.

MAMA How do you do?

ASAGAI (*Total politeness to an elder*) How do you do, Mrs. Younger. Please forgive me for coming at such an outrageous hour on a Saturday.

MAMA Well, you are quite welcome. I just hope you understand that our house don't always look like this. (*Chatterish*) You must come again. I would love to hear all about— (*Not sure of the name*) —your country. I think it's so sad the way our American Negroes don't know nothing about Africa 'cept Tarzan and all that. And all that money they pour into these churches when they ought to be helping you people over there drive out them French and Englishmen done taken away your land.

(*The mother flashes a slightly superior look at her daughter upon completion of the recitation*)

ASAGAI (*Taken aback by this sudden and acutely unrelated expression of sympathy*) Yes . . . yes . . .

MAMA (*Smiling at him suddenly and relaxing and looking him over*) How many miles is it from here to where you come from?

ASAGAI Many thousands.

MAMA (*Looking at him as she would* WALTER) I bet you don't half look after yourself, being away from your mama either. I spec you better come 'round here from time to time and get yourself some decent home-cooked meals . . .

ASAGAI (*Moved*) Thank you. Thank you very much. (*They are all quiet, then—*) Well . . . I must go. I will call you Monday, Alaiyo.

MAMA What's that he call you?

ASAGAI Oh—"Alaiyo." I hope you don't mind. It is what you would call a nickname, I think. It is a Yoruba word. I am a Yoruba.

MAMA (*Looking at* BENEATHA) I—I thought he was from—

ASAGAI (*Understanding*) Nigeria is my country. Yoruba is my tribal origin—

BENEATHA You didn't tell us what Alaiyo means . . . for all I know, you might be calling me Little Idiot or something . . .

ASAGAI Well . . . let me see . . . I do not know how just to explain it . . . The sense of a thing can be so different when it changes languages.

BENEATHA You're evading.

ASAGAI No—really it is difficult . . . (*Thinking*) It means . . . it means One for Whom Bread—Food—Is Not Enough. (*He looks at her*) Is that all right?

BENEATHA (*Understanding, softly*) Thank you.

MAMA (*Looking from one to the other and not understand-*

ing any of it) Well . . . that's nice . . . You must come to see us again—Mr.—

ASAGAI Ah-sah-guy . . .

MAMA Yes . . . Do come again.

ASAGAI Good-bye.

(*He exits*)

MAMA (*After him*) Lord, that's a pretty thing just went out here! (*Insinuatingly, to her daughter*) Yes, I guess I see why we done commence to get so interested in Africa 'round here. Missionaries my aunt Jenny!

(*She exits*)

BENEATHA Oh, Mama! . . .

(*She picks up the Nigerian dress and holds it up to her in front of the mirror again. She sets the headdress on haphazardly and then notices her hair again and clutches at it and then replaces the headdress and frowns at herself. Then she starts to wriggle in front of the mirror as she thinks a Nigerian woman might.* TRAVIS *enters and regards her*)

TRAVIS You cracking up?

BENEATHA Shut up.

(*She pulls the headdress off and looks at herself in the mirror and clutches at her hair again and squinches her eyes as if trying to imagine something. Then, suddenly, she gets her raincoat and kerchief and hurriedly prepares for going out*)

MAMA (*Coming back into the room*) She's resting now. Travis, baby, run next door and ask Miss Johnson to please let me have a little kitchen cleanser. This here can is empty as Jacob's kettle.

TRAVIS I just came in.

MAMA Do as you told. (*He exits and she looks at her daughter*) Where are you going?

BENEATHA (*Halting at the door*) To become a queen of the Nile!

(*She exits in a breathless blaze of glory.* RUTH *appears in the bedroom doorway*)

MAMA Who told you to get up?

RUTH Ain't nothing wrong with me to be lying in no bed for. Where did Bennie go?

MAMA (*Drumming her fingers*) Far as I could make out —to Egypt. (RUTH *just looks at her*) What time is it getting to?

RUTH Ten twenty. And the mailman going to ring that bell this morning just like he done every morning for the last umpteen years.

(TRAVIS *comes in with the cleanser can*)

TRAVIS She say to tell you that she don't have much.

MAMA (*Angrily*) Lord, some people I could name sure is tight-fisted! (*Directing her grandson*) Mark two cans of cleanser down on the list there. If she that hard up for kitchen cleanser, I sure don't want to forget to get her none!

RUTH Lena—maybe the woman is just short on cleanser—

MAMA (*Not listening*) —Much baking powder as she done borrowed from me all these years, she could of done gone into the baking business!

(*The bell sounds suddenly and sharply and all three are stunned—serious and silent—mid-speech. In spite of all the other conversations and distractions of the morning, this is what they have been waiting for, even* TRAVIS, *who looks helplessly from his mother to his grandmother.* RUTH *is the first to come to life again*)

RUTH (*To* TRAVIS) *Get down them steps, boy!*

(TRAVIS *snaps to life and flies out to get the mail*)

MAMA (*Her eyes wide, her hand to her breast*) You mean it done really come?

RUTH (*Excited*) Oh, Miss Lena!

MAMA (*Collecting herself*) Well . . . I don't know what we all so excited about 'round here for. We known it was coming for months.

RUTH That's a whole lot different from having it come and being able to hold it in your hands . . . a piece of paper worth ten thousand dollars . . . (TRAVIS *bursts back into the room. He holds the envelope high above his head, like a little dancer, his face is radiant and he is breathless. He moves to his grandmother with sudden slow ceremony and puts the envelope into her hands. She accepts it, and then merely holds it and looks at it*) Come on! Open it . . . Lord have mercy, I wish Walter Lee was here!

TRAVIS Open it, Grandmama!

MAMA (*Staring at it*) Now you all be quiet. It's just a check.

RUTH Open it . . .

MAMA (*Still staring at it*) Now don't act silly . . . We ain't never been no people to act silly 'bout no money—

RUTH (*Swiftly*) We ain't never had none before—*open it!*

(MAMA *finally makes a good strong tear and pulls out the thin blue slice of paper and inspects it closely. The boy and his mother study it raptly over* MAMA'S *shoulders*)

MAMA *Travis!* (*She is counting off with doubt*) Is that the right number of zeros.

TRAVIS Yes'm . . . ten thousand dollars. Gaalee, Grandmama, you rich.

MAMA (*She holds the check away from her, still looking at it. Slowly her face sobers into a mask of unhappiness*) Ten thousand dollars. (*She hands it to* RUTH) Put it away somewhere, Ruth. (*She does not look at* RUTH; *her eyes seem to be seeing something somewhere very far off*) Ten thousand dollars they give you. Ten thousand dollars.

TRAVIS (*To his mother, sincerely*) What's the matter with Grandmama—don't she want to be rich?

RUTH (*Distractedly*) You go on out and play now, baby.

(TRAVIS *exits.* MAMA *starts wiping dishes absently, humming intently to herself.* RUTH *turns to her, with kind exasperation*) You've gone and got yourself upset.

MAMA (*Not looking at her*) I spec if it wasn't for you all . . . I would just put that money away or give it to the church or something.

RUTH Now what kind of talk is that. Mr. Younger would just be plain mad if he could hear you talking foolish like that.

MAMA (*Stopping and staring off*) Yes . . . he sure would. (*Sighing*) We got enough to do with that money, all right. (*She halts then, and turn and looks at her daughter-in-law hard;* RUTH *avoids her eyes and* MAMA *wipes her hands with finality and starts to speak firmly to* RUTH) Where did you go today, girl?

RUTH To the doctor.

MAMA (*Impatiently*) Now, Ruth . . . you know better than that. Old Doctor Jones is strange enough in his way but there ain't nothing 'bout him make somebody slip and call him "she"—like you done this morning.

RUTH Well, that's what happened—my tongue slipped.

MAMA You went to see that woman, didn't you?

RUTH (*Defensively, giving herself away*) What woman you talking about?

MAMA (*Angrily*) That woman who—

(WALTER *enters in great excitement*)

WALTER Did it come?

MAMA (*Quietly*) Can't you give people a Christian greeting before you start asking about money?

WALTER (*To* RUTH) Did it come? (RUTH *unfolds the check and lays it quietly before him, watching him intently with thoughts of her own.* WALTER *sits down and grasps it close and counts off the zeros*) Ten thousand dollars— (*He turns suddenly, frantically to his mother and draws some papers out of his breast pocket*) Mama —look. Old Willy Harris put everything on paper—

MAMA Son—I think you ought to talk to your wife . . . I'll go on out and leave you alone if you want—

WALTER I can talk to her later—Mama, look—

MAMA Son—

WALTER WILL SOMEBODY PLEASE LISTEN TO ME TODAY!

MAMA (*Quietly*) I don't 'low no yellin' in this house, Walter Lee, and you know it— (WALTER *stares at them in frustration and starts to speak several times*) And there ain't going to be no investing in no liquor stores. I don't aim to have to speak on that again.

(*A long pause*)

WALTER Oh—so you don't aim to have to speak on that again? So *you* have decided . . . (*Crumpling his papers*) Well, *you* tell that to my boy tonight when you put him to sleep on the living-room couch . . . (*Turning to* MAMA *and speaking directly to her*) Yeah—and tell it to my wife, Mama, tomorrow when she has to go out of here to look after somebody else's kids. And tell it to *me,* Mama, every time we need a new pair of curtains and I have to watch *you* go out and work in somebody's kitchen. Yeah, you tell me then!

(WALTER *starts out*)

RUTH Where you going?

WALTER I'm going out!

RUTH Where?

WALTER Just out of this house somewhere—

RUTH (*Getting her coat*) I'll come too.

WALTER I don't want you to come!

RUTH I got something to talk to you about, Walter.

WALTER That's too bad.

MAMA (*Still quietly*) Walter Lee— (*She waits and he finally turns and looks at her*) Sit down.

WALTER I'm a grown man, Mama.

MAMA Ain't nobody said you wasn't grown. But you still

in my house and my presence. And as long as you are—you'll talk to your wife civil. Now sit down.

RUTH (*Suddenly*) Oh, let him go on out and drink himself to death! He makes me sick to my stomach! (*She flings her coat against him*)

WALTER (*Violently*) And you turn mine too, baby! (RUTH *goes into their bedroom and slams the door behind her*) That was my greatest mistake—

MAMA (*Still quietly*) Walter, what is the matter with you?

WALTER Matter with me? Ain't nothing the matter with *me!*

MAMA Yes there is. Something eating you up like a crazy man. Something more than me not giving you this money. The past few years I been watching it happen to you. You get all nervous acting and kind of wild in the eyes—(WALTER *jumps up impatiently at her words*) I said sit there now, I'm talking to you!

WALTER Mama—I don't need no nagging at me today.

MAMA Seem like you getting to a place where you always tied up in some kind of knot about something. But if anybody ask you 'bout it you just yell at 'em and bust out of the house and go out and drink somewheres. Walter Lee, people can't live with that. Ruth's a good, patient girl in her way—but your getting to be too much. Boy, don't make the mistake of driving that girl away from you.

WALTER Why—what she do for me?

MAMA She loves you.

WALTER Mama—I'm going out. I want to go off somewhere and be by myself for a while.

MAMA I'm sorry 'bout your liquor store, son. It just wasn't the thing for us to do. That's what I want to tell you about—

WALTER I got to go out, Mama—

(*He rises*)

MAMA It's dangerous, son.

WALTER What's dangerous?

MAMA When a man goes outside his home to look for peace.

WALTER (*Beseechingly*) Then why can't there never be no peace in this house then?

MAMA You done found it in some other house?

WALTER No—there ain't no woman! Why do women always think there's a woman somewhere when a man gets restless (*Coming to her*) Mama—Mama—I want so many things . . .

MAMA Yes, son—

WALTER I want so many things that they are driving me kind of crazy . . . Mama—look at me.

MAMA I'm looking at you. You a good-looking boy. You got a job, a nice wife, a fine boy and—

WALTER A job. (*Looks at her*) Mama, a job? I open and close car doors all day long. I drive a man around in his limousine and I say, "Yes, sir; no, sir; very good, sir; shall I take the Drive, sir?" Mama, that ain't no kind of job . . . that ain't nothing at all. (*Very quietly*) Mama, I don't know if I can make you understand.

MAMA Understand what, baby?

WALTER (*Quietly*) Sometimes it's like I can see the future stretched out in front of me—just plain as day. The future, Mama. Hanging over there at the edge of my days. Just waiting for me—a big, looming blank space—full of *nothing*. Just waiting for *me*. (*Pause*) Mama—sometimes when I'm downtown and I pass them cool, quiet-looking restaurants where them white boys are sitting back and talking 'bout things . . . sitting there turning deals worth millions of dollars . . . sometimes I see guys don't look much older than me—

MAMA Son—how come you talk so much 'bout money?

WALTER (*With immense passion*) Because it is life, Mama!

MAMA (*Quietly*) Oh— (*Very quietly*) So now it's life. Money is life. Once upon a time freedom used to be life

—now it's money. I guess the world really do change . . .

WALTER No—it was always money, Mama. We just didn't know about it.

MAMA No . . . something has changed. (*She looks at him*) You something new, boy. In my time we was worried about not being lynched and getting to the North if we could and how to stay alive and still have a pinch of dignity too . . . Now here come you and Beneatha —talking 'bout things we ain't never even thought about hardly, me and your daddy. You ain't satisfied or proud of nothing we done. I mean that you had a home; that we kept you out of trouble till you was grown; that you don't have to ride to work on the back of nobody's street-car— You my children—but how different we done become.

WALTER You just don't understand, Mama, you just don't understand.

MAMA Son—do you know your wife is expecting another baby? (WALTER *stands, stunned, and absorbs what his mother has said*) That's what she wanted to talk to you about. (WALTER *sinks down into a chair*) This ain't for me to be telling—but you ought to know. (*She waits*) I think Ruth is thinking 'bout getting rid of that child.

WALTER (*Slowly understanding*) No—no—Ruth wouldn't do that.

MAMA When the world gets ugly enough—a woman will do anything for her family. *The part that's already living.*

WALTER You don't know Ruth, Mama, if you think she would do that.

(RUTH *opens the bedroom door and stands there a little limp*)

RUTH (*Beaten*) Yes I would too, Walter. (*Pause*) I gave her a five-dollar down payment.

(*There is total silence as the man stares at his wife and the mother stares at her son*)

MAMA (*Presently*) Well—(*Tightly*) Well—son, I'm waiting to hear you say something . . . I'm waiting to hear how you be your father's son. Be the man he was . . . (*Pause*) Your wife say she going to destroy your child. And I'm waiting to hear you talk like him and say we a people who give children life, not who destroys them— (*She rises*) I'm waiting to see you stand up and look like your daddy and say we done give up one baby to poverty and that we ain't going to give up nary another one . . . I'm waiting.

WALTER Ruth—

MAMA If you a son of mine, tell her! (WALTER *turns, looks at her and can say nothing. She continues, bitterly*) You . . . you are a disgrace to your father's memory. Somebody get me my hat.

CURTAIN

ACT TWO

Scene One

Time: Later the same day.

At rise: RUTH *is ironing again. She has the radio going. Presently* BENEATHA'S *bedroom door opens and* RUTH'S *mouth falls and she puts down the iron in fascination.*

RUTH What have we got on tonight!

BENEATHA (*Emerging grandly from the doorway so that we can see her thoroughly robed in the costume Asagai brought*) You are looking at what a well-dressed Nigerian woman wears— (*She parades for* RUTH, *her hair completely hidden by the headdress; she is coquettishly fanning herself with an ornate oriental fan, mistakenly more like Butterfly than any Nigerian that ever was*) Isn't it beautiful? (*She promenades to the radio and, with an arrogant flourish, turns off the good loud blues that is playing*) Enough of this assimilationist junk! (RUTH *follows her with her eyes as she goes to the phonograph and puts on a record and turns and waits ceremoniously for the music to come up. Then, with a shout—*) OCOMOGOSIAY!

(RUTH *jumps. The music comes up, a lovely Nigerian melody.* BENEATHA *listens, enraptured, her eyes far away —"back to the past." She begins to dance.* RUTH *is dumfounded*)

RUTH What kind of dance is that?

BENEATHA A folk dance.

RUTH (*Pearl Bailey*) What kind of folks do that, honey?

BENEATHA It's from Nigeria. It's a dance of welcome.

RUTH Who you welcoming?

BENEATHA The men back to the village.

RUTH Where they been?

BENEATHA How should I know—out hunting or something. Anyway, they are coming back now . . .

RUTH Well, that's good.

BENEATHA (*With the record*)

Alundi, alundi
Alundi alunya
Jop pu a jeepua
Ang gu soooooooooo

Ai yai yae . . .
Ayehaye—alundi . . .

(WALTER *comes in during this performance; he has obviously been drinking. He leans against the door heavily and watches his sister, at first with distaste. Then his eyes look off—"back to the past"—as he lifts both his fists to the roof, screaming*)

WALTER YEAH . . . AND ETHIOPIA STRETCH FORTH HER HANDS AGAIN! . . .

RUTH (*Drily, looking at him*) Yes—and Africa sure is claiming her own tonight.

(*She gives them both up and starts ironing again*)

WALTER (*All in a drunken, dramatic shout*) Shut up! . . . I'm digging them drums . . . them drums move me! . . . (*He makes his weaving way to his wife's face and leans in close to her*) In my *heart of hearts*— (*He thumps his chest*) —I am much warrior!

RUTH (*Without even looking up*) In your heart of hearts you are much drunkard.

WALTER (*Coming away from her and starting to wander around the room, shouting*) Me and Jomo . . . (*Intently, in his sister's face. She has stopped dancing to watch him in this unknown mood*) That's my man,

Kenyatta. (*Shouting and thumping his chest*) FLAMING SPEAR! HOT DAMN! (*He is suddenly in posession of an imaginary spear and actively spearing enemies all over the room*) OCOMOGOSIAY . . . THE LION IS WAKING . . . OWIMOWEH! (*He pulls his shirt open and leaps up on a table and gestures with his spear. The bell rings.* RUTH *goes to answer*)

BENEATHA (*To encourage* WALTER, *thoroughly caught up with this side of him*) *OCOMOGOSIAY*, FLAMING SPEAR!

WALTER (*On the table, very far gone, his eyes pure glass sheets. He sees what we cannot, that he is a leader of his people, a great chief, a descendant of Chaka, and that the hour to march has come*) Listen, my black brothers—

BENEATHA OCOMOGOSIAY!

WALTER —Do you hear the waters rushing against the shores of the coastlands—

BENEATHA OCOMOGOSIAY!

WALTER —Do you hear the screeching of the cocks in yonder hills beyond where the chiefs meet in council for the coming of the mighty war—

BENEATHA OCOMOGOSIAY!

WALTER —Do you hear the beating of the wings of the birds flying low over the mountains and the low places of our land—

(RUTH *opens the door.* GEORGE MURCHISON *enters*)

BENEATHA OCOMOGOSIAY!

WALTER —Do you hear the singing of the women, singing the war songs of our fathers to the babies in the great houses . . . singing the sweet war songs? OH, DO YOU HEAR, MY BLACK BROTHERS!

BENEATHA (*Completely gone*) We hear you, Flaming Spear—

WALTER Telling us to prepare for the greatness of the time—(*To* GEORGE) Black Brother!

(*He extends his hand for the fraternal clasp*)

GEORGE Black Brother, hell!

RUTH (*Having had enough, and embarrassed for the family*) Beneatha you got company—what's the matter with you? Walter Lee Younger, get down off that table and stop acting like a fool . . .

(WALTER *comes down off the table suddenly and makes a quick exit to the bathroom*)

RUTH He's had a little to drink . . . I don't know what her excuse is.

GEORGE (*To* BENEATHA) Look honey, we're going *to* the theatre—we're not going to be *in* it . . . so go change, huh?

RUTH You expect this boy to go out with you looking like that?

BENEATHA (*Looking at* GEORGE) That's up to George. If he's ashamed of his heritage—

GEORGE Oh, don't be so proud of yourself, Bennie—just because you look eccentric.

BENEATHA How can something that's natural be eccentric?

GEORGE That's what being eccentric means—being natural. Get dressed.

BENEATHA I don't like that, George.

RUTH Why must you and your brother make an argument out of everything people say?

BENEATHA Because I hate assimilationist Negroes!

RUTH Will somebody please tell me what assimila-whoever means!

GEORGE Oh, it's just a college girl's way of calling people Uncle Toms—but that isn't what it means at all.

RUTH Well, what does it mean?

BENEATHA (*Cutting* GEORGE *off and staring at him as she replies to* RUTH) It means someone who is willing to give up his own culture and submerge himself completely in the dominant, and in this case, *oppressive* culture!

GEORGE Oh, dear, dear, dear! Here we go! A lecture on the African past! On our Great West African Heritage! In one second we will hear all about the great Ashanti empires; the great Songhay civilizations; and the great sculpture of Bénin—and then some poetry in the Bantu —and the whole monologue will end with the word *heritage!* (*Nastily*) Let's face it, baby, your heritage is nothing but a bunch of raggedy-assed spirituals and some grass huts!

BENEATHA *Grass huts!* (RUTH *crosses to her and forcibly pushes her toward the bedroom*) See there . . . you are standing there in your splendid ignorance talking about people who were the first to smelt iron on the face of the earth! (RUTH *is pushing her through the door*) The Ashanti were performing surgical operations when the English— (RUTH *pulls the door to, with* BENEATHA *on the other side, and smiles graciously at* GEORGE. BENEATHA *opens the door and shouts the end of the sentence defiantly at* GEORGE) —were still tatooing themselves with blue dragons . . .

(*She goes back inside*)

RUTH Have a seat, George. (*They both sit.* RUTH *folds her hands rather primly on her lap, determined to demonstrate the civilization of the family*) Warm, ain't it? I mean for September. (*Pause*) Just like they always say about Chicago weather: If it's too hot or cold for you, just wait a minute and it'll change. (*She smiles happily at this cliché of clichés*) Everybody say it's got to do with them bombs and things they keep setting off. (*Pause*) Would you like a nice cold beer?

GEORGE No, thank you. I don't care for beer. (*He looks at his watch*) I hope she hurries up.

RUTH What time is the show?

GEORGE It's an eight-thirty curtain. That's just Chicago, though. In New York standard curtain time is eight forty.

(*He is rather proud of this knowledge*)

RUTH (*Properly appreciating it*) You get to New York a lot?

GEORGE (*Offhand*) Few times a year.

RUTH Oh—that's nice. I've never been to New York.

(WALTER *enters. We feel he has relieved himself, but the edge of unreality is still with him*)

WALTER New York ain't got nothing Chicago ain't. Just a bunch of hustling people all squeezed up together—being "Eastern."

(*He turns his face into a screw of displeasure*)

GEORGE Oh—you've been?

WALTER *Plenty* of times.

RUTH (*Shocked at the lie*) Walter Lee Younger!

WALTER (*Staring her down*) Plenty! (*Pause*) What we got to drink in this house? Why don't you offer this man some refreshment. (*To* GEORGE) They don't know how to entertain people in this house, man.

GEORGE Thank you—I don't really care for anything.

WALTER (*Feeling his head; sobriety coming*) Where's Mama?

RUTH She ain't come back yet.

WALTER (*Looking* MURCHISON *over from head to toe, scrutinizing his carefully casual tweed sports jacket over cashmere V-neck sweater over soft eyelet shirt and tie, and soft slacks, finished off with white buckskin shoes*) Why all you college boys wear them fairyish-looking white shoes?

RUTH Walter Lee!

(GEORGE MURCHISON *ignores the remark*)

WALTER (*To* RUTH) Well, they look crazy as hell—white shoes, cold as it is.

RUTH (*Crushed*) You have to excuse him—

WALTER No he don't! Excuse me for what? What you always excusing me for! I'll excuse myself when I needs to be excused! (*A pause*) They look as funny as them black knee socks Beneatha wears out of here all the time.

RUTH It's the college *style,* Walter.

WALTER Style, hell. She looks like she got burnt legs or something!

RUTH Oh, Walter—

WALTER (*An irritable mimic*) Oh, Walter! Oh, Walter! (*To* MURCHISON) How's your old man making out? I understand you all going to buy that big hotel on the Drive? (*He finds a beer in the refrigerator, wanders over to* MURCHISON, *sipping and wiping his lips with the back of his hand, and straddling a chair backwards to talk to the other man*) Shrewd move. Your old man is all right, man. (*Tapping his head and half winking for emphasis*) I mean he knows how to operate. I mean he thinks *big,* you know what I mean, I mean for a *home,* you know? But I think he's kind of running out of ideas now. I'd like to talk to him. Listen, man, I got some plans that could turn this city upside down. I mean I think like he does. *Big.* Invest big, gamble big, hell, lose *big* if you have to, you know what I mean. It's hard to find a man on this whole Southside who understands my kind of thinking—you dig? (*He scrutinizes* MURCHISON *again, drinks his beer, squints his eyes and leans in close, confidential, man to man*) Me and you ought to sit down and talk sometimes, man. Man, I got me some ideas . . .

MURCHISON (*With boredom*) Yeah—sometimes we'll have to do that, Walter.

WALTER (*Understanding the indifference, and offended*) Yeah—well, when you get the time, man. I know you a busy little boy.

RUTH Walter, please—

WALTER (*Bitterly, hurt*) I know ain't nothing in this world as busy as you colored college boys with your fraternity pins and white shoes . . .

RUTH (*Covering her face with humiliation*) Oh, Walter Lee—

WALTER I see you all all the time—with the books tucked under your arms—going to your (*British A—a mimic*) "clahsses." And for what! What the hell you learning over there? Filling up your heads— (*Counting off on his fingers*) —with the sociology and the psychology—but they teaching you how to be a man? How to take over and run the world? They teaching you how to run a rubber plantation or a steel mill? Naw—just to talk proper and read books and wear white shoes . . .

GEORGE (*Looking at him with distaste, a little above it all*) You're all wacked up with bitterness, man.

WALTER (*Intently, almost quietly, between the teeth, glaring at the boy*) And you—ain't you bitter, man? Ain't you just about had it yet? Don't you see no stars gleaming that you can't reach out and grab? You happy?—you contented son-of-a-bitch—you happy? You got it made? Bitter? Man, I'm a volcano. Bitter? Here I am a giant—surrounded by ants! Ants who can't even understand what it is the giant is talking about.

RUTH (*Passionately and suddenly*) Oh, Walter—ain't you with nobody!

WALTER (*Violently*) No! 'Cause ain't nobody with me! Not even my own mother!

RUTH Walter, that's a terrible thing to say!

(BENEATHA *enters, dressed for the evening in a cocktail dress and earrings*)

GEORGE Well—hey, you look great.

BENEATHA Let's go, George. See you all later.

RUTH Have a nice time.

GEORGE Thanks. Good night. (*To* WALTER, *sarcastically*) Good night, *Prometheus.*

(BENEATHA *and* GEORGE *exit*)

WALTER (*To* RUTH) Who is Prometheus?

RUTH I don't know. Don't worry about it.

WALTER (*In fury, pointing after* GEORGE) See there—they get to a point where they can't insult you man to man—they got to go talk about something ain't nobody never heard of!

RUTH How you know it was an insult? (*To humor him*) Maybe Prometheus is a nice fellow.

WALTER Prometheus! I bet there ain't even no such thing! I bet that simple-minded clown—

RUTH Walter—

(*She stops what she is doing and looks at him*)

WALTER (*Yelling*) Don't start!

RUTH Start what?

WALTER Your nagging! Where was I? Who was I with? How much money did I spend?

RUTH (*Plaintively*) Walter Lee—why don't we just try to talk about it . . .

WALTER (*Not listening*) I been out talking with people who understand me. People who care about the things I got on my mind.

RUTH (*Wearily*) I guess that means people like Willy Harris.

WALTER Yes, people like Willy Harris.

RUTH (*With a sudden flash of impatience*) Why don't you all just hurry up and go into the banking business and stop talking about it!

WALTER Why? You want to know why? 'Cause we all tied up in a race of people that don't know how to do nothing but moan, pray and have babies!

(*The line is too bitter even for him and he looks at her and sits down*)

RUTH Oh, Walter . . . (*Softly*) Honey, why can't you stop fighting me?

WALTER (*Without thinking*) Who's fighting you? Who even cares about you?

(*This line begins the retardation of his mood*)

RUTH Well— (*She waits a long time, and then with resignation starts to put away her things*) I guess I might as well go on to bed . . . (*More or less to herself*) I don't know where we lost it . . . but we have . . . (*Then, to him*) I—I'm sorry about this new baby, Walter. I guess maybe I better go on and do what I started . . . I guess I just didn't realize how bad things was with us . . . I guess I just didn't really realize—(*She starts out to the bedroom and stops*) You want some hot milk?

WALTER Hot milk?

RUTH Yes—hot milk.

WALTER Why hot milk?

RUTH 'Cause after all that liquor you come home with you ought to have something hot in your stomach.

WALTER I don't want no milk.

RUTH You want some coffee then?

WALTER No, I don't want no coffee. I don't want nothing hot to drink. (*Almost plaintively*) Why you always trying to give me something to eat?

RUTH (*Standing and looking at him helplessly*) What else can I give you, Walter Lee Younger?

(*She stands and looks at him and presently turns to go out again. He lifts his head and watches her going away from him in a new mood which began to emerge when he asked her "Who cares about you?"*)

WALTER It's been rough, ain't it, baby? (*She hears and stops but does not turn around and he continues to her back*) I guess between two people there ain't never as much understood as folks generally thinks there is. I mean like between me and you— (*She turns to face him*) How we gets to the place where we scared to talk softness to each other. (*He waits, thinking hard himself*) Why you think it got to be like that? (*He is thoughtful, almost as a child would be*) Ruth, what is it gets into people ought to be close?

RUTH I don't know, honey. I think about it a lot.

WALTER On account of you and me, you mean? The way things are with us. The way something done come down between us.

RUTH There ain't so much between us, Walter . . . Not when you come to me and try to talk to me. Try to be with me . . . a little even.

WALTER (*Total honesty*) Sometimes . . . sometimes . . . I don't even know how to try.

RUTH Walter—

WALTER Yes?

RUTH (*Coming to him, gently and with misgiving, but coming to him*) Honey . . . life don't have to be like this. I mean sometimes people can do things so that things are better . . . You remember how we used to talk when Travis was born . . . about the way we were going to live . . . the kind of house . . . (*She is stroking his head*) Well, it's all starting to slip away from us . . .

(MAMA *enters, and* WALTER *jumps up and shouts at her*)

WALTER Mama, where have you been?

MAMA My—them steps is longer than they used to be. Whew! (*She sits down and ignores him*) How you feeling this evening, Ruth?

(RUTH *shrugs, disturbed some at having been prematurely interrupted and watching her husband knowingly*)

WALTER Mama, where have you been all day?

MAMA (*Still ignoring him and leaning on the table and changing to more comfortable shoes*) Where's Travis?

RUTH I let him go out earlier and he ain't come back yet. Boy, is he going to get it!

WALTER Mama!

MAMA (*As if she has heard him for the first time*) Yes, son?

WALTER Where did you go this afternoon?

MAMA I went down town to tend to some business that I had to tend to.

WALTER What kind of business?

MAMA You know better than to question me like a child, Brother.

WALTER (*Rising and bending over the table*) Where were you, Mama? (*Bringing his fists down and shouting*) Mama, you didn't go do something with that insurance money, something crazy?

(*The front door opens slowly, interrupting him, and* TRAVIS *peeks his head in, less than hopefully*)

TRAVIS (*To his mother*) Mama, I—

RUTH "Mama I" nothing! You're going to get it, boy! Get on in that bedroom and get yourself ready!

TRAVIS But I—

MAMA Why don't you all never let the child explain hisself.

RUTH Keep out of it now, Lena.

(MAMA *clamps her lips together, and* RUTH *advances toward her son menacingly*)

RUTH A thousand times I have told you not to go off like that—

MAMA (*Holding out her arms to her grandson*) Well—at least let me tell him something. I want him to be the first one to hear . . . Come here, Travis. (*The boy obeys, gladly*) Travis— (*She takes him by the shoulders and looks into his face*) —you know that money we got in the mail this morning?

TRAVIS Yes'm—

MAMA Well—what you think your grandmama gone and done with that money?

TRAVIS I don't know, Grandmama.

MAMA (*Putting her finger on his nose for emphasis*) She went out and she bought you a house! (*The explosion comes from* WALTER *at the end of the revelation and he jumps up and turns away from all of them in a fury.* MAMA *continues, to* TRAVIS) You glad about the house? It's going to be yours when you get to be a man.

TRAVIS Yeah—I always wanted to live in a house.

MAMA All right, gimme some sugar then— (TRAVIS *puts his arms around her neck as she watches her son over the boy's shoulder. Then, to* TRAVIS, *after the embrace*) Now when you say your prayers tonight, you thank God and your grandfather—'cause it was him who give you the house—in his way.

RUTH (*Taking the boy from* MAMA *and pushing him toward the bedroom*) Now you get out of here and get ready for your beating.

TRAVIS Aw, Mama—

RUTH Get on in there— (*Closing the door behind him and turning radiantly to her mother-in-law*) So you went and did it!

MAMA (*Quietly, looking at her son with pain*) Yes, I did.

RUTH (*Raising both arms classically*) *Praise God!* (*Looks at* WALTER *a moment, who says nothing. She crosses rapidly to her husband*) Please, honey—let me be glad . . . you be glad too. (*She has laid her hands on his shoulders, but he shakes himself free of her roughly, without turning to face her*) Oh, Walter . . . a home . . . *a home.* (*She comes back to* MAMA) Well—where is it? How big is it? How much it going to cost?

MAMA Well—

RUTH When we moving?

MAMA (*Smiling at her*) First of the month.

RUTH (*Throwing back her head with jubilance*) *Praise God!*

MAMA (*Tentatively, still looking at her son's back turned against her and* RUTH) It's—it's a nice house too . . . (*She cannot help speaking directly to him. An imploring quality in her voice, her manner, makes her almost like a girl now*) Three bedrooms—nice big one for you and Ruth. . . . Me and Beneatha still have to share our room, but Travis have one of his own—and— (*With difficulty*) I figures if the—new baby—is a boy, we could get one of them double-decker outfits . . . And there's a yard with a little patch of dirt where I could maybe get to grow me a few flowers . . . And a nice big basement . . .

RUTH Walter honey, be glad—

MAMA (*Still to his back, fingering things on the table*) 'Course I don't want to make it sound fancier than it is . . . It's just a plain little old house—but it's made good and solid—and it will be *ours.* Walter Lee—it makes a difference in a man when he can walk on floors that belong to *him* . . .

RUTH Where is it?

MAMA (*Frightened at this telling*) Well—well—it's out there in Clybourne Park—

(RUTH'S *radiance fades abruptly, and* WALTER *finally turns slowly to face his mother with incredulity and hostility*)

RUTH Where?

MAMA (*Matter-of-factly*) Four o six Clybourne Street, Clybourne Park.

RUTH Clybourne Park? Mama, there ain't no colored people living in Clybourne Park.

MAMA (*Almost idiotically*) Well, I guess there's going to be some now.

WALTER (*Bitterly*) So that's the peace and comfort you went out and bought for us today!

MAMA (*Raising her eyes to meet his finally*) Son—I just tried to find the nicest place for the least amount of money for my family.

RUTH (*Trying to recover from the shock*) Well—well—'course I ain't one never been 'fraid of no crackers, mind you—but—well, wasn't there no other houses nowhere?

MAMA Them houses they put up for colored in them areas way out all seem to cost twice as much as other houses. I did the best I could.

RUTH (*Struck senseless with the news, in its various degrees of goodness and trouble, she sits a moment, her fists propping her chin in thought, and then she starts to rise, bringing her fists down with vigor, the radiance spreading from cheek to cheek again*) Well—well!—All I can say is—if this is my time in life—*my time*—to say good-bye— (*And she builds with momentum as she starts to circle the room with an exuberant, almost tearfully happy release*) —to these Goddamned cracking walls!— (*She pounds the walls*) and these marching roaches!— (*She wipes at an imaginary army of marching roaches*) —and this cramped little closet which ain't now or never was no kitchen! . . . then I say it loud and good, *Hallelujah! and good-bye misery . . . I don't never want to see your ugly face again!* (*She laughs joyously, having practically destroyed the apartment, and flings her arms up and lets them come down happily, slowly, reflectively, over her abdomen, aware for the first time perhaps that the life therein pulses with happiness and not despair*) Lena?

MAMA (*Moved, watching her happiness*) Yes, honey?

RUTH (*Looking off*) Is there—is there a whole lot of sunlight?

MAMA (*Understanding*) Yes, child, there's a whole lot of sunlight.

(*Long pause*)

RUTH (*Collecting herself and going to the door of the room* TRAVIS *is in*) Well—I guess I better see 'bout Travis. (*To* MAMA) Lord, I sure don't feel like whipping nobody today!

(*She exits*)

MAMA (*The mother and son are left alone now and the mother waits a long time, considering deeply, before she speaks*) Son—you—you understand what I done, don't you? (WALTER *is silent and sullen*) I—I just seen my family falling apart today . . . just falling to pieces in front of my eyes . . . We couldn't of gone on like we was today. We was going backwards 'stead of forwards—talking 'bout killing babies and wishing each other was dead . . . When it gets like that in life—you just got to do something different, push on out and do something bigger . . . (*She waits*) I wish you say something, son . . . I wish you'd say how deep inside you you think I done the right thing—

WALTER (*Crossing slowly to his bedroom door and finally turning there and speaking measuredly*) What you need me to say you done right for? *You* the head of this family. You run our lives like you want to. It was your money and you did what you wanted with it. So what you need for me to say it was all right for? (*Bitterly, to hurt her as deeply as he knows is possible*) So you butchered up a dream of mine—you—who always talking 'bout your children's dreams . . .

MAMA Walter Lee—

(*He just closes the door behind him.* MAMA *sits alone, thinking heavily*)

CURTAIN

Scene Two

Time: Friday night. A few weeks later.

At rise: Packing crates mark the intention of the family to move. BENEATHA *and* GEORGE *come in, presumably from an evening out again.*

GEORGE O.K. . . . O.K., whatever you say . . . (*They both sit on the couch. He tries to kiss her. She moves away*) Look, we've had a nice evening; let's not spoil it, huh? . . .

(*He again turns her head and tries to nuzzle in and she turns away from him, not with distaste but with momentary lack of interest; in a mood to pursue what they were talking about*)

BENEATHA I'm *trying* to talk to you.

GEORGE We always talk.

BENEATHA Yes—and I love to talk.

GEORGE (*Exasperated; rising*) I know it and I don't mind it sometimes . . . I want you to cut it out, see—The moody stuff, I mean. I don't like it. You're a nice-looking girl . . . all over. That's all you need, honey, forget the atmosphere. Guys aren't going to go for the atmosphere—they're going to go for what they see. Be glad for that. Drop the Garbo routine. It doesn't go with you. As for myself, I want a nice— (*Groping*) —simple— (*Thoughtfully*) —sophisticated girl . . . not a poet—O.K.?

(*She rebuffs him again and he starts to leave*)

BENEATHA Why are you angry?

GEORGE Because this is stupid! I don't go out with you to discuss the nature of "quiet desperation" or to hear all about your thoughts—because the world will go on thinking what it thinks regardless—

BENEATHA Then why read books? Why go to school?

GEORGE (*With artificial patience, counting on his fingers*) It's simple. You read books—to learn facts—to get grades—to pass the course—to get a degree. That's all—it has nothing to do with thoughts.

(*A long pause*)

BENEATHA I see. (*A longer pause as she looks at him*) Good night, George.

(GEORGE *looks at her a little oddly, and starts to exit. He meets* MAMA *coming in*)

GEORGE Oh—hello, Mrs. Younger.

MAMA Hello, George, how you feeling?

GEORGE Fine—fine, how are you?

MAMA Oh, a little tired. You know them steps can get you after a day's work. You all have a nice time tonight?

GEORGE Yes—a fine time. Well, good night.

MAMA Good night. (*He exits.* MAMA *closes the door behind her*) Hello, honey. What you sitting like that for?

BENEATHA I'm just sitting.

MAMA Didn't you have a nice time?

BENEATHA No.

MAMA No? What's the matter?

BENEATHA Mama, George is a fool—honest.

(*She rises*)

MAMA (*Hustling around unloading the packages she has entered with. She stops*) Is he, baby?

BENEATHA Yes.

(BENEATHA *makes up* TRAVIS' *bed as she talks*)

MAMA You sure?

BENEATHA Yes.

MAMA Well—I guess you better not waste your time with no fools.

(BENEATHA *looks up at her mother, watching her put groceries in the refrigerator. Fnally she gathers up her things and starts into the bedroom. At the door she stops and looks at her mother*)

BENEATHA Mama—

MAMA Yes, baby—

BENEATHA Thank you.

MAMA For what?

BENEATHA For understanding me this time.

(*She exits quickly and the mother stands, smiling a little, looking at the place where* BENEATHA *just stood.* RUTH *enters*)

RUTH Now don't you fool with any of this stuff, Lena—

MAMA Oh, I just thought I'd sort a few things out.

(*The phone rings.* RUTH *answers*)

RUTH (*At the phone*) Hello—Just a minute. (*Goes to door*) Walter, it's Mrs. Arnold. (*Waits. Goes back to the phone. Tense*) Hello. Yes, this is his wife speaking . . . He's lying down now. Yes . . . well, he'll be in tomorrow. He's been very sick. Yes—I know we should have called, but we were so sure he'd be able to come in today. Yes—yes, I'm very sorry. Yes . . . Thank you very much. (*She hangs up.* WALTER *is standing in the doorway of the bedroom behind her*) That was Mrs. Arnold.

WALTER (*Indifferently*) Was it?

RUTH She said if you don't come in tomorrow that they are getting a new man . . .

WALTER Ain't that sad—ain't that crying sad.

RUTH She said Mr. Arnold has had to take a cab for three days . . . Walter, you ain't been to work for three days! (*This is a revelation to her*) Where you been, Walter Lee Younger? (WALTER *looks at her and starts to laugh*) You're going to lose your job.

WALTER That's right . . .

RUTH Oh, Walter, and with your mother working like a dog every day—

WALTER That's sad too—Everything is sad.

MAMA What you been doing for these three days, son?

WALTER Mama—you don't know all the things a man what got leisure can find to do in this city . . . What's this—Friday night? Well—Wednesday I borrowed Willy Harris' car and I went for a drive . . . just me and myself and I drove and drove . . . Way out . . . way past South Chicago, and I parked the car and I sat and looked at the steel mills all day long. I just sat in the car and looked at them big black chimneys for hours. Then I drove back and I went to the Green Hat. (*Pause*) And

Thursday—Thursday I borrowed the car again and I got in it and I pointed it the other way and I drove the other way—for hours—way, way up to Wisconsin, and I looked at the farms. I just drove and looked at the farms. Then I drove back and I went to the Green Hat. (*Pause*) And today—today I didn't get the car. Today I just walked. All over the Southside. And I looked at the Negroes and they looked at me and finally I just sat down on the curb at Thirty-ninth and South Parkway and I just sat there and watched the Negroes go by. And then I went to the Green Hat. You all sad? You all depressed? And you know where I am going right now— (RUTH *goes out quietly*)

MAMA Oh, Big Walter, is this the harvest of our days?

WALTER You know what I like about the Green Hat? (*He turns the radio on and a steamy, deep blues pours into the room*) I like this little cat they got there who blows a sax . . . He blows. He talks to me. He ain't but 'bout five feet tall and he's got a conked head and his eyes is always closed and he's all music—

MAMA (*Rising and getting some papers out of her handbag*) Walter—

WALTER And there's this other guy who plays the piano . . . and they got a sound. I mean they can work on some music . . . They got the best little combo in the world in the Green Hat . . . You can just sit there and drink and listen to them three men play and you realize that don't nothing matter worth a damn, but just being there—

MAMA I've helped do it to you, haven't I, son? Walter, I been wrong.

WALTER Naw—you ain't never been wrong about nothing, Mama.

MAMA Listen to me, now. I say I been wrong, son. That I been doing to you what the rest of the world been doing to you. (*She stops and he looks up slowly at her and she meets his eyes pleadingly*) Walter—what you ain't never understood is that I ain't got nothing, don't own nothing, ain't never really wanted nothing that wasn't for you. There ain't nothing as precious to me . . . There ain't nothing worth holding on to, money, dreams, nothing else—if it means—if it means it's going to destroy my boy. (*She puts her papers in front of him and he watches her without speaking or moving*) I paid the man thirty-five hundred dollars down on the house. That leaves sixty-five hundred dollars. Monday morning I want you to take this money and take three thousand dollars and put it in a savings account for Beneatha's medical schooling. The rest you put in a checking account—with your name on it. And from now on any penny that comes out of it or that go in it is for you to look after. For you to decide. (*She drops her hands a little helplessly*) It ain't much, but it's all I got in the world and I'm putting in your hands. I'm telling you to be the head of this family from now on like you supposed to be.

WALTER (*Stares at the money*) You trust me like that, Mama?

MAMA I ain't never stop trusting you. Like I ain't never stop loving you.

(*She goes out, and* WALTER *sits looking at the money on the table as the music continues in its idiom, pulsing in the room. Finally, in a decisive gesture, he gets up and, in a furious action, flings the bedclothes wildly from his son's makeshift bed to all over the floor—with a cry of desperation. Then he picks up the money and goes out in a hurry*)

CURTAIN

Scene Three

Time: Saturday, moving day, one week later.

Before the curtain rises, RUTH'S *voice, a strident, dramatic church alto, cuts through the silence.*

It is, in the darkness, a triumphant surge, a penetrating statement of expectation: "Oh, Lord, I don't feel no ways tired! Children, oh, glory halleujah!"

As the curtain rises we see that RUTH *is alone in the living room, finishing up the family's packing. It is moving day. She is nailing crates and tying cartons.* BENEATHA *enters, carrying a guitar case, and watches her exuberant sister-in-law.*

RUTH Hey!

BENEATHA (*Putting away the case*) Hi.

RUTH (*Pointing at a package*) Honey—look in that package there and see what I found on sale this morning at the South Center. (RUTH *gets up and moves to the package and draws out some curtains*) Lookahere—hand-turned hems!

BENEATHA How do you know the window size out there?

RUTH (*Who hadn't thought of that*) Oh—Well, they bound to fit something in the whole house. Anyhow, they was too good a bargain to pass us. (RUTH *slaps her head, suddenly remembering something*) Oh, Bennie—I meant to put a special note on that carton over there. That's your mama's good china and she wants 'em to be very careful with it.

BENEATHA I'll do it.

(BENEATHA *finds a piece of paper and starts to draw large letters on it*)

RUTH You know what I'm going to do soon as I get in that new house?

BENEATHA What?

RUTH Honey—I'm going to run me a tub of water up to here . . . (*With her fingers practically up to her nostrils*) And I'm going to get in it—and I am going to sit . . . and sit . . . and sit in that hot water and the first person who knocks to tell *me* to hurry up and come out—

BENEATHA Gets shot at sunrise.

RUTH (*Laughing happily*) You said it, sister! (*Noticing how large* BENEATHA *is absent-mindedly making the note*) Honey, they ain't going to read that from no airplane.

BENEATHA (*Laughing herself*) I guess I always think things have more emphasis if they are big, somehow.

RUTH (*Looking up at her and smiling*) You and your brother seem to have that as a philosophy of life. Lord, that man—done changed so 'round here. You know—you know what we did last night? Me and Walter Lee?

BENEATHA What?

RUTH (*Smiling to herself*) We went to the movies. (*Looking at* BENEATHA *to see if she understands*) We went to the movies. You know the last time me and Walter went to the movies together?

BENEATHA No.

RUTH Me neither. That's how long it been. (*Smiling again*) But we went last night. The picture wasn't much good, but that didn't seem to matter. We went—and we held hands.

BENEATHA Oh, Lord!

RUTH We held hands—and you know what?

BENEATHA What?

RUTH When we come out of the show it was late and dark

and all the stores and things was closed up . . . and it was kind of chilly and there wasn't many people on the streets . . . and we was still holding hands, me and Walter.

BENEATHA You're killing me.

(WALTER *enters with a large package. His happiness is deep in him; he cannot keep still with his new-found exuberance. He is singing and wiggling and snapping his fingers. He puts his package in a corner and puts a phonograph record, which he has brought in with him, on the record player. As the music comes up he dances over to* RUTH *and tries to get her to dance with him. She gives in at last to his raunchiness and in a fit of giggling allows herself to be drawn into his mood and together they deliberately burlesque an old social dance of their youth*)

BENEATHA (*Regarding them a long time as they dance, then drawing in her breath for a deeply exaggerated comment which she does not particularly mean*) Talk about—oldddddddddd-fashionedddddd—Negroes!

WALTER (*Stopping momentarily*) What kind of Negroes? (*He says this in fun. He is not angry with her today, nor with anyone. He starts to dance with his wife again*)

BENEATHA Old-fashioned.

WALTER (*As he dances with* RUTH) You know, when these *New Negroes* have their convention— (*Pointing at his sister*) —that is going to be the chairman of the Committee on Unending Agitation. (*He goes on dancing, then stops*) Race, race, race! . . . Girl, I do believe you are the first person in the history of the entire human race to successfully brainwash yourself. (BENEATHA *breaks up and he goes on dancing. He stops again, enjoying his tease*) Damn, even the N double A C P takes a holiday sometimes! (BENEATHA *and* RUTH *laugh. He dances with* RUTH *some more and starts to laugh and stops and pantomimes someone over an oper-*

ating table) I can just see that chick someday looking down at some poor cat on an operating table before she starts to slice him, saying . . . *(Pulling his sleeves back maliciously)* "By the way, what are your views on civil rights down there? . . ."

(He laughs at her again and starts to dance happily. The bell sounds)

BENEATHA Sticks and stones may break my bones but . . . words will never hurt me!

(BENEATHA *goes to the door and opens it as* WALTER *and* RUTH *go on with the clowning.* BENEATHA *is somewhat surprised to see a quiet-looking middle-aged white man in a business suit holding his hat and a briefcase in his hand and consulting a small piece of paper)*

MAN Uh—how do you do, miss. I am looking for a Mrs.— *(He looks at the slip of paper)* Mrs. Lena Younger?

BENEATHA *(Smoothing her hair with slight embarrassment)* Oh—yes, that's my mother. Excuse me. *(She closes the door and turns to quiet the other two)* Ruth! Brother! Somebody's here. *(Then she opens the door. The man casts a curious quick glance at all of them)* Uh—come in please.

MAN *(Coming in)* Thank you.

BENEATHA My mother isn't here just now. Is it business?

MAN Yes . . . well, of a sort.

WALTER *(Freely, the Man of the House)* Have a seat. I'm Mrs. Younger's son. I look after most of her business matters.

(RUTH *and* BENEATHA *exchange amused glances)*

MAN *(Regarding* WALTER, *and sitting)* Well—My name is Karl Lindner . . .

WALTER *(Stretching out his hand)* Walter Younger. This is my wife— (RUTH *nods politely)* —and my sister.

LINDNER How do you do.

WALTER *(Amiably, as he sits himself easily on a chair,*

leaning with interest forward on his knees and looking expectantly into the newcomer's face) What can we do for you, Mr. Lindner!

LINDNER (*Some minor shuffling of the hat and briefcase on his knees*) Well—I am a representative of the Clybourne Park Improvement Association—

WALTER (*Pointing*) Why don't you sit your things on the floor?

LINDNER Oh—yes. Thank you. (*He slides the briefcase and hat under the chair*) And as I was saying—I am from the Clybourne Park Improvement Association and we have had it brought to our attention at the last meeting that you people—or at least your mother—has bought a piece of residential property at— (*He digs for the slip of paper again*) —four o six Clybourne Street . . .

WALTER That's right. Care for something to drink? Ruth, get Mr. Lindner a beer.

LINDNER (*Upset for some reason*) Oh—no, really. I mean thank you very much, but no thank you.

RUTH (*Innocently*) Some coffee?

LINDNER Thank you, nothing at all.

(BENEATHA *is watching the man carefully*)

LINDNER Well, I don't know how much you folks know about our organization. (*He is a gentle man; thoughtful and somewhat labored in his manner*) It is one of these community organizations set up to look after—oh, you know, things like block upkeep and special projects and we also have what we call our New Neighbors Orientation Committee . . .

BENEATHA (*Drily*) Yes—and what do they do?

LINDNER (*Turning a little to her and then returning the main force to* WALTER) Well—it's what you might call a sort of welcoming committee, I guess. I mean they, we, I'm the chairman of the committee—go around and see the new people who move into the neighborhood and sort of give them the lowdown on the way we do things out in Clybourne Park.

BENEATHA (*With appreciation of the two meanings, which escape* RUTH *and* WALTER) Un-huh.

LINDNER And we also have the category of what the association calls— (*He looks elsewhere*) —uh—special community problems . . .

BENEATHA Yes—and what are some of those?

WALTER Girl, let the man talk.

LINDNER (*With understated relief*) Thank you. I would sort of like to explain this thing in my own way. I mean I want to explain to you in a certain way.

WALTER Go ahead.

LINDNER Yes. Well. I'm going to try to get right to the point. I'm sure we'll all appreciate that in the long run.

BENEATHA Yes.

WALTER Be still now!

LINDNER Well—

RUTH (*Still innocently*) Would you like another chair—you don't look comfortable.

LINDNER (*More frustrated than annoyed*) No, thank you very much. Please. Well—to get right to the point I— (*A great breath, and he is off at last*) I am sure you people must be aware of some of the incidents which have happened in various parts of the city when colored people have moved into certain areas— (BENEATHA *exhales heavily and starts tossing a piece of fruit up and down in the air*) Well—because we have what I think is going to be a unique type of organization in American community life—not only do we deplore that kind of thing—but we are trying to do something about it. (BENEATHA *stops tossing and turns with a new and quizzical interest to the man*) We feel— (*gaining confidence in his mission because of the interest in the faces of the people he is talking to*) —we feel that most of the trouble in this world, when you come right down to it— (*He hits his knee for emphasis*) —most of the trouble exists because people just don't sit down and talk to each other.

RUTH (*Nodding as she might in church, pleased with the remark*) You can say that again, mister.

LINDNER (*More encouraged by such affirmation*) That we don't try hard enough in this world to understand the other fellow's problem. The other guy's point of view.

RUTH Now that's right.

(BENEATHA *and* WALTER *merely watch and listen with genuine interest*)

LINDNER Yes—that's the way we feel out in Clybourne Park. And that's why I was elected to come here this afternoon and talk to you people. Friendly like, you know, the way people should talk to each other and see if we couldn't find some way to work this thing out. As I say, the whole business is a matter of *caring* about the other fellow. Anybody can see that you are a nice family of folks, hard working and honest I'm sure. (BENEATHA *frowns slightly, quizzically, her head tilted regarding him*) Today everybody knows what it means to be on the outside of *something*. And of course, there is always somebody who is out to take the advantage of people who don't always understand.

WALTER What do you mean?

LINDNER Well—you see our community is made up of people who've worked hard as the dickens for years to build up that little community. They're not rich and fancy people; just hard-working, honest people who don't really have much but those little homes and a dream of the kind of community they want to raise their children in. Now, I don't say we are perfect and there is a lot wrong in some of the things they want. But you've got to admit that a man, right or wrong, has the right to want to have the neighborhood he lives in a certain kind of way. And at the moment the overwhelming majority of our people out there feel that people get along better, take more of a common interest in the life of the community, when they share a common background. I want you to believe me when I tell you that race prejudice simply doesn't enter into it. It is a matter of the people of Clybourne Park believing, rightly or wrongly, as I say, that for the happiness of all concerned that our Negro families are happier when they live in their *own* communities.

BENEATHA (*With a grand and bitter gesture*) This, friends, is the Welcoming Committee!

WALTER (*Dumfounded, looking at* LINDNER) Is this what you came marching all the way over here to tell us?

LINDNER Well, now we've been having a fine conversation. I hope you'll hear me all the way through.

WALTER (*Tightly*) Go ahead, man.

LINDNER You see—in the face of all things I have said, we are prepared to make your family a very generous offer . . .

BENEATHA Thirty pieces and not a coin less!

WALTER Yeah?

LINDNER (*Putting on his glasses and drawing a form out of the briefcase*) Our association is prepared, through the collective effort of our people, to buy the house from you at a financial gain to your family.

RUTH Lord have mercy, ain't this the living gall!

WALTER All right, you through?

LINDNER Well, I want to give you the exact terms of the financial arrangement—

WALTER We don't want to hear no exact terms of no arrangements. I want to know if you got any more to tell us 'bout getting together?

LINDNER (*Taking off his glasses*) Well—I don't suppose that you feel . . .

WALTER Never mind how I feel—you got any more to

say 'bout how people ought to sit down and talk to each other? . . . Get out of my house, man.

(*He turns his back and walks to the door*)

LINDNER (*Looking around at the hostile faces and reaching and assembling his hat and briefcase*) Well—I don't understand why you people are reacting this way. What do you think you are going to gain by moving into a neighborhood where you just aren't wanted and where some elements—well—people can get awful worked up when they feel that their whole way of life and everything they've ever worked for is threatened.

WALTER Get out.

LINDNER (*At the door, holding a small card*) Well—I'm sorry it went like this.

WALTER Get out.

LINDNER (*Almost sadly regarding* WALTER) You just can't force people to change their hearts, son.

(*He turns and puts his card on a table and exits.* WALTER *pushes the door to with stinging hatred, and stands looking at it.* RUTH *just sits and* BENEATHA *just stands. They say nothing.* MAMA *and* TRAVIS *enter*)

MAMA Well—this all the packing got done since I left out of here this morning. I testify before God that my children got all the energy of the dead. What time the moving men due?

BENEATHA Four o'clock. You had a caller, Mama.

(*She is smiling, teasingly*)

MAMA Sure enough—who?

BENEATHA (*Her arms folded saucily*) The Welcoming Committee.

(WALTER *and* RUTH *giggle*)

MAMA (*Innocently*) Who?

BENEATHA The Welcoming Committee. They said they're sure going to be glad to see you when you get there.

WALTER (*Devilishly*) Yeah, they said they can't hardly wait to see your face.

(*Laughter*)

MAMA (*Sensing their facetiousness*) What's the matter with you all?

WALTER Ain't nothing the matter with us. We just telling you 'bout the gentleman who came to see you this afternoon. From the Clybourne Park Improvement Association.

MAMA What he want?

RUTH (*In the same mood as* BENEATHA *and* WALTER) To welcome you, honey.

WALTER He said they can't hardly wait. He said the one thing they don't have, that they just *dying* to have out there is a fine family of colored people! (*To* RUTH *and* BENEATHA) Ain't that right!

RUTH *and* BENEATHA (*Mockingly*) Yeah! He left his card in case—

(*They indicate the card, and* MAMA *picks it up and throws it on the floor—understanding and looking off as she draws her chair up to the table on which she has put her plant and some sticks and some cord*)

MAMA Father, give us strength. (*Knowingly—and without fun*) Did he threaten us?

BENEATHA Oh—Mama—they don't do it like that any more. He talked Brotherhood. He said everybody ought learn how to sit down and hate each other with good Christian fellowship.

(*She and* WALTER *shake hands to ridicule the remark*)

MAMA (*Sadly*) Lord, protect us . . .

RUTH You should hear the money those folks raised to buy the house from us. All we paid and then some.

BENEATHA What they think we going to do—eat 'em?

RUTH No, honey, marry 'em.

MAMA (*Shaking her head*) Lord, Lord, Lord . . .

RUTH Well—that's the way the crackers crumble. Joke.

BENEATHA (*Laughingly noticing what her mother is doing*) Mama, what are you doing?

MAMA Fixing my plant so it won't get hurt none on the way . . .

BENEATHA Mama, you going to take *that* to the new house?

MAMA Un-huh—

BENEATHA That raggedy-looking old thing?

MAMA (*Stopping and looking at her*) It expresses *me.*

RUTH (*With delight, to* BENEATHA) So there, Miss Thing! (WALTER *comes to* MAMA *suddenly and bends down behind her and squeezes her in his arms with all his strength. She is overwhelmed by the suddenness of it and, though delighted, her manner is like that of* RUTH *with* TRAVIS)

MAMA Look out now, boy! You make me mess up my thing here!

WALTER (*His face lit, he slips down on his knees beside her, his arms still about her*) Mama . . . you know what it means to climb up in the chariot?

MAMA (*Gruffly, very happy*) Get on away from me now . . .

RUTH (*Near the gift-wrapped package, trying to catch* WALTER'S *eye*) Psst—

WALTER What the old song say, Mama . . .

RUTH Walter—Now?
(*She is pointing at the package*)

WALTER (*Speaking the lines, sweetly, playfully, in his mother's face*)
I got wings . . . you got wings . . .
All God's children got wings . . .

MAMA Boy—get out of my face and do some work . . .

WALTER
When I get to heaven gonna put on my wings,
Gonna fly all over God's heaven . . .

BENEATHA (*Teasingly, from across the room*) Everybody talking 'bout heaven ain't going there!

WALTER (*To* RUTH, *who is carrying the box across to*

them) I don't know, you think we ought to give her that . . . Seems to me she ain't been very appreciative around here.

MAMA (*Eying the box, which is obviously a gift*) What is that?

WALTER (*Taking it from* RUTH *and putting it on the table in front of* MAMA) Well—what you all think. Should we give it to her?

RUTH Oh—she was pretty good today.

MAMA I'll good you—

(*She turns her eyes to the box again*)

BENEATHA Open it, Mama.

(*She stands up, looks at it, turns and looks at all of them, and then presses her hands together and does not open the package*)

WALTER (*Sweetly*) Open it, Mama. It's for you. (MAMA *looks in his eyes. It is the first present in her life without its being Christmas. Slowly she opens her package and lifts out, one by one, a brand-new sparkling set of gardening tools.* WALTER *continues, prodding*) Ruth made up the note—read it . . .

MAMA (*Picking up the card and adjusting her glasses*) "To our own Mrs. Miniver—Love from Brother, Ruth and Beneatha." Ain't that lovely . . .

TRAVIS (*Tugging at his father's sleeve*) Daddy, can I give her mine now?

WALTER All right, son. (TRAVIS *flies to get his gift*) Travis didn't want to go in with the rest of us, Mama. He got his own. (*Somewhat amused*) We don't know what it is . . .

TRAVIS (*Racing back in the room with a large hatbox and putting it in front of his grandmother*) Here!

MAMA Lord have mercy, baby. You done gone and bought your grandmother a hat?

TRAVIS (*Very proud*) Open it!

(*She does and lifts out an elaborate, but very elaborate,*

wide gardening hat, and all the adults break up at the sight of it)

RUTH Travis, honey, what is that?

TRAVIS (*Who thinks it is beautiful and appropriate*) It's a gardening hat! Like the ladies always have on in the magazines when they work in their gardens.

BENEATHA (*Giggling fiercely*) Travis—we were trying to make Mama Mrs. Miniver—not Scarlet O'Hara!

MAMA (*Indignantly*) What's the matter with you all! This here is a beautiful hat! (*Absurdly*) I always wanted me one just like it!

(*She pops it on her head to prove it to her grandson, and the hat is ludicrous and considerably oversized*)

RUTH Hot dog! Go, Mama!

WALTER (*Doubled over with laughter*) I'm sorry, Mama—but you look like you ready to go out and chop you some cotton sure enough!

(*They all laugh except* MAMA, *out of deference to* TRAVIS' *feelings*)

MAMA (*Gathering the boy up to her*) Bless your heart—this is the prettiest hat I ever owned— (WALTER, RUTH *and* BENEATHA *chime in—noisily, festively and insincerely congratulating* TRAVIS *on his gift*) What are we all standing around here for? We ain't finished packin' yet. Bennie, you ain't packed one book.

(*The bell rings*)

BENEATHA That couldn't be the movers . . . it's not hardly two good yet—

(BENEATHA *goes into her room.* MAMA *starts for door*)

WALTER (*Turning, stiffening*) Wait—wait—I'll get it.

(*He stands and looks at the door*)

MAMA You expecting company, son?

WALTER (*Just looking at the door*) Yeah—yeah . . .

(MAMA *looks at* RUTH, *and they exchange innocent and unfrightened glances*)

MAMA (*Not understanding*) Well, let them in, son.

BENEATHA (*From her room*) We need some more string.

MAMA Travis—you run to the hardware and get me some string cord.

(MAMA *goes out and* WALTER *turns and looks at* RUTH. TRAVIS *goes to a dish for money*)

RUTH Why don't you answer the door, man?

WALTER (*Suddenly bounding across the floor to her*) 'Cause sometimes it hard to let the future begin! (*Stooping down in her face*)

I got wings!
You got wings!
All God's children got wings!

(*He crosses to the door and throws it open. Standing there is a very slight little man in a not too prosperous business suit and with haunted frightened eyes and a hat pulled down tightly, brim up, around his forehead.* TRAVIS *passes between the men and exits.* WALTER *leans deep in the man's face, still in his jubilance*)

When I get to heaven gonna put on my wings,
Gonna fly all over God's heaven . . .

(*The little man just stares at him*)

Heaven—

(*Suddenly he stops and looks past the little man into the empty hallway*) Where's Willy, man?

BOBO He ain't with me.

WALTER (*Not disturbed*) Oh—come on in. You know my wife.

BOBO (*Dumbly, taking off his hat*) Yes—h'you, Miss Ruth.

RUTH (*Quietly, a mood apart from her husband already, seeing* BOBO) Hello, Bobo.

WALTER You right on time today . . . Right on time. That's the way! (*He slaps* BOBO *on his back*) Sit down . . . lemme hear.

(RUTH *stands stiffly and quietly in back of them, as*

though somehow she senses death, her eyes fixed on her husband)

BOBO (*His frightened eyes on the floor, his hat in his hands*) Could I please get a drink a water, before I tell you about it, Walter Lee?

(WALTER *does not take his eyes off the man.* RUTH *goes blindly to the tap and gets a glass of water and brings it to* BOBO)

WALTER There ain't nothing wrong, is there?

BOBO Lemme tell you—

WALTER Man—didn't nothing go wrong?

BOBO Lemme tell you—Walter Lee. (*Looking at* RUTH *and talking to her more than to* WALTER) You know how it was. I got to tell you how it was. I mean first I got to tell you how it was all the way . . . I mean about the money I put in, Walter Lee . . .

WALTER (*With taut agitation now*) What about the money you put in?

BOBO Well—it wasn't much as we told you—me and Willy— (*He stops*) I'm sorry, Walter. I got a bad feeling about it. I got a real bad feeling about it . . .

WALTER Man, what you telling me about all this for? . . . Tell me what happened in Springfield . . .

BOBO Springfield.

RUTH (*Like a dead woman*) What was supposed to happen in Springfield?

BOBO (*To her*) This deal that me and Walter went into with Willy—Me and Willy was going to go down to Springfield and spread some money 'round so's we wouldn't have to wait so long for the liquor license . . . That's what we were going to do. Everybody said that was the way you had to do, you understand, Miss Ruth?

WALTER Man—what happened down there?

BOBO (*A pitiful man, near tears*) I'm trying to tell you, Walter.

WALTER (*Screaming at him suddenly*) THEN TELL ME, GODDAMNIT . . . WHAT'S THE MATTER WITH YOU?

BOBO Man . . . I didn't go to no Springfield, yesterday.

WALTER (*Halted, life hanging in the moment*) Why not?

BOBO (*The long way, the hard way to tell*) 'Cause I didn't have no reasons to . . .

WALTER Man, what are you talking about!

BOBO I'm talking about the fact that when I got to the train station yesterday morning—eight o'clock like we planned . . . Man—*Willy didn't never show up.*

WALTER Why . . . where was he . . . where is he?

BOBO That's what I'm trying to tell you . . . I don't know . . . I waited six hours . . . I called his house . . . and I waited . . . six hours . . . I waited in that train station six hours . . . (*Breaking into tears*) That was all the extra money I had in the world . . . (*Looking up at* WALTER *with the tears running down his face*) Man, *Willy is gone.*

WALTER Gone, what you mean Willy is gone? Gone where? You mean he went by himself. You mean he went off to Springfield by himself—to take care of getting the license— (*Turns and looks anxiously at* RUTH) You mean maybe he didn't want too many people in on the business down there? (*Looks to* RUTH *again, as before*) You know Willy got his own ways. (*Looks back to* BOBO) Maybe you was late yesterday and he just went on down there without you. Maybe—maybe—he's been callin' you at home tryin' to tell you what happened or something. Maybe—maybe—he just got sick. He's somewhere—he's got to be somewhere. We just got to find him—me and you got to find him. (*Grabs* BOBO *senselessly by the collar and starts to shake him*) We got to!

BOBO (*In sudden angry, frightened agony*) What's the

matter with you, Walter! *When a cat take off with your money he don't leave you no maps!*

WALTER (*Turning madly, as though he is looking for* WILLY *in the very room*) Willy! . . . Willy . . . don't do it . . . Please don't do it . . . Man, not with that money . . . Man, please, not with that money . . . Oh, God . . . Don't let it be true . . . (*He is wandering around, crying out for Willy and looking for him or perhaps for help from God*) Man . . . I trusted you . . . Man, I put my life in your hands . . . (*He starts to crumple down on the floor as* RUTH *just covers her face in horror.* MAMA *opens the door and comes into the room, with* BENEATHA *behind her*) Man . . . (*He starts to pound the floor with his fists, sobbing wildly*) *That money is made out of my father's flesh . . .*

BOBO (*Standing over him helplessly*) I'm sorry, Walter . . . (*Only* WALTER'S *sobs reply.* BOBO *puts on his hat*) I had my life staked on this deal, too . . .

(*He exits*)

MAMA (*To* WALTER) Son— (*She goes to him, bends down to him, talks to his bent head*) Son . . . Is it gone? Son, I gave you sixty-five hundred dollars. Is it gone? All of it? Beneatha's money too?

WALTER (*Lifting his head slowly*) Mama . . . I never . . . went to the bank at all . . .

MAMA (*Not wanting to believe him*) You mean . . . your sister's school money . . . you used that too . . . Walter? . . .

WALTER Yessss! . . . All of it . . . It's all gone . . .

(*There is total silence.* RUTH *stands with her face covered with her hands;* BENEATHA *leans forlornly against a wall, fingering a piece of red ribbon from the mother's gift.* MAMA *stops and looks at her son without recognition and then, quite without thinking about it, starts to beat him senselessly in the face.* BENEATHA *goes to them and stops it*)

BENEATHA Mama!

(MAMA *stops and looks at both of her children and rises slowly and wanders vaguely, aimlessly away from them*)

MAMA I seen . . . him . . . night after night . . . come in . . . and look at that rug . . . and then look at me . . . the red showing in his eyes . . . the veins moving in his head . . . I seen him grow thin and old before he was forty . . . working and working and working like somebody's old horse . . . killing himself . . . and you —you give it all away in a day . . .

BENEATHA Mama—

MAMA Oh, God . . . (*She looks up to Him*) Look down here—and show me the strength.

BENEATHA Mama—

MAMA (*Folding over*) Strength . . .

BENEATHA (*Plaintively*) Mama . . .

MAMA Strength!

CURTAIN

ACT THREE

An hour later.

At curtain, there is a sullen light of gloom in the living room, gray light not unlike that which began the first scene of Act One. At left we can see WALTER *within his room, alone with himself. He is stretched out on the bed, his shirt out and open, his arms under his head. He does not smoke, he does not cry out, he merely lies there, looking up at the ceiling, much as if he were alone in the world.*

In the living room BENEATHA *sits at the table, still surrounded by the now almost ominous packing crates. She sits looking off. We feel that this is a mood struck perhaps an hour before, and it lingers now, full of the empty sound of profound disappointment. We see on a line from her brother's bedroom the sameness of their attitudes. Presently the bell rings and* BENEATHA *rises without ambition or interest in answering. It is* ASAGAI, *smiling broadly, striding into the room with energy and happy expectation and conversation.*

ASAGAI I came over . . . I had some free time. I thought I might help with the packing. Ah, I like the look of packing crates! A household in preparation for a journey! It depresses some people . . . but for me . . . it is another feeling. Something full of the flow of life, do you understand? Movement, progress . . . It makes me think of Africa.

BENEATHA Africa!

ASAGAI What kind of a mood is this? Have I told you how deeply you move me?

BENEATHA He gave away the money, Asagai . . .

ASAGAI Who gave away what money?

BENEATHA The insurance money. My brother gave it away.

ASAGAI Gave it away?

BENEATHA He made an investment! With a man even Travis wouldn't have trusted.

ASAGAI And it's gone?

BENEATHA Gone!

ASAGAI I'm very sorry . . . And you, now?

BENEATHA Me? . . . Me? . . . Me I'm nothing . . . Me. When I was very small . . . we used to take our sleds out in the wintertime and the only hills we had were the ice-covered stone steps of some houses down the street. And we used to fill them in with snow and make them smooth and slide down them all day . . . and it was very dangerous you know . . . far too steep . . . and sure enough one day a kid named Rufus came down too fast and hit the sidewalk . . . and we saw his face just split open right there in front of us . . . And I remember standing there looking at his bloody open face thinking that was the end of Rufus. But the ambulance came and they took him to the hospital and they fixed the broken bones and they sewed it all up . . . and the next time I saw Rufus he just had a little line down the middle of his face . . . I never got over that . . .

ASAGAI What?

BENEATHA That that was what one person could do for another, fix him up—sew up the problem, make him all right again. That was the most marvelous thing in the world . . . I wanted to do that. I always thought it was the one concrete thing in the world that a human being could do. Fix up the sick, you know—and make them whole again. This was truly being God . . .

ASAGAI You wanted to be God?

BENEATHA No—I wanted to cure. It used to be so important to me. I wanted to cure. It used to matter. I used to care. I mean about people and how their bodies hurt . . .

ASAGAI And you've stopped caring?

BENEATHA Yes—I think so.

ASAGAI Why?

BENEATHA Because it doesn't seem deep enough, close enough to the truth.

ASAGAI Truth? Why is it that you despairing ones always think that only you have the truth? I never thought to see *you* like that. You! Your brother made a stupid, childish mistake—and you are grateful to him. So that now you can give up the ailing human race on account of it. You talk about what good is struggle; what good is anything? Where are we all going? And why are we bothering?

BENEATHA *And you cannot answer it!* All your talk and dreams about Africa and Independence. Independence and then what? What about all the crooks and petty thieves and just plain idiots who will come into power to steal and plunder the same as before—only now they will be black and do it in the name of the new Independence— You cannot answer that.

ASAGAI (*Shouting over her*) *I live the answer!* (*Pause*) In my village at home it is the exceptional man who can even read a newspaper . . . or who ever *sees* a book at all. I will go home and much of what I will have to say will seem strange to the people of my village . . . But I will teach and work and things will happen, slowly and swiftly. At times it will seem that nothing changes at all . . . and then again . . . the sudden dramatic events which make history leap into the future. And then quiet again. Retrogression even. Guns, murder, revolution. And I even will have moments when I wonder if the quiet was not better than all that death and hatred. But I will look about my village at the illiteracy and disease and ignorance and I will not wonder long. And perhaps . . . perhaps I will be a great man . . . I mean perhaps I will hold on to the substance of truth and find my way always with the right course . . . and perhaps for it I will be butchered in my bed some night by the servants of empire . . .

BENEATHA *The martyr!*

ASAGAI . . . or perhaps I shall live to be a very old man respected and esteemed in my new nation . . . And perhaps I shall hold office and this is what I'm trying to tell you, Alaiyo; perhaps the things I believe now for my country will be wrong and outmoded, and I will not understand and do terrible things to have things my way or merely to keep my power. Don't you see that there will be young men and women, not British soldiers then, but my own black countrymen . . . to step out of the shadows some evening and slit my then useless throat? Don't you see they have always been there . . . that they always will be. And that such a thing as my own death will be an advance? They who might kill me even . . . actually replenish me!

BENEATHA Oh, Asagai, I know all that.

ASAGAI Good! Then stop moaning and groaning and tell me what you plan to do.

BENEATHA Do?

ASAGAI I have a bit of a suggestion.

BENEATHA What?

ASAGAI (*Rather quietly for him*) That when it is all over —that you come home with me—

BENEATHA (*Slapping herself on the forehead with exasperation born of misunderstanding*) Oh—Asagai—at this moment you decide to be romantic!

ASAGAI (*Quickly understanding the misunderstanding*) My dear, young creature of the New World—I do not mean across the city—I mean across the ocean; home—to Africa.

BENEATHA (*Slowly understanding and turning to him with murmured amazement*) To—to Nigeria?

ASAGAI Yes! . . . (*Smiling and lifting his arms playfully*) Three hundred years later the African Prince rose up out of the seas and swept the maiden back across the middle passage over which her ancestors had come—

BENEATHA (*Unable to play*) Nigeria?

ASAGAI Nigeria. Home. (*Coming to her with genuine romantic flippancy*) I will show you our mountains and our stars; and give you cool drinks from gourds and teach you the old songs and the ways of our people—and, in time, we will pretend that— (*Very softly*) —you have only been away for a day—

(*She turns her back to him, thinking. He swings her around and takes her full in his arms in a long embrace which proceeds to passion*)

BENEATHA (*Pulling away*) You're getting me all mixed up—

ASAGAI Why?

BENEATHA Too many things—too many things have happened today. I must sit down and think. I don't know what I feel about anything right this minute.

(*She promptly sits down and props her chin on her fist*)

ASAGAI (*Charmed*) All right, I shall leave you. No—don't get up. (*Touching her, gently, sweetly*) Just sit awhile and think . . . Never be afraid to sit awhile and think. (*He goes to door and looks at her*) How often I have looked at you and said, "Ah—so this is what the New World hath finally wrought . . ."

(*He exits.* BENEATHA *sits on alone. Presently* WALTER *enters from his room and starts to rummage through things, feverishly looking for something. She looks up and turns in her seat*)

BENEATHA (*Hissingly*) Yes—just look at what the New World hath wrought! . . . Just look! (*She gestures with bitter disgust*) There he is! *Monsieur le petit bourgeois noir*—himself! There he is—Symbol of a Rising Class! Entrepreneur! Titan of the system! (WALTER *ignores her completely and continues frantically and destructively looking for something and hurling things to floor and tearing things out of their place in his search.* BENEATHA *ignores the eccentricity of his actions and goes on with the monologue of insult*) Did you dream of yachts on Lake Michigan, Brother? Did you see yourself on that Great Day sitting down at the Conference Table, surrounded by all the mighty bald-headed men in America? All halted, waiting, breathless, waiting for your pronouncements on industry? Waiting for you—Chairman of the Board? (WALTER *finds what he is looking for—a small piece of white paper—and pushes it in his pocket and puts on his coat and rushes out without ever having looked at her. She shouts after him*) I look at you and I see the final triumph of stupidity in the world!

(*The door slams and she returns to just sitting again.* RUTH *comes quickly out of* MAMA'S *room*)

RUTH Who was that?

BENEATHA Your husband.

RUTH Where did he go?

BENEATHA Who knows—maybe he has an appointment at U. S. Steel.

RUTH (*Anxiously, with frightened eyes*) You didn't say nothing bad to him, did you?

BENEATHA Bad? Say anything bad to him? No—I told him he was a sweet boy and full of dreams and everything is strictly peachy keen, as the ofay kids say!

(MAMA *enters from her bedroom. She is lost, vague, trying to catch hold, to make some sense of her former command of the world, but it still eludes her. A sense of waste overwhelms her gait; a measure of apology rides on her shoulders. She goes to her plant, which has remained on the table, looks at it, picks it up and takes it to the window sill and sits it outside, and she stands and looks at it a long moment. Then she closes the window, straightens her body with effort and turns around to her children)*

MAMA Well—ain't it a mess in here, though? (*A false cheerfulness, a beginning of something*) I guess we all better stop moping around and get some work done. All this unpacking and everything we got to do. (RUTH *raises her head slowly in response to the sense of the line; and* BENEATHEA *in similar manner turns very slowly to look at her mother*) One of you all better call the moving people and tell 'em not to come.

RUTH Tell 'em not to come?

MAMA Of course, baby. Ain't no need in 'em coming all the way here and having to go back. They charges for that too. (*She sits down, fingers to her brow, thinking*) Lord, ever since I was a little girl, I always remembers people saying, "Lena—Lena Egglston, you aims too high all the time. You needs to slow down and see life a little more like it is. Just slow down some." That's what they always used to say down home—"Lord, that Lena Eggleston is a high-minded thing. She'll get her due one day!"

RUTH No, Lena . . .

MAMA Me and Big Walter just didn't never learn right.

RUTH Lena, no! We gotta go. Bennie—tell her . . . (*She rises and crosses to* BENEATHEA *with her arms outstretched.* BENEATHEA *doesn't respond*) Tell her we can still move . . . the notes ain't but a hundred and twenty five a month. We got four grown people in this house—we can work . . .

MAMA (*To herself*) Just aimed too high all the time—

RUTH (*Turning and going to* MAMA *fast—the words pouring out with urgency and desperation*) Lena—I'll work . . . I'll work twenty hours a day in all the kitchens in Chicago . . . I'll strap my baby on my back if I have to and scrub all the floors in America and wash all the sheets in America if I have to—but we got to move . . . We got to get out of here . . .

(MAMA *reaches out absently and pats* RUTH'S *hand*)

MAMA No—I sees things differently now. Been thinking 'bout some of the things we could do to fix this place up some. I seen a second-hand bureau over on Maxwell Street just the other day that could fit right there. (*She points to where the new furniture might go.* RUTH *wanders away from her*) Would need some new handles on it and then a little varnish and then it look like something brand-new. And—we can put up them new curtains in the kitchen . . . Why this place be looking fine. Cheer us all up so that we forget trouble ever came . . . (*To* RUTH) And you could get some nice screens to put up in your room round the baby's basinet . . . (*She looks at both of them, pleadingly*) Sometimes you just got to know when to give up some things . . . and hold on to what you got.

(WALTER *enters from the outside, looking spent and leaning against the door, his coat hanging from him*)

MAMA Where you been, son?

WALTER (*Breathing hard*) Made a call.

MAMA To who, son?

WALTER To the Man.

MAMA What man, baby?

WALTER The Man, Mama. Don't you know who The Man is?

RUTH Walter Lee?

WALTER *The Man*. Like the guys in the street say—The Man. Captain Boss—Mistuh Charley . . . Old Captain Please Mr. Bossman . . .

BENEATHA (*Suddenly*) Lindner!

WALTER That's right! That's good. I told him to come right over.

BENEATHA (*Fiercely, understanding*) For what? What do you want to see him for!

WALTER (*Looking at his sister*) We going to do business with him.

MAMA What you talking 'bout, son?

WALTER Talking 'bout life, Mama. You all always telling me to see life like it is. Well—I laid in there on my back today . . . and I figured it out. Life just like it is. Who gets and who don't get. (*He sits down with his coat on and laughs*) Mama, you know it's all divided up. Life is. Sure enough. Between the takers and the "tooken." (*He laughs*) I've figured it out finally. (*He looks around at them*) Yeah. Some of us always getting "tooken." (*He laughs*) People like Willy Harris, they don't never get "tooken." And you know why the rest of us do? 'Cause we all mixed up. Mixed up bad. We get to looking 'round for the right and the wrong; and we worry about it and cry about it and stay up nights trying to figure out 'bout the wrong and the right of things all the time . . . And all the time, man, them takers is out there operating, just taking and taking. Willy Harris? Shoot—Willy Harris don't even count. He don't even count in the big scheme of things. But I'll say one thing for old Willy Harris . . . he's taught me something. He's taught me to keep my eyes on what counts in this world. Yeah— (*Shouting out a little*) Thanks, Willy!

RUTH What did you call that man for, Walter Lee?

WALTER Called him to tell him to come on over to the show. Gonna put on a show for the man. Just what he wants to see. You see, Mama, the man came here today and he told us that them people out there where you want us to move—well they so upset they willing to pay us not to move out there. (*He laughs again*) And—and oh, Mama—you would of been proud of the way me and Ruth and Bennie acted. We told him to get out . . . Lord have mercy! We told the man to get out. Oh, we was some proud folks this afternoon, yeah. (*He lights a cigarette*) We were still full of that old-time stuff . . .

RUTH (*Coming toward him slowly*) You talking 'bout taking them people's money to keep us from moving in that house?

WALTER I ain't just talking 'bout it, baby—I'm telling you that's what's going to happen.

BENEATHA Oh, God! Where is the bottom! Where is the real honest-to-God bottom so he can't go any farther!

WALTER See—that's the old stuff. You and that boy that was here today. You all want everybody to carry a flag and a spear and sing some marching songs, huh? You wanna spend your life looking into things and trying to find the right and the wrong part, huh? Yeah. You know what's going to happen to that boy someday—he'll find himself sitting in a dungeon, locked in forever—and the takers will have the key! Forget it, baby! There ain't no causes—there ain't nothing but taking in this world, and he who takes most is smartest—and it don't make a damn bit of difference *how*.

MAMA You making something inside me cry, son. Some awful pain inside me.

WALTER Don't cry, Mama. Understand. That white man is going to walk in that door able to write checks for more money than we ever had. It's important to him and I'm going to help him . . . I'm going to put on the show, Mama.

MAMA Son—I come from five generations of people who was slaves and sharecroppers—but it ain't nobody in my family never let nobody pay 'em no money that was a way of telling us we wasn't fit to walk the earth. We ain't never been that poor. (*Raising her eyes and looking at him*) We ain't never been that dead inside.

BENEATHA Well—we are dead now. All the talk about dreams and sunlight that goes on in this house. All dead.

WALTER What's the matter with you all! I didn't make this world! It was give to me this way! Hell, yes, I want me some yachts someday! Yes, I want to hang some real pearls 'round my wife's neck. Ain't she supposed to wear no pearls? Somebody tell me—tell me, who decides which women is suppose to wear pearls in this world. I tell you I am a *man*—and I think my wife should wear some pearls in this world!

(*This last line hangs a good while and* WALTER *begins to move about the room. The word "Man" has penetrated his consciousness; he mumbles it to himself repeatedly between strange agitated pauses as he moves about*)

MAMA Baby, how you going to feel on the inside?

WALTER Fine! . . . Going to feel fine . . . a man . . .

MAMA You won't have nothing left then, Walter Lee.

WALTER (*Coming to her*) I'm going to feel fine, Mama. I'm going to look that son-of-a-bitch in the eyes and say — (*He falters*) —and say, "All right, Mr. Lindner— (*He falters even more*) —that's your neighborhood out there. You got the right to keep it like you want. You got the right to have it like you want. Just write the check and—the house is yours." And, and I am going to say— (*His voice almost breaks*) And you—you people just put the money in my hand and you won't have to live next to this bunch of stinking niggers! . . . (*He straightens up and moves away from his mother, walking around the room*) Maybe—maybe I'll just get down on my black knees . . . (*He does so;* RUTH *and* BENNIE *and* MAMA *watch him in frozen horror*) Captain, Mistuh, Bossman. (*He starts crying*) A-hee-hee-hee! (*Wringing his hands in profoundly anguished imitation*) Yasssssuh! Great White Father, just gi' ussen de money, fo' God's sake, and we's ain't gwine come out deh and dirty up yo' white folks neighborhood . . .

(*He breaks down completely, then gets up and goes into the bedroom*)

BENEATHA That is not a man. That is nothing but a toothless rat.

MAMA Yes—death done come in this here house. (*She is nodding slowly, reflectively*) Done come walking in my house. On the lips of my children. You what supposed to be my beginning again. You—what supposed to be my harvest. (*To* BENEATHA) You—you mourning your brother?

BENEATHA He's no brother of mine.

MAMA What you say?

BENEATHA I said that that individual in that room is no brother of mine.

MAMA That's what I thought you said. You feeling like you better than he is today? (BENEATHA *does not answer*) Yes? What you tell him a minute ago? That he wasn't a man? Yes? You give him up for me? You done wrote his epitaph too—like the rest of the world? Well, who give you the privilege?

BENEATHA Be on my side for once! You saw what he just did, Mama! You saw him—down on his knees. Wasn't it you who taught me—to despise any man who would do that. Do what he's going to do.

MAMA Yes—I taught you that. Me and your daddy. But I thought I taught you something else too . . . I thought I taught you to love him.

BENEATHA Love him? There is nothing left to love.

MAMA There is always something left to love. And if you ain't learned that, you ain't learned nothing. (*Looking at her*) Have you cried for that boy today? I don't mean for yourself and for the family 'cause we lost the money. I mean for him; what he been through and what it done to him. Child, when do you think is the time to love somebody the most; when they done good and made things easy for everybody? Well then, you ain't learning —because that ain't the time at all. It's when he's at his lowest and can't believe in hisself 'cause the world done whipped him so. When you starts measuring somebody, measure him right, child, measure him right. Make sure you done taken into account what hills and valleys he come through before he got to wherever he is.

(TRAVIS *bursts into the room at the end of the speech, leaving the door open*)

TRAVIS Grandmama—the moving men are downstairs! The truck just pulled up.

MAMA (*Turning and looking at him*) Are they baby? They downstairs?

(*She sighs and sits. Lindner appears in the doorway. He peers in and knocks lightly, to gain attention, and comes in. All turn to look at him*)

LINDNER (*Hat and briefcase in hand*) Uh—hello . . .

(RUTH *crosses mechanically to the bedroom door and opens it and lets it swing open freely and slowly as the lights come up on* WALTER *within, still in his coat, sitting at the far corner of the room. He looks up and out through the room to* LINDNER)

RUTH He's here.

(*A long minute passes and* WALTER *slowly gets up*)

LINDNER (*Coming to the table with efficiency, putting his briefcase on the table and starting to unfold the papers and unscrew fountain pens*) Well, I certainly was glad to hear from you people. (WALTER *has begun the trek out of the room, slowly and awkwardly, rather like a small boy, passing the back of his sleeve across the back of his mouth from time to time*) Life can really be so much simpler than people let it be most of the time. Well—with whom do I negotiate? You, Mrs. Younger, or your son here? (MAMA *sits with her hands folded on her lap and her eyes closed as* WALTER *advances.* TRAVIS *goes close to* LINDNER *and looks at the papers curiously*) Just some official papers, sonny.

RUTH Travis, you go downstairs.

MAMA (*Opening her eyes and looking into* WALTER'S)

No. Travis, you stay right here. And you make him understand what you doing, Walter Lee. You teach him good. Like Willy Harris taught you. You show where our five generations done come to. Go ahead, son—

WALTER (*Looks down into his boy's eyes.* TRAVIS *grins at him merrily and* WALTER *draws him beside him with his arm lightly around his shoulder*) Well, Mr. Lindner. (BENEATHA *turns away*) We called you— (*There is a profound, simple groping quality in his speech*) —because, well, me and my family (*He looks around and shifts from one foot to the other*) Well—we are very plain people . . .

LINDNER Yes—

WALTER I mean—I have worked as a chauffeur most of my life—and my wife here, she does domestic work in people's kitchens. So does my mother. I mean—we are plain people . . .

LINDNER Yes, Mr. Younger—

WALTER (*Really like a small boy, looking down at his shoes and then up at the man*) And—uh—well, my father, well, he was a laborer most of his life.

LINDNER (*Absolutely confused*) Uh, yes—

WALTER (*Looking down at his toes once again*) My father almost beat a man to death once because this man called him a bad name or something, you know what I mean?

LINDNER No, I'm afraid I don't.

WALTER (*Finally straightening up*) Well, what I mean is that we come from people who had a lot of pride. I mean—we are very proud people. And that's my sister over there and she's going to be a doctor—and we are very proud—

LINDNER Well—I am sure that is very nice, but—

WALTER (*Starting to cry and facing the man eye to eye*) What I am telling you is that we called you over here to tell you that we are very proud and that this is—this is my son, who makes the sixth generation of our family in this country, and that we have all thought about your offer and we have decided to move into our house because my father—my father—he earned it. (MAMA *has her eyes closed and is rocking back and forth as though she were in church, with her head nodding the amen yes*) We don't want to make no trouble for nobody or fight no causes—but we will try to be good neighbors. That's all we got to say. (*He looks the man absolutely in the eyes*) We don't want your money.

(*He turns and walks away from the man*)

LINDNER (*Looking around at all of them*) I take it then that you have decided to occupy.

BENEATHA That's what the man said.

LINDNER (*To* MAMA *in her reverie*) Then I would like to appeal to you, Mrs. Younger. You are older and wiser and understand things better I am sure . . .

MAMA (*Rising*) I am afraid you don't understand. My son said we was going to move and there ain't nothing left for me to say. (*Shaking her head with double meaning*) You know how these young folks is nowadays, mister. Can't do a thing with 'em. Good-bye.

LINDNER (*Folding up his materials*) Well—if you are that final about it . . . There is nothing left for me to say. (*He finishes. He is almost ignored by the family, who are concentrating on* WALTER LEE. *At the door* LINDNER *halts and looks around*) I sure hope you people know what you're doing.

(*He shakes his head and exits*)

RUTH (*Looking around and coming to life*) Well, for God's sake—if the moving men are here—LET'S GET THE HELL OUT OF HERE!

MAMA (*Into action*) Ain't it the truth! Look at all this here mess. Ruth put Travis' good jacket on him . . . Walter Lee, fix your tie and tuck your shirt in, you look just like somebody's hoodlum. Lord have mercy, where is my plant? (*She flies to get it amid the general bustling of the family, who are deliberately trying to ignore the nobility of the past moment*) You all start on down . . . Travis child, don't go empty-handed . . . Ruth, where did I put that box with my skillets in it? I want to be in charge of it myself . . . I'm going to make us the biggest dinner we ever ate tonight . . . Beneatha, what's the matter with them stockings? Pull them things up, girl . . .

(*The family starts to file out as two moving men appear and begin to carry out the heavier pieces of furniture, bumping into the family as they move about*)

BENEATHA Mama, Asagai—asked me to marry him today and go to Africa—

MAMA (*In the middle of her getting-ready activity*) He did? You ain't old enough to marry nobody— (*Seeing the moving men lifting one of her chairs precariously*) Darling, that ain't no bale of cotton, please handle it so we can sit in it again. I had that chair twenty-five years . . .

(*The movers sigh with exasperation and go on with their work*)

BENEATHA (*Girlishly and unreasonably trying to pursue the conversation*) To go to Africa, Mama—be a doctor in Africa . . .

MAMA (*Distracted*) Yes, baby—

WALTER Africa! What he want you to go to Africa for?

BENEATHA To practice there . . .

WALTER Girl, if you don't get all them silly ideas out your head! You better marry yourself a man with some loot . . .

BENEATHA (*Angrily, precisely as in the first scene of the play*) What have you got to do with who I marry!

WALTER Plenty. Now I think George Murchison—

(*He and* BENEATHA *go out yelling at each other vigorously;* BENEATHA *is heard saying that she would not marry* GEORGE MURCHISON *if he were Adam and she were Eve, etc. The anger is loud and real till their voices diminish.* RUTH *stands at the door and turns to* MAMA *and smiles knowingly*)

MAMA (*Fixing her hat at last*) Yeah—they something all right, my children . . .

RUTH Yeah—they're something. Let's go, Lena.

MAMA (*Stalling, starting to look around at the house*) Yes—I'm coming. Ruth—

RUTH Yes?

MAMA (*Quietly, woman to woman*) He finally come into his manhood today, didn't he? Kind of like a rainbow after the rain . . .

RUTH (*Biting her lip lest her own pride explode in front of* MAMA) Yes, Lena.

(WALTER'S *voice calls for them raucously*)

MAMA (*Waving* RUTH *out vaguely*) All right honey—go on down. I be down directly.

(RUTH *hesitates, then exits.* MAMA *stands, at last alone in the living room, her plant on the table before her as the lights start to come down. She looks around at all the walls and ceilings and suddenly, despite herself, while the children call below, a great heaving thing rises in her and she puts her fist to her mouth, takes a final desperate look, pulls her coat about her, pats her hat and goes out. The lights dim down. The door opens and she comes back in, grabs her plant, and goes out for the last time*)

CURTAIN

Paddy Chayefsky

The Tenth Man

TO TYRONE GUTHRIE

Manufactured in the United States of America by H. Wolff

The Tenth Man was first presented by Saint Subber and Arthur Cantor at The Booth Theatre, New York City, November 5, 1959, with the following cast:

(*In order of appearance*)

THE CABALIST	Arnold Marlé
THE SEXTON	David Vardi
SCHLISSEL	Lou Jacobi
ZITORSKY	Jack Gilford
ALPER	George Voskovec
FOREMAN	Jacob Ben-Ami
THE GIRL (EVELYN FOREMAN)	Risa Schwartz
ARTHUR LANDAU	Donald Harron
HARRIS	Martin Garner
THE RABBI	Gene Saks
KESSLER BOYS	Alan Manson Paul Marin
THE POLICEMAN	Tim Callaghan

DIRECTED BY Tyrone Guthrie
SETTINGS AND LIGHTING BY David Hays
COSTUMES BY Frank Thompson
ASSOCIATE: Caroline Swann

An Orthodox Synagogue

ACT ONE

Before the Morning Prayers.

ACT TWO

Scene 1: The Morning Prayers.
Scene 2: Before the Afternoon Prayers.

ACT THREE

The Exorcism.

ACT ONE

Interior of the synagogue of the Congregation Atereth-Tifereth Yisroel.

It is a poor congregation, and the synagogue is actually a converted shop. A raised platform surrounded by a railing contains the lectern and the Holy Ark. This altar is surrounded by rows of plain wooden folding chairs which constitute the seating accommodations for the congregation. On the far side of the altar is an old desk at which THE RABBI *presides when teaching Hebrew school.*

A partitioned area downstage right is THE RABBI'S *study, a crowded little cubicle containing a battered mahogany desk and chair, an old leather armchair, a worn leather couch, and piles of black prayer books. On the walls are old framed pictures of bearded patriarchs in desolate obsession over their Talmuds and perhaps a few familiar scenes from the Old Testament.*

Downstage is a metal heating unit. There is a second heating unit upstage, and a door leading apparently to a bathroom. The front door is stage left.

It is 6:30 A.M. *on a cold winter day.*

At rise, THE CABALIST *stands in the middle of the synagogue, entirely wrapped in a thick white linen prayer shawl with broad black stripes, praying silently from a heavy prayer book that rests on the railing of the altar. Suddenly he pauses in his intense devotions, clutches at the railing as if to keep himself from falling. We have the impression that he is faint, near to swooning. He is a small, bearded man, in his seventies; his face is lean and lined, his eyes sunken and hollow. He wears a small black skullcap from beneath which stick out gray forelocks and sidecurls—a testament to his orthodoxy. After a moment, he regains his strength and returns to his prayers.*

Three men hurry into the synagogue out of the oppressive cold of the street. They are THE SEXTON, SCHLISSEL *and* ZITORSKY. *They all wear heavy overcoats and gray fedoras.* SCHLISSEL *and* ZITORSKY *are in their early seventies.* THE SEXTON *is a small, nervous, bespectacled man of forty-eight. We know he is a sexton because he carries a huge ring of keys. The men rub their hands for warmth and huff and puff and dart quick looks at* THE CABALIST, *who is oblivious to their entrance.*

SCHLISSEL (*Muttering*) Close the door. (*Light pours down on the synagogue as* THE SEXTON *flicks on the wall switch.* THE SEXTON *scurries upstage to fuss with the heater in the rear of the synagogue.* SCHLISSEL *and* ZITORSKY *shuffle downstage to a small uncovered heater and stand silently—indeed a little wearily—for a moment.* SCHLISSEL *sighs*) So how goes it with a Jew today?

ZITORSKY How should it go?

SCHLISSEL Have a pinch of snuff.

ZITORSKY No, thank you.

SCHLISSEL Davis won't be here this morning. I stopped by his house. He has a cold. His daughter-in-law told me he's still in bed.

ZITORSKY My daughter-in-law, may she grow rich and buy a hotel with a thousand rooms and be found dead in every one of them.

SCHLISSEL My daughter-in-law, may she invest heavily in General Motors, and the whole thing should go bankrupt.

ZITORSKY Sure, go have children.

SCHLISSEL The devil take them all.

THE SEXTON (*Scurrying downstage; to* THE CABALIST *as he passes*) Hirschman, are you all right?

(*He flutters, a small round ball of a man, to the door of* THE RABBI'S *office, which he now opens with one of the many keys on his chain*)

SCHLISSEL Foreman won't be here today.

ZITORSKY What's the matter with Foreman?

SCHLISSEL His granddaughter today. This is the morning.

ZITORSKY Oh, that's right. Today is the morning.

SCHLISSEL Listen, it's better for everybody.

ZITORSKY Sure.

SCHLISSEL I told Foreman, I said: "Foreman, it's better for everybody." The girl is becoming violent. I spoke to her father. He said to me they live in terror what she'll do to the other children. They came home one night, they found her punching one of the little children.

ZITORSKY Well, what can you do?

SCHLISSEL What can you do? You do what they're doing. They're putting her back in the institution.

ZITORSKY Of course. There she will have the benefit of trained psychiatric personnel.

SCHLISSEL The girl is incurable. She's been in and out of mental institutions since she was eleven years old. I met the psychiatrist there, you know, when I was up there to visit Foreman last week. I discussed the whole business with him. A fine young fellow. The girl is a schizophrenic with violent tendencies.

(ZITORSKY *considers this diagnosis for a moment, then sighs*)

ZITORSKY Ah, may my daughter-in-law eat acorns and may branches spout from her ears.

SCHLISSEL May my daughter-in-law live to be a hundred and twenty,and may she live all her years in *her* daughter-in-law's house.

(THE SEXTON *has been tugging a large opened brown cardboard carton out of* THE RABBI'S *office, from which he now extracts two velvet bags which he hands to* SCHLISSEL *and* ZITORSKY. *A fifth old Jew now enters from the street, a patrician little man with a Vandyke beard and a black homburg. His name is* ALPER. *He bursts into shrill prayer as he enters*)

ALPER (*Chanting*) "As for me in the abundance of thy loving kindness will I come into thy house; I will worship toward thy holy temple in the fear of thee. How goodly are thy tents, O Jacob . . ." (*As precipitously as the prayer had begun, it now drops into nothing more than a rapid movement of lips.* THE SEXTON *acknowledges* ALPER'S *arrival with a nod and darts back into* THE RABBI'S *office, where he plunks himself behind the desk and begins hurriedly to dial the phone.* ALPER'S *voice zooms abruptly up into a shrill incantation again*) ". . . in the truth of thy salvation. Amen!"

SCHLISSEL Amen.

ZITORSKY Amen.

(ALPER *joins the other two old men and they stand in silent, rueful speculation*)

THE SEXTON (*On phone*) Hello, Harris? This is Bleyer the Sexton. Come on down today, we need you. Foreman won't be here. Davis is sick. We won't have ten men for the morning prayers if you don't come down . . . Services start in twenty minutes. Hurry up . . . Wear a sweater under your coat . . . All right . . .

(*He hangs up, takes a large ledger from the desk, and begins nervously to examine its pages*)

SCHLISSEL Hirschman slept over in the synagogue again last night. Have you ever seen such pietistic humbug?

ALPER Well, he is a very devout man. A student of the

cabala. The Rabbi speaks of him with the greatest reverence.

SCHLISSEL Devout indeed. I assure you this lavish display of orthodoxy is a very profitable business. I was told confidentially just yesterday that his board and food are paid for by two foolish old women who consider him a saint.

ALPER It can't cost them very much. He's been fasting the last three days.

SCHLISSEL And the reason he sleeps in the synagogue so frequently is because his landlady does not give him heat for his own room in the mornings.

ZITORSKY Ah, go be an old man in the winter.

ALPER I must say, I really don't know what to do with myself on these cold days.

SCHLISSEL I'm an atheist. If I had something better to do, would I be here?

ZITORSKY You know what would be a nice way to kill a day? I think it would be nice to take a trip up to Mount Hope Cemetery and have a look at my burial plot. A lovely cemetery. Like a golf course, actually. By the time one gets there and comes back, the whole day has been used up. Would you like to come? I'll pay both your fares.

ALPER Why not? I have never been to Mount Hope. I have my burial plot on Mount Zion Cemetery.

ZITORSKY Oh, that's a beautiful cemetery.

ALPER Yes, it is. My wife wanted to buy plots in Cedar Lawn because her whole family is buried there, but I wouldn't hear of it.

ZITORSKY Oh, Cedar Lawn. I wouldn't be buried in Cedar Lawn.

ALPER It's in such a bad state. The headstones tumble one on top of the other, and everybody walks on the graves.

ZITORSKY They don't take care in Cedar Lawn. My wife once said, she should rest in peace, that Cedar Lawn was the tenement of cemeteries.

ALPER A well-turned phrase.

ZITORSKY She had a way with words, God grant her eternal rest.

ALPER I'd like you to come to Mount Zion sometimes, see my plot.

ZITORSKY Maybe we could make the trip tomorrow.

SCHLISSEL Listen to these two idiots, discussing their graves as if they were country estates.

ZITORSKY Where are you buried, Schlissel?

SCHLISSEL Cedar Lawn.

ALPER Well, listen, there are many lovely areas in Cedar Lawn. All my wife's family are buried there.

ZITORSKY Come with us, Schlissel, and have a look at my grave.

SCHLISSEL Why not? What else have I got to do?

(ALPER *now slowly goes about the business of donning his prayer shawl and phylacteries, which he takes out of a velvet prayer bag. Among Jews, prayer is a highly individual matter, and peripatetic to the bargain. The actual ritual of laying on the phylacteries is a colorful one.* ALPER *extracts his left arm from his jacket and rebuttons his jacket so that his shirt-sleeved left arm hangs loose. Then, the shirt sleeve is rolled up almost to the shoulder, and the arm phylactery, a long thin black leather thong, is put on by wrapping it around the left arm seven times, three times around the palm, and three times around the middle finger. All this is accompanied by rapidly recited prayers, as is the laying on of the head phylactery. All the while* ALPER *walks, bending and twisting at the knees, raising his voice occasionally in the truly lovely words of incantation. In a far upstage corner,* THE CABALIST *huddles under his enveloping white tallith—prayer shawl—his back to everyone else, deeply involved in his personal meditations. The synagogue itself is a shabby little place, the walls yellowed and cracked, illumined by a fitful overhead bulb. There is indeed at this moment a sense of agelessness, even of primitive barbarism. During this,* THE SEXTON *has dialed a second number*)

THE SEXTON Hello? Mr. Arnold Kessler, please . . . How do you do? This is Mr. Bleyer the Sexton at the synagogue. Perhaps you recall me . . . Did I wake you up? I'm terribly sorry. As long as you're up, according to my books, your father died one year ago yesterday, on the eleventh day in the month of Shvat, may his soul fly straight to the Heavenly Gates, and how about coming down with your brother and saying a memorial prayer in your father's name? . . . Let me put it this way, Mr. Kessler. You know we can't have morning prayers without a quorum of ten men. If you and your brother don't come down we won't have a quorum . . . As a favor to me . . . Kessler, may your children be such devoted sons, and bring your brother. You are doing a good deed. Peace be with you. Hurry up.

(*He hangs up, sits frowning, totaling, up on his fingers the number of men he has, scowls. In the synagogue,* ALPHER'S *voice rises for a brief moment*)

ALPER "... and it shall be to thee for a sign upon thy hand, and for a memorial between thy eyes . . ."

(THE SEXTON *rises abruptly from his chair and bustles out of the office to the front door of the synagogue*)

THE SEXTON (*To nobody in particular*) Listen, I'm going to have to get a tenth Jew off the street somewheres. I'll be right back. Schlissel, will you please fix that bench already, you promised me.

(*He exits.* SCHLISSEL *nods and picks up a hammer. For a moment, only the singsong murmur of the rapid prayers and the upstage tapping of* SCHLISSEL'S *hammer fill the stage. The front door to the synagogue now opens, and a sixth old Jew peers in. He is a frightened little wisp of a man, named* FOREMAN. *He is obviously in a state. He darts terrified looks all about the synagogue, and then abruptly disappears back into the street, leaving the syna-*

gogue door open. Nobody noticed his brief appearance. A moment later, he is back, this time leading a slim young girl of eighteen wearing a topcoat, who is also distracted. The old man herds her quickly across the synagogue to THE RABBI'S *office, pushes her in, and closes the door behind her. She stands in* THE RABBI'S *office, almost rigid with terror.* FOREMAN *scuttles back to close the front door.* SCHLISSEL *looks up and notices* FOREMAN *and nods to him; he nods back. Like his friends,* FOREMAN *wears a heavy winter coat and a worn fedora some sizes too small for him. He stands and watches the others apprehensively. At last* ALPER *reaches the end of his laying on of the phylacteries, his voice climbing to a shrill incantation)*

ALPER (*To* FOREMAN, *moving slowly as he prays*) ". . . and it shall be for a sign upon thy hand, and for frontlets between thy eyes; for by strength of hand the Lord brought us out from Egypt. Amen!"

FOREMAN (*Muttering, his head bobbing nervously*) Amen!

ALPER I thought you weren't coming down today, Foreman.

FOREMAN (*His mouth working without saying anything. Finally, he says*) Alper . . .

ALPER You seem agitated. Is something wrong?

FOREMAN (*Staring at his friend*) Alper, I have her here.

ALPER You have who here?

FOREMAN I have my granddaughter Evelyn here. I have her here in the Rabbi's office.

ALPER What are you talking about?

FOREMAN I took her out of the house while nobody was looking, and I brought her here. I am faint. Let me sit down.

(*He sinks onto a chair. His friend regards him with concern*)

ALPER Here, David, let me take your coat.

FOREMAN Alper, I have seen such a thing and heard words as will place me in my grave before the singing of the evening service. "Blessed art Thou, O Lord, King of the Universe, who hath wrought the wonders of the world." (*Suddenly half-starting from his seat*) I must speak to Hirschman! This is an affair for Hirschman who has delved into the cabala and the forbidden mysteries of numbers.

ALPER Sit down, Foreman, and compose yourself. (FOREMAN *sinks slowly back onto his chair*) Why did you bring her here? Foreman, you are my oldest friend from our days in the seminary together in Rumni in the Province of Poltava, and I speak to you harshly as only a friend may speak. You are making too much out of this whole matter of the girl. I know how dear she is to you, but the girl is insane, for heaven's sake! What sort of foolishness is this then to smuggle her out of your son's home? To what purpose? Really, Foreman, a gentle and pious man like you! Your son must be running through the streets at this moment shouting his daughter's name. Cal him on the phone and tell him you are bringing her back to him.

(FOREMAN *stares at his friend, his pale eyes filled with tears*)

FOREMAN Alper . . .

ALPER David, my dear friend, make peace with this situation.

FOREMAN (*Whispering*) She is possessed, Alper. She has a dybbuk in her. A demon! It spoke to me. (*He stares down at the floor at his feet, a numb terror settling over his face*) It spoke to me. I went in to my granddaughter this morning to comfort her, and I said: "How are you?" And she seemed quite normal. She has these moments of absolute lucidity. (*He looks desperately at his friend again*) She seemed to know she was being taken to the institution again. Then suddenly she fell to the floor in a swoon. I said: "Evelyn, what's the matter?" And she looked up at me, and it was no longer her face, but a face so twisted with rage that my blood froze in my body. And a voice came out of her that was not her own. "Do you know my voice?" And I knew it. I knew the voice. God have mercy on my soul. I stood there like a statue, and my granddaughter lay on the floor with her eyes closed, and the voice came out of her, but her lips never moved. "David Foreman, son of Abram, this is the soul of Hannah Luchinsky, whom you dishonored and weakened in your youth, and the Gates of Heaven are closed to me." And my granddaughter began to writhe on the floor as if in the most horrible agony, and she began to laugh so loudly that I was sure my son and daughter-in-law in the living room could hear. I flung the door open in panic, and my son and daughter-in-law were sitting there talking, and they heard nothing. And I tell you shrieks of laughter were coming from this girl on the floor. And I closed the door and besought God, and finally the dybbuk was silent. May God strike me down on this spot, Alper, if every word I tell you is not true.

(ALPER *has slowly sat down on an adjacent chair, absolutely enthralled by the story. He stares at* FOREMAN)

ALPER A dybbuk?

FOREMAN (*Nodding*) A dybbuk. Could you believe such a thing?

ALPER Who did the dybbuk say she was?

FOREMAN You should remember her. Hannah Luchinsky.

ALPER The name is vaguely familiar.

FOREMAN You remember Luchinsky, the sexton of the Rumni seminary, with his three daughters? Hannah was the handsome one who became pregnant, and they threw stones at her, called her harlot, and drove her out of the city.

ALPER (*Recognition slowly coming over him*) Ooohhh.

FOREMAN I was the one who debased her.

ALPER You? You were such a nose-in-the-books, a gentle and modest fellow. Dear me. A dybbuk. Really! What an extraordinary thing. Schlissel, do you want to hear a story?

SCHLISSEL (*Coming over*) What?

ALPER (*To* ZITORSKY, *who ambles over*) Listen to this. Foreman is telling a story here that will turn your blood into water.

SCHLISSEL What happened?

FOREMAN What happened, Schlissel, was that I went in to see my granddaughter this morning and discovered that she was possessed by a dybbuk. Now, please, Schlissel, before you go into one of your interminable disputations on the role of superstition in the capitalist economy, let me remind you that I am a follower of Maimonides and . . .

SCHLISSEL What are you talking about?

FOREMAN A dybbuk! A dybbuk! I tell you my granddaughter is possessed by a dybbuk! Oh, my head is just pounding! I do not know which way to turn.

SCHLISSEL What are you prattling about dybbuks?

ALPER (*To* SCHLISSEL) The voice of Hannah Luchinsky spoke to him through the lips of his granddaughter.

ZITORSKY Oh, a dybbuk.

SCHLISSEL What nonsense is this?

ALPER (*To* FOREMAN) Are you sure?

FOREMAN (*Angrily*) Am I sure? Am I a peasant who leaps at every black cat? Have I ever shown a susceptibility to mysticism? Have you not seen me engaging Hirschman over there in violent disputation over the fanatic numerology of the cabala? Have I not mocked to his very face the murky fantasy of the Gilgul with wispy souls floating in space? Really! Am I sure! Do you take me for a fool, a prattler of old wives' tales? Really! I tell you I heard that woman's voice as I hear the cold wind outside our doors now, and saw my granddaughter writhing in the toils of possession as I see the phylactery on your brow this moment. I was a teacher of biology for thirty-nine years at the Yeshiva High School. A dedicated follower of the great Rambam who scoffed at augurs and sorcerers! For heaven's sake! Really! I report to you only what I see! (*He strides angrily away, and then his brief flurry of temper subsides as abruptly as it flared*) My dear Alper, please forgive this burst of temper. I am so distressed by this whole business that I cannot control my wits. I assure you that it is as hard for me to believe my own senses as it is for you.

ZITORSKY When I was a boy in Lithuania, there was a young boy who worked for the butcher who was possessed by the dybbuk.

SCHLISSEL (*Scornfully*) A dybbuk. Sure. Sure. When I was a boy in Poland, I also heard stories about a man who lived in the next town who was possessed by a dybbuk. I was eight years old, and, one day after school, my friends and I walked barefoot the six miles to the next town, and we asked everybody, "Where is the man with the dybbuk?" And nobody knew what we were talking about. So I came home and told my mother: "Mama, there is no man with a dybbuk in the next town." And she gave me such a slap across the face that I turned around three times. And she said to me: "Aha! Only eight years old and already an atheist." Foreman, my friend, you talk like my mother, who was an ignorant fish-wife. I am shocked at you.

FOREMAN Oh, leave me be, Schlissel. I have no patience with your pontificating this morning.

ALPER Don't let him upset you, Foreman. The man is a Communist.

FOREMAN He is not a Communist. He is just disagreeable.

SCHLISSEL My dear fellow, I have never believed in God.

Should I now believe in demons? A dybbuk. This I would like to see.

FOREMAN (*Furiously*) Then see! (*He strides to the door of* THE RABBI'S *office and wrenches the door open. The others gingerly follow him to the opened doorway and peer in.* THE GIRL—EVELYN—*stares at them, terrified. In a thunderous voice,* FOREMAN *cries out*—) Dybbuk! I direct you to reveal yourself!

(THE GIRL *stares at the four patently startled old men, and then suddenly bursts into a bloodcurdling shriek of laughter. The four old men involuntarily take one step back and regard this exhibition wide-eyed.*)

FOREMAN What is your name?

THE GIRL I am Hannah Luchinsky.

FOREMAN Who are you?

THE GIRL I am the Whore of Kiev, the companion of sailors.

FOREMAN How come you to be in my granddaughter's body?

THE GIRL I was on a yacht in the sea of Odessa, the pleasure of five wealthy merchants. And a storm arose, and all were lost. And my soul rose from the water and flew to the city of Belgorod where my soul appealed to the sages of that city. But since I was debauched they turned their backs on me.

FOREMAN And then?

THE GIRL Then my soul entered the body of a cow who became insane and was brought to slaughter and I flew into the body of this girl as if divinely directed.

FOREMAN What do you want?

THE GIRL I want the strength of a pure soul so that I may acquire that experience to ascend to heaven.

FOREMAN I plead with you to leave the body of this girl.

THE GIRL I have wandered through Gilgul many years, and I want peace. Why do you plague me? There are those among you who have done the same as I and will suffer a similar fate. There is one among you who has lain with whores many times, and his wife died of the knowledge.

ZITORSKY (Aghast) Oh, my God!

THE GIRL (*Laughing*) Am I to answer questions of old men who have nothing to do but visit each other's cemeteries?

ZITORSKY (*Terrified*) A dybbuk . . . a dybbuk . . .

FOREMAN Evelyn . . . Evelyn . . . She is again in a catatonic state.

(THE GIRL *now sits in the* RABBI'S *chair, sprawling wantonly, apparently finished with the interview. The four old men regard her a little numbly. They are all quite pale as a result of the experience. After a moment,* FOREMAN *closes the door of* THE RABBI'S *office, and the four old men shuffle in a silent group downstage, where they stand, each reviewing in his own mind the bizarre implications of what they have seen.* FOREMAN *sinks into a chair and covers his face with his hands. After a long, long moment,* ZITORSKY *speaks*)

ZITORSKY Well, that's some dybbuk, all right.

SCHLISSEL The girl is as mad as a hatter and fancies herself a Ukrainian trollop. This is a dybbuk?

ALPER I found it quite and unnerving experience.

ZITORSKY She caught me dead to rights. I'll tell you that. I was the one she was talking about there, who trumpeted around with women. Listen, when I was in the garment business, if you didn't have women for the out-of-town buyers, you couldn't sell a dozen dresses. Oh, I was quite a gamy fellow when I was in business, a madcap really. One day, my wife caught me in the shop with a model—who knew she would be downtown that day?—and from that moment on, my wife was a sick woman and died three years later, cursing my name with her last breath. That was some dybbuk, all right. How she picked me out! It gave me the shivers.

ALPER Did you notice her use of archaic language and her Russian accent? The whole business had an authentic ring to me.

SCHLISSEL What nonsense! The last time I was up to Foreman's the girl confided to me in a whisper that she was Susan Hayward. A dybbuk! Ever since she was a child Foreman has been pumping her head full of the wretched superstitions of the Russian Pale, so she thinks she is a dybbuk. The girl is a lunatic and should be packed off to an asylum immediately.

(ALPER *regards* SCHLISSEL *with a disapproving eye; he then takes* SCHLISSEL'S *arm and leads him a few steps away for a private chat*)

ALPER Really, Schlissel, must you always be so argumentative? We are all here agreed that we have a dybbuk in our company, but you always seem intent on being at odds with everyone around you. Really, look at poor Foreman, how distraught he is. Out of simple courtesy, really, for an old friend, can you not affect at least a silence on the matter? And, after all, what else have you got to do today? Ride two and a half hours to look at Zitorsky's tombstone? When you stop and think of it, this dybbuk is quite an exciting affair. Really, nothing like this has happened since Kornblum and Milsky had that fist fight over who would have the seat by the East Wall during the High Holidays.

ZITORSKY (*Ambling over*) That's some dybbuk, all right.

SCHLISSEL (*Frowning*) All right, so what'll we do with this dybbuk now that we got it?

ALPER It seems to me, there is some kind of ritual, an exorcism of sorts.

ZITORSKY Maybe we should tell the Rabbi.

SCHLISSEL A young fellow like that. What does he know of dybbuks? A dybbuk must be exorcised from the body by a rabbi of some standing. You can't just call in some smooth-shaven young fellow fresh from the seminary for such a formidable matter as a dybbuk. This Rabbi has only been here two months. He hardly knows our names.

ALPER He's right. You have to get a big rabbi for such a business.

SCHLISSEL What has to be done is we must get in touch with the Korpotchniker Rabbi of Williamsburg, who has inherited the mantle of the Great Korpotchniker of Lwów, whose fame extends to all the corners of the world.

ZITORSKY Oh, a sage among sages.

ALPER I was about to suggest the Bobolovitcher Rabbi of Crown Heights.

SCHLISSEL Where do you come to compare the Bobolovitcher Rabbi with the Korpotchniker?

ALPER I once attended an afternoon service conducted by the Bobolovitcher, and it was an exalting experience. A man truly in the great tradition of Chassidic rabbis.

ZITORSKY A sage among sages, may his name be blessed for ever and ever.

SCHLISSEL It shows how much you know. The Bobolovitcher Rabbi is a disciple of the Korpotchniker and sat at the Korpotchniker's feet until a matter of only a few years ago.

ALPER Listen, I'm not going to argue with you. Either one is fine for me.

SCHLISSEL The Korpotchniker is the number one Chassidic rabbi in the world. If you're going to involve yourself at all, why not go straight to the top?

ALPER All right, so let it be the Korpotchniker.

ZITORSKY For that matter, the Lubanower Rabbi of Brownsville is a man of great repute.

SCHLISSEL The Lubanower! Really! He's a young man, for heaven's sakes!

ALPER Zitorsky, let it be decided then that it will be the Korpotchniker.

ZITORSKY I only made a suggestion.

SCHLISSEL The question is how does one get to the Korpotchniker? One does not drop into his home as if it were a public library. One has to solicit his secretary and petition for an audience. It may take weeks.

ALPER I do think, Schlissel, we shall have to get a more accessible rabbi than that. Ah, here is Hirschman, who I am sure can give us excellent counsel in this matter.

(THE CABALIST *has indeed finished his prayers, and is shuffling downstage, a small, frightened man.* FOREMAN *leaps from his chair.*

FOREMAN Hirschman!

(*Everyone crowds around* THE CABALIST)

ZITORSKY Oh, boy, Hirschman, have we got something to tell you!

ALPER Zitorsky, please. Hirschman, you are a man versed in the cabala, a man who prays with all the seventy-two names of the Most Ancient of the Ancient Ones.

FOREMAN (*Blurting out*) Hirschman, my granddaughter is possessed by a dybbuk!

THE CABALIST (*Starting back in terror*) A dybbuk!

ALPER Foreman, please, one does not announce such a thing as baldly as that.

THE CABALIST Are you sure?

FOREMAN Hirschman, as a rule, I am given to whimsy.

THE CABALIST Was it the soul of a woman wronged in her youth?

FOREMAN Yes.

THE CABALIST I heard her cry out last night. I awoke for my midnight devotions, and as I prayed I heard the whimpering of a woman's soul. (*A strange expression of wonder settles over his face*) I have fasted three days and three nights, and I dismissed the sound of this dybbuk as a fantasy of my weakened state. For only those to whom the Ancient One has raised his veil can hear the traffic of dybbuks. Is this a sign from God that my penitence is over? I have prayed for such a sign. I have felt strange things these past days. Sudden, bursting illuminations have bleached mine eyes, and I have heard the sounds of dead and supernatural things.

(*He lifts his worn little face, his eyes wide with wonder. The others are put a little ill-at-ease by this effusive outburst.* FOREMAN, *indeed, is quite overwhelmed*)

ALPER Actually, Hirschman, all we want to know is if you knew the telephone number of the Korpotchniker Rabbi.

(THE CABALIST *with some effort brings himself back to the moment at hand*)

THE CABALIST He is my cousin. I will call him for you.

(*He moves slowly off, still obsessed with some private wonder of his own, to the phone on the outside wall of* THE RABBI'S *office*)

ALPER (*Quite awed*) Your cousin? You are the Korpotchniker's cousin, Hirschman?

ZITORSKY (*Hurrying after* THE CABALIST) You'll need a dime, Hirschman.

(*He gives* THE CABALIST *the ten-cent piece*)

ALPER Schlissel, the Korpotchniker's cousin, did you hear? Apparently, he's not such a humbug.

SCHLISSEL I tell you, he gives me the creeps, that Hirschman.

(THE CABALIST *has dialed a number on the wall phone.* FOREMAN *stands at his elbow, hunched with anxiety*)

THE CABALIST (*To* FOREMAN, *gently*) Where is she, the dybbuk?

FOREMAN In the Rabbi's office.

THE CABALIST You are wise to go to the Korpotchniker. He is a Righteous One among the Righteous Ones. We were quite close as children until I abandoned the rabbinate. (*On the phone, in soft, gentle tones*) Hello? Is this Chaim son of Yosif . . . This is Israel son of Isaac . . . And peace be unto you . . . There is a man here of my congregation who feels his granddaughter is possessed by a dybbuk and would seek counsel from my cousin . . . He will bless you for your courtesy. Peace be unto you, Chaim son of Yosif. (*He hangs the receiver back in its cradle and turns to* FOREMAN) Give me a paper and pencil. (*The others, who have crowded around to hear the phone call, all seek in their pockets for a paper and pencil and manage to produce an old envelope and a stub of a pencil between them*) That was the Korpotchniker's secretary, and you are to go to his home as quickly as you can. I will write the address down for you. It is Williamsburg in Brooklyn. And you will be received directly after the morning services.

(*He gives* FOREMAN *the address, sweeps his prayer shawl on and retires upstage again for continued devotions*)

FOREMAN Thank you, Hirschman. The eye of the Lord will be open to you in the time of your need.

ZITORSKY Oh, Williamsburg. That's quite a ride from here.

SCHLISSEL What are you talking about? Foreman, you take the Long Island Railroad to Atlantic Avenue Station, where you go down stairs, and you catch the Brooklyn subway.

ALPER Maybe, I should go along with you, David, because a simple fellow like you will certainly get lost in the Atlantic Avenue Station, which is an immense or conflux of subways

SCHLISSEL What you do, Foreman, is you take the Long Island Railroad to the Atlantic Avenue Station, where you take the Double G train on the lower level . . .

ALPER Not the Double G train.

SCHLISSEL What's wrong with the Double G?

ALPER One takes the Brighton train. The Double G train will take him to Smith Street, which is a good eight blocks' walk.

SCHLISSEL The Brighton train will take him to Coney Island.

ALPER Foreman, listen to what I tell you. I will write down the instructions for you because an innocent fellow like you, if they didn't point you in the right direction, you couldn't even find the synagogue in the morning. Where's my pencil?

(*He has taken the paper and pencil from* FOREMAN'S *numb fingers and is writing down the traveling instructions*)

FOREMAN (*Staring off at the wall of* THE RABBI'S *office*) What shall I do with the girl? I can't leave her here.

ALPER Don't worry about the girl. She knows me. I'm like a second grandfather to her.

FOREMAN I don't like to leave her. Did I do right, Alper? Did I do right, kidnaping her this morning and bringing her here? Because the psychiatrist said we must prepare ourselves that she would probably spend the rest of her life in mental institutions. The irrevocability of it! The rest of her life! I was in tears almost the whole night thinking about it. Perhaps this produced a desperate susceptibility in me so that I clutch even at dybbuks rather than believe she is irretrievably insane. Now, in the sober chill of afterthought, it all seems so unreal and impetuous. And here I am bucketing off to some forbidding rabbi to listen to mystical incantations.

ALPER The Korpotchniker is not a rogue, Foreman. He is not going to sell you patent medicine. He will advise you quite sensibly, I am sure.

FOREMAN (*Buttoning his coat*) Yes, yes, I shall go to see him. You shall have to hide her till I come back. My son has probably called the police by now, and sooner or later they will come here looking for her.

ALPER Don't worry about it. I won't leave her side for a moment.

FOREMAN I better tell her I'm going. She'll be frightened if she looks for me, and I'm not here.

(*He hurries quickly to the* RABBI'S *office, where he stands a moment, regarding* THE GIRL *with mingled fear and tenderness.* THE GIRL *has sunk into the blank detachment of schizophrenia and stares unseeingly at the floor*)

SCHLISSEL So the girl is a fugitive from the police. The situation is beginning to take on charm.

ALPER Look at Schlissel. The retired revolutionary. As long as it's against the law, he believes in dybbuks.

SCHLISSEL I believe in anything that involves a conspiracy.

(*At this point, the front door bursts open, and* THE SEXTON *returns with the announcement—*)

THE SEXTON I've got a tenth Jew!

ZITORSKY Sexton, have we got something to tell you!

SCHLISSEL (*Shushing him abruptly*) Sha! Idiot! Must you tell everyone?

THE SEXTON (*He leans back through the open door to the street and says to someone out there*) Come in, come in . . . (*A fine-looking, if troubled, young fellow in his middle thirties enters; he is dressed in expensive clothes, albeit a little shabby at the moment, as if he had been on a bender for the last couple of days. His name is* ARTHUR LANDAU. *He stands ill-at-ease and scowling, disturbed in aspect. His burberry topcoat hangs limply on him.* THE SEXTON *has scooted to an open carton, from which he takes out a black paper skullcap, nervously talking as he does*) Harris didn't come in yet?

SCHLISSEL No.

THE SEXTON The two Kessler boys, I called them on the phone, they didn't show up yet? (*He thrusts the skullcap into* ARTHUR'S *hand*) Here's a skullcap, put it on. (ARTHUR *takes the skullcap absently, but makes no move to put it on. He is preoccupied with deep and dark thoughts.* THE SEXTON *heads for the front door*) The Rabbi's not here yet?

SCHLISSEL He'll be here in a couple of minutes.

THE SEXTON It's only seven minutes to the services. Listen, I'm going to the Kesslers'. I'll have to pull them out of their beds, I can see that. I'll be right back. (*To* ARTHUR) You'll find some phylacteries in the carton there. Alper, give the man a prayer book. Sure, go find ten Jews on a winter morning.

(*He exits, closing the front door*)

FOREMAN (*As he comes out of the office*) All right, I'm going. She didn't eat anything this morning, so see she gets some coffee at least. Let's see. I take the Long Island Railroad to Atlantic Avenue Station. Listen, it has been a number of years since I have been on the subways. Well, wish me luck. Have I got money for carfare? Yes, yes. Well . . . well . . . my dear friends, peace be with you.

ALPER And with you, Foreman.

ZITORSKY Amen.

FOREMAN (*Opening the door*) Oh, it's cold out there.

(*He exits, closing the door*)

ALPER He'll get lost. I'm sure of it.

ZITORSKY Oh, have you ever seen such excitement? My heart is fairly pounding.

ALPER Oh, it's just starting. Now comes the exorcism. That should be something to see.

ZITORSKY Oh, boy.

SCHLISSEL Oh, I don't know. You've seen one exorcism, you've seen them all.

ZITORSKY You saw one, Schlissel?

SCHLISSEL Sure. When I was a boy in Poland, we had more dybbuks than we had pennies. We had a fellow there in my village, a mule driver, a burly chap who reeked from dung and was drunk from morning till night. One day, he lost his wits completely, and it was immediately attributed to a dybbuk. I was a boy of ten, perhaps eleven, and I watched the whole proceedings through a hole in the roof of the synagogue. A miracle-working rabbi who was passing through our district was invited to exorcise the dybbuk. He drew several circles on the ground and stood in the center surrounded by four elders of the community, all dressed in white linen and trembling with terror. The Miracle-Worker bellowed out a series of incantations, and the poor mule driver, who was beside himself with fear, screamed and . . . hello, Harris . . . (*This last is addressed to a very, very old man named* HARRIS, *who is making his halting way into the synagogue at this moment. He barely nods to the others, having all he can do to get into the synagogue and close the door.* SCHLISSEL *continues his blithe story*) . . . and fell to the floor. It was a marvelous vaudeville, really. I was so petrified that I fell off the roof and almost broke a leg. The Miracle-Worker wandered off to work other miracles and the mule driver sold his mule and went to America where I assume, because he was a habitual drunkard and an insensitive boor, he achieved considerable success. Our little village had a brief month of notoriety, and we were all quite proud of ourselves.

ALPER Oh, it sounds like a marvelous ceremony.

SCHLISSEL Of course, they don't exorcise dybbuks like they used to. Nowadays, the rabbi hangs a small amulet around your neck, intones, "Blessed art Thou, O Lord," and that's an exorcism.

ALPER Oh, I hope not.

SCHLISSEL Really, religion has become so pallid recently, it is hardly worth while being an atheist.

ZITORSKY I don't even know if I'll come to see this exorcism. I'm already shivering just hearing about it.

ALPER Well, you know, we are dealing with the occult here, and it is quite frightening. Hello there, Harris, how are you? (*By now, the octogenarian has removed his overcoat, under which he wears several layers of sweaters, one of which turns out to be one of his grandson's football jerseys, a striped red garment with the number 63 on it. For the rest of the act, he goes about the busi-*

ness of putting on his phylacteries. ALPER *claps his hands)* Well, let me find out if we can help this young Jew here. (*He moves toward* ARTHUR LANDAU, *smiling)* Can I give you a set of phylacteries?

ARTHUR (*Scowling—a man who has had a very bad night the night before)* I'm afraid I wouldn't have the first idea what to do with them.

ALPER You'll find a prayer shawl in one of these velvet bags here.

ARTHUR No, thank you.

ALPER (*Offering a small black prayer book)* Well, here's a prayer book anyway.

ARTHUR Look, the only reason I'm here is a little man stopped me on the street, asked me if I was Jewish, and gave me the impression he would kill himself if I didn't come in and complete your quorum. I was told all I had to do was stand around for a few minutes wearing a hat. I can't read Hebrew and I have nothing I want to pray about, so there's no sense giving me that book. All I want to know is how long is this going to take, because I don't feel very well, and I have a number of things to do.

ALPER My dear young fellow, you'll be out of here in fifteen or twenty minutes.

ARTHUR Thank you.

(*He absently puts the black paper skullcap on his head and sits down, scowling, on one of the wooden chairs.* ALPER *regards him for a moment; then turns and goes back to his two colleagues)*

ALPER (*To* SCHLISSEL *and* ZITORSKY) To such a state has modern Jewry fallen. He doesn't know what phylacteries are. He doesn't want a shawl. He can't read Hebrew.

ZITORSKY I wonder if he's still circumcised.

(ARTHUR *abruptly stands)*

ARTHUR I'd like to make a telephone call. (*Nobody hears*

him. He repeats louder) I said, I'd like to make a telephone call.

ALPER (*Indicating the wall phone*) Right on the wall there.

ARTHUR This is a rather personal call.

ALPER There's a phone in the Rabbi's office there.

(ARTHUR *crosses to* THE RABBI'S *office*)

SCHLISSEL Well, look about you, really. Here you have the decline of Orthodox Judaism graphically before your eyes. This is a synagogue? A converted grocery store, flanked on one side by a dry cleaner and on the other by a shoemaker. Really, if it wasn't for the Holy Ark there, this place would look like the local headquarters of the American Labor Party. In Poland, where we were all one step from starvation, we had a synagogue whose shadow had more dignity than this place.

ALPER It's a shame and a disgrace.

ZITORSKY A shame and a disgrace.

(*In* THE RABBI'S *office* ARTHUR *is regarding* THE GIRL *with a sour eye*)

ARTHUR Excuse me. I'd like to make a rather personal call.

(THE GIRL *stares down at the floor, unhearing, unmoving, off in a phantasmic world of her own distorted creation.* ARTHUR *sits down at* THE RABBI'S *desk, turns his shoulder to* THE GIRL, *and begins to dial a number*)

SCHLISSEL Where are all the Orthodox Jews? They have apostated to the Reform Jewish temples, where they sit around like Episcopalians, listening to organ music.

ALPER Your use of the word "apostasy" in referring to Reform Jews interests me, Schlissel. Is it not written in Sifre on Deuteronomy, "Even if they are foolish, even if they transgress, even if they are full of blemishes, they are still called sons"? So, after all, is it so terrible to be a Reform Jew? Is this not an interesting issue for disputation? Oh, my God!

(*He wheels and starts back for* THE RABBI'S *office. The same thought has been entering the other two old fellows' minds, as has been indicated by a growing frown of consternation on each of their faces. They follow* ALPER *to* THE RABBI'S *office, where he opens the door quickly and stares in at* ARTHUR LANDAU. *The latter is still seated at* THE RABBI'S *desk, waiting for an answer to his phone call; and* THE GIRL *is still in her immobilized state.* ARTHUR *casts such a baleful eye at this interruption that the three old men back out of the office and close the door. They remain nervously outside the door of the office. At last, someone responds to* ARTHUR'S *phone call*)

ARTHUR (*On the phone, shading his face, and keeping his voice down*) Hello, Doctor, did I wake you up? This is Arthur Landau . . . Yes, I know. Do you think you can find an hour for me this morning? . . . Oh, I could be in your office in about an hour or so. I'm out in Mineola. My ex-wife lives out here with her parents, you know. And I've been blind drunk for—I just figured it out—three days now. And I just found myself out here at two o'clock in the morning banging on their front door, screaming . . . (THE GIRL'S *presence bothers him. He leans across the desk to her and says*—) Look, this is a very personal call, and I would really appreciate your letting me have the use of this office for just a few minutes.

(THE GIRL *looks up at him blankly*)

THE GIRL (*Hollowly*) I am the Whore of Kiev, the companion of sailors.

(*The bizarreness of this stops* ARTHUR. *He considers it for a moment, and then goes back to the phone*)

ARTHUR (*On the phone*) No, I'm still here. I'm all right. At least, I'm still alive. (*He hides his face in the palm of one hand and rubs his brow nervously*) I've got to see you, Doc. Don't hang up on me, please. If my analyst hangs up on me, that'll be the end. Just let me talk a couple of minutes . . . I'm in some damned synagogue. I was on my way to the subway. Oh, my God, I've got to call my office. I was supposed to be in court twice yesterday. I hope somebody had the brains to apply for an adjournment. So it's funny, you know. I'm in this damned synagogue. I'll be down in about an hour, Doctor . . . Okay. Okay . . . I'm all right . . . No, I'm all right . . . I'll see you in about an hour. (*He hangs up, hides his face in the palms of both hands and slowly pulls himself together. After a moment, he looks up at* THE GIRL, *who is back to staring at the floor. He frowns, stands, goes to the door of the office, opens it, gives one last look at* THE GIRL, *and closes the door behind him. He finds himself staring at the inquiring faces of the three old men*) Listen, I hope you know there's a pretty strange girl in there.

(*The old men bob their heads nervously.* ARTHUR *crosses the synagogue to a chair and sits down, his face dark with his emotions. The three old men regard him anxiously. After a moment,* SCHLISSEL *approaches* ARTHUR)

SCHLISSEL A strange girl, you say?

ARTHUR Yes.

SCHLISSEL Did she say anything?

ARTHUR She said: "I am the Whore of Kiev, the companion of sailors."

SCHLISSEL That was a very piquant statement, wouldn't you say?

ARTHUR Yes, I think I would call it piquant.

SCHLISSEL What do you make of it?

ARTHUR (*Irritably*) Look, I'm going. I have a hundred things to do. I . . .

SCHLISSEL No, no, no. Sit down. For heaven's sakes, sit down.

ALPER (*Hurrying over*) Don't go. Oh, my, don't go. We

need you for a tenth man. We haven't had ten men in the morning in more than a week, I think.

ZITORSKY (*On* ALPER'S *tail*) Two weeks, at least.

(*At this point,* HARRIS, *who has finally divested himself of his muffler and the heavy, ribbed sweaters which were over his jacket, and is now enwrapt in a prayer shawl, bursts into a high, quavering prayer*)

HARRIS "Blessed art thou, O Lord, our God, King of the Universe, who hath sanctified us by his commandments and . . ."

(*The words dribble off into inaudibility.* ARTHUR LANDAU *darts a startled look at the old man, not being prepared for this method of prayer, and moves a few nervous steps away from the other old men, then stands rubbing his brow, quite agitated*)

ALPER (*Whispering to* SCHLISSEL) So what happened in there? Did she say anything?

SCHLISSEL Yes, she said she was the Whore of Kiev, and the companion of sailors.

ALPER Oh, dear me.

SCHLISSEL I'm afraid we shall have to get her out of the Rabbi's office because if she keeps telling everybody who walks in there that she is the Whore of Kiev, they will pack us all off to the insane asylum. And let us be quite sensible about this situation. If Foreman has kidnaped the girl, he has kidnaped her, however kindly his motives —not that I expect the police to regard a dybbuk as any kind of sensible explanation. Whatever the case, it would be a good idea to keep the girl a little less accessible. (*The wall phone rings*) Ah! I'll tell you who that is. That's Foreman's son calling to find out if Foreman and the girl are here. (*The phone rings again*) Well, if you won't answer it, I'll answer it.

(*He crosses to the wall phone*)

ALPER We could take her to my house. Everybody is still sleeping. We'll put her in the cellar.

(*The phone rings again.* SCHLISSEL *picks up the phone*)

SCHLISSEL (*On the phone*) Hello. (*He turns to the others and nods his head, indicating he was quite right in guessing the caller. The other two old men move closer to the phone*) Mr. Foreman, your father isn't here . . . Listen, I tell you, he isn't here . . . I wouldn't have the slightest idea. I haven't seen her since I was up to your house last Tuesday. Isn't she home? . . . If he comes in, I'll tell him . . . Okay . . . (*He hangs up and turns to the other two*) Well, we are in it up to our necks now.

ALPER (*Stripping off his phylacteries*) So shall we take her to my house?

SCHLISSEL All right. Zitorsky, go in and tell her we are going to take her some place else.

ZITORSKY (*Not exactly inspired by the idea*) Yeah, sure.

SCHLISSEL (*To* ZITORSKY) For heaven's sakes, Zitorsky, you don't really believe that's a dybbuk in there.

ZITORSKY If that's no dybbuk, then you go in and take her.

(SCHLISSEL *shuffles slowly to the door of* THE RABBI'S *office*)

SCHLISSEL (*Pausing at the closed office door*) It's getting kind of complicated. Maybe we ought to call Foreman's son and tell him she's here and not get involved.

ZITORSKY Oh, no!

SCHLISSEL Ah, well, come on. What can they do to us? They'll call us foolish old men, but then foolishness is the only privilege of old age. So, Alper, you'll deal with her. You know how to talk to her, and we'll hide her in your cellar. So we'll have a little excitement. (*He opens the door, and the three old men regard* THE GIRL *as she sits in sodden, detached immobility*) Listen. Alper, let's get along, you know. Before the Sexton comes back and starts asking us where we're all going.

(ALPER *nods apprehensively and takes a few steps into the office*)

ALPER (*To* THE GIRL, *who doesn't actually hear him or know of his presence*) How do you do, my dear Evelyn. This is Alper here. (*She makes no answer.* ALPER *turns to the other two*) She's in one of her apathetic states.

ZITORSKY (*Darting back into the synagogue proper*) I'll get your coat, Alper.

SCHLISSEL (*Looking around to see if* ARTHUR *is paying any attention to what's going on; he is not*) Well, take her by the arm.

ALPER Evelyn, your grandfather suggested we take you to my house. You always liked to play with the children's toys in my cellar there, you remember? Come along, and we'll have a good time.

ZITORSKY (*Giving* SCHLISSEL *an overcoat*) Here. Give this to Alper.

(*He hurries off to the front door of the synagogue*)

HARRIS (*In the process of laying on his phylacteries*) "And from thy wisdom, O Most High God, Thou shalt reserve for me . . ."

(*He dribbles off into inaudibility*)

ALPER (*Placing a tentative hand on* THE GIRL'S *shoulder*) Evelyn, dear . . .

(*She looks up, startled*)

ZITORSKY (*Leaning out the front door, searching up and down the street*) Oh, it's cold out here.

ALPER (*To* SCHLISSEL, *who is hurriedly putting on his own overcoat*) I have a feeling we're going to have trouble here.

SCHLISSEL I've got your coat here.

ALPER Evelyn . . . (*A strange animal-like grunt escapes* THE GIRL, *and she begins to moan softly*) Evelyn dear, please don't be alarmed. This is Mr. Alper here who has known you since you were born. (*He is getting a little panicky at the strange sounds coming out of* THE GIRL, *and he tries to grab her arm to help her to her feet. She bursts into a shrill scream, electrifying everybody in the synagogue with the exception of* THE CABALIST, who is *oblivious to everything.* ZITORSKY, *who has just closed the front door, stands frozen with horror.* ARTHUR, *sunk in despondency, looks up, startled. The old man,* HARRIS, *pauses briefly, as if the sound has been some distant buzzing, and then goes back to his mumbled prayers*) Evelyn, my dear girl, for heaven's sakes . . .

THE GIRL (*Screaming out*) Leave me alone! Leave me alone!

ARTHUR (*Coming to* SCHLISSEL, *who shuts the office door quickly*) What's going on in there?

SCHLISSEL It's nothing, it's nothing.

THE GIRL (*Screaming*) They are my seven sons! My seven sons!

ALPER (*Who is trying earnestly to get out of the office*) Who closed this door?

ZITORSKY (*Reaching for the front door*) I'm getting out of here.

SCHLISSEL (*To* ZITORSKY) Where are you going?

(*But* ZITORSKY *has already fled into the street*)

ARTHUR (*To* SCHLISSEL) What's all this screaming?

(ALPER, *at last out of the office, comes scurrying to* SCHLISSEL)

ALPER I put my hand on her arm to help her up, and she burst into this fit of screaming.

(ARTHUR *strides to the open doorway of the office.* THE GIRL *stares at him, hunched now in terror, frightened and at bay*)

ARTHUR (*To* SCHLISSEL) What have you been doing to this girl?

SCHLISSEL The girl is possessed by a dybbuk.

ARTHUR What?

SCHLISSEL (*To* ALPER) Zitorsky ran out in the street like a kangaroo.

ALPER Listen, maybe we should call somebody.

ARTHUR Listen, what is this?

ALPER My dear young man, there is no reason to alarm yourself. There is an insane girl in the Rabbi's office, but she appears to have quieted down.

ARTHUR What do you mean, there's an insane girl in the Rabbi's office?

ALPER Yes, she is a catatonic schizophrenic, occasionally violent, but really, go back to your seat. There is no cause for alarm.

ARTHUR Am I to understand, sir, that it is a practice of yours to keep insane girls in your Rabbi's office?

ALPER No, no. Oh, dear, I suppose we shall have to tell him. But you must promise, my dear fellow, to keep this whole matter between us. (*To* SCHLISSEL) Zitorsky, you say, took to his heels?

SCHLISSEL Absolutely flew out of the door.

ALPER Well, I really can't blame him. It was quite an apprehensive moment. I was a little shaken myself. (*He peeks into the office*) Yes, she seems to be quite apathetic again. I think we just better leave her alone for the time being.

ARTHUR Look, what is going on here?

ALPER My dear fellow, you are, of course, understandably confused. The girl, you see, is possessed by a dybbuk.

ARTHUR Yes, of course. Well, that explains everything.

ALPER Well, of course, how would he know what a dybbuk is? A dybbuk is a migratory soul that possesses the body of another human being in order to return to heaven. It is a Lurian doctrine, actually tracing back to the Essenes, I suppose, but popularized during the thirteenth century by the Spanish cabalists. I wrote several articles on the matter for Yiddish periodicals. My name is Moyshe Alper, and at one time I was a journalist of some repute. (ZITORSKY *appears in the doorway again, peering nervously in*) Come in, Zitorsky, come in. The girl is quiet again.

(ZITORSKY *approaches them warily*)

ARTHUR Look, are you trying to tell me you have a girl in there you think is possessed by some demon? Where is her mother or father or somebody who should be responsible for her?

ALPER If there were someone responsible for her, would she be insane in the first place?

ARTHUR Of course, this is none of my business . . .

ALPER You are a good fellow and let me put you at ease. The girl is in good hands. Nobody is going to hurt her. Her grandfather, who adores her more than his own life, has gone off for a short while.

ZITORSKY To Williamsburg on the Brighton train.

SCHLISSEL The Brighton train takes you to Coney Island.

ZITORSKY You said the Double G.

ALPER All right, all right.

ARTHUR Of course, this is none of my business.

ALPER (*To* ARTHUR) I can understand your concern; it shows you are a good fellow, but really the matter is well in hand.

(*The front door opens and there now enter* THE SEXTON *and two young men in their thirties, apparently the* KESSLER *boys, who are none too happy about being roused on this cold winter morning. They stand disconsolately around in the back of the synagogue*)

THE SEXTON Here are two more, the Kessler boys.

ALPER Now we'll have ten for a quorum.

ZITORSKY Kessler? Kessler? Oh, yes, the stationery store. I knew your father.

(*There is a general flurry of movement.* THE SEXTON *hurries about the ritual of baring his left arm, donning the prayer shawl and phylacteries, walking nervously about, mumbling his prayers rapidly.* ARTHUR, *quite disturbed again, looks into* THE RABBI'S *office at* THE GIRL, *then moves slowly into the office.* THE GIRL *is again in a world of her own. He closes the door and studies* THE GIRL. SCHLISSEL, ALPER *and* ZITORSKY *watch him warily, taking off their overcoats again and preparing to stay for the impending services.* HARRIS' *shrill quavering voice suddenly leaps up into audibility again*)

HARRIS "Thou shalt set apart all that openeth the womb of the Lord, and the firstling that cometh of a beast which thou shalt have, it shall belong to the Lord . . ."

SCHLISSEL (*To* ALPER) What are we going to do when the Rabbi tries to get into his office? He'll see the girl, and that will be the end of our exorcism. What shall we tell the Rabbi?

(*The front door of the synagogue opens, and* THE RABBI *comes striding efficiently in, right on cue. He is a young man in his early thirties, neatly dressed if a little threadbare, and carrying a briefcase*)

ZITORSKY Peace be with you, Rabbi.

THE RABBI Peace be with you.

ALPER (*Intercepting* THE RABBI *as he heads for his office*) How do you do, Rabbi.

(THE RABBI *nods as he strides to the door of his office, where* SCHLISSEL *blocks the way*)

SCHLISSEL We have ten men today, Rabbi.

THE RABBI Good. (*He reaches for the door to his office*) I'll just get my phylacteries.

ALPER (*Seizing* ZITORSKY'S *phylacteries*) Oh, here, use these. It's late, Rabbi.

THE RABBI (*Taking the phylacteries*) Fine. Well, let's start the services.

(*He turns back to the synagogue proper. From all around, each man's voice rises into prayer*)

THE CURTAIN FALLS

ACT TWO

Scene 1

Fifteen minutes later.

ZITORSKY *is reading the prayers. He stands before the lectern on the raised platform, singing the primitive chants.*

ZITORSKY "And we beseech thee according to thine abundant mercies, O Lord . . ."

THE SEXTON Young Kessler, come here and open the Ark. (*The younger* KESSLER *ascends the platform and opens the Ark by drawing the curtains and sliding the doors apart*)

ZITORSKY "And it came to pass, when the ark set forward, that Moses said, Rise up, O Lord, and Thine enemies shall be scattered, and they that hate Thee shall flee before Thee. For out of Zion shall go forth the Law, and the word of the Lord from Jerusalem." (*Immediately, the rest of the quorum plunges into a mumbled response: "Blessed be Thy name, O Sovereign of the World! Blessed be Thy crown, and Thy abiding place!" Jewish prayers are conducted in a reader-congregation pattern, although frequently the reader's vocalized statements and the congregation's mumbled responses merge and run along simultaneously. In this specific moment of prayer, when the Ark has been opened and the Torah is about to be taken out, the demarcation between reader and congregation is clear-cut. The sliding brown wooden doors of the Ark are now open.* THE SEXTON *is reaching in to take out the exquisitely ornamented Torah, which, when its lovely brocaded velvet cover is taken off, will show itself to be a large parchment scroll divided on two carved rollers. When* THE SEXTON *gets the Torah out, he hands it carefully to* ZITORSKY, *who has been chosen this day for the honor of holding the Torah until it is to be read from.* ZITORSKY, *who, as today's reader, has been reading along with the congregation although more audibly, now allows his voice to ring out clearly, marking the end of this paragraph of prayers)* ". . . May it be Thy gracious will to open my heart in Thy Law, and to grant my heart's desires, and those of all Thy people Israel, for our benefit, throughout a peaceful life." (*Pause*) "Magnify the Lord with me, and let us exalt His name together." (*Again, the congregation leaps into mumbled response. "Thine, O Lord, is the greatness, and the power, and the glory, and the victory, and the majesty . . ."* ZITORSKY *marches solemnly to the front of the lectern, carrying the Torah before him. Each man kisses the Torah as it passes him. There is now the ritual of removing the velvet cover, and the Torah is laid upon the lectern.* ZITORSKY, HARRIS *and* THE SEXTON *form a hovering group of three old betallithed Jews over it.* THE RABBI *stands rocking slightly back and forth to the left of the lectern. Off the raised platform, but immediately by the railing, stands* THE CABALIST, *rocking back and forth and praying.* ALPER *and* SCHLISSEL *stand at various places, mumbling their responses. The two* KESSLER *boys have removed their coats and wear prayer shawls, but still stand as close to the front door as they can.* ARTHUR LANDAU *stands, leaning against the wall of* THE RABBI'S *office, quite intrigued by the solemn prayers and rituals.* THE GIRL *is still in* THE RABBI'S *office, but she is standing now, listening as well as she can to the prayers. Her face is peaceful now and quite lovely. Again* ZITORSKY'S *voice rises to indicate the end of a paragraph of prayer)* "Ascribe all of your greatness unto our God, and render honor to the Law." (*There is now a quick mumbled conference among the three old Jews at the lectern, then* THE SEXTON *suddenly leans out and calls to the two* KESSLER *boys in the rear*)

THE SEXTON Kessler, you want to read from the Torah?

THE ELDER KESSLER No, no, no. Get somebody else.

THE SEXTON Alper? (ALPER *nods and makes his way to the lectern.* THE SEXTON'S *voice, a high, whining incantation, rises piercingly into the air, announcing the fact that Moyshe son of Abram will read from the Torah*) Rise up, Reb Moses Ha'Kohan, son of Abram, and speak the blessing on the Torah. "Blessed be He, who in His Holiness gave the Law unto his people Israel, the Law of the Lord is perfect."

CONGREGATION (*Scattered response*) "And ye that cleave unto the Lord your God are alive every one of you this day."

ALPER (*Now at the lectern, raises his head and recites quickly*) "Blessed is the lord who is to be blessed for ever and ever."

CONGREGATION "Blessed is the Lord who is to be blessed for ever and ever."

ALPER "Blessed art Thou, O Lord our God, King of the Universe, who hast chosen us from all peoples and hast given us Thy Law. Blessed art Thou, O Lord, who givest the Law."

CONGREGATION Amen!

THE SEXTON "And Moses said . . ."

(*There are now four mumbling old Jews huddled over the lectern. It all becomes very indistinguishable;* THE SEXTON'S *piercing tenor rises audibly now and then to indicate he is reading.* ALPER *moves into the reader's position and begins to read from the Torah, bending his knees and twisting his body and hunching over the Torah, peering at the meticulous Hebrew lettering inscribed therein.* SCHLISSEL *and the* KESSLER *boys find seats where they were standing, as does* THE CABALIST. THE RABBI *and* HARRIS *are seated on the raised platform. In* THE

RABBI'S *office,* THE GIRL *decides to go out into the synagogue proper. She opens the door and moves a few steps out.* ARTHUR *hears her and turns to her warily*)

THE GIRL (*Quite lucidly and amiably*) Excuse me, sir, are they reading from the Torah now?

(*She peers over* ARTHUR'S *shoulder toward the old men at the lectern*)

ARTHUR Yes, I think so.

(*He watches her carefully. She seems all right now. Still, there is something excessively ingenuous about her, a tentative, wide-eyed, gently smiling innocence*)

THE GIRL Is my grandfather here?

(*She peers nervously around the synagogue*)

ARTHUR Which one would be your grandfather?

THE GIRL (*Growing panic*) No, he's not here. I see Mr. Alper, but I don't see my grandfather.

ARTHUR I'm sure he will be back soon.

(*His calmness reassures her*)

THE GIRL (*She studies this strange young man*) I think all synagogues should be shabby because I think of God as being very poor as a child. What do you think of God as?

ARTHUR I'm afraid I think of God as the Director of Internal Revenue.

(THE GIRL *laughs brightly and then immediately smothers her laughter, aware she is in a solemn synagogue*)

THE GIRL You're irreverent. (*Frowning, she goes into* THE RABBI'S *office, plops down on his swivel chair, and swivels back and forth, very much like a child.* ARTHUR *follows her tentatively, studying her cautiously, yet taken by her ingenuousness. She darts a quick frightened look at him*) Were you in here just before?

ARTHUR Well, yes.

THE GIRL Did I—did I say anything?

ARTHUR (*Amiably*) Well, yes.

THE GIRL (*Sighing*) I see. Well, I might as well tell you.

I've been to several mental institutions. (*She looks quickly at him. He smiles at her*) You don't seem very disconcerted by that.

ARTHUR Oh, I expect it might be hard to find somebody who couldn't do with occasional confinement in a mental institution.

(*In the synagogue,* THE SEXTON *now calls* HARRIS *to read from the Torah*)

THE GIRL (*She frowns*) Did my grandfather say when he would be back or where he was going?

(*She starts from her seat frightened again*)

ARTHUR I understand he'll be back soon.

THE GIRL Are you the doctor?

ARTHUR No. You don't have to be the least bit afraid of me.

THE GIRL (*She brightens*) My grandfather and I are very close. I'm much closer to him than I am to my own father. I'd rather not talk about my father, if you don't mind. It's a danger spot for me. You know, when I was nine years old, I shaved all the hair off my head because that is the practice of really Orthodox Jewish women. I mean, if you want to be a rabbi's wife, you must shear your hair and wear a wig. That's one of my compulsive dreams. I keep dreaming of myself as the wife of a handsome young rabbi with a fine beard down to his waist and a very stern face and prematurely gray forelocks on his brow. I have discovered through many unsuccessful years of psychiatric treatment that religion has a profound sexual connotation for me. Oh, dear, I'm afraid I'm being tiresome about my psychiatric history. Really, being insane is like being fat. You can talk about nothing else. Please forgive me. I am sure I am boring you to death.

ARTHUR No, not at all. It's nice to hear somebody talk with passion about anything, even their insanity.

THE GIRL (*Staring at him*) The word doesn't bother you?

ARTHUR What word?

THE GIRL Insanity.

ARTHUR Good heavens, no. I'm a lawyer. Insanity in one form or another is what fills my anteroom. Besides, I'm being psychoanalyzed myself and I'm something of a bore about that too. You are a bright young thing. How old are you?

THE GIRL Eighteen.

ARTHUR (*Staring at her*) My God, you're a pretty kid! I can hardly believe you are psychopathic. Are you very advanced?

THE GIRL Pretty bad. I'm being instituionalized again. Dr. Molineaux's Sanitarium in Long Island. I'm a little paranoid and hallucinate a great deal and have very little sense of reality, except for brief interludes like this, and I might slip off any minute in the middle of a sentence into some incoherency. If that should happen, you must be very realistic with me. Harsh reality is the most efficacious way to deal with schizophrenics.

ARTHUR You seem well read on the matter.

THE GIRL I'm a voracious reader. I have so little else to do with myself. Will you come and visit me at Dr. Molineaux's hospital? I am awfully fond of you.

ARTHUR Yes, of course, I will.

THE GIRL It won't be as depressing an experience as you might think. If I am not in the violent ward, I will probably be allowed to go to the commissary and have an ice-cream soda with you. The worst of an insane asylum is really how poorly dressed the inmates are. They all wear old cable-stitched sweaters. I do like to look pretty. (*A vacuous look is beginning to come across her face*) They ask me to be in a lot of movies, you know, when I have time. Did you see *David and Bathsheba* with Susan Hayward? That was really me. I don't tell anybody that. They don't want me to make movies. My mother, I mean. She doesn't even go to synagogue on Saturday. You're the new Rabbi, you know. Sometimes, I'm the Rabbi, but they're all afraid of me. The temple is sixty cubits long and made of cypress and overlaid with gold. The burnished Roman legions clank outside the gates, you know. Did you see *The Ten Commandments?* I saw that Tuesday, Wednesday. I was in that. I was the girl who danced. I was in that. Mr. Hirschman is here, too, you know, and my grandfather. Everybody's here. Do you see that boy over there? Go away. Leave us alone. He's insane. He's really Mr. Hirschman the Cabalist. He's making a golem. You ought to come here, Rabbi.

ARTHUR (*Who has been listening fascinated, now says firmly*) I am not the Rabbi, Evelyn.

(*She regards him briefly*)

THE GIRL Well, we're making a golem and . . .

ARTHUR You are not making a golem, Evelyn.

(*She pauses, staring down at the floor. A grimace of pain moves quickly across her face and then leaves it. After a moment, she mumbles—*)

THE GIRL Thank you. (*Suddenly she begins to cry and she throws herself on* ARTHUR'S *breast, clinging to him, and he holds her gently, caressing her as he would a child*) Oh, I can't bear being insane.

ARTHUR (*Gently*) I always thought that since the insane made their own world it was more pleasurable than this one that is made for us.

THE GIRL (*Moving away*) Oh, no, it is unbearably painful. It is the most indescribable desolation. You are all alone in deserted streets. You cannot possibly imagine it.

ARTHUR I'm afraid I can. I have tried to commit suicide so many times now it has become something of a family joke. Once, before I was divorced, my wife stopped in to tell a neighbor before she went out to shop: "Oh, by the way, if you smell gas, don't worry about it. It's only Arthur killing himself again." Suicides, you know, kill themselves a thousand times, but one day I'll slash my wrists and I will forget to make a last-minute telephone call and there will be no stomach-pumping Samaritans to run up the stairs and smash my bedroom door down and rush me off to Bellevue. I'll make it some day—I assure you of that.

THE GIRL (*Regarding him with sweet interest*) You don't look as sad as all that.

ARTHUR Oh, I have made a profession of ironic detachment. It depresses me to hear that insanity is as forlorn as anything else. I had always hoped to go crazy myself some day since I have apparently no talent for suicide.

THE GIRL I always thought life would be wonderful if I were only sane.

ARTHUR Life is merely dreary if you're sane, and unbearable if you are sensitive. I cannot think of a more meaningless sham than my own life. My parents were very poor so I spent the first twenty years of my life condemning the rich for my childhood nightmares. Oh, I was quite a Bernard Barricade when I was in college. I left the Communist Party when I discovered there were easier ways to seduce girls. I turned from reproaching society for my loneliness to reproaching my mother, and stormed out of her house to take a room for myself on the East Side. Then I fell in love—that is to say, I found living alone so unbearable I was willing to marry. She married me because all her friends were marrying somebody. Needless to say, we told each other how deeply in love we were. We wanted very much to be happy. Americans, you know, are frantic about being happy. The American nirvana is a man and his wife watching television amiably and then turning off the lights and effortless making the most ardent love to each other. Television unfortunately is a bore and ardent love is an immense drain on one's energy. I began to work day and night at my law office, and besides becoming very successful, I managed to avoid my wife entirely. For this deceit, I was called ambitious and was respected by everyone including my wife, who was quite as bored with me as I was with her. We decided to have children because we couldn't possibly believe we were that miserable together. All this while I drove myself mercilessly for fear that if I paused for just one moment, the whole slim, trembling sanity of my life would come crashing down about my feet without the slightest sound. I went to a psychoanalyst who wanted to know about my childhood when I could barely remember whether I took a taxi or a bus to his office that day. I began to drink myself into stupors, pursuing other men's wives, and generally behaving badly. One morning, I stared into the mirror and could barely make out my features. Life is utterly meaningless. I have had everything a man can get out of life—prestige, power, money, women, children, and a handsome home only three blocks from the Scarsdale Country Club, and all I can think of is I want to get out of this as fast as I can. (*He has become quite upset by now, and has to avert his face to hide a sudden welling of tears. He takes a moment to get a good grip on himself, readopts his sardonic air and says*—) As you see, I have quite a theatrical way when I want to.

THE GIRL (*Brightly*) Oh, I think you are wonderfully wise.

ARTHUR Oh, it was said best by your own King Solomon, the wisest man who ever lived, when he wrote Ecclesiastes.

THE GIRL Oh, King Solomon didn't write Ecclesiastes. That was written by an anonymous Jewish scholar in Alexandria. I wouldn't put too much stock in it. Weariness was all the rage among the Hellenized Jews.

ARTHUR (*Staring at her*) You are an amazing kid.

(*She smiles back at him exuberantly, unabashedly showing her fondness for him. It embarrasses him, and he turns away. He opens the door, and looks out into the synagogue, where the reading of the Torah has come to an end)*

THE RABBI (*Singing out*) "Blessed art Thou, O Lord our God, King of the Universe, who has given us the Law of truth, and hast planted everywhere life in our midst. Blessed art Thou, O Lord, who givest the Law."

(*There is a scattered mumbled response from the old men in the synagogue.* ZITORSKY *now takes the Torah and holds it up above his head and chants*)

ZITORSKY "And this is the Law which Moses set before the children of Israel, according to the commandment of the Lord by the hand of Moses." (*The four men on the platform form a small group as* ZITORSKY *marches slowly back to the Ark carrying the Torah. A mumble of prayers rustles through the synagogue.* ZITORSKY'S *voice rises out*) "Let them praise the name of the Lord; for His name alone is exalted."

(*He carefully places the Torah back into the Ark. A rumble of prayer runs through the synagogue. All the men in the synagogue are standing now*)

ARTHUR (*Turning to* THE GIRL) They're putting the Torah back. Is the service over?

THE GIRL No. I have a wonderful book I want to give to you. Mr. Hirschman, our Community Cabalist, gave it to me. It is called the Book of Splendor, a terribly mystical book. And you are a mystic, you know.

ARTHUR Oh, am I?

THE GIRL Yes. I never met anyone who wanted to know the meaning of life as desperately as you do. I have to get the book for you.

(SCHLISSEL *pokes his head into the office and indicates to* ARTHUR *that he is needed outside*)

ARTHUR I think they need me outside.

(*He moves to the door*)

THE GIRL Yes, we really shouldn't have been talking during the service.

(ARTHUR *goes out of the office, closing the door behind him. He joins* SCHLISSEL, *who is a few steps away, muttering the prayers*)

ARTHUR (*Shaking his head*) What a pity, really. A lovely girl. What a pity. Now, you look like a sensible sort of man. What is all this nonsense about demons? You really should call her father or mother or whoever it is who is responsible for her.

SCHLISSEL Young man, if we called her father he would come down and take her away.

ARTHUR Yes. That would be the point, wouldn't it?

SCHLISSEL Then what happens to our exorcism?

ARTHUR What exorcism?

SCHLISSEL Listen, we've got to exorcise the dybbuk.

ARTHUR (*Aghast*) Exorcism!

(THE SEXTON *leans over the railing of the platform and admonishes them in a heavy whisper*)

THE SEXTON Sssshhhh!

(SCHLISSEL *promptly turns back to muttering his prayers.* ARTHUR *stares at him with vague disbelief*)

ARTHUR Are you serious?

(ZITORSKY'S *voice rises up loud and clear*)

ZITORSKY ". . . And it is said, and the Lord shall be king over all the earth; on that day shall the Lord be One, and His Name One."

(THE CONGREGATION, *which had been sitting, now stands again.* THE SEXTON *leans over the railing and calls to the* KESSLER *boys*)

THE SEXTON Kessler, stand up. Now is the time for your memorial prayers.

(The two KESSLER *boys nod, stand, and look unhappily down at their prayer books.* HARRIS *pokes a palsied finger onto a page to show them where to read, and the two young men now begin to read painstakingly and with no idea of what they are reading*)

KESSLER BOYS "Magnified and sanctified be His great

Name in the world which He hath created according to His will. May He establish His kingdom in your lifetime and in your days, and in the lifetime of all the house of Israel, speedily and at a near time; and say ye, Amen."

CONGREGATION Amen. "Let His Great Name be blessed for ever and ever."

KESSLER BOYS "Blessed, praised, and glorified, exalted, extolled and honored, adored, and lauded, be the Name of the Holy One, blessed be He, beyond, yea, beyond all blessings and hymns, praises and songs, which are uttered in the world, and say ye, Amen."

CONGREGATION Amen.

(*The front door to the synagogue bursts open and* FOREMAN *thrusts himself in, obviously much distraught; not so distraught, however, that he doesn't automatically join in the "Amen"*)

KESSLER BOYS "May there be abundant peace from heaven, and life for us and for all Israel; and say ye, Amen."

CONGREGATION Amen.

KESSLER BOYS "May he who maketh peace in his high places, make peace for us and for all Israel, and say ye, Amen."

CONGREGATION Amen.

(*The synagogue bursts into a quick mumble of prayers, except for* SCHLISSEL, *who scurries over to* FOREMAN. FOREMAN *stares at him, white with panic*)

SCHLISSEL What happened? You got lost? You took the Long Island Railroad to Atlantic Avenue Station, and you got lost in the Atlantic Avenue Station?

FOREMAN What Atlantic Avenue Station? I couldn't even find the Long Island Railroad!

SCHLISSEL Idiot! You are an innocent child! Really! Services are over in a minute, and I'll take you myself. (ALPER *is leaning over the railing of the platform, making obvious gestures, as if to ask what had happened.*

Even ZITORSKY *looks up from his hunched position at the lectern.* SCHLISSEL *announces in a heavy whisper, as he starts to put on his coat—)* He couldn't even find the Long Island Railway Station. (ALPER *clasps his brow.* THE SEXTON *turns around to* SCHLISSEL *and admonishes him with a heavy "Ssshhh!!!"* FOREMAN *has begun walking about, mumbling the prayers by heart, automatically a part of the service again. As he passes* SCHLISSEL, *he indicates with a jerk of his head that he would like to know of the well-being of his granddaughter)* She's all right. Don't worry about her.

(FOREMAN *nods and continues mumbling his prayers. In* THE RABBI'S *office,* THE GIRL, *who has been sitting pensively, now stands, puts her coat on, goes out of the office, calmly crosses to the rear of the synagogue, and exits through the front door. Absolutely no one is aware she has gone.* THE CONGREGATION *now bursts into a loud prayer, obviously the last one of the service, since the men on the platform begin to meander off, and all those who are still wearing their phylacteries begin to strip them off, even as they say the words of the prayer)*

CONGREGATION

"He is the Lord of the Universe, who reigned ere any creature yet was formed.

At the time when all things were made by His desire, then was His name proclaimed King.

And after all things shall have had an end, He alone, the dreadest one shall reign;

Who was, who is, and who will be in glory."

(SCHLISSEL, ALPER, ZITORSKY, *and* FOREMAN *have all rattled quickly through this final paean, impatient to close off the service, while the others continue the terminal recital. The four old men form a huddled group by the front door)*

ALL FOUR (*Rattling it off*) "And with my spirit, my body, also; the Lord is with me, and I will not fear. Amen."

ALPER Amen, what happened?
SCHLISSEL I'm taking him myself right away.
ZITORSKY What happened, you got lost?
FOREMAN I asked this fellow in the street, I said: "Could you . . ."
SCHLISSEL (*To* ALPER, *pointing to* ARTHUR) Listen, keep an eye on that fellow there. He wants to tell the Rabbi about the girl. All right, listen. I shall have to lead Foreman by the hand to Korpotchniker. All right, listen, we're going. Good-bye. Peace be unto you.
ALPER Take the Long Island Railroad to the Atlantic Avenue Station. Then take the Brighton train.
SCHLISSEL Oh, for heaven's sakes. Are you presuming to tell me how to get to Williamsburg?
ALPER All right, go already.
SCHLISSEL (*Muttering as he leads* FOREMAN *out the door*) The Brighton train. If we took the Brighton train, we would spend the day in Coney Island.

(*He exits with* FOREMAN, *closing the door. The rest of the* CONGREGATION *has finally come to the end of the service*)

CONGREGATION (*Their scattered voices rising to a coda*) "And with my spirit, my body also; the Lord is with me, and I will not fear. Amen!"
ZITORSKY *and* ALPER Amen!

(*There is a flurry of dispersion. The two* KESSLER *boys mumble good-byes and disappear quickly out into the street, buttoning their coats against the cold.* HARRIS, *who is slowly and tremblingly removing his phylacteries, continues slowly to dress himself again throughout the rest of the scene.* THE SEXTON *now scurries about, gathering the various phylacteries and prayer shawls and putting them back into the velvet prayer bags and then putting all the velvet bags and prayer books back into the cardboard carton they were all taken from, an activity he pursues with his usual frenetic desperation. Only* THE RABBI *and*

THE CABALIST *continue to say a few extra prayers: "The Thirteen Principles of Faith," etc.* THE CABALIST *reads them sitting down, hunched over his prayer book.* ALPER *and* ZITORSKY *have genuine cause for alarm concerning* ARTHUR LANDAU, *for he has ambled down to the platform, where he stands waiting for* THE RABBI *to finish his prayers. They watch* ARTHUR *guardedly.* HARRIS *suddenly decides to be communicative. He lifts his old face to* ALPER *and* ZITORSKY)

HARRIS Ah, am I thirsty!

ALPER (*Watching* ARTHUR *carefully*) Good.

(THE RABBI, *having finished his last prayer, now turns and starts down from the platform.* ARTHUR *steps forward to meet him*)

ARTHUR Rabbi . . .

THE RABBI (*Walking by him*) I'll be with you in just a moment.

(*He strides directly to his office.* ALPER *leaps to intercept him*)

ALPER Rabbi . . .

THE RABBI (*Continuing into his office*) I'll be with you in a minute, Alper. (*He goes into his office and closes the door.* ALPER *clasps his brow and shrugs.* ZITORSKY *mutters an involuntary "Oy." They both nod their heads and wait with the sufferance that is the badge of all their tribe.* ARTHUR *moves a few steps to* THE RABBI'S *door and also waits. In the office,* THE RABBI *sits down—all business—and dials a number. Then he speaks into the phone*) I'd like to make a person-to-person call to Rabbi Harry Gersh in Wilmington, Delaware. The number in Wilmington is Kingswood 3-1973 . . . Thank you . . . (*He hums a snatch of the service.* ALPER *knocks lightly on the door, and, receiving no answer, opens the door and comes into the office. He stares—open-mouthed —noting the absence of* THE GIRL. *He tugs at his Vandyke beard in contemplation*) Yes, Alper?

ALPER Well, I'll tell you, Rabbi . . . (*He scowls, a little flustered, then turns and goes out of the office*) Excuse me.

THE RABBI (*On the phone*) Locust 6-0932.

ALPER (*To* ZITORSKY) She's not there.

ZITORSKY She's not there?

ALPER I'll have to go out and look for her.

(*Frowning in contemplation,* ALPER *puts his coat on slowly and exits from the synagogue.* THE RABBI *is still on the phone. His voice rises to the pitch usually used for long-distance calls*)

THE RABBI Harry, how are you, this is Bernard here, I'm sorry I wasn't in last night, my wife Sylvia said it was wonderful to hear your voice after all these years, how are you, Shirley, and the kids, oh, that's wonderful, I'm glad to hear it. Harry, my wife tells me you have just gotten your first congregation and you wanted some advice since I have already been fired several times . . . Good, how much are you getting? . . . Well, five thousand isn't bad for a first congregation although I always thought out-of-town paid better. And what is it, a one-year contract? . . . Well, what kind of advice can I give you? Especially you, Harry. You are a saintly, scholarly, and truly pious man, and you have no business being a rabbi. You've got to be a go-getter, Harry, unfortunately. The synagogue I am in now is in an unbelievable state of neglect and I expect to see us in prouder premises within a year. But I've got things moving now. I've started a Youth Group, a Young Married People's Club, a Theatre Club which is putting on its first production next month, *The Man Who Came to Dinner,* I'd like you to come, Harry, bring the wife, I'm sure you'll have an entertaining evening. And let me recommend that you organize a little-league baseball team. It's a marvelous gimmick, I have sixteen boys in my Sunday School now . . . Harry, listen, what do I know about baseball? . . . Harry, let me interrupt you. How in heaven's name are you going to convey an awe of God to boys who will race out of your Hebrew classes to fly model rocket ships five hundred feet in the air exploding in three stages? To my boys, God is a retired mechanic . . . Well, I'm organizing a bazaar right now. When I hang up on you, I have to rush to the printer's to get some raffles printed, and from there I go to the Town Hall for a permit to conduct bingo games. In fact, I was so busy this morning, I almost forgot to come to the synagogue . . . (*He says gently*) Harry, with my first congregation, I also thought I was bringing the word of God. I stood up in my pulpit every Sabbath and carped at them for violating the rituals of their own religion. My congregations dwindled, and one synagogue given to my charge disappeared into a morass of mortgages. Harry, I'm afraid there are times when I don't care if they believe in God as long as they come to the synagogue . . . Of course, it's sad . . . Harry, it's been my pleasure. Have I depressed you? . . . Come and see us, Harry . . . Good luck . . . Of course. Good-bye.

(*He hangs up, stands, starts looking around for his briefcase, and strides out into the synagogue still searching for it. He is interrupted by* ARTHUR)

ARTHUR Rabbi, I have to hurry off, but before I go I would like to talk to you about that girl in your office. These old men tell me she is possessed by a demon and I think they are intending to perform some kind of an exorcism. I must caution you that that girl should be treated only by competent psychiatrists and the most frightful harm might come to her if she is subjected to anything like— Look, do you know about this exorcism, because I cannot believe you would tolerate any . . .

THE RABBI (*Who has been trying very hard to follow all this*) I'm afraid you have me at a disadvantage.

ARTHUR I'm talking about the girl in your office.

THE RABBI I'm somewhat new here and don't know everybody yet by name. Please be patient with me. Now, I take it you want to get married.

(*For a moment* ARTHUR *briefly considers the possibility he is not really awake*)

ARTHUR (*Pensively*) This whole morning is beginning to seem absolutely . . . Rabbi, there is a girl in your office who is insane.

THE RABBI In my office? (THE RABBI *is suddenly distracted by* ZITORSKY, *who has been wandering around the synagogue, looking up and down between the rows of chairs, and is now looking into the bathroom at the upstage end of the synagogue*) Mr. Zitorsky, what are you doing?

ZITORSKY (*To* ARTHUR, *who is moving quickly to* THE RABBI'S *office*) Well, have you ever seen such a thing? The girl has vanished into thin air.

(*He shuffles to* THE RABBI, *absolutely awe-struck by it all*)

ARTHUR (*Now examining the interior of* THE RABBI'S *office*) I suspect something more mundane, like simply walking out the door.

(*He moves quickly to the front door, which now opens, and* ALPER *returns, frowning with thought*)

ALPER (*To* ARTHUR) Well, is that something or isn't it? I looked up and down, I couldn't see her.

(ARTHUR *scowls and goes out into the street, where he stands looking up and down*)

THE RABBI Mr. Zitorsky, if you will just tell me what this is all about.

ZITORSKY (*His eyes wide with awe*) Rabbi, Mr. Foreman brought his granddaughter down this morning, and he said: "She is possessed by a dybbuk!" Well, what can you say when someone tells you something like that?

THE RABBI Oh, Mr. Foreman's granddaughter. Yes, of course, I see.

ZITORSKY So he took us into your office where she was standing, and it spoke to us! What an experience! You cannot imagine! The voice of the dybbuk spoke to us. It was like a hollow echo of eternity, and the girl's whole body was illuminated by a frame of light! Fire flashed from her mouth. All of us were there, ask Alper here, he'll tell you. I swear this on my soul! The girl began to rise into the air!

ALPER Actually, Zitorsky is coloring the story a little.

ZITORSKY (*Riveted by the marvelousness of the fantasy*) What are you talking about? You saw it with your own eyes!

ALPER Well, it was an experience, I must say.

THE RABBI And the girl has gone now.

ZITORSKY Into the air about us.

THE RABBI And where is Mr. Foreman?

ALPER He went to Brooklyn.

THE RABBI What in heaven's name for?

ALPER To see the Korpotchniker Rabbi.

THE RABBI (*Quite impressed*) The Korpotchniker?

ZITORSKY Certainly! Maybe you don't know this, but Hirschman is his cousin.

THE RABBI Mr. Hirschman? I have to admit I didn't know that.

ZITORSKY Oh, sure. Listen, Hirschman is the first-born son of the original Korpotchniker.

ALPER I am afraid we are drifting from the point.

THE RABBI (*Frowning*) The girl probably went home. Why don't you call the girl's home, Mr. Alper, and find out if she's there? I think you are a very close friend of the family.

ARTHUR (*Who has come back into the synagogue*) Well, thank God for the first rational voice I've heard today.

ALPER (*Nodding his head sadly*) Yes, I suppose I had better call her father.

ARTHUR (*Buttoning his coat*) Fine. (*Glancing at his watch*) Gentlemen, if you don't need me for anything any more, I would like to get to my analyst. Good morning.

(*He strides to the door*)

THE RABBI Peace be unto you.

(ARTHUR *pauses at the front door, a little amused at the archaic greeting*)

ARTHUR Peace be unto you, Rabbi.

(*He opens the door and goes out*)

THE RABBI Who was that fellow?

ZITORSKY Who knows? The Sexton found him on the street.

THE RABBI (*Buttoning his own coat*) Well, I have to be down at the printer's. A dybbuk. Really. What an unusual thing. Is Mr. Foreman a mystical man? By the way, Mr. Alper—Mr. Zitorsky—you weren't at the meeting of the Brotherhood last night. I think you should take a more active interest in the synagogue. Did you receive an announcement of the meeting? Please come next time. (*He finds his briefcase*) Ah, there it is, good. (*He heads for the door*) I would like to know what the Korpotchniker said about this. Will you be here later today? I'll drop in. Let me know what happens. You better call the girl's family right away, Alper. Good morning. Peace be with you.

ALPER *and* ZITORSKY Peace be with you, Rabbi.

(THE RABBI *exits. The two old men regard each other a little balefully, and then shuffle to* THE RABBI'S *office, where* ALPER *sits down and puts his hand on the phone, resting it on the receiver, quite depressed by the turn of events. In the synagogue,* THE CABALIST *is huddled in prayer, and* THE SEXTON *has gotten a broom out and is sweeping an upstage area. A long moment of hushed silence fills the stage*)

ALPER (*His hand still on the phone*) Zitorsky, let us reason this out.

ZITORSKY Absolutely.

ALPER (*The Talmudic scholar*) If I call the girl's home, there are two possibilities. Either she is home or she is not home. If she is home, why call? If she is not home, then there are two possibilities. Either her father has already called the police, or he has not called the police. If he has already called the police, then we are wasting a telephone call. If he has not called the police, he will call them. If he calls the police, then there are two possibilities. Either they will take the matter seriously or they will not. If they don't take the matter seriously, why bother calling them? If they take the matter seriously, they will rush down here to find out what we already know, so what gain will have been made? Nothing. Have I reasoned well, Zitorsky?

ZITORSKY You have reasoned well.

ALPER Between you and me, Zitorsky, how many people are there on the streets at this hour that we couldn't spot the girl in a minute? Why should we trouble the immense machinery of the law? We'll go out and find the girl ourselves.

(*They are both up in a minute, buttoning their coats and hurrying to the front door, where they pause*)

ZITORSKY (*Regarding* ALPER *with awe*) Alper, what a rogue you are!

(ALPER *accepts the compliment graciously, and they both dart out into the street. Then, out of the hollow hush of the stage,* THE CABALIST'S *voice rises into a lovely chant as he rocks back and forth, his eyes closed in religious ecstasy*)

THE CABALIST (*Singing slowly and with profound conviction*)

"I believe with perfect faith in the coming of the Messiah, and though he tarry, I will wait daily for his coming.

I believe with perfect faith that there will be a resurrection of the dead

at the time when it shall please the Creator,

blessed be His name,

and exalted the remembrance of him for ever and ever."

(*The front door opens, and* THE GIRL *comes rushing in, holding a beautifully bound leather book. She looks quickly around the synagogue, now empty except for* THE SEXTON *and* THE CABALIST, *and then hurries to* THE RABBI'S *office, which is of course also empty. A kind of panic sweeps over her, and she rushes out into the synagogue again, to* THE SEXTON)

THE GIRL Mr. Bleyer, the young man that was here, do you know . . . (*She whirls as the front door opens behind her and* ARTHUR *comes in. We have the feeling he also has been, if not running, at least walking very quickly. He and* THE GIRL *stare at each other for a moment. Then she says to him*—) I went home to get this book for you. I wanted you to have this book I told you about.

ARTHUR (*Quietly*) I just simply couldn't go till I knew you were all right.

(*For a moment they stand poised, staring at each other. Then she sweeps across the stage and flings herself into his arms*)

THE GIRL (*Crying out*) Oh, I love you. I love you. I love you . . .

(*They stand, locked in embrace.* THE CABALIST'S *voice rises again in a deeply primitive chant, exquisite in its atavistic ardor*)

THE CABALIST

"For Thy salvation I hope, O Lord! I hope, O Lord, for Thy salvation. O Lord, for Thy salvation I hope!

For Thy salvation I hope, O Lord! I hope, O Lord, for Thy salvation! O Lord, for Thy salvation I hope!"

THE CURTAIN FALLS

Scene 2

It is now several hours later. A silent, dozing quiet has settled over the synagogue. Indeed, THE CABALIST *has dozed off over a thick tome at the upstage desk on the far side of the altar, his shawl-enshrouded head lying on his book.* THE GIRL, *too, is napping, curled up in the worn leather armchair in* THE RABBI'S *office.* THE SEXTON *is sitting like a cobbler on a chair stage left.* ALPER *and* ZITORSKY *sit drowsily on two wooden chairs, center stage. Only* ARTHUR *moves restlessly around the synagogue. He looks into* THE RABBI'S *office, checking on* THE GIRL, *studies her sleeping sweetness, somehow deeply troubled. All is still, all is quiet.*

In the synagogue, THE CABALIST *awakens suddenly and sits bolt upright, as if he has just had the most bizarre dream. He stares wide-eyed at the wall in front of him. He rises, and moves slowly downstage, his face a study in quiet awe. Apparently, he has had a profoundly moving dream, and he puts his hand to his brow as if to keep his thoughts from tumbling out. An expression of exaltation spreads across his wan, lined, bearded old face. His eyes are wide with terror.*

THE CABALIST (*Whispering in awe*) "Blessed be the Lord. Blessed be the Lord. Blessed be the Lord." (*He stands now almost at the footlights, staring out over the audience, his face illuminated with ecstasy. He cries out*) Praise ye the Lord! Hallelujah! Praise ye the Lord! Hallelujah! It is good to sing praises unto our God; for it is pleasant and praise is seemly. Praise ye the Lord! Hallelujah! (ALPER *has watched* THE CABALIST *with drowsy interest.* THE CABALIST *turns and stares at him*) My dear friends, my dear, dear friends . . .

(*Tears fill his old eyes, and his mouth works without saying anything for a moment*)

ALPER Are you all right, Hirschman?

THE CABALIST (*Awed by an inner wonder*) I was studying the codification of the Law, especially those paragraphs beginning with the letters of my father's name—because today is my father's day of memorial. I have brought some honey cake here, in my father's memory. I have it somewhere in a paper bag. Where did I put it? I brought it here last night. It is somewhere around—and as I studied, I dozed off and my head fell upon the Book of Mishna. Oh, my dear friends, I have prayed to the Lord to send me a dream, and He has sent me a dream. I dreamt that I was bathing in a pool of the clearest mountain water. And a man of great posture appeared on the bank, and he said to me: "Rabbi, give me your blessing, for I go to make a journey." And I looked closely on the man, and it was the face of my father. And I said unto him: "My father, why do you call me Rabbi? For did I not lustfully throw away the white fringed shawl of the rabbinate and did I not mock the Lord to thy face? And have I not spent my life in prayer and penitence so that I might cleanse my soul?" And my father smiled upon me, and his bearded face glowed with gentleness, and he said unto me: "Rise from your bath, my son, and put upon you these robes of white linen which I have arrayed for you. For thy soul is cleansed and thou hast found a seat among the righteous. And the countenance of the Lord doth smile upon thee this day. So rise and rejoice and dance in the Holy Place. For thine is eternal peace and thou art among the righteous." Thus was the dream that I dreamt as my head lay on the Book of Mishna. (*He lifts his head and stares upward*) The Lord shall reign for ever. Thy God, O Zion, unto all generations. Praise ye the Lord. Hallelujah! (*He stares distractedly around him*) Where is the wine, Sexton? The wine! There was a fine new bottle on Friday! I have been given a seat among the righteous! For this day have I lived and fasted! I have been absolved! Hallelujah! Hallelujah!— Ah, the cakes! Here! Good!— (*He is beginning to laugh*) I shall dance before the Holy Ark! Sexton! Sexton! Distribute the macaroons that all may share this exalted day! The Lord hath sent me a sign, and the face of my father smiled upon me!

(*As abruptly as he had begun to laugh he begins to sob in the effusion of his joy. He sinks onto a chair and cries unashamedly*)

ALPER My dear Hirschman, how delighted we are for you.

THE SEXTON (*Offering some honey cake to* ZITORSKY) You want some cake there, Zitorsky?

ZITORSKY I'll have a little wine too as long as we're having a party.

(THE SEXTON *scurries off to the lectern, the bottom of which is a cabinet containing various sacramental things and wine*)

ARTHUR (*Who has been watching all this, rather taken by it*) What happened?

ALPER Mr. Hirschman has received a sign from God. His father has forgiven him, and his soul has been cleansed.

ARTHUR That's wonderful.

ZITORSKY (*To* THE SEXTON, *now pouring wine from a decanter*) I'll tell you, Bleyer, if you have a little whiskey, I prefer that. Wine makes me dizzy.

THE SEXTON Where would I get whiskey? This is a synagogue, not a saloon.

ZITORSKY (*Taking his glass of wine*) Happiness, Hirschman.

ALPER Some wine for our young friend here. (*To* ARTHUR) Will you join Mr. Hirschman in his moment of exaltation?

ARTHUR Yes, of course.

(THE SEXTON, *who is pouring the wine and sipping a glass of his own as he pours, has begun to hum a gay Chassidic tune. He hands* ARTHUR *his glass*)

ZITORSKY (*Handing his glass back for a refill*) Oh, will Schlissel eat his heart out when he finds out he is missing a party.

ALPER (*Making a toast*) Rabbi Israel, son of Isaac, I think it is fitting we use your rabbinical title—we bow in reverence to you.

THE CABALIST (*Deeply touched*) My dear, dear friends, I cannot describe to you my happiness.

ZITORSKY There hasn't been a party here since that boy's confirmation last month. Wasn't that a skimpy feast for a confirmation? Another glass, please, Sexton. Oh, I'm beginning to sweat. Some confirmation party that was! The boy's father does a nice business in real estate and all he brings down is a few pieces of sponge cake and one bottle of whiskey. One bottle of whiskey for fifty people! As much whiskey as I had couldn't even cure a toothache. Oh, boy, am I getting dizzy. When I was a boy, I could drink a whole jar of potato cider. You remember that potato cider we used to have in Europe? It could kill a horse. Oh, boy, what kind of wine is that? My legs are like rubber already.

(ZITORSKY *suddenly stamps his foot and executes a few brief Chassidic dance steps*)

ALPER This is not bad wine, you know. A pleasant bouquet.

ZITORSKY (*Wavering over to* ARTHUR) Have a piece of cake, young man. What does it say in the Bible? "Go eat your food with gladness and drink your wine with a happy mind?" Give the boy another glass.

ARTHUR (*Smiling*) Thank you. I'm still working on this one.

(THE CABALIST *suddenly raises his head and bursts into a gay Chassidic chant*)

THE CABALIST (*Bursting into song*)

"Light is sown,
sown for the righteous,
and joy for the upright,
the upright in heart.
Oh,
light is sown,
sown for the righteous . . ."

ZITORSKY (*Gaily joining in*)

"and joy for the upright,
the upright in heart.
Oh!"

(THE CABALIST *and* ZITORSKY *take each other's shoulders and begin to dance in the formless Chassidic pattern. They are in wonderful spirits*)

"Light is sown,
sown for the righteous . . ."

(THE SEXTON *and* ALPER *join in, clapping their hands and eventually joining the dance so that the four old Jews form a small ring, their arms around each other's shoulders, their old feet kicking exuberantly as they stamp about in a sort of circular pattern*)

ALL

". . . and joy for the upright,
the upright in heart."
Oh!
Light is sown,
sown for the righteous,
and joy for the upright,
the upright in heart.

(*Round and round they stomp and shuffle, singing out lustily, sweat forming in beads on their brows. The words are repeated over and over again until they degenerate, from the shortness of breath of the singers, into a "Bi-bu-bu-bi-bi-bi-bi-bi-bi-bibibi."* ARTHUR *watches, delighted. Finally,* ALPER, *gasping for breath, breaks out of the ring and staggers to a chair*)

THE CABALIST A good sixty years I haven't danced! Oh, enough! Enough! My heart feels as if it will explode!

(*He staggers, laughing, from the small ring of dancers and sits down, gasping for air*)

ALPER Some more wine, Hirschman?

THE CABALIST (*Gasping happily*) Oh!

(ZITORSKY *looks up, noticing* THE GIRL, *who, awakened by the romping, has sidled out into the synagogue and has been watching the gaiety with delight.* ZITORSKY *eyes her wickedly for a moment; then advances on her, his arm outstretched, quite the old cock-of-the-walk*)

ZITORSKY Bi-bi-bi-bi-bi-bi-bi . . .

(*He seizes her in his arms and begins to twirl around, much to her delight. She dances with him, her skirts whirling and her feet twinkling, laughing at the sheer physical excitement of it all.* ZITORSKY *supplies the music, a gay chant, the lyrics of which consist of: "Bi-bi-bi-bi-bi-bi-bi-bi . . ."*)

THE CABALIST The last time I danced was on the occasion of the last Day of the Holiday of Tabernacles in 1896. I was seventeen years old. (*A sudden frightened frown sweeps across his face. He mutters*) Take heed for the girl, for the dybbuk will be upon her soon.

ALPER (*Leaning to him*) What did you say, Israel son of Isaac?

(THE CABALIST *turns to* THE GIRL *dancing with* ZITORSKY, *and stares at her*)

THE CABALIST Let the girl rest, Zitorsky, for she struggles with the dybbuk. Behold. (THE GIRL *has indeed broken away from* ZITORSKY *and has begun an improvised dance of her own. The gaiety is gone from her face and is re-*

placed by a sullen lasciviousness. The dance she does is a patently provocative one. She dances slowly at first, and then with increasing abandon and wantonness. ZITORSKY *recoils in horror.* THE GIRL *begins to stamp her feet and to whirl more and more wildly. Her eyes grow bold and flashing and she begins to shout old Gypsy words, a mongrel Russian, Oriental in intonation.* THE CABALIST *now slowly moves to* THE GIRL, *who, when she becomes aware of his coming close, abruptly stops her dance and stands stock-still, her face a mask of extravagant pain.* THE CABALIST *regards her gently*) Lie down, my child, and rest.

(*At this quiet suggestion,* THE GIRL *begins to sway as if she is about to faint*)

THE GIRL (*Barely audible*) I feel so faint, so faint.

(*She sinks slowly to the floor, not quite in a swoon, but on the verge.* ARTHUR *races to her side*)

ARTHUR Do we have any water here?

ALPER Wine would be better. Sexton, give her some wine.

(THE SEXTON *hurries with someone's glass*)

ARTHUR (*Holding* THE GIRL'S *head*) Is she a sickly girl?

ALPER (*Bending over them*) She was never sick a day in her life.

THE SEXTON Here's the wine.

ZITORSKY (*To* THE SEXTON) Did I tell you? Did I tell you?

THE GIRL I feel so faint. I feel so faint.

ARTHUR (*Bringing the glass of wine to her lips*) Sip some of this.

THE GIRL (*Murmuring*) Save me . . . save me . . .

THE CABALIST The dybbuk weakens her. I have seen this once before.

THE SEXTON (*To* ZITORSKY) When you told me about this dybbuk, I didn't believe you.

ZITORSKY So did I tell you right?

THE SEXTON Oh, boy.

ARTHUR Help me get her onto the chair in there.

ALPER Yes, of course.

THE SEXTON Here, let me help a little.

(*Between them, they manage to get* THE GIRL *up and walk her slowly to* THE RABBI'S *office, where they gently help her lie down on the leather sofa*)

THE CABALIST (*To* ZITORSKY) They haven't heard from Mr. Foreman yet?

ZITORSKY No, we're waiting.

THE CABALIST (*Frowning*) It is not that far to Williamsburg. Well, the girl will sleep now.

(*He walks slowly to the door of* THE RABBI'S *office, followed by a wary* ZITORSKY. ALPER *returns to the synagogue proper to join the other old men, and, for the briefest of moments,* ARTHUR *finds himself alone with* THE GIRL, *holding her head gently in his arms. Suddenly he kisses her brow and lightly strokes her hair. He rises quickly as the others return*)

ARTHUR I think she's fallen asleep.

ALPER Thank heavens for that.

ARTHUR Look, I'm going to call her family. She may be quite ill. I think we'd all feel a lot better if she were in the hands of a doctor. If one of you will just give me her home telephone number . . . (*Just a little annoyed, for nobody answers him*) Please, gentlemen, I really don't think it's wise to pursue this nonsense any longer.

THE CABALIST It is not nonsense. I do not speak of dybbuks casually. As a young man, I saw hundreds of people come to my father claiming to be possessed, but, of all these, only two were true dybbuks. Of these two, one was a girl very much like this poor girl, and, even before the black candles and the ram's horn could be brought for the exorcism, she sank down onto the earth and died. I tell you this girl is possessed, and she will die, clutching at her throat and screaming for redemption unless the dybbuk is exorcised. (*He stares at the others and nods his head*) She will die. Wake the girl. I will take her to the Korpotchniker myself.

ALPER Zitorsky, wake the girl. I will get her coat. Sexton, call a taxicab for Rabbi Israel. (ALPER, *who had been reaching for* THE GIRL'S *coat, is stayed by* ARTHUR. *He looks up at the young man*) Young man, what are you doing?

ARTHUR Mr. Alper, the girl is sick. There may be something seriously wrong with her.

ALPER Young man, Rabbi Israel says she is dying.

ARTHUR Well, in that case certainly, let me have her home telephone number.

ALPER (*Striding into* THE RABBI'S *office*) You are presuming in matters that are no concern of yours.

ARTHUR (*Following*) They are as much my concern as they are yours. I have grown quite fond of this girl. I want her returned to the proper authorities, right now. If necessary, I shall call a policeman. Now, let's have no more nonsense.

(ALPER *sinks down behind the desk, glowering. A moment of silence fills the room. Then* THE CABALIST, *who has been standing in the rear of the office and watching with quiet interest, says—*)

THE CABALIST The young man doesn't believe in dybbuks?

ARTHUR I'm afraid not. I think you are all behaving like madmen.

(THE CABALIST *considers this answer for a moment*)

THE CABALIST I will tell you an old Chassidic parable. A deaf man passed by a house in which a wedding party was going on. He looked in the window and saw all the people there dancing and cavorting, leaping about and laughing. However, since the man was deaf and could not hear the music of the fiddlers, he said to himself: "Ah, this must be a madhouse." Young man, because you are deaf, must it follow that we are lunatics?

ARTHUR You are quite right. I did not mean to mock your

beliefs, and I apologize for it. However, I am going to call the girl's father, and, if he wants to have the girl exorcised, that's his business. (*He sits down behind the desk, puts his hand on the receiver, and looks up at* ALPER) Well?

THE CABALIST Give him the number, Mr. Alper. (ALPER *fishes an old address book out of his vest pocket, thumbs through the pages, and hands the open book to* ARTHUR, *who begins to dial*) There is no one home in the girl's house. Her father, who wishes only to forget about the girl, has gone to his shop in the city, and, at this moment, is overeating at his lunch in a dairy restaurant. The stepmother has taken the younger children to her sister's. The girl's doctor has called the police and has gone about his rounds, and the police are diffidently riding up and down the streets of the community, looking for an old Jew and his granddaughter. (ARTHUR *says nothing, but simply waits for an answer to his ring.* THE CABALIST *sits down on the arm of the couch to contemplate. At last he says—*) I cannot understand why this young man does not believe in dybbuks.

ALPER It is symptomatic of the current generation, Rabbi Israel, to be utterly disillusioned. Historically speaking, an era of prosperity following an era of hard times usually produces a number of despairing and quietistic philosophies, for the now prosperous people have found out they are just as unhappy as when they were poor. Thus when an intelligent man of such a generation discovers that two television sets have no more meaning than one or that he gets along no better with his wife in a suburban house than he did in their small city flat, he arrives at the natural assumption that life is utterly meaningless.

THE CABALIST What an unhappy state of affairs.

(ARTHUR *returns the receiver to its cradle*)

ARTHUR (*Muttering*) Nobody home.

THE CABALIST (*To* ARTHUR) Is that true, young man, that you believe in absolutely nothing?

ARTHUR Not a damn thing.

THE CABALIST There is no truth, no beauty, no infinity, no known, no unknown.

ARTHUR Precisely.

THE CABALIST Young man, you are a fool.

ARTHUR Really. I have been reading your book—the Book of Zohar. I am sure it has lost much in the translation, but, sir, any disciple of this abracadabra is presuming when he calls anyone else a fool.

(ARTHUR *produces from his jacket the book* THE GIRL *gave him, and extends it to* THE CABALIST, *who accepts it, frowning*)

THE CABALIST You have been reading the Book of Zohar. Dear young man, one does not read the Book of Zohar, leaf through its pages, and make marginal notes. I have entombed myself in this slim volume for sixty years, raw with vulnerability to its hidden mysteries, and have sensed only a glimpse of its passion. Behind every letter of every word lies a locked image, and behind every image a sparkle of light of the ineffable brilliance of Infinity. But the concept of the Inexpressible Unknown is inconceivable to you. For you are a man possessed by the Tangible. If you cannot touch it with your fingers, it simply does not exist. Indeed, that will be the epithet of your generation—that you took everything for granted and believed in nothing. It is a very little piece of life that we know. How shall I say it? I suggest it is wiser to believe in dybbuks than in nothing at all.

ARTHUR Mr. Hirschman, a good psychiatrist—even a poor one—could strip your beliefs in ten minutes. You may think of yourself as a man with a God, but I see you as a man obsessed with guilt who has invented a God so he can be forgiven. You have invented it all—the guilt, God, forgiveness, the whole world, dybbuks, love, passion, fulfillment—the whole fantastic mess of pottage—because it is unbearable for you to bear the pain of insignificance. None of these things exist. You've made them all up. The fact is, I have half a mind to let you go through with this exorcism, for, after all the trumpetings of rams' horns and the bellowing of incantations and after the girl falls in a swoon on the floor—I assure you, she will rise up again as demented as she ever was, and I wonder what bizarre rationale and mystique you will expound to explain all that. Now, if the disputation is at an end, I am going to call the police.

(*He picks up the receiver again and dials the operator*)

ALPER Well, what can one say to such bitterness?

THE CABALIST (*Shrugs*) One can only say that the young man has very little regard for psychiatrists.

(*The front door to the synagogue bursts open, and* FOREMAN *and* SCHLISSEL *come hurtling in, breathing heavily and in a state of absolute confusion.* ALPER *darts out into the synagogue proper and stares at them*)

SCHLISSEL Oh, thank God, the synagogue is still here!

ALPER Well?

SCHLISSEL (*He can hardly talk, he is so out of breath*) Well, what?

ALPER What did the Korpotchniker say?

SCHLISSEL Who knows?! Who saw the Korpotchniker?! We've been riding in subways for four hours! Back and forth, in this train, in that train! I am convinced there is no such place as Williamsburg and there is no such person as the Korpotchniker Rabbi! I tell you, twice we got off at two different stations, just to see daylight, and, as God is my witness, both times we were in New Jersey!

FOREMAN Oh, I tell you, I am sick from driving so much.

ALPER Idiot! You didn't take the Brighton train!

SCHLISSEL We took the Brighton train! (*He waves both arms in a gesture of final frustration*) We took all the trains! I haven't had a bite to eat all morning. Don't tell me about Brighton trains! Don't tell me about anything! Leave me alone, and the devil take your whole capitalist economy! (ZITORSKY, THE SEXTON *and* THE CABALIST *have all come out to see what the noise is all about. Even* ARTHUR *is standing in the office doorway, listening to all this*) We asked this person, we asked that person. This person said that train. That person said this train. We went to a policeman. He puts us on a train. The conductor comes in, says: "Last stop." We get out. As God is my witness, New Jersey. We get back on that train. The conductor says: "Get off next station and take the other train." We get off the next station and take the other train. A man says: "Last stop." We get out. New Jersey!

(*In* THE RABBI'S *office,* THE GIRL *suddenly sits bolt upright, her eyes clenched tight in pain, screaming terribly, her voice shrill with anguish*)

FOREMAN (*Racing to her side*) Oh, my God! Evelyn! Evelyn! What is it?!

(THE GIRL *clutches at her throat and screams*)

THE GIRL Save me! Save me! Save me!

(ZITORSKY *and* THE SEXTON *begin to mutter rapid prayers under their breath*)

ALPER (*Putting his arm around* FOREMAN) David, she's very ill. We think she may be dying.

(ARTHUR *has raced to* THE GIRL. *He sits on the couch beside her and takes her in his arms*)

ARTHUR Call a doctor.

FOREMAN (*In panic, to* ALPER) He says I should call a doctor.

(ARTHUR *puts his hand to his brow and shakes his head as if to clear it of shock and confusion*)

ALPER (*Crossing to* THE CABALIST) Save her, Rabbi Israel. You have had your sign from God. You are among the righteous.

(ARTHUR *turns slowly and regards the silent betallithed form of the little* CABALIST)

ARTHUR (*To* THE CABALIST, *his voice cracking under emotions he was unaware he still had*) For God's sakes, perform your exorcism or whatever has to be done. I think she's dying.

(THE CABALIST *regards* ARTHUR *for a moment with the profoundest gentleness. Then he turns and, with an authoritative voice, instructs* THE SEXTON)

THE CABALIST Sexton, we shall need black candles, the ram's horn, prayer shawls of white wool, and there shall be ten Jews for a quorum to witness before God this awesome ceremony.

THE SEXTON Just plain black candles?

THE CABALIST Just plain black candles.

(THE SEXTON *is already hurrying into his coat.* ALPER *moves quietly up to* FOREMAN *standing in the office doorway, and touches his old friend's shoulder in a gesture of awe and compassion.* FOREMAN, *at the touch, begins to cry and buries his shaking old head on his friend's shoulder.* ALPER *embraces him*)

ZITORSKY (*In the synagogue, to* SCHLISSEL) I am absolutely shaking—shaking.

(ARTHUR, *having somewhat recovered his self-control, sinks down behind the desk, frowning, confused by all that is going on, and moved by a complex of feeling he cannot understand at all*)

THE CURTAIN FALLS

ACT THREE

Half an hour later.

At rise, THE GIRL *is sitting in* THE RABBI'S *office, perched on the couch, nervous, frightened, staring down at her restlessly twisting fingers.* FOREMAN *sits behind* THE RABBI'S *desk, wrapped in his own troubled thoughts. He wears over his suit a long white prayer shawl with thick black stripes, like that worn by* THE CABALIST *throughout the play.*

Indeed, all the men now wear these ankle-length white prayer shawls, except ARTHUR, *who, at rise, is also in* THE RABBI'S *office, deep in thought.*

THE CABALIST *stands downstage left, his prayer shawl hooded over his head; he is leafing through a volume, preparing the prayers for the exorcism.*

THE SEXTON *is standing by the wall phone, the receiver cradled to his ear, waiting for an answer to a call he has just put in. He is more or less surrounded by* ALPER, SCHLISSEL, *and* ZITORSKY.

ZITORSKY How about Milsky the butcher?

ALPER Milsky wouldn't come. Ever since they gave the seat by the East Wall to Kornblum, Milsky said he wouldn't set foot in this synagogue again. Every synagogue I have belonged to, there have always been two kosher butchers who get into a fight over who gets the favored seat by the East Wall during the High Holy

Days, and the one who doesn't abandons the congregation in a fury, and the one who does always seems to die before the next High Holy Days.

SCHLISSEL Kornblum the butcher died? I didn't know Kornblum died.

ALPER Sure. Kornblum died four years ago.

SCHLISSEL Well, he had lousy meat, believe me, may his soul rest in peace.

(THE SEXTON *has hung up, recouped his dime, reinserted it, and is dialing again*)

ZITORSKY (*To* THE SEXTON) No answer?

(THE SEXTON *shakes his head*)

THE SEXTON I'm calling Harris.

SCHLISSEL Harris? You tell an eighty-two-year-old man to come down and make a tenth for an exorcism, and he'll have a heart attack talking on the phone with you.

THE SEXTON (*Dialing*) Well, what else am I to do? It is hard enough to assemble ten Jews under the best of circumstances, but in the middle of the afternoon on a Thursday it is an absolute nightmare. Aronowitz is in Miami. Klein the furrier is at his job in Manhattan. It is a workday today. Who shall I call? (*He waits for someone to answer*) There are many things that I have to do. The tapestries on the Ark, as you see, are faded and need needlework, and the candelabras and silver goblet for the saying of the Sabbath benediction are tarnished and dull. But every second of my day seems to be taken up with an incessant search for ten Jews . . . (*On the phone*) Hello, Harris. Harris, this is Bleyer the Sexton. We need you badly down here in the synagogue for a quorum . . . If I told you why, you wouldn't come . . . All right, I'll tell you, but, in God's name, don't tell another soul, not even your daughter-in-law . . .

SCHLISSEL My daughter-in-law, may she grow like an onion with her head in the ground.

THE SEXTON (*On the phone*) Hirschman is going to exorcise a dybbuk from Foreman's granddaughter . . . I said, Hirschman is . . . A dybbuk That's right, a dybbuk . . . Right here in Mineola . . . That's right. Why should Mineola be exempt from dybbuks?

ALPER (*Thinking of names*) There used to be a boy came down here every morning, about eight, nine years ago—a devout boy with forelocks and sidecurls—a pale boy, who was studying to be a rabbi at the seminary.

THE SEXTON (*On the phone*) Harris, this is not a joke.

SCHLISSEL Chwatkin.

ALPER That's right, Chwatkin. That was the boy's name. Chwatkin. Maybe we could call him. Does he still live in the community?

SCHLISSEL He's a big television actor. He's on television all the time. Pinky Sims. He's an actor.

ZITORSKY Pinky Sims? That's a name for a rabbinical student?

THE SEXTON Put on your sweater and come down.

ALPER (*To* THE SEXTON, *who has just hung up*) So Harris is coming?

THE SEXTON Yes, he's coming. So with Harris, that makes eight, and I am frankly at the end of my resources. I don't know who else to call.

ALPER This is terrible. Really. God manifests Himself in our little synagogue, and we can't even find ten Jews to say hello.

THE SEXTON I shall have to go out in the street and get two strangers. (*Putting on his coat*) Well, I don't look forward to this at all. I will have to stop people on the street, ask them if they are Jewish—which is bad enough —and then explain to them I wish them to attend the exorcism of a dybbuk—I mean, surely you can see the futility of it.

ALPER (*To* THE CABALIST, *who is crossing now en route to the office*) We can only get eight. A disgrace. Really. We shall not have the exorcism for lack of two Jews.

THE SEXTON (*On his way out*) All right, I'm going.
(*He exits*)

ZITORSKY (*To* SCHLISSEL) In those days when I was deceiving my wife, I used to tell her I was entertaining out-of-town buyers. I once told her I was entertaining out-of-town buyers every night for almost three weeks. It was a foolhardy thing to do because even my wife could tell business was not that good. So one night she came down to my loft on Thirty-Sixth Street and walked in and caught me with—well, I'm sure I've told you this story before.

SCHLISSEL Many times.

(THE CABALIST *enters the office. Upon his entrance,* THE GIRL *stands abruptly, obviously deeply disturbed and barely in control of herself. She turns from* THE CABALIST *and shades her eyes with her hand to hide her terror.* FOREMAN *looks up briefly. He seems to be in a state of shock.* THE CABALIST *sits down on the couch, letting his heavy prayer shawl fall back on his shoulders, and studies his hands folded patiently between his knees. After a moment, he speaks*)

THE CABALIST (*Quietly*) Dybbuk, I am Israel son of Isaac. My father was Isaac son of Asher, and I wear his fringed shawl on my shoulders as I talk to you. (*Upon these words,* THE GIRL *suddenly contorts her form, as if seized by a violent cramp. She clutches her stomach and bends low, and soft sobs begin to come out of her*) Reveal yourself to me.

THE GIRL (*In the voice of the dybbuk*) I am Hannah Luchinsky.

(*In the synagogue,* ALPER, SCHLISSEL, *and* ZITORSKY *begin to edge—quite frightened—to the open office door.* ARTHUR *watches from his seat behind* THE RABBI'S *desk*)

THE CABALIST Why do you possess this girl's body?

THE GIRL (*Twisting and contorting; in the voice of the*

dybbuk) My soul was lost at sea, and there is no one to say the prayers for the dead over me.

THE CABALIST I will strike a bargain with you. Leave this girl's body through her smallest finger, doing her no damage, not even a scratch, and I shall sit on wood for you for the First Seven Days of Mourning and shall plead for your soul for the First Thirty Days and shall say the prayers for the dead over you three times a day for the Eleven Months and light the Memorial Lamp each year upon the occasion of your death. I ask you to leave this girl's body.

(THE GIRL *laughs quietly*)

THE GIRL (*In the voice of the dybbuk*) You give me short weight, for you will yourself be dead before the prayers for the new moon.

(*In the office doorway, the three old men shudder.* FOREMAN *looks up slowly.* THE CABALIST *closes his eyes*)

THE CABALIST (*Quietly*) How do you know this?

THE GIRL (*In the voice of the dybbuk*) Your soul will fly straight to the Heavenly Gates and you will be embraced by the Archangel Mihoel.

THE CABALIST Then I enjoin the Angel of Death to speed his way. Dybbuk, I order you to leave the body of this girl.

(THE GIRL's *face suddenly flashes with malevolence*)

THE GIRL (*In the voice of the dybbuk, shouting*) No! I seek vengeance for these forty years of limbo! I was betrayed in my youth and driven to the Evil Impulse against my will! I have suffered beyond belief, and my spirit has lived in dunghills and in piles of ashes, and I demand the soul of David son of Abram be cast through Gilgul for the space of forty years times ten to gasp for air in the sea in which I drowned . . .

FOREMAN (*Standing in terror*) No! No!

THE GIRL (*In the voice of the dybbuk*) . . . so that my

soul may have peace! A soul for a soul! That is my bargain.

FOREMAN (*Shouting*) Let it be then! Leave my granddaughter in peace and I will give my soul in exchange.

THE CABALIST (*With ringing authority*) The disposition of David son of Abram's soul will not be decided here. It's fall and ascent has been ordained by the second universe of angels. The bargain cannot be struck! Dybbuk, hear me. I order you to leave the body of this girl through her smallest finger, causing her no pain nor damage, and I give you my word, prayers will be said over you in full measure. But if you abjure these words, then must I proceed against you with malediction and anathema.

THE GIRL (*Laughs*) Raise not thy mighty arm against me, for it has no fear for me. A soul for a soul. That is my bargain.

(THE GIRL *suddenly begins to sob*)

THE CABALIST (*To* ALPER) We shall have to prepare for the exorcism.

ALPER I thought that would be the case.

THE GIRL (*Sitting down on the couch, frightened, in her own voice*) I am so afraid.

FOREMAN There is nothing to fear. It will all be over in a minute, like having a tooth pulled, and you will walk out of here a cheerful child.

SCHLISSEL (*Ambling back into the synagogue proper with* ZITORSKY *and* ALPER) I tell you, I'd feel a lot better if the Korpotchniker was doing this. If you are going to have a tooth pulled, at least let it be by a qualified dentist.

ZITORSKY I thought Hirschman handled himself very well with that dybbuk.

SCHLISSEL (*To* ALPER *and* ZITORSKY) If I tell you all something, promise you will never throw it back in my face.

ZITORSKY What?

SCHLISSEL I am beginning to believe she is really possessed by a dybbuk.

ZITORSKY I'm beginning to get used to the whole thing.

(THE CABALIST *has stood and moved upstage to the rear wall of the synagogue, where he stands in meditation.* FOREMAN *is sitting again, somewhat numb, beside his granddaughter. After a moment,* THE GIRL *speaks*)

THE GIRL I am very frightened, Arthur.

ARTHUR (*Rises*) Well, I spoke to my analyst, as you know, and he said he didn't think this exorcism was a bad idea at all. The point is, if you really do believe you are possessed by a dybbuk . . .

THE GIRL Oh, I do.

ARTHUR Well, then, he feels this exorcism might be a good form of shock treatment that will make you more responsive to psychiatric therapy and open the door to an eventual cure. Mr. Hirschman assures me it is a painless ceremony. So you really have nothing to be frightened of.

THE GIRL Will you be here?

ARTHUR Of course. Did you think I wouldn't?

(FOREMAN *moves slowly out into the synagogue, as if to ask something of* THE CABALIST)

THE GIRL I always sense flight in you.

ARTHUR Really.

THE GIRL You are always taking to your heels, Arthur. Especially in moments like now when you want to be tender. I know that you love me or I couldn't be so happy with you, but the whole idea of love seems to terrify you, and you keep racing off to distant detachments. I feel that if I reached out for your cheek now, you would turn your head or, in some silent way, clang the iron gates shut on me. You have some strange dybbuk all of your own, some sad little turnkey, who drifts about inside of you, locking up all the little doors, and saying,

"You are dead. You are dead." You do love me, Arthur. I know that.

ARTHUR (*Gently*) I wish you well, Evelyn. We can at least say that.

THE GIRL I love you. I want so very much to be your wife. (*She stares at him, her face glowing with love. She says quietly*) I will make you a good home, Arthur. You will be very happy with me. (*He regards her for a moment, caught by her wonder. He reaches forward and lightly touches her cheek. She cannot take her eyes from him*) I adore you, Arthur.

ARTHUR (*With deep gentleness*) You are quite mad.

(*They look at each other.* ARTHUR *stands*)

THE GIRL You think our getting married is impractical.

ARTHUR Yes, I would say it was at the least impractical.

THE GIRL Because I am insane and you are suicidal.

ARTHUR I do think those are two reasons to give one pause.

THE GIRL Well, at least we begin with futility. Most marriages take years to arrive there.

ARTHUR Don't be saucy, Evelyn.

THE GIRL (*Earnestly*) Oh, Arthur, I wouldn't suggest marriage if I thought it was utterly unfeasible. I think we can make a go of it. I really dc. I know you have no faith in my exorcism . . .

ARTHUR As I say, it may be an effective shock therapy.

THE GIRL But we could get married this minute, and I still think we could make a go of it. I'm not a dangerous schizophrenic; I just hallucinate. I could keep your house for you. I did for my father very competently before he remarried. I'm a good cook, and you do find me attractive, don't you? I love you, Arthur. You are really very good for me. I retain reality remarkably well with you. I know I could be a good wife. Many schizophrenics function quite well if one has faith in them.

ARTHUR (*Touched by her earnestness*) My dear Evelyn . . .

THE GIRL I don't ask you to have faith in dybbuks or gods or exorcisms—just in me.

(*He gently touches her cheek*)

ARTHUR How in heaven's name did we reach this point of talking marriage?

THE GIRL It is a common point of discussion between people in love.

(*He kneels before her, takes her hand between his*)

ARTHUR (*Tenderly*) I do not love you. Nor do you love me. We met five hours ago and exchanged the elementary courtesy of conversation—the rest is your own ingenuousness.

THE GIRL I do not remember ever being as happy as I am this moment. I feel enchanted. (*They are terribly close now. He leans to her, his arm moving to embrace her. And then he stops, and the moment is broken. He turns away, scowls, stands*) You are in full flight again, aren't you?

ARTHUR I reserve a certain low level of morality which includes not taking advantage of incompetent minors.

THE GIRL Why can't you believe that I love you?

ARTHUR (*Angrily*) I simply do not believe anybody loves anyone. Let's have an end to this. (*He is abruptly aware that their entire love scene has been observed by the old men, who are clustered together in the open doorway of* THE RABBI'S *office, beaming at them. With a furious sigh,* ARTHUR *strides to the door and shuts it in the old men's faces. He turns back to* THE GIRL, *scowling*) Really, this is all much too fanciful. Really, it is. In an hour, you will be back to your institution, where I may or may not visit you.

(THE GIRL *sits down slowly*)

THE GIRL If I were not already insane, the thought that I might not see you again would make me so.

ARTHUR I don't know what you want of me.

THE GIRL (*One step from tears*) I want you to find the meaning of your life in me.

ARTHUR But that's insane. How can you ask such an impossible thing?

THE GIRL Because you love me.

ARTHUR (*Cries out*) I don't know what you mean by love! All it means to me is I shall buy you a dinner, take you to the theatre, and then straight to our tryst, where I shall reach under your blouse for the sake of tradition while you breathe hotly in my ear in a pretense of passion. We will mutter automatic endearments, nibbling at the sweat on each other's earlobes, all the while gracelessly fumbling with buttons and zippers, cursing under our breath the knots in our shoelaces, and telling ourselves that this whole comical business of stripping off our trousers is an act of nature like the pollination of weeds. Even in that one brief moment when our senses finally obliterate our individual alonenesses, we will hear ringing in our ears the reluctant creaking of mattress springs.

(THE GIRL *stares at him, awed by this bitter expostulation*)

THE GIRL You are possessed.

ARTHUR At your age, I suppose, one still finds theatrical charm in this ultimate of fantasies, but when you have been backstage as often as I have, you will discover love to be an altogether shabby business of cold creams and costumes.

THE GIRL (*Staring at him*) You are possessed by a dybbuk that does not allow you to love.

ARTHUR (*Crying out again in sudden anguish*) Oh, leave me alone! Let's get on with this wretched exorcism!

(*He strides to the door, suddenly turns, confused, disturbed, and would say something, but he doesn't know what. He opens the door to find the old men patiently waiting for him with beaming smiles. This disconcerts him and he turns to* THE GIRL *again and is again at a loss for words. She stares at the floor*)

THE GIRL We could be very happy if you would have faith in me.

(*He turns and shuffles out of* THE RABBI'S *office*)

ARTHUR (*To the old men*) It was tasteless of you to gawk at us.

(*He continues into the synagogue, trailed by the old men. He sits, and is immediately surrounded by the old men*)

FOREMAN Are you interested in this girl, young man, because my son is not a rich man, by any means, but he will give you a fine wedding, catered by good people, with a cantor . . .

ZITORSKY And a choir.

FOREMAN . . . Possibly, and a dowry perhaps in the amount of five hundred dollars which, believe me, is more than he can afford. However, I am told you are a professional man, a lawyer, and the father of the bride must lay out good money for such a catch.

ALPER *and* ZITROSKY Sure . . . Absolutely.

FOREMAN Of course, the girl is an incompetent and you will have to apply to the courts to be appointed the committee of her person . . .

ALPER . . . A formality, I assure you, once you have married her.

FOREMAN As for the girl, I can tell you first hand, she is a fine Jewish girl . . .

ZITORSKY Modest . . .

ALPER Devout . . .

FOREMAN . . . And she bakes first-rate pastries.

ARTHUR (*Staring at the gay old men with disbelief*) You

are all mad, madder than the girl, and if I don't get out of here soon, I shall be as mad as the rest.

ZITORSKY A beauty, young man. Listen, it is said—better a full-bosomed wife than to marry a Rothschild.

SCHLISSEL Leave the man alone. We have all been miserably married for half a century ourselves. How can you in good faith recommend the institution?

ALPER The girl is so obviously taken with him. It would be a good match.

FOREMAN (*Anxiously*) Perhaps, he is married already.

ALPER (*To* ARTHUR) My dear fellow, how wonderful to be in love.

ARTHUR I love nothing!

THE CABALIST Yes. The girl is quite right. He is possessed. He loves nothing. Love is an act of faith, and yours is a faithless generation. That is your dybbuk.

(*The front door of the synagogue opens, and* THE SEXTON *slips quickly in, quietly closing the door*)

ARTHUR (*To* THE CABALIST) Don't you think it's time to get on with this exorcism?

THE CABALIST Yes.

(*He moves to the door of* THE RABBI'S *office, where he regards the supine form of* THE GIRL *on the couch*)

ALPER (*To* THE SEXTON) Did you get anybody?

(THE SEXTON *moves in his nervous way down into the synagogue. He has obviously been on the go since he left; sweat beads his brow, and he is breathing heavily*)

THE SEXTON (*Unbuttoning his coat and wiping his brow*) Gentlemen, we are in the soup.

SCHLISSEL You couldn't find anybody?

THE SEXTON Actually, we have nine now, but the issue of a quorum has become an academic one. Oh, let me catch my breath. The Rabbi will be here in a few minutes.

ALPER The Rabbi?

THE SEXTON I saw him on Woodhaven Boulevard, and he said he would join us. Harris is on his way already. I saw him coming down the hill from his house. But the whole matter is academic.

ALPER You told the Rabbi we need him to exorcise the girl's dybbuk?

THE SEXTON Well, what else was I to say? He asked me what I needed a quorum for at one o'clock in the afternoon, and I told him, and he thought for a moment, and he said: "All right, I'll be there in a few minutes." He is quite a nice fellow, something of a press agent perhaps, but with good intentions. Oh, I am perspiring like an animal. I shall surely have the ague tomorrow. I have been running all over looking for Jews. I even went to Friedman the tailor. He wasn't even in town. So let me tell you. I was running back here. I turned the corner on Thirty-Third Road there, and I see parked right in front of the synagogue a police patrol car.

(*The others start*)

ALPER (*Looking up*) Oh?

THE SEXTON That's what I mean when I say we are in the soup.

SCHLISSEL Did they say something to you?

THE SEXTON Sure they said something. I tell you, my heart gave such a turn when I saw that police car there. They were sitting there, those two policemen, big strapping cossacks with dark faces like avenging angels, smoking cigarettes, and with their revolvers bulging through their blue overcoats. As I walked across the street to the synagogue, my knees were knocking.

ALPER When was this? It was just now?

THE SEXTON Just this second. Just before I came in the door . . . Hello, Harris, how are you?

(*This last to the octogenarian, who, bundled in his heavy overcoat, muffler, and with his hat pulled down on his head, has just entered the synagogue*)

ZITORSKY (*To* THE SEXTON) So what happened?

HARRIS (*In his high shrill voice, as he unbuttons his over-*

coat) Gentlemen! Have you heard about this dybbuk?

SCHLISSEL Harris, we were all here at the time he called you.

THE SEXTON Harris, did you see the police car outside?

SCHLISSEL So what did the policeman say?

THE SEXTON (*Unbuttoning his collar and wiping his neck with a handkerchief*) This big strapping fellow with his uniform full of buttons looks up, he says: "You know a man named David Foreman? We're looking for him and his granddaughter, a girl, eighteen years old." Well?! Eh! Well, are we in the soup or not?

(SCHLISSEL *goes to the front door, opens it a conspiratorial crack, and looks out*)

ARTHUR I don't think the police will bother you if you get your exorcism started right away. They won't interrupt a religious ceremony, especially if they don't know what it is.

THE CABALIST (*Who has made up his own mind*) Sexton, fetch the black candles, one for each man.

(THE SEXTON *scurries to* THE RABBI'S *office, where the black candles are lying on the desk, wrapped in brown grocery paper*)

ARTHUR (*Moving to the front door*) I'll stand by the door and talk to the police if they come in.

SCHLISSEL (*Closing the front door*) They're out there all right.

THE CABALIST (*He looks about the little synagogue, immensely dignified now, almost beatified in his authority. The others wait on his words*) I shall want to perform the ablutions of the Cohanim. Is there a Levite among you?

SCHLISSEL I am a Levite.

THE CABALIST You shall pour the water on my hands.

(THE SEXTON *scoots across the synagogue, carrying black candles to everyone*)

HARRIS (*Looking distractedly about*) What are we doing now? Where is the dybbuk?

ALPER Harris, put on a prayer shawl.

HARRIS (*Moving nervously to the office door*) Is this actually a serious business then? Where is the dybbuk? Tell me because Bleyer the Sexton told me nothing . . . (*His words drift off into a mumble. He enters the office, sees* THE GIRL *sitting rigidly on the chair. He starts at the sight of her, snatches a prayer shawl from the carton, and, quite in terror, darts back into the synagogue*)

THE CABALIST There is nothing in the Book of Codes which gives the procedure for exorcism, so I have selected those passages to read that I thought most apt. For the purpose of cleansing our souls, we shall recite the Al-chait, and we shall recite that prayer of atonement which begins: "Sons of man such as sit in darkness." As you pray these prayers, let the image of God in any of His seventy-two faces rise before you.

ALPER (*Crossing into* THE RABBI'S *office*) I'll get the books.

THE SEXTON (*Giving* SCHLISSEL *a metal bowl and a pitcher*) Fill it with water.

SCHLISSEL I'm an atheist. Why am I mixed up in all this?

ALPER We do not have a quorum. Will this be valid?

THE CABALIST We will let God decide.

THE SEXTON When shall I blow the ram's horn?

THE CABALIST I shall instruct you when.

HARRIS (*Putting on his shawl*) What shall I do? Where shall I stand?

ZITORSKY (*To* HARRIS) Stand here, and do not be afraid. (FOREMAN *comes out of* THE RABBI'S *office carrying a long white woolen prayer shawl, which he gives to* ARTHUR)

FOREMAN (*To* ARTHUR) I will show you how to put it on. (*He helps* ARTHUR *enshroud himself in the prayer shawl.*

SCHLISSEL *comes out of the washroom carefully carrying his brass bowl and the pitcher filled with water. He goes to* THE CABALIST, *who holds his white hands over the basin.* SCHLISSEL *carefully pours the water over them.* THE CABALIST *speaks with great distinctness*)

THE CABALIST "Blessed art Thou, O Lord our God, King of the Universe, who hath sanctified us by his commandments, and has commanded us to cleanse our hands."

ALL Amen.

(*The others watch until the last of the water has been poured over his hands. A sudden silence settles over the synagogue. They are all standing about now, eight men, cloaked in white, holding their prayer books.* THE CABALIST *dries his hands on a towel handed to him by* SCHLISSEL. *He puts the towel down, rolls his sleeves down, takes his long shawl and, with a sweep of his arms, raises it over his head, lifts his face, and cries out*—)

THE CABALIST "Thou knowest the secrets of eternity and the most hidden mysteries of all living. Thou searchest the innermost recesses, and tryest the reins and the heart. Nought is concealed from thee, or hidden from thine eyes. May it then be thy will, O Lord our God and God of our fathers, to forgive us for all our sins, to pardon us for all our iniquities, and to grant us remission for all our transgressions."

(*As one, the other old men sweep their shawls over their heads and begin the ancient recital of their sins. They all face the Ark, standing in their places, bending and twisting at the knees and beating upon their breasts with the clenched fists of their right hands. They all pray individually, lifting their voices in a wailing of the spirit.* ARTHUR *remains silent*)

ALL

"For the sin which we have committed before thee under compulsion, or of our own will;

And for the sin which we have committed before thee in hardening of the heart!
For the sin which we have committed before thee unknowingly":

ZITORSKY
"And for the sin which we have committed before thee with utterance of the lips."

FOREMAN
"For the sin which we have committed before thee by unchastity";

SCHLISSEL
"For the sin which we have committed before thee by scoffing";

HARRIS
"For the sin which we have committed before thee by slander;
And for the sin which we have committed before thee by the stretched-forth neck of pride":
(*It is a deadly serious business, this gaunt confessional. The spectacle of the eight men, cloaked in white, crying out into the air the long series of their sins and their pleas for remission, has a suggestion of the fearsome barbarism of the early Hebrews. They stand, eyes closed, and in the fervor of communication with God, their faces pained with penitence. The last of the old men,* HARRIS, *finally cries out the last lines of supplication, his thin voice all alone in the hush of the synagogue*)
"And also for the sins for which we are liable to any of the four death penalties inflicted by the court—stoning, burning, beheading, and strangling; for thou art the forgiver of Israel and the pardoner of the tribes of Jeshurun in every generation and beside thee we have no king, who pardoneth and forgiveth."
(*Again, the silence falls over the stage*)

THE CABALIST "Children of men, such as sit in darkness and in the shadow of death, being bound in affliction and iron, He brought them out of darkness, and the shadow of death."

THE OTHERS "Children of men, such as sit in darkness and in the shadow of death, being bound in affliction and iron, He brought them out of darkness, and the shadow of death."

THE CABALIST "Fools because of their transgressions, and because of their iniquities are afflicted."

THE OTHERS "Fools because of their transgressions and because of their iniquities are afflicted."

THE CABALIST "They cry unto The Lord in their trouble, and He saveth them out of their distress."

(*The repetition of the lines has its cumulative effect on* ARTHUR. *His lips begin to move involuntarily, and soon he has joined the others, quietly muttering the words*)

ARTHUR *and* THE OTHERS "They cry unto The Lord in their trouble, and He saveth them out of their distress."

THE CABALIST "Then He is gracious unto him and saith":

ARTHUR *and* THE OTHERS "Then He is gracious unto him and saith":

THE CABALIST "Deliver him from going down to the pit; I have found a ransom."

ARTHUR *and* THE OTHERS "Deliver him from going down to the pit; I have found a ransom."

THE CABALIST Amen.

ARTHUR *and* THE OTHERS Amen.

THE CABALIST Bring the girl in, Mr. Foreman.

(FOREMAN *nods and goes into* THE RABBI'S *office*)

ALPER (*To* SCHLISSEL) I don't like it. Even if the Rabbi comes, there will only be nine of us. I am a traditionalist. Without a quorum of ten, it won't work.

SCHLISSEL (*Muttering*) So what do you want me to do?

(*In* THE RABBI'S *office,* FOREMAN *touches* THE GIRL'S *shoulder, and she starts from her comalike state and looks at him*)

FOREMAN Come. It is time.

(*She nods nervously and sits up. There is a vacuous look about her, the vague, distracted look of the insane*)

THE GIRL (*Quite numbly*) Where are you taking me? My mother is in Rome. They put the torch to her seven sons, and they hold her hostage. (*She rises in obedience to her grandfather's arm as he gently escorts her out of the office into the synagogue proper. All the while she maintains a steady drone of rattling gibberish*) Where were you yesterday? I asked everybody about you. You should have been here. We had a lot of fun. We had a party, and there were thousands of people, Calebites and Bedouins, dancing like gypsies.

(*She suddenly lapses into a sullen silence, staring at the ground, her shoulders jerking involuntarily. The others regard her uneasily*)

THE SEXTON Shall I take the ram's horn out?

THE CABALIST Yes.

(THE SEXTON *produces the horn-shaped trumpet from the base of the pulpit. The front door of the synagogue now opens, and a tall, strapping young* POLICEMAN, *heavy with the authority of his thick blue overcoat, steps one step into the synagogue. He stands in the open doorway, one hand on the latch of the door, his attitude quite brusque—as if he could not possibly get his work done if he had to be polite*)

THE POLICEMAN Is Rabbi Marks here?

(ALPER *throws up his arms in despair. The others alternately stare woodenly at* THE POLICEMAN *or down at the floor.* ARTHUR, *still deeply disturbed, rubs his brow.* THE CABALIST *begins to pray silently, only his lips moving in rapid supplication*)

THE SEXTON No, he's not.

THE POLICEMAN I'm looking for a girl named Evelyn Foreman. Is that the girl?

(*He indicates* THE GIRL)

ALPER (*Moving away, muttering*) Is there any need, Officer, to be so brusque or to stand in an open doorway so that we all chill to our bones?

THE POLICEMAN (*Closing the door behind him*) Sorry.

SCHLISSEL (*To* ZITORSKY) A real cossack, eh? What a brute. He will take us all to the station house and beat us with night sticks.

THE POLICEMAN (*A little more courteously*) A girl named Evelyn Foreman. Her father has put out a call for her. She's missing from her home. He said she might be here with her grandfather. Is there a Mr. David Foreman here?

(*Nobody says anything*)

ALPER You are interrupting a service, Officer.

THE POLICEMAN I'm sorry. Just tell me, is that the girl? I'll call in and tell them we found her.

(SCHLISSEL *suddenly advances on* THE POLICEMAN)

SCHLISSEL First of all, where do you come to walk in here like you were raiding a poolroom? This is a synagogue, you animal. Have a little respect.

THE POLICEMAN All right, all right, I'm sorry. I happen to be Jewish myself.

(ALPER *looks up quickly*)

ALPER You're Jewish? (ALPER *turns slowly to* THE SEXTON) Sexton, our tenth man.

THE SEXTON Alper, are you crazy?

ALPER A fine, strapping Jewish boy. (*To* THE POLICEMAN) Listen, we need a tenth. You'll help us out, won't you?

SCHLISSEL (*Strolling nervously past* ALPER) Alper, what are you doing, for God's sakes?

ALPER We have to have ten men.

SCHLISSEL What kind of prank is this? You are an impossible rogue, do you know that?

ALPER (*Taking* SCHLISSEL *aside*) What are you getting so excited about? He doesn't have to know what it is. We'll tell him it's a wedding. I think it's funny.

SCHLISSEL Well, we will see how funny it is when they take us to the basement of the police station and beat us with their night sticks.

ALPER Night sticks. Really, Schlissel, you are a romantic. (*Advancing on* THE POLICEMAN) I tell you, Officer, it would really help us out if you would stay ten or fifteen minutes. This girl—if you really want to know—is about to be married, and what is going on here is the Ritual of Shriving.

ZITORSKY Shriving?

ALPER A sort of ceremony of purification. It is a ritual not too commonly practiced any more, and I suggest you will find it quite interesting.

HARRIS (*To* SCHLISSEL) What is he talking about?

SCHLISSEL Who knows?

(THE POLICEMAN *opens the door and calls to his colleague outside*)

THE POLICEMAN I'll be out in about ten minutes, Tommy, all right? (*He opens the door wider for* THE RABBI, *who now comes hurrying into the synagogue, still carrying his briefcase*) Hello, Rabbi, how are you?

(THE RABBI *frowns, a little confused at* THE POLICEMAN'S *presence*)

THE RABBI Hello, Officer, what are you doing here?

(*He moves quickly to his office, taking stock of everything as he goes: the seven old men and* ARTHUR *in their white shawls, and* THE GIRL *standing woodenly in the center of the synagogue.* ALPER *and* ZITORSKY *greet him with hellos, at which he nods back*)

THE POLICEMAN They've asked me to make a tenth for the shriving.

THE RABBI (*Frowning as he darts into his office*) Shriving? (*He opens his desk to get out his own large white shawl, unbuttoning his coat as he does. He notes* ALPER, *who has followed him to the doorway*) What is the policeman doing here?

ALPER We needed a tenth.

(*In the synagogue,* THE POLICEMAN *speaks amiably to* ZITORSKY)

THE POLICEMAN This is the girl, isn't it? (ZITORSKY *nods his head bleakly*) What's really going on here?

(*In* THE RABBI'S *office,* THE RABBI *sweeps his large shawl over his shoulders*)

ALPER We have said Al-chait and a prayer of atonement, and we are waiting now just for you.

(THE RABBI *frowns in troubled thought, slips his skullcap on as he slips his fedora off. In the synagogue,* ZITORSKY *shuffles to* SCHLISSEL)

ZITORSKY (*Indicating* THE POLICEMAN *with his head, he mutters*) He knows, he knows.

SCHLISSEL Of course. Did Alper expect to get away with such a collegiate prank?

(*In* THE RABBI'S *office,* THE RABBI *finishes a rapid, silent prayer, standing with his eyes closed. He looks up at* ALPER *now*)

THE RABBI I would rather not take any active role in this exorcism. I am not quite sure of my rabbinical position. But it would please me a great deal to believe once again in a God of dybbuks. (*He walks quickly past* ALPER *out into the synagogue.* ALPER *follows*) Well, we are ten.

(*A silence falls upon the gathered men*)

FOREMAN May God look upon us with the eye of mercy and understanding and may He forgive us if we sin in our earnestness.

THE OTHERS Amen.

THE CABALIST Sexton, light the candles. (THE SEXTON *lights each man's candle.* THE CABALIST *advances slowly to* THE GIRL, *who stands slackly, her body making small occasional jerking movements, apparently in a schizophrenic state.* THE CABALIST *slowly draws a line before* THE GIRL *with the flat of his toe. He speaks quietly*) Dybbuk, I draw this line beyond which you may not come. You may not do harm to anyone in this room. (*The old men shift nervously in their various positions around the synagogue.* THE CABALIST *turns to* THE SEXTON) Open the Ark. (THE SEXTON *moves quickly up to the altar and opens the brown sliding doors of the Ark, exposing the several scrolls within, standing in their handsome velvet coverings.* THE CABALIST *moves slowly back to his original position; he says quietly*—) Dybbuk, you are in the presence of God and His Holy Scrolls. (THE GIRL *gasps*) I plead with you one last time to leave the body of this girl. (*There is no answer*) Then I will invoke the curse of excommunication upon your pitiable soul. Sexton, blow Tekiah. (THE SEXTON *raises the ram's horn to his lips, and the eerie, frightening tones shrill out into the hushed air*) Sexton, blow Shevurim. (*Again,* THE SEXTON *raises the ram's horn and blows a variation of the first hollow tones*) Sexton, blow Teruah. (*A third time,* THE SEXTON *blows a variation of the original tones*) Sexton, blow the Great Tekiah, and, upon the sound of these tones, dybbuk, you will be wrenched from the girl's body and there will be cast upon you the final anathema of excommunication from all the world of the living and from all the world of the dead. Sexton, blow the Great Tekiah.

(*For the fourth time,* THE SEXTON *raises the ram's horn to his lips and blows a quick succession of loud blasts. A silence falls heavily on the gathered men, the notes fading into the air. Nothing happens.* THE GIRL *remains as she was, standing slackly, her hands making involuntary little movements.* FOREMAN'S *head sinks slowly on his chest, and an expression of deep pain covers his face.* THE CABALIST *stares steadily at* THE GIRL. *Suddenly,* ARTHUR *begins to moan softly, and then with swift violence a horrible scream tears out of his throat. He staggers one brief step forward. At the peak of his scream, he falls heavily down on the floor of the synagogue in a complete faint. The echoes of his scream tingle momentarily in the high corners of the air in the synagogue. The others stand petrified for a moment, staring at his slack body on the floor)*

ALPER My God. I think what has happened is that we have exorcised the wrong dybbuk.

(THE POLICEMAN *starts toward* ARTHUR'S *limp body*)

THE POLICEMAN All right, don't crowd around. Let him breathe.

THE CABALIST He will be all right in a moment.

ZITORSKY If I didn't see this with my own eyes, I wouldn't believe it.

THE RABBI Mr. Hirschman, will he be all right?

THE CABALIST Yes.

SCHLISSEL (*With simple devoutness*) Praise be to the Lord, for His compassion is everywhere.

(HARRIS *sinks down onto a chair, exhausted and terrified by the whole experience.* THE RABBI *moves slowly down and stares at* ARTHUR *as* SCHLISSEL, ZITORSKY *and* ALPER *help him to a chair*)

ALPER How are you, my dear fellow?

ARTHUR (*Still in a state of shock*) I don't know.

THE SEXTON (*Coming forward with some wine*) Would you like a sip of wine?

ARTHUR (*Taking the goblet*) Yes, thank you very much. (*Turning to look at* THE GIRL) How is she?

(*Her schizophrenic state is quite obvious.* ARTHUR *turns back, his face furrowed and his eyes closed now in a mask of pain*)

SCHLISSEL Was it a painful experience, my friend?

ARTHUR I don't know. I feel beyond pain. (*Indeed, his hands are visibly trembling as if from cold; his face is rigid and masklike. Words become more difficult to say*) I feel as if I have been reduced to the moment of birth, as if the universe has become one hunger.

(*He seems to be almost on the verge of collapse*)

ALPER A hunger for what?

ARTHUR (*Whispering*) I don't know.

THE CABALIST For life.

(*At these words,* ARTHUR *sinks back into his chair, exhausted*)

ARTHUR Yes, for life. I want to live. (*He opens his eyes and begins to pray quietly*) God of my fathers, you have exorcised all truth as I knew it out of me. You have taken away my reason and definition. Give me then a desire to wake in the morning, a passion for the things of life, a pleasure in work, a purpose to sorrow . . . (*He slowly stands, for a reason unknown even to himself, and turns to regard the slouched figure of* THE GIRL) Give me all of these things in one—give me the ability to love. (*In a hush of the scene, he moves slowly to* THE GIRL *and stands before her crouched slack figure*) Dybbuk, hear me. I will cherish this girl, and give her a home. I will tend to her needs and hold her in my arms when she screams out with your voice. Her soul is mine now—her soul, her charm, her beauty—even you, her insanity, are mine. If God will not exorcise you, dybbuk, I will. (*To* THE GIRL) Evelyn, I will get your coat. We have a lot of things to do this afternoon. (*He turns to the others*) It is not a simple matter to get somebody released from an institution in New York. (*He starts briskly across to* THE RABBI'S *office and pauses at the door*) Officer, why don't you just call in and say you have located the girl and she is being brought to her father. (*To* MR. FOREMAN) You'd better come along with us. Would somebody get my coat? We will need her father's approval. We shall have to stop off at my office and have my secretary draw some papers.

(MR. FOREMAN *has hurriedly gotten* THE GIRL'S *coat,* ARTHUR'S *coat, and his own. In this rather enchanted state, these three drift to the exit door*)

THE POLICEMAN Rabbi, is this all right?

THE RABBI Yes, quite all right.

ARTHUR (*Pausing at the door, bemused, enchanted*) Oh —thank you all. Good-bye.

ALL Good-bye.

ZITORSKY Go in good health.

ALPER Come back and make a tenth for us sometime.

(ARTHUR *smiles and herds* THE GIRL *and* FOREMAN *out of the synagogue. The door closes behind them*)

SCHLISSEL (*Sitting with a deep sigh*) Well, what is one to say? An hour ago, he didn't believe in God; now he's exorcising dybbuks.

ALPER (*Pulling up a chair*) He still doesn't believe in God. He simply wants to love. (ZITORSKY *joins the other two*) And when you stop and think about it, gentlemen, is there any difference? Let us make a supposition . . .

(*As the curtain falls, life as it was slowly returns to the synagogue. The three old men engage in disputation,* THE CABALIST *returns to his isolated studies,* THE RABBI *moves off into his office,* THE SEXTON *finds a chore for himself, and* THE POLICEMAN *begins to button his coat*)

THE CURTAIN FALLS

Lillian Hellman

Toys in the Attic

FOR RICHARD WILBUR

Manufactured in the United States of America by H. Wolff

Toys in the Attic was first presented by Kermit Bloomgarden at the Hudson Theatre, New York City, on February 25, 1960, with the following cast:

(IN ORDER OF APPEARANCE)

CARRIE BERNIERS	Maureen Stapleton
ANNA BERNIERS	Anne Revere
GUS	Charles McRae
ALBERTINE PRINE	Irene Worth
HENRY SIMPSON	Percy Rodriguez
JULIAN BERNIERS	Jason Robards, Jr.
LILY BERNIERS	Rochelle Oliver
TAXI DRIVER	William Hawley
THREE MOVING MEN	Clifford Cothren, Tom Manley, Maurice Ellis

DIRECTED BY Arthur Penn
SETTING AND LIGHTING BY Howard Bay
COSTUMES BY Ruth Morley

Place: The Berniers house in New Orleans.

ACT ONE

SIX P.M. on a summer day.

ACT TWO

EIGHT A.M. the following morning.

ACT THREE

Shortly after.

ACT ONE

Place: The BERNIERS' *living room, the entrance porch to the house, and a small city garden off the porch. The house is solid middle-class of another generation. The furniture is heavy and old. Everything inside and outside is neat, but in need of repairs. The porch has two rocking chairs and is crowded with plants. The garden has a table and chairs that have been painted too often and don't stay together very well. It is a house lived in by poor, clean, orderly people who don't like where they live.*

At rise: ANNA BERNIERS, *carrying her gloves and purse and still wearing her hat, pushes open the blinds of the windows that give on the garden. She lifts a large camellia pot and puts it outside. She pours a glass of water on the plant and moves back into the room to take off her hat.* ANNA *is a nice-looking woman, calm and quiet. She is about forty-two.* CARRIE BERNIERS *appears from the street, climbs the porch steps, and sits down in a porch chair. She is about thirty-eight, still pretty, but the prettiness is wearing thin and tired. She fans herself, rocks back and forth, the chair creaks and sways, and, wearily, she rises and moves to the other chair.*

CARRIE (*As she hears* ANNA *moving about in the kitchen*) That you, Anna?

ANNA (*Her voice*) Just got home.

CARRIE Hot.

ANNA Paper says a storm.

CARRIE I know. I'll take the plants in.

ANNA I just put them out. Let them have a little storm air.

CARRIE I don't like them out in a storm. Worries me. I don't like storms. I don't believe plants do, either.

ANNA (*Appears in the living room with a broom and a dust rag; speaks out toward the porch*) Did you have a hard day?

CARRIE He let me leave the office after lunch. "You're looking a little peaked, Miss Berniers, from the heat." I said I've been looking a little peaked for years in heat, in cold, in rain, when I was young, and now. You mean *you're* hot and want to go home, you faker, I said. Only I said it to myself.

ANNA We had a private sale at the store. Coats. Coats on a day like this. There was a very good bargain, red with black braid. I had my eye on it for you all last winter. But—

CARRIE Oh, I don't need a coat.

ANNA Yes, you do. Did you go to the park? I wanted to, but the sale went so late. Old lady Senlis and old lady Condelet just sat there, looking at everything, even small coats. How can rich people go to a sale on a day like this?

CARRIE I feel sorry for them. For all old ladies. Even rich ones. Money makes them lonely.

ANNA (*Laughs*) Why would that be?

CARRIE Don't you feel sorry for old ladies? You used to.

ANNA When my feet don't hurt and I don't have to sell them coats at a sale. Was it nice in the park?

CARRIE I didn't go to the park. I went to the cemetery.

ANNA (*Stops dusting, sighs*) Everybody still there?

CARRIE I took flowers. It's cool there. Cooler. I was the only person there. Nobody goes to see anybody in summer. Yet those who have passed away must be just as lonely in summer as they are in winter. Sometimes I think we shouldn't have put Mama and Papa at Mount Olive cemetery. Maybe it would have been nicer for them at Mount Great Hope with the new, rich people. What would you think if we don't get buried at Mount Olive with Mama and Papa?

ANNA Any place that's cool.

CARRIE I bought you a small bottle of Eau d'haut Alpine. Cologne water of the high Alps, I guess. (*Holds up a package*) Your weekly present. What did you buy me, may I ask, who shouldn't?

ANNA Jar of candied oranges.

CARRIE Oh, how nice. We'll have them for a savory. Do you know I read in our travel book on England that *they* think a proper savory is an anchovy. Anchovy after dinner. They won't make me eat it. What are you doing?

ANNA Nothing. I'm going to clean.

CARRIE Oh, don't. Sunday's cleaning day. Was this house always so big?

ANNA It grew as people left it.

CARRIE I want to tell you something I've never told you before. I never, ever, liked this house. Not even when we were children. I know *you* did, but I didn't.

ANNA You know I liked it?

CARRIE I don't think Julian ever liked it, either. That's why we used to have our supper out here on the steps. Did you ever know that's why I used to bring Julian out here, even when he was a baby, and we'd have our supper on the steps? I didn't want him to find out about the house. Julian and I. Nice of Mama and Papa to let us, wasn't it? Must have been a great deal of trouble carrying the dishes out here. Mama had an agreeable nature.

ANNA I carried the dishes out.

CARRIE Did you? Yes, so you did. Thank you, Anna. Thank you very much. Did you mind eating with Mama and Papa— (*Points off*) —in that awful oak tomb?

ANNA Yes, I minded.

CARRIE Well, it sure was a nice thing to do. I never knew

you minded. Funny how you can live so close and long and not know things, isn't it?

ANNA Yes, indeed. I called Mr. Shine today. He said he hadn't had an inquiry in months. He said we should reduce the price of the house. I said we would, but there wasn't anything to reduce it to.

CARRIE (*Gets up, goes into the living room*) Oh, somebody'll come along will like it, you'll see.

ANNA Nobody's ever liked this house, nobody's ever going to.

CARRIE You always get mean to the house when something worries you. What's the matter?

ANNA And you always go to the cemetery.

CARRIE (*Opens the waist of her dress*) Just cooler. I so much like the French on the graves. *Un homme brave, mort pour la cité pendant la guerre*— Sounds better in French. A man gallant is so much more than just a gallant man. Nobody in our family's ever been killed in a war. Not Grandpapa, not Papa— Why, don't you think?

ANNA Some people get killed, some people don't.

CARRIE (*Laughs*) Papa always said he was scared to death and ran whenever he could. But Papa said just anything. Julian didn't like it when he said things like that. No little boy would. Papa shouldn't have talked that way.

ANNA Papa's been dead twenty-two years, Carrie. You should have taken it up with him before this.

CARRIE No letter for two weeks. I went to the main post office today, and said I was sure there'd been some confusion. Would they please call the other Berniers and see if a letter was there. And Alfie said, "Carrie, there are no other Berniers in New Orleans. There are some live in Biloxi, Mississippi, with a hardware store, but the central government of the United States does not give money to Louisiana to make calls to Mississippi, although maybe you could change that if you said it was Julian who had written the letter he didn't write." I was angry, but I didn't show it. How do you know it's Julian I am talking about, I said. We're expecting letters from Paris and Rome in reply to inquiries about our forthcoming tour.

(*She stops suddenly, run down*)

ANNA Julian's busy. That's all.

(GUS, *a colored man of about thirty-five, carrying a block of ice, comes up the porch steps*)

GUS You home?

ANNA We're home.

(GUS *goes off toward the kitchen*)

CARRIE (*Goes toward the piano*) I bought a book called *French Lessons in Songs.* I don't believe it. Never been two weeks before in his whole life. (*Softly, slowly*) I telephoned to Chicago and the hotel manager said Julian and Lily had moved months ago. Why didn't Julian tell us that?

ANNA (*Quietly*) I knew. I knew last week. Two letters came back here with address unknown. Carrie, Julian's married, he's moved away, he's got a business to take care of, he's busy. That's all.

CARRIE He's never been too busy to write or phone to us. You know that.

ANNA I know things have changed. That's as it should be.

CARRIE Yes, of course. Yes.

GUS (*Puts his head into the room*) Icebox all on one side. Miss Anna, you all sure need a new icebox. You all ought to treat yourselves.

ANNA You know, Gus, colored people are getting to talk just like white people. Kind of a shame.

GUS Ought to treat yourselves. Get a new little house, new little icebox. No more Julian to worry about. Just yourselves now to treat good.

CARRIE It's true. You getting to talk just like that white trash in my office. Just yourselves now and all that. (*With force*) Well, what do you think? We *are* going to treat ourselves good. We're going to sell this house and never come back. We're going on a great, big, long trip. For a *year,* or five. What do you think of that?

GUS (*To* ANNA) Ought to get yourselves a nice cat. I'll water the yard for you. Where are you going this time?

CARRIE Where we were always going. To Europe.

GUS You told me that last year. And I stopped the ice. And you told me around seven years back when Julian went on his other business trip, and I stopped the ice then— (*He laughs*) When I stop it now?

CARRIE (*Angry, too upset*) Very soon. *Very* soon. You hear me, Gus? *Very* soon. And if you just don't believe me you come around to church Sunday and hear us take a solemn oath right in church. We don't break a solemn oath in church.

GUS That's good. Lot of people do.

CARRIE How dare you, Gus? When I say a solemn oath in church?

ANNA (*To* GUS) There's food in the icebox. Help yourself.

CARRIE Remember, Gus, when Julian and I used to eat out there and you and your sister and brother'd walk past and stare at us, and Julian would go tell Mama we wanted more food, and he'd bring it to you himself?

GUS Yes'm. Came in handy. Just like now.

(*He exits from the porch. He picks up a garden hose and disappears to the rear of the house*)

CARRIE (*Looks at* ANNA) Why did I tell him that about Europe?

ANNA I don't know.

CARRIE Let's get out our travel books this evening and write out all our plans.

ANNA No. Don't let's ever speak about it, until we're ready to go, or think about it, or listen to each other, or tell Gus—I don't want to write things down again.

CARRIE It was you who wanted to wait last time. After the wedding.

ANNA It was you, Carrie.

CARRIE For a very good reason. Could we give them a smaller wedding present? Lily is a very rich girl and the one thing a very rich girl knows about is sterling silver. Her mother gave them ten thousand dollars. What would Lily have thought of us?

ANNA I don't know. I don't think she cares about things like that. Lily was so in love with Julian—

CARRIE Oh, I imagine even in love you take time off to count your silver.

CARRIE (*Softly*) We could still go to Europe this year. Do you want to? How much money have we got? Did you make the deposit this week?

ANNA Twenty-eight hundred and forty-three dollars. No, I didn't have time.

CARRIE (*Quickly*) Oh, it's too hot tonight. Should we treat ourselves and go out for supper? It's been so long since we ate in a restaurant. Let's start doing our French lessons again because we'll need them now for the trip— (*She moves to the piano and plays and sings the next speech*) "*Une chambre pour deux dames.*" Have you one room for two ladies? "*Ah non! Trop chère!*" Oh no! Too expensive! "*Merci, M'sieur. Trop chère.*" We'll stay in Paris, of course, for just as long as we want. Then we'll go to Strasbourg, have the famous pâté, and put flowers on the graves of Mama's relatives.

ANNA I'll have the pâté. You put flowers on the graves of Mama's relatives.

CARRIE Remember the night Julian told us about the marriage? He said that night we would all go to Europe together, the way we always planned. Mama would want us to put flowers on the graves in Strasbourg. She would, Anna, and so we must.

ANNA I don't know what the dead would like. Maybe Mama's changed.

CARRIE As soon as we do set a date for departure, I'll have my evening dress fixed. No, I won't. Pink's no good for me now. I've kind of changed color as I got older. You, too. Funny. To change color. *"C'est trop chère, M'sieur."* I don't want to go if we have to say that all the time.

ANNA We've always said it, we always will say it. And why not?

CARRIE I just think it would be better not to go to Europe right now.

ANNA (*Laughs*) We weren't going.

CARRIE Save enough until we can go real right. That won't take long. Maybe just another year.

ANNA A year is a long time—now.

CARRIE If you want to go, just let's get up and go. (*In sudden, false excitement*) Come on. Let's do. I can't tell you how much I want to go— (*Points to the piano*) That and a good piano. Every time there's a wishbone I say I want a good life for Julian, a piano, a trip to Europe. That's all. You know, even if we can't go to Europe we could afford a little trip to Chicago. The coach fares are very cheap—

ANNA I don't think we should run after Julian and Lily and intrude on their lives.

CARRIE Who's doing that? What an unpleasant idea. (*As* ANNA *starts toward the kitchen*) We haven't got twenty-eight hundred and forty-three dollars. I took out a thousand dollars yesterday and sent it to Chicago. I didn't know then that Julian had moved from the hotel. But I am sure they'll forward the money—I signed the wire with love from Anna and Carrie, so he knows it comes from you, too.

ANNA (*Slowly*) I don't think you should have done that.

CARRIE But I knew you would want to send it—

ANNA How do you know what I would want?

CARRIE (*Slowly, hurt*) Shouldn't I know what you want for Julian? (*When* ANNA *does not answer*) I'm sorry our trip will have to wait a little longer, but—

ANNA I'm sorry, too. But it's not the trip. Nor the money. We are interfering, and we told ourselves we wouldn't.

CARRIE But if he needs money—

ANNA Needs it? Julian has a good business. Why do you think he needs it?

CARRIE He's always needed it. (*Quickly*) I mean I don't mean that. I mean it's because the letter didn't come. Anyway, even people with a good business can use a little money— You think I did wrong?

ANNA Yes, I do.

(*She exits*)

CARRIE (*Calling after* ANNA) Julian won't be angry with me. He never has been. I'll just telephone to him and say— (*She makes a half move to the phone*) But there's no place to phone to. Anna, what do you think? (*There is no answer. After a second she moves back to the piano and begins to play. During her speech* ALBERTINE PRINE *and* HENRY SIMPSON *appear in the garden.* ALBERTINE PRINE *is a handsome woman of about forty-five, dressed with elegance, but in no current fashion. She speaks carefully, as if she were not used to talking very much. Her movements are graceful and quiet.* HENRY *is a colored man of about forty-five. He is dressed in a summer suit, but he carries a chauffeur's cap.* MRS. PRINE *stops as she hears the piano*)

ALBERTINE Is the older one Miss Caroline?

HENRY (*Laughs*) They call her Carrie. No. Miss Anna is the older one.

ALBERTINE (*Smiles*) You laugh at me. But I only met them twice before the marriage. Two long dinners. Many savage tribes have a law that people must eat alone, in silence. Sensible, isn't it? (*She moves toward the porch steps, then stops*) Perhaps it would be best if you went in. I'm not good at seeing people any more, and there will be much chatter. (*He doesn't answer her. She laughs*) Very well. But I am sure it's hot in there. Would you tell them I'm out here?

HENRY (*Gently*) *You* have come to call on *them.*

ALBERTINE Nice to live this close to the river. I still like it down here. Soggy and steaming. The flowers aren't strong enough to cover the river smells. That's the way it should be. Very vain of flowers to compete with the Mississippi. My grandmother lived on this street when I was a little girl, and I liked it then. I used to pretend I slept under the river, and had a secret morning door up into this street. What are you holding?

HENRY A chauffeur's cap.

ALBERTINE You win many small battles. Never mind. Wear it if you must. Put it on now and say I am here.

HENRY No. Just go and ring the bell.

(*She smiles and moves up the porch steps.* ANNA *comes back into the room, dressed in an apron and carrying a tray*)

ANNA (*To* CARRIE) I'm making jambalaya for you.

CARRIE Isn't that nice?

(*The bell rings.* CARRIE *jumps and runs to the door*)

ALBERTINE (*To* CARRIE) Hello, Miss Anna.

CARRIE (*Amazed*) Mrs. Prine. Mrs. Prine. Do come in. (*She moves ahead of* ALBERTINE, *calling*) Mrs. Prine is here. Isn't that nice?

ANNA (*Moves forward*) Mrs. Prine, it's gracious of you to come. We should have come to call on you.

CARRIE (*Flustered*) We're relatives now, after all. We did phone, three times. But, of course, you never got the messages.

ALBERTINE (*To* CARRIE) Yes, I did get them, Miss Anna.

ANNA *I* am Anna.

ALBERTINE Forgive me.

ANNA (*Turns to* CARRIE) And this is Carrie. Close your dress.

CARRIE Oh, my goodness. (*She turns away and nervously buttons her dress*) You must forgive me—

ANNA How are you, Mrs. Prine? Are you spending the summer across the lake?

ALBERTINE No. I've closed the lake house. Now that Lily is married, I stay right here in summer. I don't like the country.

CARRIE Not like the country. My. I never heard anybody say a thing like that before. It takes courage to just up and say you don't like the country Everybody likes the country.

ALBERTINE Do they? I see so few people.

ANNA (*Quickly*) You must be lonely without Lily.

ALBERTINE No.

CARRIE Oh. Goodness.

ALBERTINE I've come at your supper time—

ANNA And we'd like to share it with you.

CARRIE Oh, please do stay. I'll just go and primp myself—

ALBERTINE No, thank you. I eat at midnight. It's my bad habit to live at night and sleep the days away.

CARRIE Lily said that— Well, she just said that.

ALBERTINE I suppose it was hard on a child, a young girl, not to have her mother available during the day. But perhaps it was just as well. What time do you expect Lily and Julian?

CARRIE Expect them? Expect them? We haven't heard for seventeen days—

ALBERTINE Lily left a message that they'd be here tonight. I came to say—

ANNA (*As* CARRIE *turns to her*) They'd be *here* tonight? We've had no word, Mrs. Prine.

CARRIE (*In great excitement*) The Chicago train comes in at seven. Have we time to get to the station? I'll phone. It's never on time. I'll get dressed right away. Are there enough shrimps? Is there crayfish bisque left? We can still buy some wine—Get dressed, Anna—

ALBERTINE Miss Carrie, they are not on the Chicago train.

CARRIE You said you had a message—

ALBERTINE Yes, Lily spoke with Henry on the phone. She said they would be coming here tonight.

CARRIE Then they *must* be on that train—

ALBERTINE No. The call was not from Chicago. The call came from here.

CARRIE (*Carefully*) It could not have come from here.

ALBERTINE I am sure of it, Miss Carrie, because I saw Lily two nights ago.

CARRIE Saw her? Here? Here? (*After a second*) What did Lily say?

ALBERTINE I didn't speak to her. She was moving back and forth in front of the house as if she wished to come in and didn't wish to come in.

CARRIE (*After a pause*) You saw your daughter, after a whole year, walking in front of your house and you didn't speak to her? I don't understand, Mrs. Prine.

ALBERTINE That's quite all right.

ANNA (*Softly*) But we need to understand.

ALBERTINE (*Turns her head, looks at* CARRIE *and then at* ANNA) Strange. Sometimes I can't tell which of you is speaking. (*To* CARRIE) Your manner, Miss Carrie, is so, well, so Southern. And then, suddenly, you are saying what I had thought Miss Anna might say. It is as if you had exchanged faces, back and forth, forth and back.

CARRIE (*Sharply*) Did you see Julian?

ALBERTINE There. That's what I mean. No. Julian was not with Lily. I have simply had a mesage saying they would be here this evening. I have told you all I know.

CARRIE (*To* ANNA) What should we do? (*To* ALBERTINE) What are you going to do?

ALBERTINE I will go home now and ask you to tell Lily

that I will come again in the morning. Please tell them that the house is mostly closed up, but by tomorrow I can make them comfortable.

CARRIE Oh, no. Julian will want to be here.

ALBERTINE Ah, I am sure they prefer to stay here, but—

ANNA There must be a good reason why Julian hasn't told us he is in town. If we seem upset, Mrs. Prine, it is because we are not accustomed to—

ALBERTINE —daughters who walk in the night and mothers who do not speak to daughters who walk in the night. I really don't know why Lily didn't come in to me, nor why I didn't ask her. Good night. Thank you. (*She moves out, followed by* ANNA, *followed by a dazed* CARRIE. HENRY *is waiting in the garden.* ALBERTINE *moves toward him, then turns toward the porch*) I think you have met Henry Simpson. Miss Anna and Miss Carrie Berniers, Henry.

HENRY Good evening.

(ALBERTINE *takes his arm and they exit*)

CARRIE (*Softly*) Is *that* the man Lily calls Henry? *That* man was there in a white coat when we went for dinner, but I didn't know that was the Henry. You mean he's a nigger? I never heard anybody introduce a nigger before. I'm sorry I didn't say something. I never think of things in time. (*She turns, sees* ANNA *has gone back to the living room, and moves to join her*) That man Lily called Henry is a nigger. Is he a chauffeur? What is he? Last time, he was a butler. Introduces us to a nigger— (*Sits down, desperate*) Do you believe that strange woman? Do you believe they're in town?

ANNA Maybe Lily's pregnant. They arrived and wanted to go to a doctor first so they could tell us the good news. I'm sure something like that—

CARRIE She's not pregnant.

ANNA How do you know?

CARRIE Girls like Lily don't have babies right away. Too

full of good times the first year of marriage, I can tell you that.

ANNA What do you know about the first year of marriage?

CARRIE I just know.

ANNA How? From books you don't read any more?

CARRIE You're saying that again. Teasing me again. No, I don't read much any more, and I don't play the piano, or put ice on my face, or walk for wild flowers— (*Very loudly, as if she were going to cry*) I get tired now after work and that terrible man. All I want to do is have a little something to eat and play casino, and— Don't you like to play casino with me, is that what you're saying?

ANNA Not every night. I like to read—

CARRIE You don't ever have to play casino again. Read whenever you like, but don't nag me about it. You used to do it with Julian, too. Some people read and some people learn other ways— I think she's crazy, that Mrs. Prine. And you know what? I don't believe they're in New Orleans without coming here. (*Lamely*) Do you? What do you think?

ANNA I think it's happened again. And he feels bad and doesn't want to tell us.

CARRIE Well, that's natural enough. Who wants to come home and say they've failed? What do you mean? *What's* happened again?

ANNA (*Gently*) You understand me.

(*She rises and exits toward the kitchen*)

CARRIE I don't think it's nice of us to guess this way. We don't know anything, and yet here we are— (*But* ANNA *has left the room*) A great many men take a long time to find themselves. And a lot of *good* business men just aren't worth bowing to. Goodness. Look at the people in my office. Dull, stupid—ugly, too. I don't like ugly people. I just can't help it, and I'm not ashamed any more to say it. (ANNA *comes back carrying a tray of food*) Are you going to *eat?*

ANNA I always have. I think it's best to continue.

CARRIE You're just as worried and nervous as I am. You always talk cold when you get nervous. Anna. Please. When he comes, don't be cold. Please. It will hurt him—

ANNA Why do you so often make it seem as if I had always been severe and unloving? I don't think it's true.

CARRIE I don't believe I do that. It's you who gave him everything, long before I was old enough to help. But sometimes you go away from us both, and, well, it worries Julian when you do that.

ANNA (*Takes a bankbook from her pocket*) Here is the savings bankbook. Give it to him.

CARRIE (*Deeply pleased*) Oh, thank you. I'll give it to him when we're alone and Lily doesn't see. (ANNA *sits at the table, and puts food on* CARRIE'S *plate.* CARRIE *moves about*) It's only for a short time. We'll have it back. After all, in a sense, this money is his. We lent it to him and he paid us back. This is the very money he paid us back, Anna. So, in a sense, its his.

ANNA Do come and eat.

CARRIE You're thinking that what I just said is foolish. You're thinking that you never understood where he got the money to pay for your operation—

ANNA You know very well where he got it: He played in a dangerous poker game.

CARRIE I'm not so sure. I often wondered—

ANNA The shrimps are getting cold.
(*She begins to eat*)

CARRIE I can't eat. I don't know how you can. (*Sighs, then brightens*) You know, it sounds strange, but I am positive he will make a fortune someday.

ANNA A fortune isn't necessary. A job is.

CARRIE All those self-made men at the office. Like Mr. Barrett. No interest in anything. Making fun of opera and poetry and women. Mean, too, ever since he tried to put his hands on me years ago. Pig. Things can go wrong for a long time and then suddenly everything in a man's life clears up— Have you a headache, Anna? Do your eyes worry you tonight? Can I get you something?

ANNA I haven't a headache. And if I had I wouldn't know the remedy. A prescription put up fresh each time Julian fails.

CARRIE Oh, don't be sad. I'm not. I feel cheerful. Place and people and time make things go wrong, and then all of a sudden— (*There is the offstage noise of a car. She jumps up, runs to the window, stares out, nods at what she sees. Slowly, suddenly cool and calm, she turns back to* ANNA) I am going to wait on the porch. Please don't show what you feel. Welcome him as he should always be welcomed in this, his house.

(*She moves to the porch.* JULIAN'S *voice is heard offstage*)

JULIAN Is that my Carrie on the porch?

CARRIE (*Laughs with enormous pleasure*) Yes, that's your Carrie on the porch. I can still jump. Shall I jump and you will catch me? (*In the middle of her speech, as she begins a jump movement, a* TAXI DRIVER *appears carrying a very large number of packages and valises*) Oh. (JULIAN *and* LILY BERNIERS *appear. He is a handsome, tall man of about thirty-four.* LILY *is a frail, pretty girl of about twenty-one. She moves behind him.* JULIAN'S *arms and hands are filled with valises and packages*)

JULIAN Don't jump. I have no hands to catch you. (*Grinning, he moves up the steps as* CARRIE *waits for him. He puts the valises down and takes her in his arms, lifting her from the ground*) Darling Carrie-Pie.

CARRIE Julian.

(*He kisses her, puts her down. She clings to him a minute and follows him as he moves quickly into the house and toward* ANNA. LILLY *follows* CARRIE. ANNA *stands waiting for him, smiling warmly. When he kisses* ANNA *it is quite different—no less warm, but different—from his greeting to* CARRIE. ANNA *moves away from him and toward* LILY)

ANNA My dear Lily, how good to see you.

CARRIE (*To* JULIAN) One year and six days. (*As she hears* ANNA'S *greeting to* LILY) Lily! I didn't see you. (*Kisses* LILY. LILY *smiles and kisses her*) Forgive me. One year and six days. I was so excited that I didn't see you—

JULIAN (*To the* TAXI DRIVER, *who comes in carrying the valises and packages*) Bring them in. Bring them in. I'm hungry, Anna. Hungry for your cooking. Not a good restaurant in Chicago. Would *not* know a red pepper if they saw one.

CARRIE There's crayfish in the icebox, thank God, and jambalaya on the table—

JULIAN Then go and get them. I'm weak. *Very,* very weak.

ANNA (*Laughs*) You don't look it.

CARRIE Sit down, dear—

(*She starts to run off to the kitchen. Before she does,* JULIAN *hands the* TAXI DRIVER *several bills. She peers at them.* JULIAN *laughs*)

JULIAN Don't be nosey. He deserves them. No porters at the station because the train came in early.

TAXI DRIVER (*Stares at the bills*) Thank you, sir. Thank you— (*Puzzled*) The train came in—

JULIAN (*Quickly*) All right. Good-bye. (*Gives him another bill*) Buy your baby something from me.

TAXI DRIVER Thank you, sir. But I have to say in frank and complete honesty that I haven't got a baby.

JULIAN (*Gives him another bill*) Then take this and get one and name it Julian.

(*The* TAXI DRIVER *laughs and exits*)

ANNA You still say that to waiters and taxi drivers? That

means you've been in a poker game. And what train came in early?

CARRIE (*Very quickly*) Anna, go get the crayfish. And make fresh, hot coffee. Lily, shall I take you to your room? Oh, my no, it needs cleaning. Well, just sit down. Anna, get the crayfish for Julian.

ANNA There are no crayfish.

JULIAN (*Is eating the dinner on the table with great pleasure*) We'll go out later and have them with champagne. (*To* ANNA) The same dress?

ANNA The same dress. You look tired, Lily. Can I get you something?

LILY I am tired. Julian doesn't like me to be tired.

JULIAN I don't like anybody to be tired. But it was a long trip, darling— (*As if he is prompting her*) Wasn't it a long trip, Lily?

LILY Yes. When it happened. It was long when it happened.

JULIAN Lily.

LILY (*Quickly, to* CARRIE *and* ANNA) It was a very long trip. Longer than going.

ANNA The wedding day. My how it rained. And Julian put his new coat round your pretty dress and the drawing room was full of flowers. Remember?

LILY (*Smiling, suddenly uplifted, happy*) Did it rain? I don't remember. It was all days to me: Cold and hot days, fog and light, and I was on a high hill running down with the top of me, and flying with the left of me, and singing with the right of me— (*Softly, as if she is worn out*) I was doing everything nice anybody had ever done nice.

ANNA (*Touched*) Nice.

LILY What were you doing when I was doing all that, Julian?

JULIAN (*His mouth very full*) Being my kind of happy.

LILY You're always happy.

JULIAN I am glad you think that, darling.

ANNA You've given us no news. How is the shoe factory?

JULIAN What shoe factory?

(*There is a long silence. He is grinning and eating.* ANNA *moves toward the window, and takes in a plant.* CARRIE, *standing behind* JULIAN, *holds up her hand in an attempt to stop* ANNA'S *questions.* ANNA *sees it and ignores it*)

ANNA (*Carefully*) The shoe factory that you bought in Chicago.

JULIAN Oh, *that* shoe factory. It's gone.

ANNA Don't be flip with me, Julian.

CARRIE (*Gesturing wildly*) He's not. He's just trying to explain—

JULIAN (*Turns, sees* CARRIE, *laughs, catches the gesturing hand*) No, I'm not. I'm not trying to explain anything. (*To* ANNA) I was being flip. I forget that you worry about the money I lose.

ANNA It's not the money— It's that you don't seem to care. And the money was—

JULIAN Lily's money.

LILY My money? Doesn't matter about my money. I don't want money.

CARRIE (*To* LILY) You mustn't worry about it. Not worth it.

LILY I'm not worried about money, Miss Carrie.

CARRIE I suppose rich people always worry about money. People like us have to learn there are more important things.

LILY I said I wasn't worried about money, Miss Carrie.

CARRIE Well, you mustn't.

JULIAN (*To* ANNA) The factory was a crooked sell. The machinery wasn't any good. I didn't know anything about shoe machinery and I never should have thought I did. Man who sold it to me faked the books. That's all.

CARRIE (*Softly*) That could happen to anybody.

JULIAN (*Laughs*) No. Not to anybody. Just me.

CARRIE That's not true. And you mustn't ever believe it.

JULIAN Darling Carrie. Hiding her hopes that I would come home with Chicago over my shoulder, dressed in pure gold, bringing candied oranges to hang in your hair. Well, that's just what I've done. Your hair don't look nice, Carrie-Pie.

ANNA (*Rises, crosses to the pile of dishes to carry them out*) We can help you.

CARRIE Yes, indeed we can. Julian, come in the kitchen and help me wash the dishes.

JULIAN No, ma'am. And you're never going to wash dishes again.

ANNA I don't wish to ask questions that you might not like, Julian. But it's uncomfortable this way. Your mother was here, Lily. She said she had seen you, had a message from you. She said she would come back tomorrow. (*To* JULIAN, *who has turned to stare at* LILY) So this is not your first night in town. You need not explain, but I thought we should.

JULIAN We've been in New Orleans for a week, at the hotel. I had a good reason for that. It was no neglect of you. I even came by and stared in at you— (*Points outside*) —the first hour back. You were playing casino and Anna was yawning. You look tired, both of you. You need a long, long good time. (*To* ANNA) This time, no need to be sad. I used to tell you: never was any good; never came out anywhere.

ANNA I am sad that you think it all so easy, so unimportant, so—"Never came out anywhere." I guess not, although I don't think those words mean very much.

CARRIE (*To* ANNA, *in a voice used once before*) I won't have that kind of talk. This is a happy, joyous night. Julian is home and that's all we need to know. It's a happy, joyous night.

(ANNA *exits*)

LILY (*To* JULIAN) I didn't see my mother, I didn't go

in. And I only sent the message today. I knew we'd arrive here, anyway, so— (*Softly, when there is no answer*) —I disobeyed you. But not much. Have I done harm?

JULIAN No.

(CARRIE, *listening, pretending she isn't, is idly playing on the piano with one hand*)

LILY I know you told me not to see anybody. But you didn't tell me why or anything. You just kept leaving the hotel. I want to see my mother. I want to talk with my mother.

JULIAN (*Smiles*) I'm glad to hear that. I've never heard you want that before.

LILY Are you angry with me?

JULIAN (*Smiles at her, shakes his head, moves away*) Carrie, stop that awful sound, darling. Just wait for the good piano—

CARRIE (*Laughs*) No, I'd only find out I couldn't really play.

(JULIAN *has moved out to porch and is hauling in valises.* LILY *rises and follows him*)

JULIAN (*Calling to* CARRIE) You all been to the opera?

CARRIE No. We'll wait until Europe.

JULIAN (*Laughs*) Still talking about Europe?

CARRIE Oh, we'll go someday. You'll see.

JULIAN (*Bringing in valises*) Someday soon?

(*He goes out again for more*)

CARRIE In a few years. Plenty of time. We're not that old.

(*She moves quickly out of the room*)

JULIAN Yes, you are. Old enough to have fun. Have to crowd it in now, Carrie, both of you. Crowd it in fast. (*Smiling at* LILY) You, too. Twenty-one is very, very old.

LILY (*She has followed him to the porch*) Tell me you're not angry with me.

JULIAN (*His arms heavy with valises*) I am not angry

with you. Have I ever been angry with you? Why do you ask me that so often?

LILY (*As she steps aside*) Julian, who is the lady you talked to on the train?

JULIAN (*Too lightly*) Which lady?—I talk to everybody.

LILY The not such a young lady with the sad face.

JULIAN Most ladies on trains are not so young and have sad faces. I often wondered why. (*He tries to pass her*) Move, darling.

LILY The one you were with today and yesterday and—

JULIAN (*Turns, stares at her*) Where did you see me?

LILY I don't know. Just on the street. In front of the hotel—

JULIAN No, you didn't.

LILY No, I didn't. That's the first lie I ever told you, Julian.

JULIAN Then it's one more than I ever told you.

(*Carrying the valises, he moves into the living room.* LILY *follows him*)

LILY I saw you in Audubon Park. On a bench. By the ducks.

JULIAN Have you told anybody?

LILY No.

JULIAN Don't. The lady would be in trouble. And so would we.

LILY And in that little restaurant. At a table—

JULIAN Oh, Lily.

LILY I didn't mean to walk after you, to follow you. But I was so lonely in the hotel room, locked up the way you asked me to be.

JULIAN All right, darling, all right. Don't follow me, Lily, ever again. That's not the way to be married. (LILY *hesitates, as if to say something, then exits*) Hey, everybody. Come and get your presents. Hey, where is everybody?

CARRIE (*Appears in the garden, runs up the porch, speaks*

in a whisper) Julian. I want to speak to you. Come here.

JULIAN Can't. You come here.

CARRIE Sssssh. (*He comes to the porch. She sits down on the porch steps*) Come here. I've got a nice secret. And this is where we always told nice secrets.

JULIAN You come here. *I* got nice secrets. Where's Anna? Anna!

CARRIE Ssh. Ssh.

JULIAN (*Sits beside her*) What's the matter with you?

CARRIE (*Gives him the savings bankbook*) No need for Lily to see. You'll just tell her it's yours. More than twenty-eight hundred dollars. And we don't need any of it, not any of it, so don't say anything— (*He takes her hands, kisses them. She is very moved. Softly, embarrassed*) Don't say anything, please. And if that isn't enough, we can manage other things, too.

JULIAN (*Stares at the book, then rises and calls out*) Anna!

CARRIE Anna doesn't want any thanks—

(ANNA *comes into the room*)

JULIAN (*Enters the room, holds out the bankbook*) God bless you. All my life it's been this way.

ANNA (*Smiles*) You are our life. It is we who should thank you.

(*He takes her in his arms*)

JULIAN How many, many times?

CARRIE (*Comes into the room*) You paid it back, always.

JULIAN You know I didn't. But this time I will.

CARRIE Of course you will. But Lily doesn't have to know about all this— So ssh.

JULIAN Stop ssshing me and come here and sit down and stop talking. (*He puts* CARRIE *in a chair and motions to* ANNA *to be seated. Then he leans down to unwrap the boxes and open the valises. The boxes are dressmaker boxes, and he pulls from them two fancy evening dresses.*

They are too grand for anything less than a ball. CARRIE *leans forward, stares at them*) For a ball. Wear them the second time at the opera, if you like. But I don't think dresses like these should be worn twice in the same city, do you? Everybody in Paris will talk, and we can't have that. (*He opens another box*) Maybe you can wear them again when you get to Strasbourg. (*Points his finger at* CARRIE) Not to the cemetery. I bet the opera house there is drafty— (*He has taken out two fur pieces and arranged them over the dresses*) No, No. I've got things mixed up. (*He begins to fumble in another box*) Or so the lady said. The furs are for breakfast or something. (*He is now holding up two fur-trimmed opera coats. They are royal in feeling*) *These* are for the dresses. And maybe they can be worn the second time. (*He moves to arrange them over* ANNA *and* CARRIE. CARRIE'S *is much too large and she looks drowned. He points to the other boxes and valises*) Suits for traveling. Dresses for informal evenings, whatever that is. (*Pulls out frothy, very youthful negligees*) For flirtations on Italian terraces. (*Drapes them over* ANNA *and* CARRIE. *He goes to* CARRIE *with a large rather flashy necklace*) Garnets. Your birthstone. Next time, pearls. (*He drapes over* ANNA'S *arm a large gold mesh bag*) Remember when old lady Senlis used to come along swinging her gold mesh bag, and your eyes would pop out wondering what was in it? Look and see what's in this one.

ANNA (*Softly*) What is all this, Julian?

JULIAN It is that we're rich. Just open your gold mesh bag with diamond initials—Anna, *diamond* initials—and see what's inside.

CARRIE (*Loud, nervous giggle*) The only thing could be, is a certificate to an insane asylum.

JULIAN (*Takes an envelope from the purse*) You're wrong. A certificate to a boat called the *Ottavia,* sailing day after tomorrow. Two rooms, one of them a parlor. Think of that, a parlor on a boat. (*He takes the envelope to* CARRIE) Look at it, look at it. Of course, we had always planned to go together. But I won't be able to go with you, darling, not this time, big business here, and all that. But we'll join you in a few months—

CARRIE (*Dully*) We'll wait for you.

JULIAN No, you won't. No more waiting for anything.

ANNA (*Softly*) Where does all this come from, Julian?

JULIAN All over town. I just went in places and said bring out the best for two pretty ladies who are on their way. On their way.

ANNA You know what I mean.

JULIAN I know what you mean. They were bought with my money. Mine. Yours. Ours. We're rich. How do you like that, how do you like it?

CARRIE We'll like it fine—when it happens. (*Giggles*) Rich. Us!

JULIAN What are you doing?

CARRIE Trying to make a neat package.

JULIAN Stop it. (*When she doesn't*) I said to stop it. Nothing's going back this time. Listen to me. Now listen to me. We're rich. (LILY *comes into the room. She is in her slip and is carrying a hairbrush. He smiles at her*) Aren't we rich?

LILY Mama's rich, I guess.

JULIAN No, us, us. I've been telling you for a week.

LILY There are three men at the back door. From a trucking company—

JULIAN Tell them to bring them in, darling. (*She exits*) Right in here. Now you're going to see something.

CARRIE (*Stares at the boat tickets*) Are these real boat tickets? I mean, stamped and bought?

JULIAN Bought and stamped. Look. It's going to be this way. The first money is for us to have things. Have fun. After that, I promise you, we'll invest. And like all people with money, we'll make more and more and more until we get sick from it. Rich people get sick more than we do. Maybe from worry.

ANNA Poor people, too. Like me, right now. (*Very sharply*) Where did you get this money, Julian?

CARRIE Oh, now don't start that tone. You know very well he's been in a poker game.

JULIAN No, she doesn't know that, and you don't either. (*Two* MOVING MEN *appear, carrying a fancy, highly carved spinet. There is a big sign on the spinet lettered* CARRIE) Come in. Just put it down. (*Motions to* CARRIE) By that lady.

(*The* MEN *carry the spinet to* CARRIE *and place it near her*)

CARRIE My God.

(*Another* MOVING MAN *comes in wheeling a large refrigerator on a dolly. The first two* MEN *move to help him*)

JULIAN And put that by this lady (*He motions toward* ANNA. *They wheel the refrigerator and place it almost in front of* ANNA. LILY *comes back into the room*) Good. (*He pulls out several large bills*) Thank you. Buy the babies something from me. (*To the head* MOVING MAN) Name the next one Julian.

MOVING MAN There ain't going to be no next one. Thank you.

(*They exit*)

LILY Why do you always say that? We'll name our son Julian. Don't you believe—

JULIAN (*Laughs*) Insurance. That's all.

CARRIE (*To* LILY) You're in your slip. In front of men.

JULIAN Can't harm them.

CARRIE I never heard of such a thing. Answering the door in your underwear. Don't you mind?

JULIAN I mind that you haven't looked at your piano. Think, Carrie, a fine new piano, what you always wanted, right in front of you— Play it. Play it for me, Carrie, the way we used to always say.

(*She puts out her hand, touches a note, takes her hand away and puts it over her face*)

JULIAN (*Softly, smiling*) I know. Take your time.

ANNA What is all this? Answer me, please, Julian.

JULIAN I'm going to tell you all about it someday soon. I can't now. But I'll tell you this much, I didn't play poker. All I did was sell some real estate.

ANNA You never owned any real estate.

JULIAN No. But I do now, see?

ANNA No, I don't see. I don't see at all.

JULIAN Once I liked somebody and they liked me, and she thought I was kind to her. So years go by and she hears about a good thing, and gives me the tip on it. And the tip works. Boy, how it worked. Now let it go. I'll tell you soon, but in the meantime I give my word because she could be in bad trouble. Now stop worrying, and sit back— (*He guides* ANNA'S *hand to refrigerator door, opens it, pulls an envelope from it*) I finished the deal and collected the money at two o'clock today. At two-eighteen, I rang the bells of Mr. Maxwell Shine. And so here's the mortgage to the house. (*Kneels; softly*) Look, Anna, first time in our lives, first time in our father's life. You have a house, without worry or asking him to wait. Remember when I was a kid and the time you took me with you and you made me tell Mr. Shine how I wouldn't have anyplace to live unless— Christ God, how I hated— Do you remember?

ANNA I remember.

JULIAN Well, there'll never be such things to say again. Not for any of us. (*He rises and shouts*) Not ever, ever. (*To* CARRIE) I wrote your Mr. Barrett a letter last night. I wrote it three times. "Your petty angers, the silk stockings at Christmas that were always cheaper ɪt salary. Miss Caroline Berniers will not re- ɪrk." (CARRIE *rises, makes a sound in her* ɴds *staring at him. He turns to* ANNA) For ɪ wrote that Miss Anna Berniers was resigning ɪ coat department because she was leaving for ɴded European tour. (*He sits down.* ANNA *lifts* ad *and stares at him. There is a long silence*)

Say something.

ANNA I can't say something.

JULIAN I know, I know. All came so fast. Well, we don't have to say things to each other, never did. Just sit back and have fun. That's all I want. (*To* LILY) And for you— Give me the wedding ring. (*Sharply she pulls back from him*) Give it to me. (*He takes the ring from her finger*) Twenty dollars in a pawnshop, and I polished it, and prayed you wouldn't mind, or say anything. (*He takes from his pocket, and puts on her finger, a very large diamond ring*) With this, I you wed again, and forever.

LILY Please give me my ring.

JULIAN (*Now he holds up her hand so that she can see her new diamond ring*) Look, darling, look at it. Superstitious? (*He looks at* LILY, *then at* CARRIE, *then at* ANNA) Please don't cry or look it, all of you. (*He takes an envelope from his pocket, goes to each of them as he speaks, lets them look into the envelope*) One hundred and fifty thousand dollars, less peanuts— (*Motions to the packages*) —for this. Seventy-five thousand for my partner, seventy-five thousand for me. My lawyer said I shouldn't carry all that cash around, rich people don't carry cash, not more than ten or twenty dollars, so other people pay the bills. But I said I'll carry this, I like it— Hey, did you hear—my lawyer. *I've* got a *lawyer*. What do you think of that? (CARRIE *has paid little attention to the money in the envelope, but* ANNA *is staring at it*) Ain't counterfeit. Twenty, five thousand dollar bills; fifty, one thousand dollar bills— You'll believe it all by tomorrow. Big, successful Julian, the way you wanted me. The man who was never good at anything except living on his sisters, and losing his wife's money. I never minded failure much, you minded. But you know what? I like things this way: Making bargains, talking big— I don't take my hat off in elevators any more— (*Laughs with great pleasure and picks up a large package*) Now to *important* business. Last night I drew up a budget list, you know, the way we used to. Only where we put carfare for the week, I put champagne, and where we put lunch money, sixty cents each, I put caviar. You'll like caviar.

CARRIE I hate caviar. The one time I ever ate it, I hated it. Just hated it.

JULIAN (*Holds up the package*) Champagne. *And* caviar, Carrie-Pie. You'll learn to like it. (*He starts toward the kitchen*) We're going to have a champagne-caviar party just for us. Sit down and play the piano.

(*He exits*)

CARRIE (*Softly*) Since when do you give me orders? (*Very loudly*) I said since when do you give me orders? (ANNA *puts up a hand, as if to quiet her*) I don't believe it all. I don't believe it. (*When* ANNA *doesn't answer her*) We have no jobs. (*To* LILY) What is this all about?

LILY I want my ring. I was married in my ring.

CARRIE I asked you a question, Lily.

LILY I didn't hear you.

CARRIE What is this all about? Where did Julian get this money?

LILY I don't know, ma'am. A lady came to Chicago and phoned him, and he went to see her, and everything changed and he said we were coming here, and she was on the train, and he didn't want me to know. She calls him every night at six o'clock.

CARRIE I'm not talking about women. That's not my business. I'm talking about this— (*She motions around*) Europe day after tomorrow! Has he gone crazy? What does he think we are, fine ladies with maids and secretaries who can move whenever they like? Whore's clothes. I wouldn't be seen in this. Not seen in them. (*Turns on* ANNA) For God's sake take off that stuff. What are you doing?

ANNA (*Who is reading the mortgage document*) Trying to understand.

CARRIE (*In a whisper*) Does it really say—

ANNA Yes. It really says we own this house.

CARRIE This house. This awful house. He's changed. He even talks different. Didn't he know we hated this house, always, always, always.

ANNA You used to tell him how much we liked it, and the garden, and the street, and the memories of Mama and Papa.

CARRIE You know very well I said all that to keep him from being ashamed of the house and what we didn't have—

ANNA (*Hands her the paper*) Well. We've been rewarded.

LILY I want my ring. I was married in my ring. (*She holds up her hand*) This is a vulgar ring.

CARRIE (*Points to a tiny pin she is wearing*) Topaz is my birthstone. How could he forget when he gave me this pin with the first job he ever lost. I even wear it at night—

LILY I want my married ring.

CARRIE You said that before.

(LILY *runs toward the table, picks up the ring. As she does, the phone rings, and she continues the run that will bring her to the phone*)

LILY Hello. (*A slight pause*) No, ma'am. No, he isn't. This is his wife. What is *your* name?

(*She stares at the phone and then hangs up. After a second, she puts on the old ring and, with a violent movement, throws the diamond toward the window. It hits the window and drops.* JULIAN *comes into the room carrying an ice bucket, two bottles of champagne, glasses and two very large jars of caviar*)

JULIAN I heard the phone. Didn't the phone ring?

ANNA (*After a second*) No.

JULIAN (*Pouring*) Now. (*To* CARRIE, *points to the piano*) Why aren't you playing? And you took off— Put the pretty clothes on so I can be proud.

CARRIE (*Sharply*) All of them?

LILY The phone did ring. It was that lady who calls every evening. I told her you weren't here. I don't know why I said it, but I did.

JULIAN I have business with that lady. I've told you that before. I was to meet her this evening. It's not easy for her to call me and I can't call her. Did she say she'd call back tonight? (LILY *shakes her head*) Why did you tell her I wasn't here?

LILY I didn't know I was going to do it. Please forgive me. It wasn't nice.

JULIAN Not nice, wasn't it? You know what I think it wasn't? Respectful. (*He moves toward* CARRIE) Re-spect-ful— Respectful. I don't think I can spell that word. I never used it before. But I like it. (*He hits his chest*) A man. Respect. That's what you always said, success isn't everything but it makes a man stand straight, and you were right. (*He hands a glass of champagne to* ANNA *and offers caviar. He speaks to* CARRIE) You want to know something? I bring you a piano, I ask you to play it for me, you don't. I don't think that's respectful. (*He laughs*) I like that word. (CARRIE *sits down at the piano and begins to play. She fumbles, as if she is thinking of something else, then plays a waltz.* JULIAN *moves to* LILY, *gives her a glass, whirls her around, kisses her hair)* I forgive you, my infant bride. (*He looks at her hand*) Where's your ring?

(ANNA *rises, crosses, and picks up the ring*)

LILY I don't know.

JULIAN You don't know?

ANNA I have it. I was looking at it.

(JULIAN *smiles, kisses* LILY'S *hair. The music stops sharply and he turns to* CARRIE)

JULIAN More, more. It's a party. We're having a party. (*To* ANNA) Dance?

(*He pulls her to her feet, whirls her around, the long evening coat tangled in her legs*)

CARRIE Anna. You look like a fool. Like a real fool.

JULIAN What's the matter? (*Moving to* CARRIE. *He hands her a glass of champagne. Staring at him, she sips it*) Good? (*He spoons out a large amount of caviar, sings*) *Avez-vous les chambres, Monsieur Hotel-keeper? Non, ils ne sont pas trop chères.* Nothing is too expensive now. Send up two pounds *de* caviar *pour* breakfast *pour ma soeur et moi.* (*He leans over her with the caviar*) Now.

(*He forces her mouth open.* JULIAN *laughs*)

CARRIE You're laughing at me. You've never laughed at me before. (*She rises, shrilly*) You're laughing at me.

JULIAN No, I wasn't. I'm just happy. I'm giving a party— (*He looks at* ANNA, *who has her head hung; at* LILY, *who looks sad and tearful*) What's the matter with everybody? (*He drinks his champagne. He pours himself another drink, bolts it, stares at them*) We're not having a very nice party. What's the matter?

CURTAIN

ACT TWO

Early Thursday morning. The spinet and the refrigerator are as they were the night before. ANNA, *in a housedress, is lowering the plants from the window into the garden. On a chair is a large, old-fashioned trunk-type suitcase; near the suitcase are two pairs of shoes.* ANNA *sits down, and begins to polish the shoes with rag and paste.* CARRIE *enters carrying a coffee pot. She is dressed and has on her hat. She sits down and pours herself a cup of coffee.*

CARRIE Is your headache better?

ANNA I didn't have a headache.

CARRIE You said you did.

ANNA No, I didn't.

CARRIE Last night, before you went to bed, you said your eyes were bothering you, you had a headache.

ANNA No.

CARRIE I think everybody's going crazy. I really do. No wonder you can't remember what you said. I don't think I slept an hour. I'd close my eyes, and say I don't believe it, when I get up— (*Points to the spinet, the boxes, etc.*) —that thing, and that, won't be there, and it will be years ago. He stayed out in the garden drinking by himself till late last night. (*Points inside*) Still asleep?

ANNA I suppose so.

CARRIE How could *you* have slept last night? Mama used to say you could sleep through anything.

ANNA Mama believed that lack of sleep was a sign of good breeding. Do you remember the time she said she hadn't slept for two years? (*Points inside*) Yes, I heard Lily, if that's what you mean.

CARRIE She rattled around half the night. She went out, she came back, she went out. She's a very strange girl. I remember thinking that the first time I ever met her. (*Points around the room*) And she doesn't know any more about all this than we do. That's not natural in a good marriage. In a good marriage a man doesn't have secrets from his wife.

ANNA How do you know?

CARRIE It's not natural in a good marriage, I can tell you that.

ANNA We don't know anything about a good marriage or a bad one. I read somewhere that old maids are the true detectives of the human heart. But I don't want to be a detective of other people's hearts. I'm having enough trouble with my own.

CARRIE I know you are. I know you're just as worried as I am. I know that's why you're having headaches again.

ANNA I said I didn't have a headache.

CARRIE I'll get you something for it. Julian pampers Lily as if she were a child. He never treated us that way, always boasted of our good sense.

ANNA He didn't marry us.

CARRIE Nobody wants a child for a wife.

ANNA There's no sense telling your opinions about marriage to me. I don't know anything about it.

(*She gets up, carries a pair of shoes to the valise, wraps them in paper, and packs them*)

CARRIE What are you doing?

ANNA Put your clothes out. I'm going to wash and iron today.

CARRIE What for?

ANNA (*Turns to stare at her*) Europe.

CARRIE We'll miss the eight-thirty streetcar. (*When there is no answer*) We'll miss the eight-thirty streetcar.

(*When there is no answer*) I know what Julian said. But I get the mail before Mr. Barrett, and if Julian did write such a letter I'll just throw it out. You better go down to the store and get somebody to do the same for you. (*Very sharply, when* ANNA *does not answer*) *We have no jobs.* They're not easy to get and we're not young. You told me all my life what that would mean to us. You said that as long as we could work and save a little then we could get sick when we were old, and take care of Julian, and not end as Mama and Papa did.

ANNA Julian has come home rich. We can get sick now.

CARRIE Rich! Do you really believe this foolishness? Julian rich! God knows what he's been up to. God knows when and how it will blow up. Doesn't it worry you?

ANNA Yes. It worries me. But I think we should go to Europe. He wants us to go.

CARRIE What do you mean, he wants us to go? You make it sound as if we're in his way.

ANNA I don't know what I mean.

CARRIE Go to Europe. What are you talking about? What's going to happen when trouble comes if we're not here to take care of it?

ANNA Why do you think trouble will come?

CARRIE Because it always has. You know very well what I mean. Well, you go to Europe and I'll go to work.

ANNA (*Laughs*) All right.

CARRIE If Mr. Samuel Barrett has seen the letter, I'll apologize. Mr. Barrett likes people to apologize. Nineteen years of faithful work matter for something. (*Giggles*) Ho, ho. I'd like to see you in Europe alone.

(LILY *appears from the bedroom. She has on a dress and over the dress she has on a nightgown. She stares at* CARRIE *and* ANNA *as if she didn't know who they were*)

ANNA Morning. (*She rises to pour* LILY *a cup of coffee*) Julian want his breakfast?

LILY I don't know. (*She points to the left side of the room*) He slept in there.

CARRIE Mama and Papa's room.

LILY He thought I was asleep when he went in there, but I wasn't.

CARRIE No, you certainly weren't. You moved around most of the night. Are you dressed or undressed? Well, I'm off to work.

LILY My. It's awfully hot to go to work.

CARRIE Yes. And sometimes it's awfully cold.

(*She exits toward the porch. As she moves out,* MRS. PRINE *appears in the garden.* HENRY *stands outside the garden fence. During the scene between* LILY *and* ALBERTINE, *he will occasionally be seen moving back and forth*)

ALBERTINE Good morning.

CARRIE Good morning.

(CARRIE *hurries off. At the sound of her mother's voice,* LILY *runs to the porch, stares at her mother and runs back into the room*)

LILY Oh. Where are my shoes? (*Stares down at herself, sees that she is barefoot, hestitates*) Oh. (*Runs out again to the porch and down to the garden*) Mama. I don't know why I did that.

(ALBERTINE *moves toward her and they kiss*)

ALBERTINE I come calling much too early. I forget that other people sleep at night.

LILY I didn't.

ALBERTINE I know.

LILY What did Henry tell you?

ALBERTINE That you were out, er, visiting, and wanted to speak with me.

LILY Yes. I didn't want Henry to come and get me. I didn't need his help.

ALBERTINE He said the neighborhood worried him at two o'clock in the morning.

LILY How did he know where I was?

ALBERTINE You told him on the phone.

LILY Did I? I don't remember—I was mean to Henry. Did he tell you that?

ALBERTINE No.

LILY (*After a second*) I'm sorry I spoke that way.

ALBERTINE How are you, Lily? I haven't seen you in a whole year. The garden wing of the house is being cleaned for you. You are very welcome, and I've come to say that to Julian.

LILY Thank you. It's nice that you want us. Do you?

ALBERTINE You are thinner, Lily. Have you been well?

LILY Do you?

ALBERTINE Do I what?

LILY Do you really want me to come home again?

ALBERTINE I'll come later. You must be tired from your —night's exercise.

LILY (*Quickly*) Mama, don't go. Please. I need help. Your help. I'll start at the start and try not to take long and say things nice and clear—

ALBERTINE There's no need. Don't distress yourself. I've guessed your trouble and I've brought you a check. (*She takes a check from her bag and puts it on the garden table*) Will you and Julian come and dine at eight? Then you'll decide if you wish to move in, or, if in this heat, you prefer the lake house. I've always meant to give you the lake house, Lily, and tomorrow we'll go around and have Warkins do the papers. (*When there is no answer*) At eight?

LILY What does Mrs. Warkins look like? Does she speak in a low voice?

ALBERTINE I don't know. I haven't seen her in years, and then only once or twice.

LILY You haven't seen anybody in years, except Henry, of course. How old is Mrs. Warkins?

ALBERTINE I know little about her, Lily. It's bad enough

to know Warkins. I remember her as a tall woman with a sad face. Possibly from being married to a lawyer.

LILY Is she in love with Mr. Warkins?

ALBERTINE (*Smiles, shrugs*) That is a remarkable idea. Thank God I've never been in a position to find out. Let's waste our time saying things like each to his own taste, and shaking our heads in gossip, but let's do it another time.

LILY Please don't smile and shrug, Mama. It always makes me nervous. You are angry because I was mean to Henry last night, and he told you.

ALBERTINE He told me nothing.

LILY *I was mean to Henry*. That was bad of me, wasn't it?

ALBERTINE (*Wearily, softly*) I don't know.

LILY Well, tell him I'm sorry.

ALBERTINE You have been saying you are sorry, in space, for many years.

LILY You *are* angry now.

ALBERTINE Oh, Lily.

LILY I don't know what makes me speak so wrong. All I want is to tell you, and have you help me. But I get things out of order—Mama, I'm in trouble.

ALBERTINE I know Julian lost the factory. Well, perhaps he doesn't belong in a large city. He'll find something here. In the meantime—

(*She picks up the check and hands it to* LILY)

LILY What is it, Mama?

ALBERTINE (*Slowly, too patiently*) I told you. It's a check. A check is for money. Money. It's five thousand dollars. It's yours. Oblige me by not speaking of it again.

LILY Don't be angry with me.

ALBERTINE (*After a second*) Oh, Lily. Something always happens between us.

LILY If I could only speak in order, then I wouldn't—

ALBERTINE Don't fret. Everybody talks too much, too many words, and gets them out of order.

LILY I know you think that. I know you do. That's what makes it so hard. It's that you never talk much, and you look down on people who don't do it very well.

ALBERTINE You said you were in trouble. Do you wish to tell me about it?

LILY You speak so severely, Mama.

ALBERTINE Please, Lily, let us cease this talking about talking. Tell me or do not tell me.

LILY (*Quickly, loudly*) Mama, we're rich.

ALBERTINE Who?

LILY Julian.

ALBERTINE When you say rich, do you mean *money* rich or spiritual rich, or moral rich or—

LILY You're teasing me. Money rich.

ALBERTINE Well, isn't that nice. Julian didn't lose the factory?

LILY Yes, he lost it. We got rich some other way. There were phone calls from a lady and Julian would talk so I couldn't understand, and then we came here, and it all has to do with the lady, I think, and something else—

ALBERTINE (*Very quickly*) Never mind. Never mind. He'll probably tell me. What good news, Lily. I must say I hadn't expected it. Forgive my bringing the check. How impertinent of me to take for granted that Julian needed it. Don't tell him, just tear it up. Tonight we'll have a celebration—if I still know how. Shall we dine at Galatoire's? (*When there is no answer, she stares at* LILY) What trouble are you in?

LILY First we lived in a big hotel in Chicago, and I didn't like it, and didn't have anything to do. Then we moved to a little, poor hotel and I learned to cook in the bathroom, and Julian and I were close together, and he didn't have his friends any more, and he was sad and sweet and often he stayed with me all day, in bed, and we'd read or sleep, and he'd tell me about things. We were never really hungry, but I'd have to watch the meat and give him my share when he wasn't looking because he likes meat, and I was very happy.

ALBERTINE How often the rich like to play at being poor. A rather nasty game, I've always thought. You had only to write me.

LILY It wasn't a game, it wasn't. It was just after he lost all his money in the factory—

ALBERTINE *Your* money in the factory. You like being poor and you're not going to be. Is that the trouble you are in? I can't be sorry for you, Lily. I don't think Julian would have liked the meat game for very long; and neither would you if the shortage had lasted much longer. (*Laughs*) Cheer up. Good fortune isn't as bad as it seems.

LILY You're laughing at me, and you shouldn't. Julian will leave me now.

ALBERTINE Why?

LILY He is different. Things have changed.

ALBERTINE Marriages change from day to day and year to year. All relations between people. Women, of course, have regrets for certain delicate early minutes, but— There is no answer to that.

LILY Did you, Mama? Did you have those regrets?

ALBERTINE I don't remember. I don't think so. Your father and I had very little together. And so we had little to regret.

LILY I don't mean my father.

ALBERTINE (*After a long silence*) I came here because you were in trouble, or so you said. Not because I am. When I come to you for that reason, feel free to say what you wish. Until then, please do not.

LILY Julian couldn't have me last night, and when I cried he said please not to, that— And so I went out and walked and walked. I had never seen that street before. I heard noise way up, and I went in. There were people and a woman stood before them on a box. The people talked about themselves right out loud. One woman had lost a leg but she said it was growing back and she proved it.

(*There is a long pause*)

ALBERTINE My. Are you dozing off?

LILY And a man stood up and said how he used to drink and use a gun. And the lady on the box kept saying, "Truth, truth is the way to life, and the one way, the only way. Open your hearts with this knife and throw them here." (*Throws up her arm*) She had a knife in her hand—

ALBERTINE Do sit down, Lily.

LILY And she kissed the knife—

(*She kisses her hand in imitation*)

ALBERTINE Strange tastes people have. Don't kiss your own hand again, please.

LILY (*Sits down, speaks quietly*) Everybody left and there I was. The woman said, "You want me, child?" And I said, "Could I buy your knife?" "No," she said. "The knife is not for sale." But I wanted it more than I ever wanted anything and, well— (*Smiles, slyly*) —finally, we swapped something— And when it was in my hand, for the first time in my life, I just said everything, and asked. The lady said the knife of truth would dress me as in a jacket of iron flowers and though I would do battle, I would march from the battle cleansed. Then I fell asleep—

ALBERTINE Your many religious experiences have always made me uneasy, Lily—

LILY When I woke up I knew that I must begin my struggle up the mountain path of truth by asking you—

ALBERTINE You telephoned at two this morning to speak with me about a journey up a mountain path of truth?

LILY And Henry came instead, and made me get in the car, and brought me *here*. He stood in the way— But he can't. Because I must ask truth, and speak truth, and act with truth, now and forever.

ALBERTINE Do you think this is the proper climate? So hot and damp. Puts mildew on the truth.

LILY Did you sell me to Julian, Mama?

(ALBERTINE *rises, comes to* LILY, *stares at her, and takes her by the shoulders*)

ALBERTINE (*Softly*) Lily, take hold of yourself. Take hold.

LILY Answer me.

ALBERTINE You are my child, but I will not take much more of this.

LILY (*In a cry*) Mama, Mama, I didn't mean to hurt you. (*Puts her hand on* ALBERTINE'S *chest*) But it's so bad for me. Julian may leave me now, and he's all I ever had, or will, or want— Mama, did he marry me for money?

ALBERTINE He married you because he loved you. Shame on you, Lily. You are looking for pain, and that makes me sad and always has.

LILY I told you there is another woman. I saw them. I followed them and they went places where people wouldn't see them and they talked. And she has something to do with his getting rich.

ALBERTINE Do you intend him never to speak to another woman? I don't know what you are talking about, getting rich, but it's good for people to have money of their own. The day comes when they don't like taking it from others. I know people thought of Julian as a charming man who didn't care about such things. But I never thought so.

LILY Last night when I lay waiting for him, and he knew it, he said he'd had too much champagne and he wanted to sleep alone. It's been like that since the lady came to Chicago.

ALBERTINE You've learned women's chitchat very fast.

I'm not good at this, but since we've started I can tell you everybody wants to sleep alone sometimes— (*Laughs*) —maybe most of the time.

LILY He liked to come to bed with me. You didn't know that, did you?

ALBERTINE I have not read it in the newspaper. But, as you know, I'm a large stockholder, and if you'd like it reported in detail— (*She breaks off, puts her hand over her eyes*) Forgive me.

LILY You'd never believed anybody could want me. I didn't believe it, either. I was so scared at first that I— But there I was, good for the man I loved. He said I was better than anybody, and that I must learn to cook because he'd always believed that a woman who was good in the bedroom was good in the kitchen— (*She laughs happily*) And I did learn. What do you think of that?

ALBERTINE I think well of it.

LILY (*Softly*) I was beloved, Mama, and I flourished. Now I'm frightened. Help me.

ALBERTINE (*Gently*) How can I help you when I don't understand what you're talking about? Are you really saying that if Julian stayed dependent on you, all would be safe, but if he has money for himself, and need not crawl to you—

LILY That's an ugly way to speak, Mama.

ALBERTINE On your struggle up the mountain path, you will find that truth is often ugly. It burns. (*After a second*) I don't believe there is any other woman, but in any case, be wise enough to wait and find out.

LILY I don't want to be wise, ever, Mama, ever. I'm in love.

ALBERTINE Then be happy that Julian has finally had a little luck. Lily, he would have come to hate your money. *That* was the danger I feared for you.

LILY I never wanted us to have money. I hate money. You know that, Mama.

ALBERTINE Then be very careful. Same thing as loving it. (*The phone rings and* LILY *wheels and makes a dash for the house. At the same minute,* ANNA, *who has been moving in and out of the room, packing the valise, now turns from the valise and crosses to the phone.* LILY *falls over the porch steps and rolls to the ground.* HENRY *runs toward her*)

LILY Anna! Anna!

ALBERTINE Lily.

ANNA (*Into the phone*) I will wake him. Just a minute. (*She moves out.* ALBERTINE *moves to help* LILY *rise*)

LILY (*Calling to* ANNA) That's the woman. I want to speak to her. I want to ask her—

(*She makes a sudden, violent movement up the porch steps*)

ALBERTINE No. (*Very sharply*) No.

(HENRY *touches* LILY'S *arm as if to keep her from moving*)

LILY (*To* HENRY) Leave me alone. I told you that last night. I told it to you years ago when I rolled down the hill. I meant to roll down the hill and kill myself, but you didn't know it.

HENRY I knew it.

(JULIAN *appears in the living room, dressed in a robe, the envelope of money in his pocket. He moves to the phone*)

JULIAN Hello. Sorry about the call last night. I was dying to tell you the good news, but of course I couldn't call you back. Did the cough medicine work? Did you have a good night's sleep? This is the great day, so stop worrying. Everything went fine. Got it right here in my pocket, nice clean bills. Eleven o'clock, waving a fortune at you. Where we agreed. (*He listens, smiling*) I did everything the way you told me, only better. Don't worry about me. He just beats women. (*Gently, affectionately*) I'll be there. Good-bye, my dear. (ANNA *enters the living room carrying a glass of juice and a dress.* JULIAN *takes the juice from* ANNA, *kisses her*) What's good for breakfast?

ANNA Pancakes?

JULIAN (*Looks around at the old dress she is packing*) Why are you taking all that old stuff? Throw out everything old. (*Stares at* ANNA) What's the matter with you. You look terrible.

ALBERTINE (*Through the window*) Morning, Julian.

(ANNA *exits toward the kitchen*)

JULIAN Well, look who's here. Hello. (*He starts out for the porch, stops, kicks aside a few packages, grabs a small one and runs out*) A present for you.

ALBERTINE Thank you.

(*He turns to* LILY)

JULIAN Hello, darling. (*Stares at her*) What's the matter with you? (LILY *shakes her head. He kisses her, and moves toward* ALBERTINE, *with whom he shakes hands. He sees* HENRY *and they shake hands*) How's the fishing? Been up the bayou?

HENRY Been up. But nobody got anything. Except crayfish.

JULIAN Anybody asked what I missed most in Chicago, I'd have said a bayou, a bowl of crayfish, a good gun for a flight of wild ducks coming over— Going to buy a little place up there, first thing. You're welcome all the time. (*Sees that* LILY *has not moved and is staring at the ground*) What's the matter, Lily? (*When she doesn't answer, he speaks to* ALBERTINE) I sure manage to depress my ladies. Never used to be that way. Do I depress you?

ALBERTINE (*Laughs*) I'm very glad to see you.

(*She has now unwrapped the package and taken out a flame-red lace mantilla supported by a giant comb. She arranges it on her head*)

JULIAN What's it meant for?

ALBERTINE I don't know.

JULIAN When do you wear it?

ALBERTINE I'll wear it for reading in bed. How very nice of you to bring it to me.

JULIAN (*As if the tone of thanks puzzles him*) How nice of *you*. You put it on. Nobody else— (*Turns to* LILY) Lily, did you show your mama your new ring? (LILY *shakes her head*) Oh. Go and get your ring and show your mama. (LILY *hesitates and then moves inside. He smiles ruefully at* ALBERTINE, *points to the mantilla*) Silly present, isn't it? It cost a lot.

ALBERTINE (*Laughs*) Nice to buy, nice to get, silly presents. Who wants a roast of beef?

(*She removes the mantilla and carefully folds it*)

JULIAN (*Smiles with pleasure*) That's what I thought— (*Confidentially, points inside*) I think I bought, got, brought— Well, they're sort of upset and they don't think I know it. I should have had sense enough to know that when you've been poor and wanted things you couldn't have, your stomach gets small and you can't eat much right away. I brought too much, and everything too grand, and, well. Guess they got a little sick. They're so happy that it comes out unhappy. You know how it is?

ALBERTINE I don't think so.

JULIAN It's a crazy old world. For years, they— (*Points inside*) —tell me about what's going to be, what I'm going to do, you know, get rich and big time. The more I fail, the louder they cheer me with what we're all going to have, want. And so all my life I dream about coming up those steps carrying everything, and I make up what they will say, and what I will say— (*Smiles*) Well, when it came, I guess it was hard to believe, maybe even frightened them, I never thought of that, and I just bought anything if it cost a lot, and made Carrie sick on caviar, and everybody acted scared, and like they were going to cry. Lily did cry— Natural enough. You know?

ALBERTINE (*Carefully*) No, I don't know. You've had good fortune and brought it home. There's something sad in not liking what you want when you get it. And something strange, maybe even mean. (*Sharply, as if in warning*) Nobody should have cried about your good fortune, nobody should have been anything but happy.

JULIAN No, no. You don't understand. They're happy. They just haven't had time— I scared them, Europe and a house and fancy things all in a day. Who wouldn't be scared? They thought I'd come home broke— God knows I always had— You don't know about that, but *they* do, and they got ready to give me all they had, and tell all the same nice lies about how the next time. And then there I come, strutting like a kid— (*Laughs with great pleasure*) Rich. Rich. Rich. (*As a child would say it*) I'm as good as you now. Isn't that true?

ALBERTINE (*Laughs*) I'm not sure.

JULIAN We'll have to have long talks and consultations.

ALBERTINE About money? I don't think so. I like it very much. But it makes dull talk.

JULIAN Oh, I just bet you don't really think that. (*He pokes her with his finger; she stares at him and sits very straight*) That's just the way *you* people want *us* to think. Not dull at all. Why, I had more fun this week— Know what I did?

(*He pokes her again. She reacts sharply and* HENRY *laughs. She turns to look at* HENRY *and then turns back to* JULIAN, *smiling*)

ALBERTINE Henry doesn't like people to poke me, do you, Henry?

HENRY I never saw anybody do it before.

JULIAN I went to see a man I hated the two times I ever saw him and the many times I heard about him. Once when he teased me as a boy, and once when he made fun of me as a man. (*He stops, remembers, sighs*) I guess he's the only man I ever hated. Well, I went right in his office and said I got something you want, and I'll take a hundred and fifty thousand dollars for it. After he said all about being crazy, and to get the hell out, he said, "Get your money from women—your sisters or your wife. You married her for it"— (JULIAN *rises, speaks softly to* ALBERTINE) Did people think that? Did they?

ALBERTINE I don't see people. I never thought it.

JULIAN (*Leans down, kisses her hand*) Maybe I'll knock you down later, I said to him, but right now let's keep our minds on a hundred and fifty thousand dollars delivered a week from today. (*To* ALBERTINE) Want to see?

(*He takes the envelope from his pocket and holds it open for her*)

ALBERTINE (*Laughs*) It does look nice. I don't think I ever saw anything larger than a hundred-dollar bill.

JULIAN I tell you, the rich don't have any fun with money.

ALBERTINE Smells rather nice, too.

JULIAN I put a little cologne water on it. (*As he puts the envelope back in his pocket*) One hundred and fifty thousand dollars. Do people like you think it's a lot of money?

ALBERTINE It's money. (*Very deliberately pokes him*) People like me think it's a good beginning. It's not a great fortune, but if you want one it will start you off.

JULIAN You know, I think so, too. (*Smiles at her*) Isn't it funny? I liked you, but I never talked easy with you before. Now you just seem to me like anybody else.

ALBERTINE I'm sorry.

JULIAN (*Leans over and kisses her cheek*) I didn't mean it quite like that. I just mean that you always scared me, and now you don't. I guess most people like you scared me. (*Smiles*) I was kind of, well, kind of broken. I knew it, but I showed off to keep— (*He points inside*)

—them from— (*He turns to* HENRY) It's bad for a man to feel gone. (*Then, very gaily*) Like a miracle. I go in to see this bastard shaking, and I come out knowing I did fine, knowing I'm going to be all right forever. You understand it wasn't just the money?

ALBERTINE (*Laughs*) I don't understand very much. Why don't you wait and tell me when you can?

JULIAN All I mean, you do something right. *Just right.* You know a man's got to have what you've got—very different from trying to get a job or selling something he don't want. I just sat there calm and smiling until he got through trying to find out how I, *I,* bought two acres of swamp land before he did, and how I could know how much he needed it. I thought to myself, so this is the way the big boys do it, you poor fool for being so scared all your life. So I said, "Get through, will you, I got a board of directors meeting and have no more time for you." (*Laughs with pleasure*) I don't know where I got that from. Maybe the movies. You and my lawyer can attend to the rest, so agree or don't agree, I don't want to be in the room with you too long. He got white but he didn't say anything, so I got up and started out and he said, "All right. Give us two weeks to draw the papers"— My lawyer said, "Fair enough, sir," and I guess it was the "sir" that made me angry because I said, "No. I'll take it next Tuesday at two o'clock. Have it ready." And I walked out the happiest man in town. I paid back my life some way or other— (GUS *appears carrying ice*) You can lose for just so long— When you win, everything on you grows bigger, know what I mean? (*He laughs and pokes* ALBERTINE)

ALBERTINE And I grow black and blue.

GUS Hi. Home to stay?

JULIAN Gus, just look at that new icebox. (GUS *turns, stares in through the porch door*) Bought it more for you than for them.

GUS In Chicago they keep it in the parlor?

JULIAN Gus, my old friend Gus. You're going to have that farm, kid. Go find it and start with this.

(*He hands* GUS *several large bills.* GUS *looks at them, but doesn't take them*)

GUS You at that again?

JULIAN This time I made it. Throw the ice away—

(*He shoves the money into* GUS' *hand*)

GUS Julian, I don't want that kind of trouble again.

JULIAN Nobody'll come for it this time. I'm telling you the truth. And there's as much more as you want. Now get going and find the farm.

GUS Who the hell wants a farm? Got enough trouble. Where'd you make up the farm from?

(*He goes around the garden and disappears*)

JULIAN He said since we were kids about a farm— People talk about what they want, and then— How's that?

ALBERTINE I guess most of us make up things we want, don't get them, and get too old, or too lazy, to make up new ones. Best not to disturb that, Julian. People don't want other people to guess they never knew what they wanted in the first place.

JULIAN That's real sad. I know what I want and *I'm* going to be happy getting it.

ALBERTINE Well, I like nice, rich, happy relatives, although I never had any. But I have bad news for you, Julian—it's not simple being happy, and money doesn't seem to have much to do with it, although it has to do with other things more serious.

(CARRIE *comes in, moving slowly. She stops when she sees the group*)

JULIAN Morning. Where you been?

CARRIE I—I've been downtown.

JULIAN Buying things, I hope. (*To* ALBERTINE) My sisters are going to Europe tomorrow. Isn't that fine, after years of—

CARRIE Your sisters are not— (*Then, softly*) come inside, please.

JULIAN What's the matter?

CARRIE (*Starts toward the steps, sharply*) Come inside.

JULIAN (*Playfully, but with meaning*) Carrie, stop talking like that. You got a new man on your hands. You got to talk to me different now, like I'm a tycoon. (*To* ALBERTINE) What's a tycoon? How much, I mean?

ALBERTINE Miss Carrie can tell you. She works for one.

JULIAN Barrett? Is he? I don't want to be like Barrett—

CARRIE He knows what you think of him. He'd already read your letter when I got there. I can't tell you what I felt. All I could think to say was that it was a joke and you'd be down later to apologize.

JULIAN (*After a second*) Did you? Did you really say that? Don't ever say that again, Carrie. That's one of things I don't ever have to do any more. That's one of things money's going to buy us all.

CARRIE I want to see you alone, Julian.

JULIAN I don't think you should have gone to see him at all. We'll talk about it another time. I'm busy today. (*She wheels around, angry.* JULIAN *is grinning at* ALBERTINE) How you like me? See? Got no time for small matters.

CARRIE Small matters? After nineteen years. He said he didn't believe you wrote the letter. He said I wrote it, that it was like me, that he always had known about— (*She gasps*) —things in me. After nineteen years of loyalty— I want you to get dressed and go tell him that if you owe him an apology, he owes me an apology for the awful words he said—

JULIAN (*To* ALBERTINE) That's how tycoons act toward loyal ladies?

ALBERTINE I don't know how they act toward loyal ladies.

CARRIE Julian—

ALBERTINE I do know tycoons are not romantic about money and the happiness it buys.

JULIAN Ah, can't I be romantic for a month?

(CARRIE *moves into the living room and stands waiting*)

ALBERTINE All right. We'll give you a month. After a month I suggest venality. You'll find more people understand it and are less suspicious of it. Right now it's my impression that everyone around here thinks you held up a bank.

JULIAN No, a poker game. Or a jewel robbery. Hey, Lily. Lily! Come and show your mama your ring. Lily! (*To* ALBERTINE) *You* don't think I stole the money, do you? (*He looks at his watch, then moves quickly toward the porch as* LILY *appears*)

ALBERTINE (*Because* JULIAN *is going up the steps of the porch, and because she speaks very softly, he does not hear her*) No. I think I know where you got it.

JULIAN (*As he passes* LILY, *he picks up her left hand*) Go show your mama— Where's your ring?

LILY Somewhere.

JULIAN Where is somewhere?

LILY Don't be angry, please—

JULIAN Why not? (*He moves into the room, sees* CARRIE, *smiles*) Seen a large diamond ring?

CARRIE Up to yesterday we never had such problems. How does one look for a diamond ring? Julian, he said bad things to me. Julian. (*He doesn't answer, and starts to leave the room*) Julian. Please answer me.

JULIAN Answer you what?

CARRIE Once, and not long ago, you'd have known by my face, and you'd have kissed me and said, "What is it, my Carrie?"

(*Behind* CARRIE, ANNA *appears carrying a breakfast tray. She stops*)

JULIAN (*Gently*) What is it, my Carrie?

CARRIE I want to talk to you— Let's go by ourselves, the way we used to—

JULIAN I'm due downtown—

CARRIE You have no time for me. We're coming apart, you and I—

JULIAN What are you talking about?

CARRIE You've come home in all this mystery, and not said a word with me alone—

JULIAN When I take you to the boat tomorrow, I'll tell you all about "this mystery"—

CARRIE I want to speak to you now. Now.

JULIAN (*Softly*) Did you always use that tone with me? Did you? (*To* ANNA) Did you? (*When she doesn't answer*) Say something, so I can tell the way you talk to me.

ANNA Breakfast.

JULIAN (*Takes the tray from her*) Will you press a shirt for me?

(*She nods and moves off with him*)

CARRIE You're saying no to me, when I need you?

JULIAN I'm not saying no to you. I'm saying that I'm busy.

(*He sings as he exits*)

ALBERTINE (*To* LILY, *who is on the porch*) What did you do with the ring?

LILY I don't want it.

ALBERTINE He will be hurt. I suggest that you pretend that you do want it.

LILY I don't want it.

(CARRIE, *nervously moving about, comes to stand at the window and to listen to the voices in the garden*)

ALBERTINE There are many ways of loving. I'm sure yours must be among them. Put white flowers in your hair, walk up your mountain path of truth with a white banner in your hand and as you drop it on his head, speak of love.

LILY I gave her the ring and she gave me the knife.

ALBERTINE I beg your pardon?

HENRY (*Quickly*) I know what she means.

LILY I gave the lady the ring and she gave me the knife. I didn't want the ring, and I didn't know Julian would care. But I will go and tell him the truth now and— (*She starts into the room*)

ALBERTINE You asked my advice and here it is: You do too much. Go and do nothing for a while. Nothing. I have seen you like this before. (*With force*) I tell you now, do nothing. (*To* HENRY) You know the address of the upstairs knife lady?

LILY Mama, don't make fun of her—

ALBERTINE No, indeed. We will try to find your ring. Decide whether your costume is meant for day or night, and rest yourself. (*Softly*) Lily, don't tell Julian about the ring. (LILY *nods and enters the house. She sees* CARRIE, *smiles at her, and exits toward the kitchen.* ANNA *appears carrying a shirt and crosses the room toward the kitchen*) Well, there it is.

HENRY You are not wise with Lily.

ALBERTINE No. I never was. Well, it's been a good year, hasn't it? The best I ever had.

HENRY Nothing has happened.

ALBERTINE I know Lily. You do, too.

HENRY She is jealous and scared—

ALBERTINE And nothing I say will stop her from being foolish. And of course there is another woman. But Julian isn't sleeping with her. (*Laughs*) They raised him to be a very, very moral man.

HENRY Very, very moral men sometimes sleep with women. I think.

ALBERTINE But it shows on them. Do you think he's sleeping with another woman?

HENRY He's not sleeping with her, and he won't. But he used to.

ALBERTINE Yes? (*When there is no answer*) Cy Warkins is the man he's talking about, Cy Warkins who bought what he calls his two acres of swamp land. I'm not sure why Cy wanted it so much, but if it's down by the river I can make a good guess. Warkins owns fifty percent of the stock of the interstate agreement to take the railroad route along the docks. (*Laughs*) If my guess is right, he must have been surprised that Julian knew about the best kept secret in years. I regret not being there when Julian told him. But who told Julian? Mrs. Warkins? (HENRY *does not answer*) She never liked Warkins and that was the only thing I ever knew about her. But she must be forty now. (*When there is no answer*) But of course she wasn't always forty. (*She points inside*) They knew each other? And she told him about the railroad? I'm not gossiping, you know that.

HENRY I think that's what happened. She was in love with Julian once. She hates Warkins and has wanted to leave for years. Maybe this is the money to leave with.

ALBERTINE (*Softly, in a new tone, as if it is forced out of her, and she is ashamed*) How do you know about Mrs. Warkins? Please.

HENRY I don't know about her any more, but I used to. She's a cousin to me.

ALBERTINE (*Stares at him, and then laughs*) She's part colored? Isn't that wonderful! Did Warkins know when he married her?

HENRY He doesn't know now. But Julian did, and didn't care. She's a foolish woman and grateful for such things.

ALBERTINE That's understandable, God knows.

HENRY Not to me. I am not grateful, nor ungrateful, nor any word like that.

ALBERTINE Nor should you be. You are in a bad humor with me this morning. You are disapproving. What have I done or said?

HENRY (*Softly*) You look tired.

ALBERTINE (*Rises, goes to him*) The world has many people who make things too hard for too little reason, or none at all, or the pleasure, or stupidity. We've never done that, you and I.

HENRY Yes, we've done it. But we've tried not to.

(ALBERTINE *touches his hand.* HENRY *smiles and puts her hand to his face.* ALBERTINE *turns and, as she does, she sees* CARRIE *in the window.* ALBERTINE *pauses, turns slightly to where* CARRIE *has been sitting as if to ask herself what* CARRIE *could have heard*)

ALBERTINE Are you writing a book, Miss Carrie?

CARRIE (*Softly*) This is our house, Mrs. Prine.

ALBERTINE (*Sighs*) Indeed.

(HENRY *takes her arm and they move off.* LILY *comes running into the room, holding her right hand in her left hand. She is followed by* ANNA, *who carries a bottle and gauze bandage.* LILY *runs toward the hall, calling out*)

LILY Julian, I—I cut my hand.

ANNA Lily.

LILY Julian. I cut my hand. (*Then she turns and calls out loudly toward the garden*) Mama. Mama. I cut my hand.

CARRIE Your mama has left with her friend.

(JULIAN *appears, rubbing his wet hair with a bath towel*)

JULIAN What's the matter?

LILY I cut my hand.

JULIAN (*He picks up* LILY'S *hand, holds it for* ANNA *to bandage*) It's a deep one. You ought not to have rusty knives in the kitchen.

(ANNA *looks up as if she is about to speak, but changes her mind*)

LILY Ouch. (*She turns her hand toward* JULIAN. *He kisses it and she gently touches his face. She rubs her thigh*) And last night I fell in here and hit my leg. You could cure that, too. Please. Make me cured, Julian. Let's go to bed and maybe you'll be pleased with me— Maybe. (*She puts his hand on her breast.* ANNA *turns away;* CARRIE *stands staring at them*) And if you're pleased with me, then all the bad will go away, and I will pray for it to be that way. But if you're not, I'll understand, and won't ask why— (*She laughs gaily, slyly, and presses his hand on her breast*) But *if* you are pleased with me, darling— (JULIAN *leans down to kiss her*) I have missed you.

(*He picks her up in his arms and begins to move out of the room*)

CARRIE (*Sucks in her breath; loudly*) I read in a French book that there was nothing so abandoned as a respectable young girl.

JULIAN (*Laughs*) That's true, thank God. (*He leans down to kiss* LILY'S *hair*) Otherwise nobody could stand them.

(LILY *laughs merrily*)

CARRIE (*Comes toward them*) You didn't fall in here last night. When I turned on the light—

LILY Yes, ma'am. I fell. I didn't see the spinet—

(JULIAN, *carrying* LILY, *exits*)

CARRIE You did not fall against the spinet. You were on this side of the room, hitting—

ANNA Carrie.

CARRIE She was hitting herself against that table. Just doing it. I saw her. I tell you, I saw her.

ANNA I believe you.

CARRIE He doesn't know she went out last night. He doesn't know she gave her ring away—to some woman— She's told him lies. She lies to him, she tricks him. I think she's a crazy girl— (*Points to the garden*) And that woman knows it. I think there's a crazy girl in there—

ANNA (*Softly, as if to herself*) She cut her hand, quite deliberately and calmly, with a knife she took from a valise. She said a kind of prayer over the knife—

CARRIE (*Moves swiftly toward* ANNA) You saw her do that? You saw her cut herself? I tell you she's crazy. (*She moves toward the door, right*)

ANNA No.

CARRIE How can you stand what's happening here? He comes home with all this money nonsense. He's married to a crazy girl. I think he's in bed with a girl—

ANNA —he wanted. It's not our business.

CARRIE It is our business that our brother sells something to Mr. Cyrus Warkins for a fortune Mr. Cyrus Warkins doesn't want to pay. Warkins is a powerful and dangerous man in this town, and Julian would be a baby in the hands of such a man—

ANNA What are you talking about?

CARRIE I don't know all it means. (*Points out to the garden*) But I heard them say this money, or whatever, has to do with Warkins' wife.

ANNA He slept with Charlotte Warkins ten years ago. It's been over that long.

CARRIE How do you know such a thing? How do *you* know?

ANNA Because he told me.

CARRIE I don't believe you. You're a liar.

ANNA Be quiet, Carrie.

CARRIE You've made it up, you always made up things like that. It didn't happen. He was an innocent boy— (ANNA *laughs.* CARRIE *unbuttons the neck of her dress as if she were choking*) He would never have told *you.* He would have told me. He was closer to me— There he is, another man, not our brother, lost to us after all the years of work and care, married to a crazy little whore who cuts her hand to try to get him into bed— (*Points to the garden*) The daughter of a woman who keeps a nigger fancy man. I'll bet she paid Julian to take that crazy girl away from her—

ANNA Stop that talk. You know that's not true. Stop talking about Julian that way.

CARRIE Let's go and ask him. Let's go and ask your darling child. Your favorite child, the child you made me work for, the child I lost my youth for— You used to tell us that when you love, truly love, you take your chances on being hated by speaking out the truth. (*Points inside*) Go in and do it.

ANNA All right. I'll take that chance now and tell you that you want to sleep with him and always have. Years ago I used to be frightened that you would try and I would watch you and suffer for you.

CARRIE (*After a second, in a whisper*) You never said those words. Tell me I never heard those words. Tell me, Anna. (*When there is no answer*) You were all I ever had. I don't love you any more.

ANNA That was the chance I took.

CURTAIN

ACT THREE

CARRIE is as she was. ANNA'S suitcases are on the porch. She enters, puts another suitcase below the piano, and exits. Offstage, there is a loud whistling, from JULIAN. CARRIE crosses to the spinet and begins to pick out the melody he is whistling. He enters, dressed except for his shirt, and carrying his coat. He is singing and he smiles pleasantly at CARRIE.

JULIAN (*Singing*)
This is the big day, this is the great day
This is the Berniers day.
Never been one, no, never never,
Never been such a Berniers day.
Never been such a day before.
Going to be more and plenty more.
Oh, it's money day, the end of trouble day,
And going to be more and plenty more.
Never been such a day before.
Not for Mama, not for Papa,
Not for Sister, not for Brother—
Going to be more and plenty more.
(*Shouts off*) Anna! Where's my shirt?

CARRIE (*Softly*) Do you know that all I want in this world is what will be good for you?

JULIAN And I for you (ANNA *appears carrying his shirt. He crosses to take it from her, puts it on, and sings to* ANNA)
Now every day she going to be
She going to be a Berniers day.

Say every day she going to be
She going to be a Berniers day,
And for Mama and for Papa
And for Sister and for Brother
Going to be just a Berniers day.

(*To* ANNA) It's the best day of my life since I won the bag of marbles from old Gus. You made me give them back. You said he was a poor colored boy. But I was a poor white boy so I didn't know what you were getting so fancy about. Well, I'm on my way to the best day. (*To* CARRIE, *pointing to valise*) Getting packed? Getting excited?

CARRIE (*Pats the spinet*) I'll practice today and tonight I'll give a little concert for you and we'll sing all the pieces you used to like.

(ANNA *begins to move out of the room*)

JULIAN Er. We'll be leaving today. (ANNA *stops, turns.* CARRIE *rises*) We'll be going. (*Nervously*) And *you'll* be leaving tomorrow, so just one day. 'Course I'll wait until tomorrow if you need me—

CARRIE Where are you going?

JULIAN Maybe a camping trip, maybe New York—

CARRIE A few weeks?

JULIAN I don't know. No. A year or so. And then back here, of course. This is where I belong. Where I want to be, where I was meant to be. (*Overcheerful*) And by that time you world travelers will be back and—

CARRIE *You* want to go? Or *Lily* wants to go?

JULIAN Never seen New York, either of us.

CARRIE Lily wants to go.

JULIAN I don't know. I just decided. We'll come back, don't worry, and—

(*He crosses to the chest and takes out savings bankbook*)

CARRIE Why did you suddenly decide to go? Why?

JULIAN (*Holds up the bankbook*) Some people got a family Bible. We got a savings bankbook. (*Softly, to*

CARRIE) Don't look like that. (*Points inside*) She's young and— I don't think she wanted to come back. I didn't think about it before but— And maybe we should be alone for a while. That's all. (*Points to the bankbook*) Twenty thousand going in here this morning. Twenty thousand dollars. That going to be enough? (*Laughs with pleasure*) For six months maybe? Enough?

ANNA I don't know anything about twenty thousand dollars.

JULIAN You got to learn fast. Fast, I say. What was the word Mama used to use?

CARRIE (*In a cry*) Julian, don't go—

ANNA (*Very fast*) *Faner. Elle commence a se faner.* The leaf came in the spring, stayed nice on the branch in the autumn until the winter winds would blow it in the snow. Mama said that in that little time of holding on, a woman had to make ready for the winter ground where she would lie the rest of her life. A leaf cannot rise from the ground and go back to the tree, remember that. I remember it. But when it came there was nothing I could do.

JULIAN (*Gently, touches her*) Mama was mean.

CARRIE (*Shrilly*) Anna always says something about Mama when things are wrong. Always. Mama wasn't mean to you. Just to us.

JULIAN Did you think I liked it that way? Did you? Mama had a tough time, I guess. That often makes people mean. (*Softly, to* ANNA) You're still on the tree, still so nice and pretty, and when the wind does come, a long time from now, I'll be there to catch you with a blanket made of warm roses, and a parasol of dollar bills to keep off the snow. Dollar bills make a mighty nice parasol, I just bet you. (*Smiles*) For another good lady, too. (*As if to himself*) Well, I'm off to give them to her. I'll walk right down Sailor's Lane and she'll be waiting for me. I'll take her arm, we'll have a cup of coffee, and I'll try to say thank you. No, I won't. People are always saying thank you so they can forget what they said it for. (*Holds up one envelope*) I'll just hand this to her and say, "Have a good life, baby," and then I'll walk her down to the depot and put her on the train. A happy day. (*Holds up other envelope*) Then I'll go around and bank our share. That'll make me respectable, won't it?

ANNA (*After a second*) Is she *fanée?*

JULIAN Yes. A long time ago.

ANNA Then wish her well from me.

JULIAN I will.

CARRIE Is the lady going to New York?

JULIAN I don't know where she's going. I guess so. Doesn't everybody go to New York? (LILY, *on the last of* CARRIE'S *speech, comes into the room.* JULIAN *turns and grins at her*) Want to go to New York, or a fishing trip to Canada, or the Grand Canyon, or— Today?

LILY With you?

JULIAN (*Crosses to her, holds her face with his hand*) How would you like that? Time we found a place. Wherever.

LILY You and me?

JULIAN You and me.

LILY In a room?

JULIAN (*Laughs*) In a room, or a boat, or a tent—

LILY Just you and me. And will the not happening, happen to us again?

JULIAN (*Sharply*) Lily, stop that. I was tired and I had too much to drink last night. And I was nervous the last few days and am now. Any man will tell you that happens. (*Then, smiling*) Only you must never talk such things with any man, hear me?

LILY (*Giggles*) I won't.

(*She drops the knife from her right hand. She looks down at it as if surprised*)

JULIAN (*Leans down, picks up the knife, stares at it*) What in the name of God is this?

LILY The knife of truth. Will you swear on it? Swear that you will keep me with you whatever—

JULIAN For Christ's sake, Lily. What the hell's the matter with you? (*He drops the knife on the table*) Stop talking foolish and stop playing with knives. Maybe kiddies should marry kiddies. But I'm thirty-four. Stop talking about last night and what didn't happen, because it's the kind of thing you don't talk about. Can't you understand that? (*Gently*) Now go pack your bags and go tell your mama we're going away.

LILY (*Laughing with pleasure*) Can I say we're going away forever? Just us.

JULIAN Forever. Just us. (*Turns, sees* CARRIE *and* ANNA, *and stops*) I mean we'll come back here, or the folks will come to us— (*Very fast*) You'll see. You'll come to visit us, we'll come to visit you— Buy us a little house up the bayou. Sometimes I wish I had gone on up the bayou years ago—

ANNA You did.

JULIAN Maybe I should have stayed. They said I was better with a muskrat boat than any Cajun, better with a gun. A nice little shack and a muskrat boat, all the bobwhite you could ever want— (*After a second*) Fine morning to be talking like this.

ANNA (*Sharply*) Go on.

LILY (*She runs toward* JULIAN, *holds him; he puts his arms around her*) Will you be coming back for me?

JULIAN What? What are you talking about? Lily, for Christ's sake. (*He kisses her, moves away; stops, looks pleadingly at all of them*) What's the matter? Please.

It's the best day of my life. Please somebody look happy.

ANNA Go on. (*He smiles, moves out at a run.* LILY *follows him to the porch. He turns and kisses her and runs off. After a second,* LILY *sits down on the porch, as though she is very tired.* ANNA *speaks to* CARRIE) I wanted to be around the children he will have. I wanted something nice to grow old for. I held on to that and prayed for it. (*Very softly*) This time he will go forever.

CARRIE I don't believe it. You must have your headaches again. He will not go forever, or even for long—

ANNA This time I say he will go forever. You lusted and it showed. He doesn't know he saw it, but he did see it, and some day he'll know what he saw. (*With great violence*) You know the way that happens? You understand something, and don't know that you do, and forget about it. But one night years ago I woke up and knew what I had seen in you, and always seen. It will happen that way with him. It has already begun.

CARRIE I told you I didn't love you any more. Now I tell you that I hate you. We will have to find a way to live with that.

ANNA I don't think so.

(*She moves out to the porch on her way to the garden*)

LILY Will he come back for me, Miss Anna?

ANNA What's the matter with you, child? You must go and dress and pack your things. Julian won't be long and he'll want you to be ready. Shall I call your mother?

LILY She talked cold to me. (*She imitates her mother*) "Try not to excite yourself, Lily. Try to make yourself clear, Lily." But when she talks to Henry— (*In another voice; soft and gentle*) "Lily has gone to bed. Sit down. What shall we read tonight?" (*In her own voice*) And one night she said to him, "Oh, God, make the time when we can be alone; make it come before we are both too old to have pleasure from peace." (*Softly*) She would have paid anything for that time. Did she? Did she pay Julian? Is that why he took me?

ANNA (*Very sharply*) How dare you speak that way of Julian? What a bitter thought about a man who loves you.

LILY No. Who would want me for any other reason?

ANNA (*As she moves away*) Your modesty does not excuse you.

LILY I love him, Miss Anna. If he said he loved somebody else— Well, I'd just go away and he'd be rid of me. But this way—I know you understand.

ANNA A woman who marries a man she loves should have a little more happiness from it and talk a little more sense. That's all I understand.

LILY I've upset you, Miss Anna.

ANNA Yes. You're rather an expert.

(*She disappears around the garden.* CARRIE *has been sweeping the living room. She now moves to sweep the porch*)

LILY Cleaning day? (CARRIE *does not answer*) Do you like to sweep? I like to mop.

CARRIE Have you done much? Twice, say?

LILY I'm sorry you don't like me. I wanted you to.

CARRIE (*Gestures inside*) I would like to sweep the porch. Would you—

LILY Last night, in bed, Julian was thinking, I watched him. And thinking isn't the way to make love.

CARRIE I don't know much about gentlemen in bed and I don't want to learn from you.

LILY Haven't you ever slept with a man?

(CARRIE *turns and stares at* LILY)

CARRIE Shall we have a pillow fight or make fudge? I don't like these girlish confidences.

LILY I only thought you might like to know he was thinking of you, although, of course, I can't be sure. And maybe of Miss Anna, but most probably not.

CARRIE You'll be leaving here in an hour. Be satisfied with that victory and don't trust me with your dreams.

LILY Oh, Miss Carrie. I wanted you to like me.

CARRIE There is no need to worry about me any more.

LILY Oh, I do. And I will. I'm frightened of you.

CARRIE (*Angrily*) Your favorite word. Did it ever occur to you that other people are frightened, too?

LILY You? No. No, indeed. Of what, Miss Carrie?

CARRIE Of my hair which isn't nice any more, of my job which isn't there any more, of praying for small things and knowing just how small they are, of walking by a mirror when I didn't know it would be there— (*She gasps*) People say "Those Berniers girls, so devoted. That Carrie was pretty, and then one day she wasn't; just an old maid, working for her brother." They are right. An old maid with candied oranges as a right proper treat each Saturday night. We didn't see people any more, I guess, because we were frightened of saying or hearing more than we could stand. (*Very angrily*) There are lives that are shut and should stay shut, you hear me, and people who should not talk about themselves, and that was us.

LILY Why don't you come away with us, Miss Carrie?

CARRIE Stop sticking your baby pins into me. Go inside and pray that another woman won't do it to you. I want to clean the porch.

LILY There is another woman. I've seen her. Nobody believes me.

CARRIE I believe you.

LILY I don't know who she is. Do you?

CARRIE Your mother knows. Ask her.

LILY (*Giggles*) I just bet that's true. But Mama won't tell me because she doesn't like me and doesn't tell me things.

(*Runs to* CARRIE) You know what does the harm? I keep thinking that Mama paid Julian to marry me. And then sometimes I think that's not true; he does love me. God made him love me because God knew how much I needed him. (*Smiles; ingratiating*) He just worships you, Miss Carrie, and I know he confides in you. Did he ever tell you Mama paid him? (*Grabs* CARRIE'S *arm and, in the force of the movement, throws* CARRIE *off balance*) Tell me. Be good to me. Tell me.

CARRIE (*Pulls away*) I tell you what I think: You're going to drive him crazy.

(*She starts to move off.* LILY *grabs her*)

LILY Did my Mama—

CARRIE (*Angry*) I don't know what she did. All he told us was that he had fallen in love and was going to be married.

LILY (*In a transport of pleasure*) Oh. (*Laughing with happiness*) Miss Carrie; Miss Carrie! (*She pirouettes*) He told you he was in love! Isn't that nice?

CARRIE I remember wondering why he had picked that Sunday to tell us. Anna was going to the hospital the next morning for her eye operation. None of us had ever been in a hospital before, and we didn't know about the costs, and being in a ward, and all of that. So Julian came home and told about you, and then he said that Anna was going to have the best room in the hospital and he had called the great Dr. Kranz in Philadelphia, and the great Dr. Kranz was already on the train. He wouldn't let Anna say a word, said he won the money in a poker game. I don't know— Anna was more worried about that than about her eyes. And she fussed and fussed and never liked the fancy room and the uppity private nurses. But Dr. Kanz did a wonderful operation and when she came out of it, the first thing she said to Julian was, "My eyes were not made to make all this trouble for you." And he said a beautiful thing to her, he said, "Look, I'd give my both arms and one leg for you, but not two legs, so maybe I don't love you as much as I think," and how we all laughed. (*She smiles at* LILY) A few days later he brought you to see Anna. Do you remember?

LILY (*Who has been staring at* CARRIE) Yes.

CARRIE I was happy that Julian was to be married.

LILY You said so. (*Very loudly, as if out of control*) I didn't believe you.

CARRIE Oh, I could have stopped the marriage, even you must have guessed that.

LILY Even I. But you didn't stop it because you knew my mother had paid Julian—I'm glad I helped Miss Anna, I really am—would go on paying him, and you didn't have to worry about a little girl who didn't mean anything more to anybody than a bank check.

CARRIE I have said none of that: You have been looking for it, and you would have found it in anything I, or anybody else, could say.

LILY I don't mind, not much. It's better to know. I will take Julian any way I can have him. *If* I can have him. I feel most bad and sad, Miss Carrie, because what he married me for, he doesn't need any more. Isn't that true?

CARRIE I don't know. Take your questions to Mrs. Cyrus Warkins. She'll be in New York. You can have many a cozy evening.

LILY She's coming with us?

CARRIE No. She's going on the morning train.

LILY I see. Is she a tall, dark lady?

CARRIE I've never seen her. But Henry is tall and dark and she's his cousin, so perhaps. Your mother was very amused that the great lawyer Warkins had married a part nigger and didn't know it.

LILY Does Julian love her?

CARRIE I used to think I knew about Julian. I didn't. Ask your mother and her fancy man. They said Julian and the woman were together years ago. And my sister confirms the alliance.

LILY (*Giggles too loudly*) Together? Alliance? Together in bed? Alliance in bed? What a funny way to say it. Julian told me that you talked like an old maid when you were twelve years old, and that Gus used to say you kept your vagina in the icebox, that he'd seen it there and shut the door fast.

CARRIE (*Very loudly*) Stop that filthy talk. Julian never said a thing like that—

LILY Oh, please, I didn't mean to offend you. Julian said it in fun. Afterwards in bed, we always talked fun. That's almost the best time, when you laugh and say things you'd never say anyplace else, and it's all in honor bright. It's then that you ask about other girls, everybody does Julian told me, and every man thinks it's a big bore he's got to get through for the next time, if you know what I mean. Julian said there was only one woman that ever mattered, long ago, and I wasn't to worry— (*She laughs*) —and that she was married to a bastard who beat her, and if he ever made money he'd give it to her to get away. (*She smiles*) So now she's coming with us. What will they do with me? (*She screams*) It pains me. I can't tell you. I'll ask her not to come. (*She turns and runs up the porch and into the room, toward the phone*) I'll tell her I don't blame her, of course, and I'll swear on my knife of truth that if I have just one more year— (*Grabs the phone book, drops it, holds it out to* CARRIE) Please find it for me.

CARRIE Mrs. Warkins isn't home. She's waiting for Julian.

LILY (*Runs toward the porch*) I'll run.

CARRIE Put your clothes on first. You've got a long way to go in your underwear.

LILY (*Stares down at her nightgown*) Please you go, Miss Carrie.

CARRIE Oh, I don't think so

LILY Say I'm not angry, not anything like that. Say I know what it is to love and if at the end of a year, she wants and Julian wants— Well, then. Then.

CARRIE I don't think I could say those things.

LILY You don't talk the way you did. You talk real mean.

CARRIE In the last day I lost my brother, my sister, my job. That's all I had to lose. Perhaps it's the fear of losing people that makes us talk nice or better. (*Very loudly, sharply*) Don't you think? Don't you think maybe?

LILY Do I talk different?

CARRIE You are still the baby-rich girl, teething on other people. In a few years I think you'll have to start doing something for yourself.

LILY A few years? A few days will be too late, a few minutes— What time is it? What time is Julian going to take her away?

CARRIE (*Carefully*) I did not say he was going to take her away. He has gone to meet Mrs. Warkins, evidently to give her a share.

LILY What time is it? I know Mr. Cyrus Warkins, he's Mama's lawyer. Mrs. Warkins is a sad lady, if she's the one who was on the train.

CARRIE She's ailing, I've always heard, and doesn't go into society. But I suppose the real reason is that she's part nigger and thought somebody would find out. Julian didn't mind. Imagine that. He didn't mind.

LILY Why should he? I don't mind Henry's being colored. I like negro people, and Jewish, and once I met two Irish ladies. I just hate Henry because he's Henry.

(*There is a long pause; as if* LILY *has dozed*)

CARRIE (*Watching* LILY, *sighs*) Your mind wanders, doesn't it? Go pack your bags now.

LILY You're a fine lady. He'd listen to you. Miss Carrie, please call Mr. Cyrus Warkins.

CARRIE I will not call Mr. Cyrus Warkins. His wife is not going to New York with me.

LILY Mama should call him. Where's Mama? She went for my ring. Will Mr. Warkins listen to me. Nobody does. (*She runs to pick up the phone book, opens it, and drops the book*) Don't you want to help me? It's hot.

CARRIE Wait for your Mama.

LILY It will be too late.

CARRIE I think so.

LILY You're teasing me. It's not nice to tease me and to pretend that you're not (*As* CARRIE *moves away*) Miss Carrie, please.

CARRIE (*Sharply*) What do you want of me? What is that you want?

LILY I don't want to be in the room alone. (*Points down to the telephone*) It's for the best, the best for everybody, isn't it?

CARRIE What's the sense of answering you? You just go on talking and talking.

LILY No, please. Please. Isn't it best for everybody?

CARRIE I don't know about everybody. I'm not used to thinking that way. I just think about what's best for us, for Julian.

LILY That's what I want, too. What's best for Julian. Please tell me.

CARRIE (*Carefully, as if anxious to impress the words*) I don't know that I can. The people in the bank always talk of Mr. Warkins as a low-high-born man, tough and tricky, with plenty of riffraff friends to do his dirty work. Julian isn't fit to deal with such a man and God knows what could happen. Warkins is not a man to joke with.

LILY (*After the words "what could happen,"* LILY *has picked up the phone and given the operator the number "LaFitte 1707." Her voice is firm*) Tell Mr. Warkins that Lily Berniers, Lily Prine, must speak to him immediately and does not wish to be kept waiting. (*Waiting, she smiles at* CARRIE) I think that's the way Mama would say it. Oh, hello, Mr. Cyrus, this is Lily. (*She puts the phone down, wipes her hand on her nightgown, picks up the phone, waits*) Mr. Cyrus, you mustn't blame anybody if I tell you something. Will you promise a sacred promise on the life of your child?

CARRIE He hasn't got a child.

LILY But you haven't got a child. (*Pause*) Then why did you make a sacred promise on a child you haven't got? You mustn't joke with me, Mr. Cyrus, you must not. Oh. I see. Well, please tell your wife I'm not mad a bit. That's first. Just ask her to give me one more year with Julian and then I'll promise— Well, that's all. Just ask her that. (*She listens*) I wouldn't like to say because I don't understand much myself. Why does it matter? I don't see why it should. Oh. Well, Miss Carrie heard— (CARRIE *wheels about*) A *lady* heard Henry say it. Henry? Why, the Henry of my mother—you know. Just that once, a long time ago, Julian had been kind to your wife, and that maybe she was helping him now. I don't know how Henry knew. (*After a second*) Oh, yes. I do. Henry is cousin to Mrs. Warkins. Yes, cousin. (*She waits, looks puzzled*) Mr. Cyrus? Mr. Cyrus? No, I don't think your wife's coming here. If she were, I could have asked her myself. I thought you could go right away, before she gets on the train— (*To* CARRIE) He wants to know where he can find her to give her my message. (*Into phone*) I don't know.

CARRIE Something about Sailor's Lane near the depot.

LILY Something about Sailor's Lane near the depot. Yes. Nobody's done anything bad, you understand, Mr. Cyrus, and tell her I know that, but I'd just like to ask to have Julian for one more— Mr. Cyrus? Well, thank you. (*She puts the phone down, sits, smiles*) He says he sure will go talk to her.

(CARRIE *sighs, waits, and then turns away.* ANNA *comes*

into the room, dressed in a suit. She looks at LILY, *who does not notice her. She crosses to the table and picks up the envelope with the boat tickets*)

ANNA We can't go together now. What would you like to do about these boat tickets?

CARRIE We can't go together *now?* I don't know what you mean. Were we ever going?

ANNA I thought so. When Julian brought these home to us, he thought so.

CARRIE How strange you are. Did Julian think that? I suppose so; one piece of nonsense makes for ten. We never in our lives had any intention of going, you know that as well as I do.

(ANNA *picks up the valise, takes it to the porch and exits*)

LILY I did right, just exactly. Didn't I? And I'll take the knife of truth and swear to keep my word—

CARRIE Yes. But would you do it someplace else? It would be nice to see you in a dress. Why don't you try it?

LILY Oh. All right.

(*She exits.* CARRIE *sits down, as if exhausted. She looks at her watch.* ANNA *comes back into the room, wearing a hat now, and carrying a coat*)

ANNA You never wanted to go to Europe? Never meant to go?

CARRIE How do you know such things? You go on talking the way you always talked, saying you like or want what you always said. (ANNA *doesn't answer.* CARRIE *begins to recite in a make-fun singsong*)

"On the fairest time of June
You may go, with sun or moon
Or the seven stars to light you
Or the polar ray to right you,"—

Do you still like it, all the nights you read it to us?

ANNA Yes. (*Slowly*) I don't know. I suppose it doesn't mean much to me any more.

CARRIE I can hear you, all your cultured evenings. (*Recites*)
"To see the laurel wreath on high suspended,
That is to crown our name when life is ended."

ANNA (*Standing near the piano, she plays*) And you this? So deeply felt, your favorite.

CARRIE Was it?

ANNA (*Smiles*) And the candied oranges I brought each week?

CARRIE I was sick of them ten years ago.

ANNA (*Softly*) Well, people change and forget to tell each other. Too bad—causes so many mistakes. (*She crosses to the table, takes a ship's ticket from the envelope, puts the envelope back on the table*) I've taken my ticket, left yours in the envelope. You'll explain about that to Julian.

CARRIE What are you talking about?

ANNA I'll spend the night at the hotel. I'm going to Europe tomorrow.

CARRIE (*Moves toward her, stares at her, starts to laugh*) You will be lonely.

ANNA That's all right. I always have been.

CARRIE You will look very silly, a middle-aged, scared-to-death woman, all by herself, trying to have a good time.

ANNA You will stay here until you sell the house?

CARRIE I don't believe you mean to go anywhere. It's just too crazy. You've never been anyplace in your life.

ANNA (*Moves toward the door*) We have said good-bye.

CARRIE You're showing off. You're just plain showing off. You're not going anywhere— (*As* ANNA *reaches the door*) You can't go before Julian. It would kill him to know that anything was wrong between us.

ANNA You don't love me, but you want me to stay with you.

CARRIE We will find a way to live.

ANNA No.

CARRIE You need me. You always have. Julian, everybody, always thought you the strong and sturdy—

ANNA And you the frail, the flutterer, the small. That's the way you wanted them to think. I knew better. Our patched-together supper, a little talk, sometimes a book, long ago on the piano, a game of casino, your bath, then mine, your room and my room, two doors closed.

CARRIE All those years of nights, all the things you knew and never said. Does everybody live like that, or just two old maids?

ANNA I loved you and so whatever I knew didn't matter. You wanted to see yourself a way you never were. Maybe that's a game you let people play when you love them. Well, we had made something together, and the words would have stayed where they belonged as we waited for our brother to need us again. But our brother doesn't need us any more, and so the poor house came down.

CARRIE I think our brother will need us. Now or someday. And we must stay together for it (*Softly*) You're the kind of woman with no place to go, no place to go. (*Smiles*) You see? Some of those nights I thought about you, too. We must find a way to live.

ANNA I don't wish to find a way to live with you. I am a woman who has no place to go, but I am going, and after a while I will ask myself why I took my mother's two children to be my own.

CARRIE Go unpack your bags.

ANNA (*With great force*) Pretend it's last week. You've just told the girls in the bank that you can't have coffee, you have to hurry home, that Anna will be mad at you for being late, that Anna gives the orders to the soft and tender you. Go back and pretend it's still last week. (*She moves out to the porch, picks up a camellia plant and carries it down the steps.* MRS. PRINE *appears.* HENRY *is with her, he waits beyond the garden fence*) Will I look very foolish carrying a camellia plant to Europe?

ALBERTINE I don't think so. It's most becoming. Soft around the face.

(LILY *appears. She is dressed, has on her hat, and is neat and cheerful*)

LILY (*To* ANNA) Are you coming to New York with us? I would like that, Miss Anna.

ANNA You shouldn't like it, and I'm not coming with you. (*She moves around the side of the house*) I guess two plants ain't more foolish than one.

LILY Good-bye, Mama. We're going away. Good-bye. (*Smiles*) I know that will make you happy.

ALBERTINE Here's your ring, Lily.

LILY Oh. Thank you. I had forgotten— Oh. Madame Celeste gave it to you?

ALBERTINE Madame Celeste sold it to me.

LILY That's not fair, is it? Now I must give her back the knife of truth. (*She turns as if to leave*) I'd like to keep it, but she'd never sell it.

ALBERTINE (*Very sharply*) Sit down. (LILY *sits down;* ALBERTINE *sits opposite her, and speaks very quietly, but as if the words had been rehearsed*) I've had enough of whatever you're doing. However innocent is your innocence, I've had enough. More important, it is leading you into dangerous alleys. Not even for you will I again spend time in what you call an upstairs room with a morphine addict who holds séances to cover up what she sells.

LILY (*In a fury*) I don't believe you, I don't believe you, I don't believe you. You want to take my friend from me—

ALBERTINE I am tired. I am sad. It is not good to know that my child swore fidelity to such a woman, and gave her wedding ring as proof.

LILY My friend is a sweet friend. I gave her my ring because she loved me and gave me courage—

ALBERTINE You are a pure girl and I believe you. Now listen: I am going to give you a good-bye present. Try to make use of it: the pure and the innocent sometimes bring harm to themselves and those they love and, when they do, for some reason that I do not know, the injury is very great.

LILY (*Who hasn't heard a word*) You have talked this way about my friend because you want to bring me pain. Henry makes plans to pain me— (*Outside the fence,* HENRY *turns*) As you lie in bed with him, Henry makes the plans and tells you what to do.

ALBERTINE (*Pleasantly, turns toward* HENRY) Is that what we do in bed? (*To* LILY) You think that's what we do in bed? You're wrong. It's where I forget the mistakes I made with you.

HENRY Stop it.

ALBERTINE (*Ignores him; as if she is out of his control*) If something is the matter with you, come home and I will care for you, as I should, as I should. But if nothing is the matter with you, have pity and leave me alone. I tried with you all your life, but I did not do well, and for that I ask your pardon. But don't punish me forever, Lily.

LILY (*Softly*) Is something the matter with me, Mama? (HENRY *moves toward* ALBERTINE *and holds up his hand.* ALBERTINE *stares at him, then nods*)

ALBERTINE (*Very gently*) No, darling. Certainly not.

LILY If Julian leaves me—

ALBERTINE Julian loves you, Lily.

LILY I have sent a message and will keep my word. If Mrs. Warkins will give me one year—

ALBERTINE (*After a second*) You sent a message to Mrs. Warkins? Why?

LILY Oh, because. I spoke to Mr. Warkins and told him to ask her to wait for Julian for one more year. (ALBERTINE *moves forward.* HENRY *moves toward her.* ALBERTINE *turns and stares at* HENRY) After that, if Julian doesn't want me— Where would I ever go, who would ever want me? I'm trouble, we all know that. I wouldn't have anywhere to go.

ALBERTINE (*After a long pause*) You will come home to me. You are my child.

LILY (*Warmly, sweetly*) Thank you, Mama. Nice of you. But I couldn't go home to you any more, as long as—

HENRY If it ever happens, I won't be there. I won't be there.

LILY Oh, thank you, Henry. That will be fine.

(*On the first part of* LILY'S *speech,* HENRY *sees* JULIAN *in the street.* HENRY *makes a sudden move toward him, stops.* JULIAN *appears, stumbling toward the house. His face and hands are cut and bruised. He has been beaten, and one leg is injured. He moves toward the garden in great pain; his face is so stern that the people who see him know that to assist him would be to undignify him.* ANNA, *who has seen him from the back of the house, starts toward him, then moves swiftly back as if on an errand.* LILY *does not move, but makes a loud sound.* JULIAN *tries to go up the steps of the porch, slips, and then clings to pillar of the porch.* CARRIE *moves toward him, and then backs into the room.* HENRY *goes toward* JULIAN, *but* JULIAN *puts up a hand, and* HENRY *halts*)

JULIAN I took Charlotte to her brother's house. She'll be all right, but not her face. She's safe there, I think— Do you know what Charlotte I'm talking about?

HENRY Yes.

JULIAN She'd better not stay where she is. Just in case. Not in this town.

HENRY All right.

(*Painfully, slowly,* JULIAN *moves into the room.* CARRIE, *standing near the phone, points toward it*)

CARRIE (*Softly*) Doctor?

JULIAN No. (ANNA *comes in carrying a basin and bandages*) My friend. My poor friend. All she wanted, saved for, thought about— (*He gasps as if he is sick*) —to get away forever. Standing there, standing in the alley, they slashed us up.

ALBERTINE (*Who is standing on the porch; softly*) Who?

JULIAN I don't know who. I saw two men and then I didn't see anything else. Two thugs he sent—

ALBERTINE Who sent?

JULIAN (*In a shout*) Mr. Cyrus Warkins sent his men to meet us. (*He takes the money envelope from his coat pocket where it has been arranged as if it were a handkerchief, crumbles it, and throws it to the ground*) Nobody knew she came to Chicago to tell me, nobody knew she put up the money for the land, nobody knew her name. Tell her I swear it, I swear it. (*To* ANNA, *who comes toward him with bandages*) Go away. (*To* HENRY) I told *nobody*. Tell her I swear it on my life—

HENRY No need to tell her that.

JULIAN *But somebody did know. Somebody told him.* My friend—wanted to help me, took a dangerous chance and did— (*Softly*) You should see her. You should see her. Make her know I never spoke her name.

ALBERTINE She will not think you did. I am certain she will not think you did.

JULIAN (*Points to the envelope*) That's what's left of the money.

ALBERTINE Shall I go to the police for you, Julian?

JULIAN I went. High up, to Drummond.

ALBERTINE Then perhaps—

JULIAN No. I don't know what the thugs looked like— No matter what I said I could see Drummond saying to himself that I made it up, never could have had fifty dollars in my pocket, not less a hundred fifty thousand—

ALBERTINE Shall I go to Warkins?

JULIAN What for? Is he going to tell you who told him, who he hired to beat us up— What for?

ALBERTINE I don't know.

JULIAN Christ, what a mess-ass I am. She handed me the whole deal, told me every move to make, a baby could have done it.

(*His leg collapses and he falls to the floor. Slowly, painfully he lifts himself, moves toward the chair and table.* ALBERTINE *turns away, as if the sight is painful. As* JULIAN *falls to the floor,* LILY *makes a dash to the porch.* ALBERTINE *moves toward her; puts out a hand to hold her*)

LILY Mama, I did it.

ALBERTINE Are you very sure you love him?

LILY Mama, I did it. God forgive me.

ALBERTINE Go in and sit by him. Just sit by him and shut up. Can you do that? Can you have enough pity for him not to kill him with the truth? Can you love him enough to go by him, sit down— (*Very softly, with great violence*) *—and be still?* (LILY *nods*) Then go and do it. (LILY *moves into the house and timidly approaches* JULIAN)

JULIAN I don't look nice. Take off your hat, baby. We ain't going nowhere. There ain't nothing to go with.

LILY May I wash your face?

JULIAN Don't look like that. I'm all right. Nobody ever beat me up before, or slashed a friend.

CARRIE Things can happen.

JULIAN What did you say?

CARRIE I said bad things happen to people. Doesn't mean anything.

JULIAN I mean the way you said it. Say it that way again.

CARRIE I don't know what you mean. Why don't you go rest yourself, darling. Good hot bath—

JULIAN (*Turns to stare at her*) Why you start to purr at me? As if I'd done something good— (*Moves toward her*) You're smiling. What the hell's there to smile at? You *like* me this way? (*After a second, turns to stare at the room*) Pretty, all this. And the mortgage, and the tickets to Europe, and all the fun to come. Pretty, wasn't it?

CARRIE We didn't want them. (*To* ANNA) Did we?

ANNA No, we didn't want them.

JULIAN Don't talk that way. Won't do me any good. Assing it up all my God damned life, all my life it's been the same. (*With violence*) Nobody ever beat me up before. Nobody's ever going to beat me up again.

(*There is a pause.* LILY, *who has been washing* JULIAN'S *face, turns away.* CARRIE *sighs and moves to the porch door. Then, as if a decision has been made, she moves out to the porch and leans down to pick up* ANNA'S *luggage*)

ALBERTINE (*Very sharply, to* CARRIE) Mean to see a man stoke his pride. The meanest sight in the world. Don't you think?

CARRIE Let's be glad nothing worse happened. We're together, the three of us, that's all that matters.

ALBERTINE I counted four.

CARRIE I mean the four of us.

ALBERTINE Someday you will tell him about Lily? Then there will be three of you. Before you tell him, let me know. I will want to come for her.

CARRIE (*Points inside*) All that stuff has to go back, and the debts, got to find ourselves jobs. So much to do.

(CARRIE *picks up the valise and moves into the room*)

JULIAN Old saying, money is a real pure lady and when the world began she swore herself an oath never to belong to a man who didn't love her. I never loved her and she guessed it. Couldn't fool her, she got good sense. (*Softly, desperately*) Nobody ever beat me up before. Maybe once it starts—

CARRIE There's bad luck and there's good luck. That's all.

JULIAN I guess so. Well, I've had the bad. Maybe I got a little good luck coming to me. Other men make it easy.

Plenty of room in this world for everybody. Just got to fight for it. Got to start again, start again.

(*He rises.* LILY *moves to help him*)

CARRIE I'm going to get something nice to make soup with. You always liked a good soup when you didn't feel well. Meat and marrow, the way you like it. (*As she gets to the porch door*) Tomorrow's another day. (JULIAN, *leaning on* LILY, *moves out.* CARRIE, *leaving the house, passes* HENRY *and* ALBERTINE *in the garden*) Good-bye, Mrs. Prine.

(*She exits. After a second* HENRY *puts his hand on* ALBERTINE'S *shoulder*)

HENRY Good-bye.

(HENRY *exits.* ANNA *crosses to pick up her large valise, and at the same time* ALBERTINE *rises to exit*)

CURTAIN

BIOGRAPHICAL NOTES

TENNESSEE WILLIAMS

I first met Tennessee Williams when he visited the Random House offices in 1940, unheralded and unknown, with the script of a play called *Battle of Angels* under his arm. I liked it well enough to send it over to Lawrence Langner at the Theatre Guild, who tried it out—with conspicuous lack of success—in Boston, with Miriam Hopkins in the lead.

Tennessee Williams, undaunted by this initial failure, returned to New Orleans, and in 1945 leaped overnight into the ranks of America's leading playwrights with *The Glass Menagerie*. *A Streetcar Named Desire,* produced two years later, was an even bigger hit, winning both a Pulitzer Prize and the New York Drama Critics' Circle Award. There followed, in rapid succession, such other blockbusters as *Summer and Smoke* (1948), *The Rose Tattoo* (1950), *Cat on a Hot Tin Roof* (1954—and another Pulitzer Prize winner), *Sweet Bird of Youth* (1959) and *Period of Adjustment* (1960).

Williams, no one to abandon a project because the public would have none of it, even found time to rewrite that first galling failure, *Battle of Angels,* and rechristen it *Orpheus Descending* in 1957.

Camino Real, which opened in New York on March 19, 1953, survived for only sixty performances, but is considered by many Williams' most provocative and ambitious play. It already has been revived once, and undoubtedly will be seen again.

Williams' real name is Thomas Lanier Williams. He was born in Columbus, Mississippi, on March 26, 1914, but moved North with his family to St. Louis when he was twelve—a move that proved unfortunate for them all. Thomas suffered more than the others. His health broke down, and eventually he returned to the South to live with his grandparents. He wrote some poetry during his adolescent years, but became so ashamed of it, when he grew up he changed his name to Tennessee. Why Tennessee? "Well," explains the author, "the Williamses had once fought the Indians for Tennessee, and I had already discovered that the life of a young writer was going to be something similar to the defense of a stockade against a band of savages."

Before Williams hit the jackpot with *The Glass Menagerie,* his jobs included running an all-night elevator in an apartment hotel, working as a teletype operator for the U. S. Engineers, doubling as waiter and cashier in a New Orleans beanery, and ushering at the Strand Theatre on Broadway. Today, unmarried, he lives in luxury in Key West, Florida.

WILLIAM INGE

William Inge was born in Independence, Kansas (not to be confused with the metropolis of the same name in Missouri that boasts Harry Truman and Ginger Rogers), on May 3, 1913. He was the youngest of a family of five, and the only one who conceived a passion for the theatre. He lost a year of schooling, in fact, when he became the youngest member of a troupe that toured the countryside and played under a tent.

Inge graduated from the University of Kansas in 1935, then worked for a master's degree in English at Peabody in Nashville. From 1938 to 1943 he taught drama at Stephens College for Women in Columbia, Missouri, working under a great lady who had been the toast of Broadway in her day: Miss Maude Adams. In 1943 Inge became drama, music, and movie critic for the St. Louis *Star-Times.* From 1946 to 1949 he taught English at Washington University in St. Louis.

Inge had done a bit of desultory writing in his salad days, including two fair-to-middling plays, but his first box-office success did not come until 1949, when the Theatre Guild's production of *Come Back, Little Sheba,* starring Shirley Booth and Sidney Blackmer, won the unanimous acclaim of the critics. *Picnic* (1953) and *Bus Stop* (1955) were even more emphatic successes, and *The Dark at the Top of the Stairs,* included in this volume, turned out to be his biggest hit of all.

William Inge lives in New York today, a bachelor, and commutes between Manhattan and Hollywood, where his services are in constant demand—and at a fabulous stipend.

DORE SCHARY

Dore Schary, the author and co-producer of *Sunrise at Campobello,* was born in Newark, New Jersey, on August 31, 1905, and graduated to his present eminence on Broadway by way of newspaper work, acting, producing plays in the Catskill "borscht" circuit (where, as is detailed in *Act One,* he was a contemporary of Moss Hart) and a long and increasingly important career in Hollywood.

Schary's first Hollywood job was as a junior writer at Columbia—a fifty-dollar-a-week niche that he achieved at the very time that all the banks closed in 1932. Schary celebrated by marrying Miriam Svet, a rising young painter from his home town of Newark (they now have three grown children). From Columbia, he moved onward and upward to Selznick and RKO, finally succeeding Louis B. Mayer in the exalted post of monarch of all he surveyed at MGM. That job endured for over eight stormy years, all of which put together gave him neither the satisfaction nor the acclaim he achieved with *Sunrise at Campobello,* which opened for a long Broadway run on January 30, 1958, with Mrs. Eleanor Roosevelt in the audience.

Subsequently, Mr. Schary has written *The Highest Tree,* adapted *The Devil's Advocate,* and co-produced *A Majority of One* and *The Unsinkable Molly Brown.*

Ralph Bellamy, who created the role of Franklin D. Roosevelt in the stage play of *Sunrise at Campobello,* repeated his success, again under the direction of Mr. Schary, in a faithful and inspiring motion-picture adaptation in 1960.

A Raisin in the Sun, winner of the New York Drama Critics' Circle Award as the best play of the 1958-1959 season, is Lorraine Hansberry's first play to achieve production, but she has been engrossed in the world of the theatre ever since, as a child, she was taken to see *Dark of the Moon* in her native Chicago.

Miss Hansberry was born in 1930, attended the University of Wisconsin and Roosevelt College in Chicago, and moved to New York in 1950. She lives now in Greenwich Village with her husband, Bob Nemiroff, a songwriter and music publisher.

In 1957 another music publisher named Philip Rose, a friend of the Nemiroffs, determined to produce *A Raisin in the Sun*. The necessary capital was raised with the aid of a veritable army of small but enthusiastic investors. For months no New York theatre could be found to house the play, but ecstatic notices from out-of-town tryouts had a magical effect, and *A Raisin in the Sun* opened triumphantly at the Ethel Barrymore Theatre on March 11, 1959. At the conclusion of the premiere, Sidney Poitier, best-known member of the cast, jumped down to the orchestra and carried Miss Hansberry onstage, where the audience cheered her for ten solid minutes.

John McClain, in the New York *Journal American*, hailed *A Raisin in the Sun* as "a wonderfully emotional evening." Walter Kerr in the New York *Herald Tribune*, called it "an honest, intelligible, and moving experience." John Chapman, in the New York *News*, was most enthusiastic of all. "*A Raisin in the Sun*," he wrote, "is a beautiful, lovable play—a work of theatrical magic in which the usual barrier between audience and stage disappears."

Paddy Chayefsky must be considered television's greatest gift to the legitimate theatre, because it was with such masterful TV scripts as *Marty, Bachelor Party, Middle of the Night,* and *The Catered Affair* that his name first became known to the playgoing public.

Chayefsky was born in the Bronx in New York City in 1923, and was educated at De Witt Clinton High School and C.C.N.Y. He enlisted in the Army during World War II and was sent to Germany, where he ran afoul of a booby trap; while convalescing in an Army hospital, he wrote the book and lyrics for a servicemen's musical that enlisted the interest of Producer Garson Kanin.

Chayefsky's *Marty* was the first TV play to be successfully transformed into a motion picture. It won the Academy Award. His first original screenplay, *The Goddess,* won the Critics' Prize at the 1958 Brussels Film Festival. His first play for Broadway, *Middle of the Night,* ran for almost two years, with Edward G. Robinson in the lead.

It remained for *The Tenth Man,* however, superbly directed by Tyrone Guthrie, to establish Paddy Chayefsky once and for all in the very top rank of contemporary American playwrights. The play was originally called *The Dybbuk from Woodhaven,* and was considered a dubious commercial prospect on its tryout tour. By the time it opened at the Booth Theatre in New York, on November 5, 1959, all the rough edges had been ironed out, and by ten the next morning the line before the box office was a block long. "All we need in the theatre," acclaimed Brooks Atkinson in the New York *Times,* "are writers, directors, and actors. In *The Tenth Man* they are happily met in a new play for the first time this season: a happy marriage of literary imagination and affection for people."

LILLIAN HELLMAN

Lillian Hellman is one of a score of subsequently famous literary folk who cut their eyeteeth in the strange but exciting publishing house presided over by the late Horace Liveright. There she demonstrated for the first time the fierce dedication to her ideals, the limitless capacity for work, and the constant striving for perfection that has ever since characterized her career. Tough, unyielding, brilliant, she is also capable of an understanding and compassion that found expression in her tender care of the author Dashiell Hammett in the tragic twilight of his career.

Miss Hellman was born in New Orleans in 1905, and moved with her family to New York five years later. She returned frequently to New Orleans for long visits, and went to public schools both there and in Manhattan. She attended both New York University and Columbia, but did not graduate.

Herman Shumlin persuaded her to leave Liveright's to become his chief play reader (she "discovered" Vicki Baum's *Grand Hotel*), and it was he who produced her first smash hit in 1934—*The Children's Hour.* Close on its heels came *Days to Come* (1936), *The Little Foxes* (1939), *Watch on the Rhine* (1941), *The Searching Wind* (1944), *Another Part of the Forest* (1946), and *The Autumn Garden* (1951), not to mention several remunerative detours to Hollywood, mostly under the aegis of the persuasive Sam Goldwyn.

Toys in the Attic, which opened at the Hudson Theatre on February 25, 1960, is one of Miss Hellman's most substantial hits. "It brings the theatre back to life," exulted Richard Watts, Jr., in the New York *Post;* and John Chapman, in the *News,* proclaimed "Lillian Hellman has jolted the theatre out of its childishness with a smackingly vigorous drama!"